Fishing
Western New York

Help Us Keep This Guide Up to Date

Every effort has been made by the author and editors to make this guide as accurate and useful as possible. However, many things can change after a guide is published—trails are rerouted, regulations change, techniques evolve, facilities come under new management, etc.

We would love to hear from you concerning your experiences with this guide and how you feel it could be improved and kept up to date. While we may not be able to respond to all comments and suggestions, we'll take them to heart and we'll also make certain to share them with the author. Please send your comments and suggestions to the following address:

The Globe Pequot Press
Reader Response/Editorial Department
P.O. Box 480
Guilford, CT 06437

Or you may e-mail us at:

editorial@GlobePequot.com

Thanks for your input.

A **FALCON** GUIDE®

AUG 2005

Fishing
Western New York

S P I D E R   R Y B A A K

FALCON®

GUILFORD, CONNECTICUT
HELENA, MONTANA

AN IMPRINT OF THE GLOBE PEQUOT PRESS

/A/FALCONGUIDE ®

All photos by Ray Hrynyk
Text design by Casey Shain
Maps created by Trailhead Graphics © The Globe Pequot Press

ISSN 1548-1573
ISBN 0-7627-2870-1

Manufactured in the United States of America
First Edition/First Printing

To Susan . . . still.

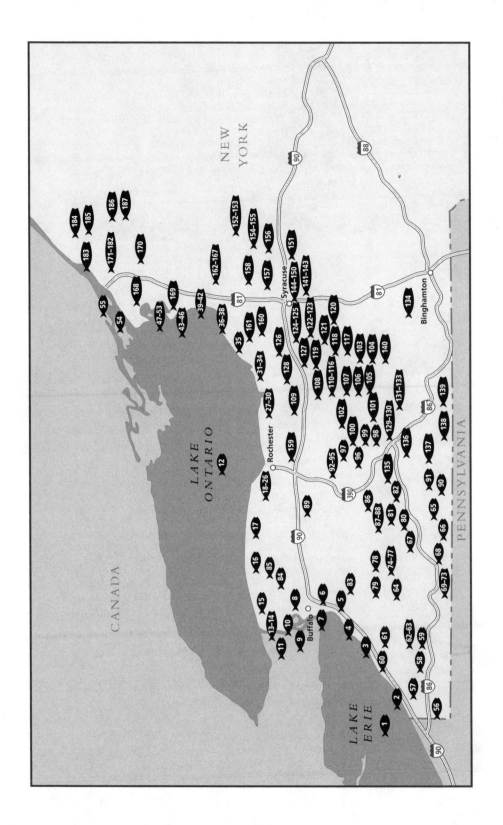

Contents

Acknowledgments

Completing a work this ambitious all by myself would have taken more years than I have left—not to mention gas money and time away from Susan, the cats, and my favorite fishing spots. An army of people helped me with everything from locating obscure sites and popular hot spots to setting me up with lodging, guides, local experts, regional fishing techniques, site dimensions, stocking statistics, maps . . . You get the picture. Mentioning everyone would add twenty or more pages to the book. So here's a list of those I bugged most of all (at least twenty times) at all hours: Frank Flack, Joe Evans, Dave Kosowski, Les Wedge, Russ Davall, Dan Bishop, Bill Hilts Jr., Jim Hanley, John Kopy, John Rucando, Stephen Litwhiler, Larry Muroski, Bart Patten, Stan Olette, Alberta Bennett, Brad Hammers, Jeff Robins, Web Pearsall, Brad Whitcomb, David Henderson, Todd Frank, J. Michael Kelly, Paul Keesler, and Mark Maghran.

Introduction

Western New York has some of the world's finest waterworks—natural and man-made, often side by side. For instance, just downstream of Niagara Falls, one of the Natural Wonders of the World, the rapids brush the Niagara Power Project, an engineering marvel that reaches out of the gorge's walls like a temple to Neptune. The last leg of the Genesee River runs through Rochester, tumbling over a series of urban waterfalls. Wild beaver live in the locks in downtown Oswego. Letchworth State Park (the Grand Canyon of the East), Watkins Glen (often called the Eighth Wonder of the World), Lake Ontario's bluffs (shoreline drumlins eroded into fantastic spires and chimneys), and Nelson Swamp (home of the world's oldest eastern white pine) are just a few of this half of the state's famous features. And the majority is right at the road.

Indeed, New York is so rich in water, it has more shoreline than some island nations. And all of it, from the Great Lakes to the tiny brooks streaming down the faces of the Allegheny foothills, is loaded with fish. The New York State Department of Environmental Conservation is charged with maintaining these fisheries. Unlike the rest of the bureaucracy, this agency does its job efficiently and productively. A recent Cornell University study estimates that freshwater fishing in New York generates a positive economic impact of $3.6 billion annually.

Just about anything that swims in the temperate waters of the Western Hemisphere can be found here. You can troll for trophy salmon or muskies; fly fish for monster steelhead, brown trout, largemouth bass, and northern pike; jig for 10-pound walleyes and world-class lake trout; use live bait for ancient and bizarre-looking critters like bowfins, eels, burbots, and gars; or simply sit on shore and dunk worms for bullheads, sunfish, perch, carp, sheepsheads, suckers—you name it.

You name the setting, too. From backcountry brooks crowned in cathedral-like foliage to urban docks illuminated by street lights, New York's got it all. And while there's no guarantee you'll land a leviathan, you're sure to catch enough fish to keep you daydreaming for years to come.

New York's Wildlife

While puma sightings have been reported all over upstate New York in the past decade, their numbers are so small, you've got a better chance of catching a fish called Wanda than seeing a mountain lion.

About the most dangerous critter you are likely to encounter is a black bear. These can show up just about anywhere in rural New York: I've run into two of them in forty-five years of fishing, and both snuck away. Still, if you see one clumsily lumbering down the trail or splashing upcreek toward you, make enough noise to be noticed, then make yourself as big as you can.

Happy angler with walleye taken from the "State Ditch," New Erie Canal (site 159), near Jacks Reef.

And then there are coyotes, 11,000 by some estimates. Corrupted by timber wolf genes, they are fully 30 percent larger than the western variety. And though their howls have probably cut some camping trips short, there is no record of one hurting a human. Several have crossed my path over the years, but when they caught wind of me, they split so fast that I was left wondering if I ever saw one in the first place.

Besides dump ducks (gulls), the friendly skies over the state's waterways are loaded with kingfishers, blue herons, cormorants, wild ducks, and Canada geese. Loons thrive in remote waters and large bodies with swampy areas. Bald eagles are making a comeback, and you can expect to see them on popular streams like the Salmon River.

Insects are so ubiquitous and plentiful, they can really bug you. Yellow jackets and bald-faced hornets have sent more than one angler diving for cover. In late spring, blackflies rule the air over backcountry creeks. Some are so aggressive, an old-timer once told me he's seen them chase trout. While that's stretching things a bit, they can swarm in such numbers from mid-May through June, especially in the Fish Creek and Salmon River drainages, they'll drive an unprotected fly fisher off a stream in the middle of a mayfly hatch. What's more, not all insect repellents discourage them—indeed, some actually seem to sound the dinner bell. Those containing DEET work well. Most roadside streams and lakes are sprayed to keep blackflies in check, but waters in wild forests and wilderness areas are not.

Finally, we have a lot of mosquitoes, attempts at eradication notwithstanding. They've become particularly troublesome lately because some carry the West Nile virus, a pathogen known to be fatal to crows and humans. These tiny vampires are especially active at dusk and dawn, near shore around ponds, lakes, canals, and slow-moving rivers. They don't cotton to insect repellents. Those who are allergic to harsh chemicals, or simply wish to avoid them, should wear Bug-Out or similar mesh garments over their regular clothes.

New York's Weather

New York has a temperate climate with an average temperature of about 48 degrees Fahrenheit. But that doesn't mean we don't get wild swings. Most winters, temperatures drop below zero. Indeed, several winters in the 1990s saw record-breaking snowfall and temperatures so cold, some self-proclaimed environmentalists burned their copies of Al Gore's *Earth in the Balance* for kindling. Syracuse, in the heart of the state, averages 120 inches of snow annually, a statistic that earns it the distinction of being the snowiest city in the country. The Tug Hill Plateau region, stretching from the north shore of Oneida Lake to about Watertown, is blessed with a meteorological phenomenon known as lake effect, in which cold winds blowing over the warmer waters of Lake Ontario generate enough snow to blanket the countryside from the east shore to the Adirondack foothills with an average of 200 inches each winter. While Lake Ontario's bays and ponds and shallow bodies like Oneida Lake develop ice caps thick enough to support pick-up trucks, most lakes in this half of the state only get ice thick enough to walk on; and in some years (most

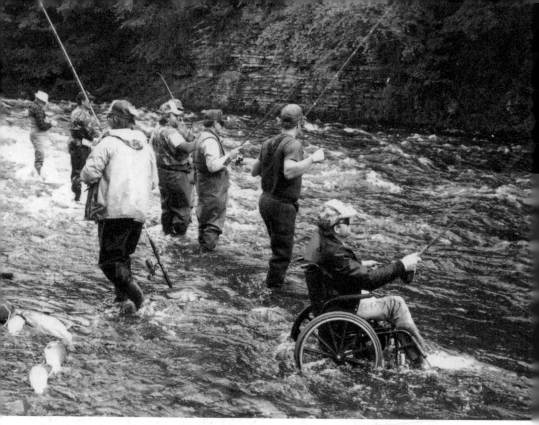

Autumn fishing on the Lower Salmon River (site 37).

recently in 2001), it's so thin that only the brave and suicidal dare to tread on it.

Summer is very humid and hot. Temperatures vary with sea level. The Finger Lakes region sees a lot of days in the high 70s and 80s. The St. Lawrence River lowlands are normally 5 degrees cooler, and the Tug Hill Plateau can be as much as 10 degrees cooler.

Spring and fall are the reason many New Yorkers put up with winter and summer. Temperatures range from 55 to 65. And while many complain it is always cloudy or raining, the truth is, the sun shines about half the time.

Finding Your Way

Maps were drawn from a variety of sources. In most cases, actual mileage was recorded by visiting the site. However, odometers aren't created equal, and when combined with factors like weather, rest stops, and garage sales, readings can vary. While every attempt has been made to present accurate distances, please accept them as approximations at best.

Including charts of the Great Lakes wasn't practical for a book of this scope. If you're going to go out beyond sight of land, especially if there's a chance you might cross into Canadian waters, it's a good idea to have a GPS on board—and lake charts. Maptech, in cooperation with Nautical Data International, Inc., offers

Digital Charts: Chart Navigator software covering the open waters of Lakes Erie and Ontario. In addition, marine facilities and topo maps of the U.S. shoreline are included. For more information, call (888) 839–5551 or visit www.maptech.com.

Catch-and-Release

One thing all competent anglers with average luck can expect to do in New York is catch fish. So many, in fact, that some will have to be released eventually for reasons ranging from the fish being out of season or too small, to catching more than you feel like cleaning, to simply not feeling like killing anymore. Of course, there are also those who practice catch-and-release religiously. Whatever the reason, it is in the best interest of all concerned for the critter to be released unharmed. Here are some simple pointers to ensure you release a fish with a future instead of a dead fish swimming.

- Avoid going after big fish with ultralight tackle. The cruel, frustrating struggle for freedom can exhaust them beyond recovery.

- Only use a net when absolutely necessary. Nets tear mouths, rip gills, break fins and teeth, scratch eyes, and remove slime, an important barrier against harmful bacteria.

- Keep the fish submerged in water, even when unhooking it.

- If you must remove a fish from the water, always wet your hands before touching it, and place it on something wet.

- If the fish is hooked deep in the tongue, guts, or gills, cut the line. Fish are bleeders, and an internal wound as small as a pinhole can be fatal. By leaving the hook in place, healing will occur around it as it rusts away. No hook is worth a life.

- Never lift a pike by squeezing its eyes with your fingers.

- Keep fingers out of a fish's gills.

Fish Consumption Advisory

While the doctor may tell you fish is healthy for you, the state advises that you eat no more than 0.5 pound of fish per week caught from any of the state's waters, including municipal reservoirs. What's more, the *New York State Department of Environmental Conservation Fishing Regulations Guide* lists three pages of streams and lakes from which you should only eat 0.5 pound per month or none at all.

Best Times to Fish

All fish feed most actively around dusk and dawn. Some biologists and successful anglers claim the moon influences feeding, and commercial calendars such as Rick Taylor's "Prime Times" list the best days and most productive hours. Still, some fish

*Releasing a nice Oswego
River brown trout (site 35).*

like catfish, eels, and walleyes feed best at night, especially when there's no moon, while yellow perch and northern pike feed best during daylight. The rest—from trout, salmon, and bass to muskies, crappies, and sunfish—feed whenever they feel like it.

Security Notice

The terrorist incidents of September 11, 2001, commonly referred to as 9/11, have taken a big bite out of fishing opportunities. In the name of national security, the government has slapped a security zone around all dangerous waterfront structures. For instance, anglers are forbidden to fish within 1,000 yards of nuclear power plants and must stay at least 25 yards away from all bridge abutments. For further information, contact the Coast Guard at (716) 843–9570.

Regulations

New York has so many fishing regulations, it takes the *Department of Environmental Conservation Fishing Regulations Guide* about forty pages just to list them all. Pick up the pamphlet when you buy a license, memorize the general regulations in the front of the book, then check the special regulations by county to see if additional rules apply to the spot you're going to fish.

Public Fishing Rights

The state has purchased easements along hundreds of miles of streams. These sites are normally posted with yellow signs announcing PUBLIC FISHING STREAM. Access is limited to the stream and the band of land 33 feet from the bank. Activities other than fishing are prohibited.

Camping

Generally, primitive camping is allowed on state land in all state forests.

- Groups numbering up to nine can spend up to three nights at any given site. Larger groups and longer stays require a permit from the local forest ranger.

- As a rule, camp must be set up at least 150 feet away from any road, trail, or source of water. Exceptions exist, however, in sites designated by a CAMP HERE disk.

- Primitive sites that are not in campgrounds are on a first-come, first-served basis and cannot be reserved.

- Lean-tos are not for exclusive use and must be shared.

Many state parks have campgrounds, and some even rent rustic cabins. Contact the park directly (see State Parks in the appendix for addresses and phone numbers) for informational brochures.

How to Use This Guide

Numerous books have been written about fishing in New York. However, none has covered every spot—there are so many that the task would be of encyclopedic proportions. This book is also limited in scope: It only includes waters that are open to the public and are relatively easy to access.

The book is broken down into five regions: Great Lakes Region, Western New York Region: Inland Waters, Finger Lakes Region, Central New York, and Thousand Islands Region. (For information about fishing sites in the eastern part of the state, see *Fishing Eastern New York*.) Every region's major sites will be named, numbered, and described the following way:

Key species: This section will include all the fish commonly sought in the spot.

Description: Each site will be described. Lakes will have their acreage or square miles given, as well as average and maximum depths. Streams will contain information on their sources, lengths, and mouths.

Tips: Site-specific tips will be given here.

The fishing: This section will provide details on the fishery, stuff like typical sizes, bait and habitat preferences, state stocking statistics (in some cases, fish stocked by local clubs or county and federal hatcheries will be included), and special regulations.

Directions: How to get there from the nearest major town. Since one of the main focuses of this book is to introduce traveling anglers to the state's fishing, the directions will be the easiest way to go—not the shortest. For streams, the major routes paralleling them will be given.

Additional information: This section will contain on-site camping information, boat launches, campgrounds, bank-fishing access, and other site-specific information.

Contact: State and local agencies to contact for information on the area. Phone numbers, addresses, and Web sites are listed in the appendix.

Lettered sites below numbered ones include access points and campgrounds.

Map Legend

Featured Fishing Site	🐟 20
Interstate Highway	90
U.S. Highway	89
State Highway	83
County, Local, or Forest Road	280
Trail	– – – – –
Railroad	┼┼┼┼┼┼┼┼┼
State Line	– · – – · –
Campground	Λ
Parking	℗
Dam	/
Lock	˅
Bridge	⌒
River, Creek, or Drainage	——
Reservoir, Lake, or Pond	●

Fish Species of New York

Brook Trout, or Speckled Trout *(Salvelinus frontinalis)*

General description: This beautiful fish normally has a deep olive back decorated with a labyrinth of wormlike markings. Spots on its sides are red and blue, and a white line traces its reddish lower fins. A member of the char family, its mouth and appetite are bigger than your average trout's.

Distribution: The state's official fish, brookies are also called natives or speckled trout and can be found in clear, cold brooks, streams, ponds, and lakes throughout the state. They are the fish of choice for anglers hiking to remote streams flowing through the Tug Hill Plateau.

Additional information: Brookies assume their most striking colors in autumn when they're ready to spawn. Males often have bright red bellies and large hooked jaws. Their propensity for eagerly taking worms, salted minnows, flies, small spoons, and spinners—you name it—has earned them the distinction of being the easiest trout to catch. The state's smallest trout, most range from 4 to 10 inches long, but fish around 18 inches are possible. As of press time, there was no state record. The most recent titleholder was disqualified in April 2003 because the trout was taken from a pond stocked with splake. State senior aquatic biologist Rich Preall, one of the loudest critics of splake, says his department will not accept entries from any waters stocked with them, or from waters in which brood-stock brook trout are released. (Stocking reports are available on the state Department of Environmental Conservation Web site, www.dec.state.ny.us.) Entries must weigh at least 4 pounds.

Lake Trout *(Salvelinus namaycush)*

General description: Like brookies, this delicious member of the char family isn't exactly the brightest fish in the tank. It has a relatively big mouth and an appetite to match. Its back is generally gray or green; the sides are silvery or gray and speckled with light spots. The belly is white, and its tail is forked.

Distribution: Another native New Yorker, this species prefers cold, deep water and is often sought in depths exceeding 100 feet. The greatest populations are found in Lake Ontario, the deepest Indian River Lakes, Adirondack ponds and lakes, and the Finger Lakes.

Additional information: One of the larger trout, lakers easily reach 20 inches, and 30-plus-inch fish are common in Lake Ontario. They spawn in autumn in shallow water over gravel. The state record, caught in Lake Erie on August 9, 2003, is 41 pounds, 8 ounces.

Brown Trout *(Salmo trutta)*

General description: Sporting deep brown backs, this species' color lightens into golden sides splashed with red and brown spots surrounded by light halos. Sometimes the red spots are so bright, they look like burning embers. Mature males sport kypes (curved lower jaws) that are often so extremely hooked, they seem deformed.

Distribution: Imported back in the 1830s from Germany, browns found America to their liking and have prospered. Far more tolerant of warm water than brookies or lakers, they do well in every kind of clean, oxygenated water, from deep lakes to shallow streams.

Additional information: Purist fly fishers consider the brown the savviest of trout. Its propensity for hitting a well-presented dry fly has endeared the species to some of the world's most famous authors—Dame Juliana Berners, Issak Walton, William Butler Yeats, and Ernest Hemingway, to name a few. Especially colorful when they spawn in autumn, browns assume a brilliance that perfectly complements Earth's most colorful season. The state record, caught in Lake Ontario on June 10, 1997, is 33 pounds, 2 ounces.

Rainbow Trout and Steelhead *(Oncorhynchus mykiss)*

General description: This species has a deep green back that melts into silvery sides. A pink stripe stretching from the corner of the fish's jaw to the base of its tail is what gives it its name. The upper half of its body, upper fins, and entire tail are splattered with black spots.

Distribution: Native to the West Coast, rainbows were introduced to New York in the nineteenth century and have been here ever since. They can be found in deep, cool lakes and cold streams throughout the state. Relatively easy to catch, they are often stocked in inhospitable urban creeks because biologists know the vast majority will likely be caught way before summer heats the water to unbearable temperatures. Those that survive the early season generally do all right by finding cool spring holes or migrating downstream to a cold lake.

Additional information: Anadromous rainbows are called steelhead and sometimes chromers. A few lake-dwelling domestic rainbows and steelhead run up tributaries in autumn to feast on brown trout and salmon eggs, often spending the entire winter. Come spring, they run upstream en masse to spawn, providing some of the year's most exciting fishing action. The state record, caught in Lake Ontario on May 22, 1985, is 26 pounds, 15 ounces.

Atlantic Salmon, or Landlocked Salmon *(Salmo salar)*

General description: The only salmon native to the state, Atlantic salmon generally have deep brown backs that quickly dissolve to silvery sides splattered with irregularly shaped spots, which are often crossed.

Distribution: At one time Lake Ontario boasted the greatest population of landlocked Atlantic salmon in the world. A combination of pollution, construction of dams on natal streams, and sterility caused by a vitamin deficiency linked to eating exotic forage (alewives and smelt) wiped them out. Currently a token presence is maintained in Lake Ontario by stocking. The state releases over 365,000 fingerlings in the lake annually. In addition, local, state, and federal agencies chip in by unloading surplus fish from hatcheries and research laboratories.

Additional information: Atlantic salmon are the only salmon that survive the spawning ordeal, often returning to spawn a second and sometimes even a third time. Considered the classiest salmon, catching one, especially on a fly, is many a fly-fishing purist's greatest dream. Atlantic salmon spawn in autumn. The state record, caught in Lake Ontario on April 5, 1997, is 24 pounds, 15 ounces.

Chinook Salmon, or King Salmon
(Oncorhynchus tshawytscha)

General description: A silvery fish with a green back, it has black spots along the upper half of its body, including the fins and the entire tail. When they're ready to spawn, they become a dark olive-brown, and the males develop a kype (hooked jaw). The inside of the mouth is entirely black.

Distribution: The largest of the Pacific salmon, chinooks were introduced into Lake Ontario in the late 1960s. Currently upwards of 1.5 million are stocked annually by the state. Individuals easily reach 35 pounds, and the species has become one of the lake's most important game fish.

Additional information: The most exciting fishing occurs roughly from mid-September through mid-November, when mature three-and-a-half-year-old fish ascend tributaries to spawn. The average size is 25 pounds; however, a few precocious one-and-a-half-year-olds (females are called jennies, and males are called jacks), averaging 8 pounds, are also present. Kings spawn in autumn and die soon afterward. The state record, caught in the Lower Salmon River on September 7, 1991, is 47 pounds, 13 ounces.

Coho Salmon, or Silver Salmon (Oncorhynchus kisutch)

General description: Another Pacific salmon, the coho is a silvery fish when actively feeding in the lake but develops red sides when it stops eating and heads upstream to spawn. The upper half of its body has black spots, but only the upper quarter of its tail and the lower half of its dorsal fin are spotted. Another identifying factor is that its mouth is black but not its gums.

Distribution: The state maintains their presence in Lake Ontario by stocking upwards of 225,000 annually.

Additional information: Cohos spawn between mid-September and mid-November in the same streams as chinooks. While they're only about a third the size of kings, their sizzling runs, spectacular leaps, and incredible stamina endear them to legions of anglers. For some strange reason, Lake Ontario's cohos grow larger than those in the Pacific Ocean, and 30-pounders are caught in the Salmon River each year. The fish spawn in autumn and then die. The state record—and the International Game

Fish Association's all-tackle world record—was caught in the Lower Salmon River on September 27, 1989, and weighed 33 pounds, 4 ounces.

Cisco, or Lake Herring *(Coregonus artedi)*

General description: This silvery fish has a rounded, cigarlike body and is often described as resembling an oversize smelt.

Distribution: They are present in deep, cold lakes like Skaneateles.

Additional information: Primarily plankton eaters, ciscos will take dry flies, tiny garden worms, small minnows, and spoons. They spawn in autumn. The state record, caught in Lake Lauderdale on January 25, 1990, is 5 pounds, 7 ounces.

Lake Whitefish *(Coregonus clupeaformis)*

General description: These fish generally have brown or blue backs that fade into silvery sides and white bellies.

Distribution: Formerly distributed widely throughout the state, pollution has run them out of most of their range. However, they are still found in cool, deep places like Lake of the Woods and Lake Ontario.

Additional information: Zebra mussels feed on the same phytoplankton that lake whitefish eat, prompting some experts to warn they will wipe out the whitefish in waters occupied by both. Others counter that zebra mussels simply redistribute the biomass by laying their waste on the floor, causing explosions in populations of bottom-feeding invertebrates, which whitefish also eat. While the jury is still out on the zebra mussel question, most scientists agree alewives are definitely a threat: They feed heavily on whitefish fry and can send the population into a nose-dive. The state record, caught in Lake Pleasant on August 29, 1995, is 10 pounds, 8 ounces.

Largemouth Bass, or Bucketmouth *(Micropterus salmoides)*

General description: The largest member of the sunfish family, this species is dark green on the back, with the color lightening as it approaches the white belly. A horizontal row of large black splotches runs along the middle of the side, from the gill plate to the base of the tail. Its trademark is its huge head and mouth. The ends of the mouth reach past the eyes. This is one of two species the Department of Environmental Conservation includes under the heading of black bass in the state *Fishing Regulations Guide.*

Distribution: Found in lakes, ponds, and sluggish streams throughout the state.

Additional information: Found in all the lower forty-eight states and inclined to hit artificial lures of every description, the largemouth bass is America's favorite game fish. It'll hit just about anything that moves and is notorious for its explosive, heart-stopping strikes on surface lures. This species spawns in the spring when water temperatures range from 62 to 65 degrees Fahrenheit. The state record, caught in Buckhorn Lake on September 11, 1987, is 11 pounds, 4 ounces.

Smallmouth Bass, or Bronzeback
(Micropterus dolomieu)

General description: Brownish in color, it is easily differentiated from the large-mouth because the ends of the mouth occur below the eyes. One of America's most popular fishes, it is granted equal status with the bucketmouth in most bass tournaments. This is one of two species the Department of Environmental Conservation includes under the heading of black bass in the state *Fishing Regulations Guide.*

Distribution: Found in lakes and streams throughout the state.

Additional information: Bronzebacks spawn in late spring and early summer when water temperatures range from 61 to 65 degrees Fahrenheit. The state record, caught in Lake Erie on June 4, 1995, is 8 pounds, 4 ounces.

Muskellunge *(Esox masquinongy)*

General description: The largest member of the pike family, this long, sleek species commonly reaches 35 pounds. The back is a light green to brownish yellow, and the sides can have dark bars or blotches. Its most prominent feature is its duck-billed mouth filled with razor-sharp teeth. Only the upper halves of the gill covers and cheeks have scales, a fact normally used to differentiate muskies from northern pike and pickerel.

Distribution: The Great Lakes system, Allegheny River watershed, and lakes like Chautauqua, Waneta, and Lamoka.

Additional information: The Ohio River and Great Lakes strains occur in the state. Muskies spawn in late April through early May when water temperatures range from 49 to 59 degrees Fahrenheit. The state record, caught in the St. Lawrence River in 1957, is 69 pounds, 15 ounces.

Caution: Keep your fingers out of the gill rakers; they are sharp enough to shred human flesh.

Tiger Muskie, or Norlunge

General description: This species is a cross between a male northern pike and a muskie. Its body is shaped the same as a true muskie, but its colors are more vivid, and its sides have wavy, tigerlike stripes. Its teeth are razor sharp.

Distribution: Although tigers occur naturally in some places like the St. Lawrence River, the vast majority of the population is man-made, stocked in lakes and rivers to provide trophy fishing and to control runaway populations of hardy panfish like white perch.

Additional information: These strikingly beautiful hybrids are sterile. The state record, caught in the Tioughnioga River on May 25, 1990, is 35 pounds, 8 ounces.

Caution: Keep your fingers out of the gill rakers; they are sharp enough to shred human flesh.

Northern Pike, or Pikeasaurus *(Esox lucius)*

General description: The medium-size member of the pike family, this long, slender fish is named after a spear used in combat during the Middle Ages. Its body is the same as the muskie's, but its color is almost invariably green, and it has large, oblong white spots on its sides. Its cheeks are fully scaled, but only the top half of its gill plates are. Its teeth are razor sharp.

Distribution: Found in large and midsize rivers and lakes throughout the state.

Additional information: Spawns in April through early May in water temperatures ranging from 40 to 52 degrees Fahrenheit. The state record, caught in Great Sacandaga Lake on September 15, 1940, is 46 pounds, 2 ounces.

Caution: Keep your fingers out of the gill rakers; they are sharp enough to shred human flesh.

Chain Pickerel *(Esox niger)*

General description: The smallest member of the pike family, its body is shaped exactly like its larger cousins, but its green sides are overlaid in a yellow, chain mail–like pattern. Its teeth are razor sharp.

Distribution: Ponds and lakes throughout the state.

Additional information: Spawns in early spring in water temperatures ranging from 47 to 52 degrees Fahrenheit. The state record, caught in Toronto Reservoir in 1965, is 8 pounds, 1 ounce.

Caution: Keep your fingers out of the gill rakers; they are sharp enough to shred human flesh.

Walleye *(Stizostedion vitreum)*

General description: The largest member of the perch family, it gets its name from its big opaque eyes. The walleye's back is dark gray to black and fades as it slips down the sides, which are often streaked in gold. It has two dorsal fins; the front one's last few spines have a black blotch at their base. Its teeth are pointed and can puncture but won't slice. Nocturnal critters, walleyes often enter shallow areas to feed. If the moon is out, their eyes catch and hold the beams, spawning ghost stories and extraterrestrial sightings by folks who see the eerie lights moving around in the water.

Distribution: Found in lakes and rivers throughout the state.

Additional information: Walleyes spawn in early spring when water temperatures range from 44 to 48 degrees Fahrenheit. The state record, caught in Allegheny Reservoir on May 22, 1994, is 16 pounds, 7 ounces.

Sauger *(Stizostedion canadense)*

General description: The second largest member of the perch family, saugers look like walleyes. They can be differentiated from their larger cousins by the two rows of black crescent markings running the length of their front dorsal fin. In addition, they lack a white spot at the bottom tip of their tail and anal fin.

Distribution: Although historically found in the Great Lakes drainage, currently their only large population is in Lake Champlain.

Additional information: Sauger spawn in the spring. The state record, caught in the Lower Niagara River on September 30, 1990, is 4 pounds, 8 ounces.

Yellow Perch *(Perca flavescens)*

General description: This popular panfish has a dark back that fades to golden yellow sides overlaid with five to eight dark vertical bands. Sometimes its lower fins are traced in bright orange.

Distribution: Found in every type of water throughout the state.

Additional information: Spawns from mid-April through May when water temperatures range from 44 to 54 degrees Fahrenheit. The state record, caught in Lake Erie in April, 1982, is 3 pounds, 8 ounces.

Black Crappie *(Pomoxis nigromaculatus)*

General description: Arguably the most delicious of the state's panfish, this member of the sunfish family has a dark olive or black back and silver sides streaked with gold and overlaid with black spots and blotches. The front of its dorsal fin has seven or eight sharp spines followed by a soft fan.

Distribution: The state's most common crappie, it is found in still to slow-moving water throughout the state.

Additional information: Spawns in late spring when water temperatures range from 57 to 73 degrees Fahrenheit. The state record, caught in Duck Lake on April 17, 1998, is 3 pounds, 12 ounces.

White Crappie *(Pomoxis annularis)*

General description: This species looks pretty much the same as its black cousin, but it is generally lighter and only has six spines on its dorsal fin.

Distribution: Found in lakes, ponds, and slow rivers throughout the state.

Additional information: Spawns late spring and early summer when water temperatures range from 57 to 73 degrees Fahrenheit. The state record, caught in Kinderhook Lake on December 18, 1988, is 3 pounds, 9 ounces.

Bluegill *(Lepomis macrochirus)*

General description: One of the most popular sunfishes, its color varies. It has anywhere from five to eight vertical bars running down its sides, a deep orange breast, and a dark blue, rounded gill flap.

Distribution: Lakes, ponds, and slow-moving rivers throughout the state.

Additional information: Ounce for ounce, bluegills are the sportiest fish. Fly fishing for them with wet flies and poppers is very popular. The species spawns in shallow, muddy areas near vegetation in summer. The state record, caught in Kohlbach Pond on August 3, 1992, is 2 pounds, 8 ounces.

Pumpkinseed *(Lepomis gibbosus)*

General description: This popular sunfish is the most widespread in the state. Its color ranges from bronze to dark green, and its gill flap has an orange-red spot on its end.

Distribution: Ponds, lakes, and slow-moving streams throughout the state.

Additional information: Spawns in shallow, muddy areas near vegetation in early summer. The state record, caught in Indian Lake on July 19, 1994, is 1 pound, 9 ounces.

Rock Bass, or Redeye or Googleye *(Ambloplites rupestris)*

General description: This popular member of the sunfish family resembles bass more closely than do pumpkinseeds and bluegills. It is dark brown to deep bronze in color, heavily spotted in black, and has big red eyes.

Distribution: Found in rocky, shallow areas of streams and lakes throughout the state.

Additional information: Spawns over rocky areas in late spring and early summer. The state record, caught in the Ramapo River on May 26, 1984, is 1 pound, 15 ounces.

Channel Catfish *(Ictalurus punctatus)*

General description: The largest indigenous member of the catfish family, it has a dark brown back, a white belly, a forked tail, and barbels around its mouth. Juveniles up to 24 inches have black spots on their sides. Spines on the dorsal and pectoral fins can inflict a nasty wound.

Distribution: Found in deep channels of lakes and large rivers throughout the state, often in heavy currents.

Additional information: Spawning takes place in summer when water temperatures reach between 75 to 85 degrees Fahrenheit. The state record, caught in Brant Lake in eastern New York on June 21, 2002, is 32 pounds, 12 ounces.

Brown Bullhead *(Ameiurus nebulosus)*

General description: Having a dark brown back and white belly, this member of the catfish family has barbels around its mouth. A relatively square tail distinguishes it from the channel catfish.

Distribution: The bullhead's tolerance to high temperatures and low oxygen levels allows it to live in places other fish can't. It is found in virtually every type of water.

Additional information: Spawns in muddy areas from late June through July. Both parents guard the schooling fry for the first few weeks of life. The state record, caught in Sugarloaf Pond on April 26, 1998, is 6 pounds, 9 ounces.

White Perch, or Silver Bass *(Morone americana)*

General description: A member of the temperate bass family Percichthyidae, this species' back can range in color from olive to silvery gray. Its sides are pale olive or silver.

Distribution: Common in the Great Lakes drainage. Although they can be found in lakes, they are generally a river fish.

Additional information: Especially common in the New Erie Canal and Oswego Canal systems, most locals don't differentiate between these and white bass—they simply call both silver bass. White perch spawn from mid-May through mid-June when the water temperature reaches 52 to 59 degrees Fahrenheit. The state record, caught in Lake Oscaletta on September 21, 1991, is 3 pounds, 1 ounce.

White Bass, or Silver Bass *(Morone chrysops)*

General description: Same as white perch but has bold lateral stripes.

Distribution: Throughout the Great Lakes drainage. Mainly found in lakes, their populations have boom and bust cycles. One year, huge rafts can be seen on the surface in places like Onondaga Lake; the next year, they seem as rare as hen's teeth.

Additional information: Most locals don't differentiate between these and white perch, simply calling both silver bass. White bass spawn in late spring. The state record, caught in Furnace Brook on May 2, 1992, is 3 pounds, 6 ounces.

Burbot, or Ling or Lawyer *(Lota lota)*

General description: Looking like a cross between a bullhead and an eel, this species' color is yellow-brown overlaid with a dark mottled pattern. It has a single barbel on its chin and deeply embedded scales that are so tiny, they are almost invisible.

Distribution: Cold, deep lakes and rivers in the Great Lakes and Susquehanna River drainages.

Additional information: Found in water up to 700 feet deep, individuals range from 12 to 20 inches. They are the only freshwater fish in the state that spawns in winter. Females lay up to one million eggs at a time. The state record, caught in Black River Bay on February 14, 1991, is 16 pounds, 12 ounces.

Freshwater Drum, or Sheepshead *(Aplodinotus grunniens)*

General description: Overall color is silvery with a blue to olive-brown back and a white belly.

Distribution: Great Lakes and Mohawk, Hudson, and Susquehanna River drainages.

Additional information: Sheepsheads have small round teeth for crushing snails and have a taste for zebra mussels. They use muscles around their swimming bladders to produce drumming sounds. Spawning takes place in the summer from July through September. The state record, caught in Ganargua Creek on May 26, 1995, is 24 pounds, 7 ounces.

Common Carp *(Cyprinus carpio)*

General description: A brown-colored, large-scaled fish with orange fins, it has two barbels on each side of its upper jaw. Some are leatherlike with no scales or spotted with disproportionately large scales.

Distribution: Native to Eurasia, the species was introduced into American waters around 1830 and found the habitat good. They thrive in warm water and can be found everywhere from the Great Lakes to abandoned canals, farm ponds, and in the lower reaches of creeks and brooks.

Additional information: Like many introduced species, carp suffer an image problem. Recently, however, traveling European anglers have discovered the state's tremendous carp fishery, and the species is gaining cult status. A good way to catch them is to find a spot that looks fishy and still-fish with a piece of baked potato about the size of a bouillon cube, a marble-size piece of white bread, or several kernels of canned corn. They will also hit worms. One of the most exciting ways to catch them is to sight-fish in a sluggish creek, slowly working the bait to the fish. They spawn in late spring when the water temperature reaches 62 degrees Fahrenheit. The state record, caught in Tomhannock Reservoir on May 12, 1995, is 50 pounds, 4 ounces.

American Eel *(Anguilla rostrata)*

General description: A snakelike fish with a pointed head, its dorsal fin starts midway down its back, wraps around the end, and becomes continuous with the caudal and anal fins, reaching halfway up the belly.

Distribution: These fish are found throughout the Great Lakes and Hudson River drainages and in the New Erie Canal.

Additional information: Nocturnal by nature, eels are often caught at night on worms by bullhead anglers fishing in swamps and marshes and by walleye anglers fishing large minnows on the bottom in canals or in holes below dams. After hatching in the Atlantic Ocean, the larvae migrate to fresh water, where individuals live for varying lengths of time before maturing and returning to the Sargasso Sea to spawn and die, a life cycle known as catadromous. Mature adults migrate back to sea in autumn. The eel's life span is unknown, but one was kept in captivity for eighty-eight years. Females migrate for great distances inland, while males stay close to the sea. The state record, caught in Cayuga Lake on July 25, 1984, is 7 pounds, 14 ounces.

Bowfin, or Dog Fish *(Amia calva)*

General description: Easily recognized by its primitive appearance, it has a long flat head, a large mouth full of sharp teeth, a dorsal fin running along most of its back, and a rounded tail. Males have a large spot at the upper corner of the base of the tail.

Distribution: Mostly found in the Great Lakes drainage; however, some inland waters like Lake Neatahwanta are loaded with them.

Additional information: The sole surviving member of the Amiiformes family, a species that was around when dinosaurs roamed the countryside, bowfins spawn in shallow water in the spring. The state record, caught in Bashakill Marsh on June 5, 2000, is 12 pounds, 8 ounces.

White Sucker, or French Trout or Rubber Lips
(Catostomus commersoni)

General description: A large-scaled, cylindrically shaped fish, its back and sides are olive-brown, and it has a white belly. They normally range from 10 to 20 inches.

Distribution: Throughout the state in just about every kind of water, from small streams to the Great Lakes.

Additional information: Although their flesh is sweet in the early spring, it gets funky as the water warms up. About the only use most anglers have for white suckers is for bait. Their young are among the hardiest minnows, capable of living for hours while hooked through the back. Many anglers kill them needlessly, and this is a waste because suckers are valuable forage for everything from pike and bass to muskies, walleyes, and trout. The state record, caught in the Hudson River on May 13, 1994, is 5 pounds, 3 ounces.

Rainbow Smelt *(Osmerus mordax)*

General description: A cylindrically shaped silver fish with an olive back, it generally sports a noticeable silver stripe and a pink or blue iridescence along it sides. It has a large mouth for a small fish, with two large canine teeth on the roof of the mouth. They normally range from 6 to 9 inches but can reach 13 inches.

Distribution: Found in the Great Lakes and Lake Champlain, they have been introduced into numerous waters throughout the state, including some Finger Lakes.

Additional information: Smelt are considered a delicacy wherever they are found. They ascend small streams in the spring to spawn and are often taken in large quantities with dip nets. There is no state record.

GREAT LAKES REGION

ombined, the five Great Lakes (Superior, Michigan, Huron, Erie, and Ontario) flood 94,560 square miles, an area stretching from the heart of North America to its east coast. Although Russia's Lake Baikal is the deepest and largest body of fresh water in the world, the Great Lakes cover more surface area. The border between Canada and the United States runs roughly across their center. New York contains the United States' entire share of Lake Ontario, the Niagara and St. Lawrence Rivers, and about 20 percent (the southeastern end) of Lake Erie.

The only way to do justice to these massive diversified fisheries is to break them down into components. The Lake Erie and Lake Ontario sites will concentrate on the lakes; bays, tributaries, and outlets will be treated as individual sites. In the case of feeder streams like the Genesee and Black Rivers, whose fisheries in the lower reaches are influenced by seasonal runs of Lake Ontario species, only the stretch from their mouths to the first barrier impassable by fish will be reviewed in this section. The remainder will be covered in the regional section. For instance, the Upper Salmon River is in the Central New York region.

Keep in mind that both lakes and their tributaries upstream to the first barrier impassable by fish are governed by the Great Lakes Special Regulations listed in the *New York State Department of Environmental Conservation Fishing Regulations Guide.* Like the seasons, the rules change regularly, often according to geographic location and sometimes without rhyme or reason (for instance, the daily limit for rainbow trout in all Jefferson County tributaries is one), so check each new printing of the regulations.

In the fall of 2000, roughly 6,000 waterfowl washed up on Lake Erie's eastern shore. Studies showed they had died of Type E botulism, a paralytic disease commonly affecting fish-eating birds but also fatal to humans. The following summer, bottom-feeding fish—specifically freshwater drum (sheepshead), smallmouth bass, rock bass, stone cats, channel catfish, mudpuppies, and lake sturgeon—began washing up on shore from the same cause. Since the disease hadn't been eradicated by the time this book went to press, you are advised not to touch sickly fish or dead fish and birds found in the water or on the beach.

1. Lake Erie (see maps on pages 23, 24, and 26)

Key species: Muskellunge, smallmouth bass, walleye, steelhead, channel catfish, and yellow perch.

Description: The fourth largest Great Lake and the eleventh largest freshwater body in the world, Lake Erie is relatively shallow, averaging about 60 feet deep. Lacking the great depths of its sister lakes makes it one of the most productive warm-water fisheries on the planet, all 9,910 square miles of it.

Angler with a nice bronzeback taken in Lake Erie (site 1).

Tips: Drag scented or salted tubes on jigheads along bottom for smallmouths.

The fishing: Ever since being brought back from the dead in the 1970s, Lake Erie has been famous for smallmouth bass and walleyes. The bass average 3 pounds, and you can expect at least one 4-pounder per trip—fifty-fish days are common. They are mostly targeted with soft plastics—everything from craws and 3-inch minnows to curly-tailed grubs and lizards. Walleyes average 6 pounds, but so many fish over 12 pounds have been caught, no one keeps track anymore. They are mostly taken by trolling crankbaits ranging from Rattlin' Rogues and Poe's Super Cedars to Hot 'N Tots. Yellow perch, typically ranging between 10 and 14 inches, are taken with worms, minnows, and small lures. Huge muskies up to 50 pounds can show up anytime and are often caught on crankbaits targeting bass. However, serious muskie hunters target trophies by trolling large crankbaits. Steelhead ranging from 3 to 20 pounds are caught offshore by trolling spoons and plugs and off piers with worms and egg sacs. Monster channel catfish up to 30 pounds are targeted in stream mouths with cut bait and chicken liver.

The lake possesses so many smallmouths, it boasts a special season for trophy bass. From the first Saturday in May until the regular season opener, anglers are

Lake Erie: Barcelona to Dunkirk · Lower Chautauqua Creek

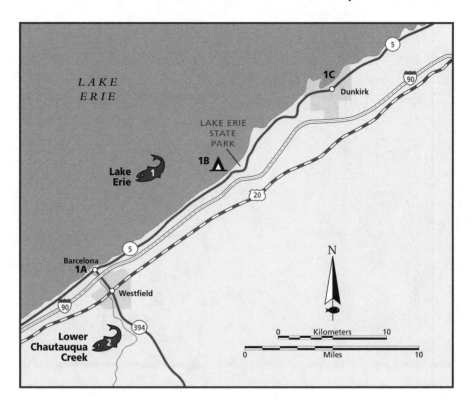

entitled to keep one bass daily at least 15 inches long. In 2002 the state was considering stocking brown trout into the lake. If the program works as expected, Lake Erie will contain "football browns" by press time and trophies a couple of years later.

This lake is governed by the special Great Lakes regulations found in the state *Fishing Regulations Guide*.

Directions: NY 5 parallels the lake, coming so close to the water half the time, motorists can see it.

Additional information: If you are going to fish offshore and aren't sure where the international border is, carry a Canadian fishing license. The local visitors bureaus offer a free *Greater Niagara Hot Spot Fishing Map: Erie and Niagara County Fishing Guide*.

Contact: New York State Department of Environmental Conservation Region 9, Chautauqua County Visitors Bureau, and Buffalo Niagara Convention & Visitors Bureau.

Lake Erie: Silver Creek to Evangola State Park · Lower Cattaraugus Creek

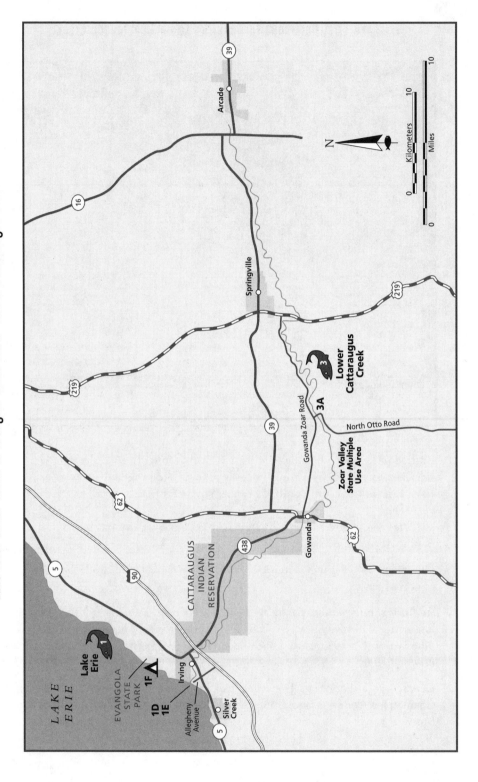

1A. Barcelona Harbor Boat Launch/Dan Reed Pier Park
(see map on page 23)

Description: This facility offers a three-lane paved ramp, parking for seventy-five rigs, and shore-fishing access. A launch fee is charged during peak season, from around a week before Memorial Day through a week after Labor Day.

Directions: At the US 20/NY 394 intersection in the village of Westfield, head northwest on NY 394 for almost 2 miles to NY 5 and turn east.

1B. Lake Erie State Park *(see map on page 23)*

Description: This 355-acre fee area offers ninety-seven no-frills campsites, ten cabins, hot showers, a picnic area, and a 0.75-mile beach.

Directions: From Dunkirk, take NY 5 west for about 5 miles.

1C. Dunkirk Harbor Ramp/City Pier Park *(see map on page 23)*

Description: A large pier with a parking strip down the middle, bait shop, double-lane concrete ramp, parking for fifty rigs, and shore-fishing access.

The fishing: The lake off the harbor is one of the best spots around for catching smallmouth bass ranging from 2 to 7 pounds. In the early season drag rubber worms, curly-tailed grubs, or just about any other soft plastic on bottom in 15 to 25 feet of water. By mid-July the bass move out to water from 25 to 35 feet deep. Toward season's end they're even deeper, up to 40 feet. Catfish ranging from 6 to 18 pounds are partial to this area and respond to cut bait, strips of salmon milt, and gobs of salmon skein.

Directions: On Central Avenue in the heart of Dunkirk.

1D. Town of Hanover Launch

Description: This facility boasts hard-surface ramps, parking for about seventy-five rigs, and additional parking for about thirty cars.

Directions: From Silver Creek, take NY 5 east for about 2 miles, turn north on Allegheny Avenue, then turn right about 0.25 mile later at the sign.

1E. Cattaraugus Creek Harbor Public Access

Description: This site has parking for about ten cars.

The fishing: The mouth of Cattaraugus Creek is protected by a long, tall breakwall. Anglers stand at its base and target steelhead averaging 5 pounds with spinners, crankbaits, and egg sacs in autumn and spring. This is also a popular spot for trophy channel catfish up to 25 pounds. They like meat (big minnows, chicken liver, cut bait, and shrimp) fished on bottom in deep holes.

Directions: Follow directions to site 1D, but instead of turning off Allegheny Avenue, continue to its end.

Lake Erie: Sturgeon Point to Buffalo Harbor and Nearby Creeks

1F. Evangola State Park *(see map on page 24)*

Description: Sprawling over 700 scenic acres, this fee area offers eighty-something campsites, a long stretch of beach, a snack bar, and showers. The campground is open May through mid-October; free day use off season.

Directions: From Buffalo, take NY 5 west for about 15 miles.

1G. Sturgeon Point Public Access

Description: This fee area offers paved launch ramps, parking for over a hundred rigs, additional parking for over a hundred cars, and shore-fishing access. A launch fee is charged only in summer.

The fishing: Shore anglers find the breakwall a productive spot for catching steelhead in autumn and spring with egg sacs and perch and smallmouth bass in spring and summer with minnows, crayfish, and plugs. Additionally, the lake off Sturgeon Point is famed for post-spawn smallmouths ranging from 1 to 5 pounds. They can be taken from June through mid-July in 15 to 25 feet of water with scented tubes, Carolina-rigged 4-inch finesse worms, or bucktail jigs. Some huge walleyes also come around early in the season and can be taken by drifting worm rigs or casting minnow crankbaits like Smithwick Rogues and Divin' Rat-L-Traps. From fall through spring, fish the 40- to 60-foot depths about 3 miles offshore for yellow perch up to 15 inches.

Directions: Head west on NY 5 for about 2.5 miles from Highland-on-the-Lake and turn right on Sturgeon Point Road.

1H. Buffalo Harbor

Description: Averaging 30 feet deep, the harbor's waves break against downtown Buffalo's west bank. Five miles of breakwall protect it from the worst Lake Erie can dish out.

The fishing: Compared to the rest of the lake, the smallmouth bass and walleye fisheries are poor here. However, trophy muskies and huge walleyes move into the area in November, lured by schools of bait seeking refuge in the harbor's warmer waters. Most are targeted by trolling large crankbaits. The minimum length for muskies is 54 inches.

Additional information: Formerly heavily industrialized, the harbor has a lot of shore-fishing access but is best fished from a boat. The NFTA Small Boat Harbor and Marina, the country's largest freshwater marina, boasts 14 concrete ramps, loading docks, parking for 1,000 rigs, shuttle service to the parking lot, modern rest rooms, and a restaurant. Open May 15 through November 30; a launch fee charged during peak periods.

Directions: Off Furhmann Boulevard in Buffalo.

2. Lower Chautauqua Creek *(see map on page 23)*

Key species: Steelhead.

Description: A clear, pool/riff stream for about the first mile below the Westfield Waterworks' barrier, this creek slowly widens and deepens. Around the NY 5 bridge, it reaches the same gradient as Lake Erie, becoming wadeable flat water punctuated with deep spots.

Tips: Float a little piece of worm or a whole garden worm below a pencil bobber.

The fishing: Experts classify this creek as New York's second most productive Lake Erie tributary (Lower Cattauraugus Creek, site 3, is numero uno) for steelhead. The state stocks roughly 50,000 steelhead annually. From autumn through spring, returnees ranging from 3 to 15 pounds stage heart-pounding runs. They hit egg sacs, in-line spinners, and Hot Shots.

Directions: Head north out of the hamlet of Westfield on NY 394 for almost 2 miles to NY 5, turn west, and travel for about 0.5 mile.

Additional information: The state owns public fishing rights on both banks from the mouth to about 500 yards upstream of the NY 5 bridge.

Contact: New York State Department of Environmental Conservation Region 9 and Chautauqua County Visitors Bureau.

3. Lower Cattaraugus Creek *(see map on page 24)*

Key species: Steelhead.

Description: Roughly 65 miles long, the lower portion stretches from Springville Dam to the mouth, some 30 miles, and includes the fabulous Zoar Valley, a gorge with cliffs soaring up to 300 feet above the water. A shallow stream at the dam, it grows steadily, becoming river-size by the time it flows into Lake Erie.

Tips: From ice-out through March, cast spoons like Little Cleos and Dardevles around the mouth for steelhead.

The fishing: Steelhead are this stream's bread-and-butter fish. From October through March, they migrate inland all the way to the Springville Dam—water levels permitting. However, most fish are caught downstream of Gowanda. They take egg sacs, worms, in-line spinners, and yarn flies.

Additional information: About half way between NY 5/US 20 and I–90, the stream enters the Seneca Nation of Indians' Cattaraugus Reservation and largely remains on their territory for about 10 miles, to roughly 500 yards below Gowanda's Aldrich Street Bridge. A tribal license, but not a New York state license, is needed to fish the nation's waters. The visitors bureau's *Greater Niagara Hot Spot Fishing*

Map: Erie and Niagara County Fishing Guide contains a map showing where Indian territory is.

Directions: NY 438 parallels the creek from Irving to Gowanda.

Contact: New York State Department of Environmental Conservation Region 9, Cattaraugus Indian Reservation, and Buffalo Niagara Convention & Visitors Bureau.

3A. Public Access *(see map on page 24)*

Description: This site offers shore access and parking for about ten cars.

The fishing: After heavy autumn rains and during winter thaws and spring runoff, steelhead up to 15 pounds are present in the gorge.

Additional information: This spot is a little upstream of the Zoar Valley. Some anglers launch rubber rafts and canoes here, float into the Zoar Valley State Multiple Use Area, and take out at the US 62 bridge in downtown Gowanda.

Directions: Take Gowanda Zoar Road for about 6 miles east from Gowanda and turn south on North Otto Road (CR 11).

4. Eighteenmile Creek (Erie County) *(see map on page 26)*

Key species: Brown trout, steelhead, and channel catfish.

Description: About the size of an average trout stream, this creek has many personalities, ranging from shallow water sliding over bedrock to trout-friendly pocket water, riffles, and pools.

Tips: Use egg sacs immediately after ice-out.

The fishing: Although the state stocks the headwaters with about 750 9-inch brown trout each year, this creek is best known for steelhead—roughly 40,000 5-inchers are stocked annually. They trickle back to their childhood haunts during the fall salmon runs to pig out on salmon eggs and again in the spring to spawn. Chromers typically range from 6 to 12 pounds and like egg sacs, yarn flies, and ⅛-ounce in-line spinners like Aglia Streamers. Monster channel catfish up to 25 pounds hang out in the holes at the creek's mouth during warm weather and like chicken livers, cut bait, salmon milt, and skein.

Directions: Head north out of Highland-on-the-Lake on Lake Shore Road for about a mile and turn east on South Creek Road, which parallels the creek for about 4 miles.

Contact: New York State Department of Environmental Conservation Region 9 and Buffalo Niagara Convention & Visitors Bureau.

4A. Hoback Flats Public Access *(see map on page 26)*

Description: Parking for twenty cars.

Directions: Head south out of Buffalo on NY 5 for about 10 miles, turn east on South Creek Road and travel about 1 mile to the hamlet of North Evans, then turn left on Versailles Road and travel a few hundred yards.

Additional information: The state owns fishing rights stretching from a few hundred yards downstream of the access site, upstream to the US 20 bridge.

5. Cazenovia Creek *(see map on page 26)*

Key species: Steelhead.

Description: Formed by the confluence of the east and west branches, this stream flows west for about 11 miles and feeds the Buffalo River. Running largely through populated areas, it has a moderate gradient and relatively clear water.

Tips: Work tiny Flatfish and in-line spinners through the flat water.

The fishing: Savvy locals have been catching salmonids in this stream for as long as they've been stocked in Lake Erie. Though not great in number, steelhead ranging from 3 to 10 pounds are available fall through spring and are normally targeted with egg sacs and fresh salmon skein.

Directions: NY 16 parallels the creek from East Aurora to Buffalo.

Additional information: State fisheries biologist Mike Wilson says his office started an annual stocking program in 2003 in which 10,000 steelhead were released. If the program takes off, substantial numbers of steelhead in the 2- to 3-pound range should start running in 2005, and they'll be bigger each year after that. The lower reaches are good canoe water.

Contact: New York State Department of Environmental Conservation Region 9 and Buffalo Niagara Convention & Visitors Bureau.

6. Buffalo Creek *(see map on page 26)*

Key species: Walleye, smallmouth bass, steelhead, and brown trout.

Description: The headwaters of the Buffalo River, this stream twists and turns every chance it gets, meandering for a dizzying 35 miles or so before reaching its destination on the outskirts of Buffalo.

Tips: Cast Wooly Worms in the fall for brown trout.

The fishing: State fisheries biologist Joe Evans says the area around the mouth of this stream is a popular local hot spot for post-spawn walleyes and smallmouths. Walleyes can go anywhere from 2 to 8 pounds, and the bronzebacks reach 4 pounds.

Both respond to worms and crankbaits. Steelhead tour from late fall through spring and are taken on egg sacs and worms. The headwaters in Wyoming County are stocked with 2,500 yearling brown trout averaging 8.5 inches and 200 two-year-olds. They like worms and salted minnows fished deep in spring and in-line spinners and flies summer and fall.

Directions: NY 354 parallels the creek on the outskirts of Buffalo, and NY 78 parallels its headwaters.

Additional information: There are no formal public access sites, but posted signs are few, and most folks enter the stream anywhere it comes close to the road and at bridges.

Contact: New York State Department of Environmental Conservation Region 9 and Buffalo Niagara Convention & Visitors Bureau.

7. Buffalo River

Key species: Walleye, smallmouth bass, and steelhead.

Buffalo River

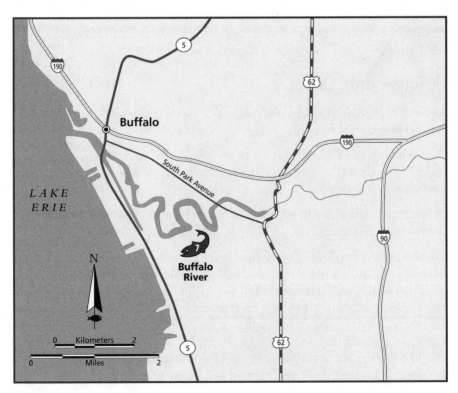

Description: Flowing through Buffalo, the state's second largest city, this Lake Erie tributary got dumped on quite a bit in the past. Indeed, in the 1960s about all that plied its sticky waves were brown nasties—not trout, either. Currently the stuff flowing through it resembles water again, prompting some to proclaim it one of the state's greatest environmental success stories.

Tips: Cast rattling crankbaits for post-spawn walleyes and smallmouths.

The fishing: This urban stream attracts spawning runs of walleyes, and some stay in the city for the first few weeks of the season. They range from 3 to 10 pounds and are taken by trolling crankbaits and drifting worms, plain and on spinner harnesses. Smallmouth bass also run the stream to spawn. They can reach over 5 pounds and are taken on worms and crayfish. Roughly 20,000 yearling steelies are stocked annually, and each spring they return to downtown for some spawning action. They hit egg sacs, worms, yarn flies, and small lures. The river has a history of being a walleye fishery, and according to Jim Hanley, Erie County's sport fishing coordinator, the state is conducting a walleye stocking program aimed at restoring a residential population.

Directions: The river meanders around Buffalo's south side and is paralleled near its mouth by South Park Avenue and Ohio Street.

Additional information: A fishing access site on Harlem Road has parking for fifteen cars.

Contact: New York State Department of Environmental Conservation Region 9 and Buffalo Niagara Convention & Visitors Bureau.

8. Tonawanda Creek

Key species: Walleye, northern pike, largemouth bass, smallmouth bass, black crappie, and brown trout.

Description: While the last 13 miles or so of the creek have been channeled and made into the New Erie Canal, the water upstream of Pendleton occupies the natural course and snakes east for about 40 scenic miles.

Tips: Cast crankbaits like Bomber Long "A"s and Rat-L-Traps through deep pools in May and June for walleyes.

The fishing: Walleyes from 18 to 25 inches are available year-round. However, the most productive time to fish is from opening day through mid-June, when many of the Lake Erie and Niagara River fish who swam into the creek to spawn are still around. Most locals target them with crankbaits and jigs tipped with minnows, worms, or scented curly-tailed grubs, or by drifting worms or trolling night crawlers on spinner rigs. Northern pike in the 18- to 22-inch range are plentiful, and 10-pounders are available. They respond to live minnows and spinnerbaits. Largemouth bass average 2 to 4 pounds, and bigger ones are present. They hang

Tonawanda Creek

around docks, windfalls, and vegetation and respond to Zara Spooks, soft plastic jerkbaits, and 7- to 10-inch worms jerked on the surface or just below it and to jig-'n'-pigs worked in slop and along weed edges. Bronzebacks are usually small, from 12 to 14 inches. They love crayfish, worms, and spinnerbaits. Black crappies typically range from 9 to 12 inches, but dream-size 14-inchers and better are taken regularly. They like minnows, Beetle Spins, and wet flies worked around structure and windfalls. South of Attica, the state annually stocks roughly 2,500 brown trout averaging 9 inches and 200 two-year-olds averaging 14 inches. They respond to garden worms and red worms in early spring and night crawlers and flies the rest of the season.

Directions: Tonawanda Creek Road and NY 5 parallel much of the stream's warmwater fishery, and NY 98 runs along the trout sections.

Additional information: The creek forms the Niagara-Erie County line. A couple miles upstream of NY 93, the creek enters the Tonawanda Indian Reservations, and nonresidents are urged to get permission before fishing on Indian territory—problem is, they're very slow in returning calls.

Contact: New York State Department of Environmental Conservation Region 9.

9. Upper Niagara River

Key species: Muskellunge, northern pike, smallmouth bass, largemouth bass, and walleye.

Description: The outlet of Lake Erie, this stream starts out at a brisk pace in Buffalo, steadily accelerates to rapids, and ends up diving over Niagara Falls—all in the span of about 16 miles.

Tips: In autumn flatline "The Triangle" (the area between Strawberry Island, the northern tip of Grand Island, and Frenchman Creek) with large crankbaits like Swim Wizzes and Depth Raiders for trophy muskellunge.

The fishing: Muskie anglers have always considered the upper river one of the best bets in the entire Great Lakes region for catching a trophy. Twenty-five-pounders are plentiful, and going for a 40-pounder is a realistic goal. Fish for them by drifting large minnows up to 18 inches long, casting large jerkbaits and bucktail spinners, or trolling huge plugs. Northerns average 5 pounds and love ambushing spinnerbaits and buzzbaits worked in marinas and weedy shelves along the bank. Pikeasaurus enthusiasts nail numerous fish in the 10- to 15-pound class by drifting alewives or shiners on bottom or suspending them below bobbers and fishing tight to weed edges. Smallmouths aren't as plentiful or as big as their Lake Erie cousins, but there are enough trophies to make fishing for them worthwhile. Work bucktail jigs or jigheads tipped with curly-tailed grubs and tubes along drops and around structure, including construction debris. Lately the largemouth bass fishery has been exploding. Jim Hanley, Erie County sport fishing coordinator, says an 8-pound-4-ounce

Upper Niagara River

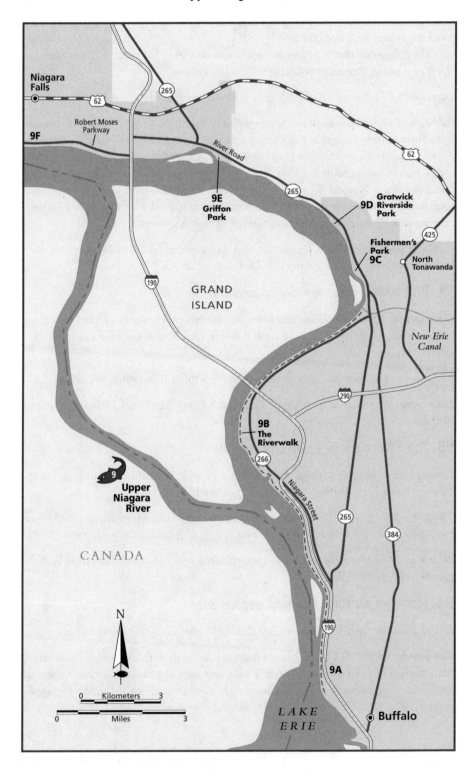

trophy was caught in 2001. He suggests working jig-'n'-pigs and spinnerbaits along weed edges in heavy current. Walleyes are in the river year-round, but the greatest numbers can be found in spring and fall. Cast crankbaits or work jigs along deep weed edges and over boulder fields.

The Niagara River is governed by the special Great Lakes regulations found in the state *Fishing Regulations Guide*.

Directions: NY 265 and Robert Moses Parkway parallel the river.

Additional information: Boats are prohibited north of Grand Island to prevent folks from getting caught in the current and being swept over the falls. The visitors bureau publishes a free fishing map (*Greater Niagara Hot Spot Fishing Map*). There are no public campgrounds on the river, but numerous private ones are in the area. Niagara Falls, a Natural Wonder of the World, is popular with honeymooners and tourists. The cities on both sides of the cataract are loaded with motels and features ranging from theme parks and aquariums to gambling casinos.

Contact: New York State Department of Environmental Conservation Region 9 and Buffalo Niagara Convention & Visitors Bureau.

9A. Bird Island Pier *(see map on page 35)*

Description: This 2-mile-long pier separates the Niagara River from the Black Rock Canal. It was recently renovated by the Army Corps of Engineers and now has a safety railing.

The fishing: The pier is a local hot spot for everything that swims in Lake Erie.

Directions: Access is at Broderick Park (take Ferry Street off Niagara Street) in Buffalo.

9B. The Riverwalk *(see map on page 35)*

Description: Shoulder parking areas along a 14-mile recreational trail hugging the Niagara River from Buffalo to the mouth of the Erie Canal.

The fishing: This trail offers numerous spots to shore fish. Every species in the river comes within range of bank anglers in the spring and fall.

Directions: Niagara Street (NY 266), which turns into River Road north of Buffalo, parallels the Riverwalk.

9C. Fishermen's Park *(see map on page 35)*

Description: Parking for five cars and about 150 yards of great shore-fishing access.

The fishing: Most folks come here to leisurely still-fish with live bait for everything from catfish and sheepshead to white bass and sunfish. However, spin fishers do well casting crankbaits or swimming 3-inch scented curly-tailed grubs for small-mouths ranging from 1 to 2.5 pounds and an occasional walleye up to 8 pounds.

Directions: Off River Road (NY 265) on the west side of North Tonawanda.

9D. Gratwick Riverside Park Public Access *(see map on page 35)*

Description: This fee area offers a paved ramp, parking for fifty rigs, picnic tables, and 300 yards of shore fishing.

Directions: On River Road (NY 265) in the village of North Tonawanda.

9E. Griffon Park Shore Public Access *(see map on page 35)*

Description: This tiny park offers a paved ramp, parking for ten rigs, and shore-fishing access on the channel (called the Little Niagara River) flowing between Cayuga Island and the mainland.

The fishing: The river channel from Cayuga Island to about 1 mile upstream is a muskie hot spot.

Directions: Off Buffalo Avenue on the south edge of the city of Niagara Falls.

9F. Niagara Reservation State Park *(see map on page 35)*

Description: A mile-long sidewalk hugs the river from the falls upstream. Huge pay-to-park lots are at the falls, and a no-fee parking area for about five cars is about 1 mile upstream of the falls.

The fishing: Steelhead averaging 5 pounds move into this fast water (the nastiest rapids this side of the Colorado River) autumn through spring, and smallmouth bass up to 18 inches hang out in the pockets in summer and fall. Both species take crankbaits and streamers, and the chromers take egg sacs, too.

Directions: Off the southbound lane of Robert Moses Parkway in Niagara Falls.

10. New York State Power Authority Reservoir
(see map on page 38)

Key species: Smallmouth bass and walleye.

Description: This 1,900-acre impoundment holds water diverted from the Upper Niagara River at night for use in generating power by the lower river's generators by day.

Tips: As your bait approaches shore, reel in quickly to avoid hooking up on rocks.

The fishing: Just about every species found in the Upper Niagara River, including muskies, can be found here. However, smallmouth bass ranging from 12 to 16 inches and walleyes from 18 to 22 inches are the most often sought game fish. They take minnows, worms, and crankbaits.

Directions: Take Lockport Road east from Niagara Falls to the edge of town, turn north on Military Road (NY 265) and follow it for about 1 mile.

Lower Niagara River - Wilson and Olcott Areas

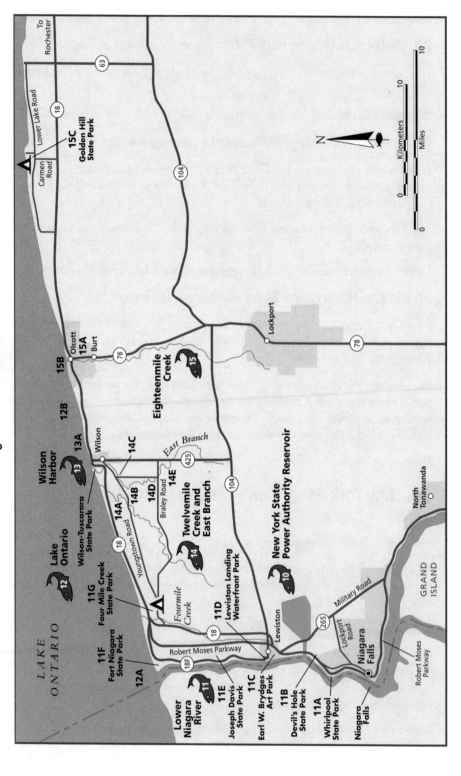

To Rochester

Lower Lake Road

Carmen Road

15C
Golden Hill State Park

63

18

104

Lockport

78

Eighteenmile Creek

15

Olcott
15A Burt
15B

78

12B

13A

Wilson

14C

East Branch

425

14E
14B **14D**

Braley Road

Twelvemile Creek and East Branch

14

104

New York State Power Authority Reservoir

10

Military Road

Lockport Road

265

North Tonawanda

GRAND ISLAND

Robert Moses Parkway

Niagara Falls

Wilson Harbor

13

Wilson-Tuscarora State Park

Youngstown Road

18

Fourmile Creek

18

Lake Ontario

12

11G
Four Mile Creek State Park

11F
Fort Niagara State Park

12A

18F

LAKE ONTARIO

Lower Niagara River

11

11E
Joseph Davis State Park

11C
Earl W. Brydges Art Park

Robert Moses Parkway

18

Lewiston

11D
Lewiston Landing Waterfront Park

11B
Devil's Hole State Park

11A
Whirlpool State Park

Niagara Falls

Robert Moses Parkway

N

10
Kilometers
0

10
Miles
0

10
0

Additional information: The reservoir park has parking for about twenty-five cars, a playground, picnic facilities, and toilets. Boating is not allowed.

Contact: New York State Department of Environmental Conservation Region 9 and Niagara County Tourism and Convention Corporation.

11. Lower Niagara River

Key species: Lake trout, steelhead, chinook salmon, coho salmon, brown trout, muskellunge, walleye, smallmouth bass, channel catfish, and white bass.

Description: Flowing from Niagara Falls to its mouth on Lake Ontario, a distance of about 12 miles, this stretch of river is half raging rapids slicing through a spectacular gorge and half mild-mannered stream guided by steep, wooded slopes.

Tips: In the spring back-troll crankbaits on bottom in the fast water between the Niagara Power Project and the first set of river-wide rapids about 0.25 mile upstream.

The fishing: Each spring schools of lake trout ranging from 5 to 20 pounds ascend the river to spawn. They are taken mostly by trolling Kwikfish and Flatfish. Steelhead up to 15 pounds are present in rapids year-round, especially from fall through spring. During cold weather they like egg sacs, skein, and worms bounced along bottom. When the water starts warming up, they'll take in-line spinners, crankbaits, and streamers. Fall sends massive runs of chinook salmon up to 40 pounds and coho salmon up to 20 pounds into the river. Fish for them with egg sacs or gobs of fresh skein treated with Pro-Cure. Lake-run, football-size brown trout run about the same time salmon do and hit egg sacs and worms.

Muskellunge ranging from 20 to 30 pounds rule the slow water north of Lewiston. They respond to large crankbaits like Hookers flatlined on lead-core line. Walleyes ranging from 2 to 10 pounds can be caught just about anywhere. The favorite local technique is to drift spinner-rigged Yellow Sally flies tipped with worms in the eddies of places like Stella Niagara and in the mouth of the river. Jigging with bucktails tipped with worms, minnows, or leeches or with bladebaits also works well. Scrappy smallmouth bass up to 16 inches are all over the rapids and will hit anything from worms and minnows to curly-tailed grubs and diving crankbaits. Huge catfish up to 20-something pounds prowl deep eddies and can be taken on live minnows and cut bait fished on bottom. Although their numbers have been down recently, white bass from 5 to 10 inches still concentrate below the Niagara Power Project's turbines. They hit worms, small crankbaits, and curly-tailed grubs worked through the turbulence.

The Niagara River is governed by the special Great Lakes regulations found in the state *Fishing Regulations Guide*.

Directions: Robert Moses Parkway parallels the river from the falls to NY 104 in Lewiston, and NY 18F parallels it from there all the way to Fort Niagara State Park at the mouth.

Whitewater smallmouth bass from the Niagara Gorge (site 11).

Additional information: The international border between the United States and Canada runs down the middle of the river. Boat fishers have two options: Stay on the east half or carry a Canadian license.

Contact: New York State Department of Environmental Conservation Region 9 and Niagara County Tourism and Convention Corporation.

11A. Whirlpool State Park Gorge Access *(see map on page 38)*

Description: An environmentally friendly Civilian Conservation Corps–era stone stairway leads down to an abandoned trolley grade that follows the river for a couple miles in both directions. If you head downstream for about 1 mile, you'll find stairs leading up to Devil's Hole State Park.

The fishing: Trophy lake-run salmonids and resident smallmouths up to 18 inches hang out in the oxygenated water. The area is challenging to fish because of its monster rapids and huge boulders calved off the soaring cliffs. But the spectacular scenery and chance to catch a trophy salmonid just about any time of year make the effort worthwhile.

Directions: This park is located about 2 miles north of Niagara Falls, off the south lane of Robert Moses Parkway. After parking, follow the rim railing downstream (north) for about 0.25 mile to the stairs.

Additional information: During the evening the New York Power Authority draws water from the Upper Niagara River to fill its power reservoir. Come morning, it closes its intake pipes, and the river rises dramatically. If you see it coming up, back off to higher ground.

11B. Devil's Hole State Park Gorge Access *(see map on page 38)*

Description: An environmentally friendly Civilian Conservation Corps–era stone staircase winds down to a trail at the bottom of the gorge. An old trolley grade, eroded in one spot to just a few inches wide, skirts the bottom. If you head upstream on the trail for about 1 mile, you'll find the stairs leading up to Whirlpool State Park.

The fishing: See site 11A.

Directions: The park is about 3 miles north of the city of Niagara Falls, off the south lane of the Robert Moses Parkway.

Additional information: See site 11A.

11C. Earl W. Brydges Art Park *(see map on page 38)*

Description: A 202-acre state park specializing in cultural events, it also offers trails down gentle slopes to two fishing access landings on quiet stretches of the river. In addition, adventurous types can strike out on their own to fish the park's rugged mile-long shoreline stretching to the Niagara Power Project's Robert Moses Power Plant.

Directions: Entrances on South Eighth Street and South Fourth Street in the village of Lewiston.

11D. Lewiston Landing Waterfront Park *(see map on page 38)*

Description: This fee area offers a double-lane paved ramp with parking for thirty rigs, picnic tables, and toilets.

Directions: Located on Water Street on west edge of the village of Lewiston.

11E. Joseph Davis State Park *(see map on page 38)*

Description: Spread over more than 200 acres, this park offers parking for five cars and about 300 yards of shore fishing on a quiet stretch of the Niagara River.

Directions: Head north out of Lewiston on NY 18F for a little under 2 miles.

11F. Fort Niagara State Park *(see map on page 38)*

Description: Sprawling over 240 acres, including a stretch of Lake Ontario Beach and the Niagara River, this fee area offers shore fishing, a paved boat launch on the Niagara, parking for a hundred rigs, and rest rooms.

Directions: Located on the northern edge of Youngstown, off NY 18F.

Additional information: Standing at the mouth of the Niagara River, the fort was built by the French during the French and Indian War, but they lost it to the British. Ceded to America in 1796, our troops used it to stage their unsuccessful invasion of Canada during the War of 1812. The British recaptured it briefly but returned it after the conflict. The United States stationed troops at the fort until 1963. Currently, it is staffed in summer by Revolutionary War reenactors.

11G. Four Mile Creek State Park *(see map on page 38)*

Description: Spread over 248 acres, including a long stretch of Lake Ontario Beach, this fee area isn't on the Niagara River—but it's close, only about 3 miles east of the mouth. It offers more than 250 campsites (100 electric), showers, toilets, and access to Fourmile Creek. A day-use fee is charged noncampers in-season, the third weekend of April through October.

The fishing: Fourmile Creek gets minor autumnal runs of salmonids, water levels permitting, and small groups of ripe, bragging-size steelhead in the spring.

Directions: Head north out of Youngstown on NY 18 for 3 miles, turn left on Four Mile Drive, and continue for a couple hundred yards.

12. Lake Ontario *(see maps on pages 38, 55, 58, 66, 78, 85, 89, and 91)*

Key species: Chinook salmon, coho salmon, lake trout, brown trout, steelhead, rainbow trout, landlocked Atlantic salmon, smallmouth bass, walleye, channel catfish, yellow perch, and rock bass.

Description: Big enough to fit the state of Hawaii and still have room left over for the current charter fleet to make a living fishing in the channels between the islands, Lake Ontario is an exercise in relativity. The tiniest Great Lake, it measures 193 miles long by 53 miles wide, averages 282 feet deep, and has a maximum depth of 803 feet.

Tips: In spring flatline Junior ThunderSticks off planer boards around tributary mouths, in 3 to 7 feet of water, for brown trout averaging 7 pounds.

The fishing: A lake this size naturally spawns a lot of fish tales. Most are true. Constantly improving water quality, copious forage, lamprey control, and the annual stocking of millions of salmon and trout by Canadian and New York authorities conspire to make this place one of the world's top fisheries. And while a new exotic critter seems to crop up every year (spiny water fleas and round gobies are recent illegal immigrants), threatening to trash the habitat, Lake Ontario continues to pump out trophies in massive quantities. Indeed, chinook salmon over 40 pounds; coho salmon, lake trout, and brown trout weighing 30-something pounds; rainbow trout (including steelhead) over 20 pounds; walleyes exceeding 10 pounds; 5-pound smallmouth bass; and 20-pound catfish are caught so often, anglers are getting spoiled.

The lake has a reputation for spitting out record fish—and controversy. For instance, the current International Game Fish Association's all-tackle record coho salmon is a 33-pound-4-ouncer caught on September 27, 1989, in the Salmon River. Problem is, it may be a chinook/coho salmon hybrid, a species so new that it doesn't have an official name yet ("Kingho"?). Indeed, it's not even certain whether the breed is created naturally by the current washing chinook milt over coho eggs or by man accidentally corrupting the ingredients in the hatchery. Experts claim the only definitive way to tell them apart is to examine the innards. Anglers skeptical of scientists reading animal entrails claim the species is a mutant form of coho, attributing it to the witch's brew of antibiotics, growth hormones, and pharmaceuticals (they aren't screened out by sewage treatment plants) lining the lake's floor, making it akin to a mad biologist's aquarium. Staying abreast of the times, the IGFA recently added a chinook/coho hybrid listing and recognizes a 35-pound-8-ouncer caught in the Salmon River on October 21, 2001, as the all-tackle world record.

Most anglers go for salmonids by dragging lures through the targeted species' preferred water temperature. Brown trout and landlocked salmon seek water around 60 degrees Fahrenheit, coho and chinook salmon like it around 54 degrees, steelhead and rainbows are partial to 55 degrees, and lake trout are fond of 50 degrees. Recently retired state fisheries biologist Les Wedge uses another popular technique. "The fish most likely to bite are the hungry ones" says Wedge, "and they cruise temperatures their forage prefers. Smelt like a cool 45 degrees, while alewives like it around 65 degrees." Find the ideal temperature layer and troll cut bait through it. Look for smallmouth bass on deep boulder fields and drop-offs, where they eagerly take live minnows and crayfish, bucktail jigs, and jigheads tipped with minnows, scented curly-tailed grubs, or tubes.

In May and November huge walleyes in the 5- to 13-pound range mill around the mouths of major rivers like the Niagara, Oswego, and Black. Target them on cloudy days and at night by casting jigs and SpinFlexes tipped with worms or curly-tailed grubs and by flatlining ThunderSticks, Bomber Long "A"s, or worms on spinner rigs. From June through October they are back in the lake, hanging out on boulder fields 20 to 40 feet deep or suspended 15 to 30 feet down over 50 to 80 feet of water. Monster channel catfish the size of miniature Minotaurs (15 to 25 pounds) thrive in the deep holes of river mouths. Fish for them on bottom along eddies and current breaks with strips of salmon milt, cut bait, and large minnows. Yellow perch up to 14 inches and rock bass exceeding 1 pound can be found near shore in water up to 40 feet deep. They are especially drawn to boulder fields, piers, riprap, break-walls, and any other insect- and crayfish-rich cover. They strike everything from worms and minnows to small lures.

Lake Ontario is governed by the special Great Lakes regulations found in the state *Fishing Regulations Guide*.

Directions: Woven from many roads and blazed by square green signs bearing a pair of soles stepping over waves, the Seaway Trail runs the length of the lake.

Additional information: Halfway out in the lake an invisible line separates the United States from Canada. If you're going to be fishing in the open lake—especially in the main shipping channel—and don't know the border, carry New York and Canadian fishing licenses. Numerous annual fishing tournaments like the LOC (Lake Ontario Counties) spring and fall derbies and the Lake Ontario Pro-Am Salmon Team Tournament are held each year; details are available at tourism offices. Sites 12A through 12I below are great offshore hot spots.

Contact: New York State Department of Environmental Conservation Regions 6, 7, 8, and 9; Buffalo Niagara Convention & Visitors Bureau; Niagara County Tourism and Convention Corporation; Orleans County Tourism; Greater Rochester Visitors Association (Monroe County); Wayne County Office of Tourism; Cayuga County Tourism; Oswego County Promotion & Tourism; 1000 Islands International Tourism Council (Jefferson County); and Seaway Trail, Inc.

12A. Niagara Bar *(see map on page 38)*

Description: Niagara Bar is the popular name given to the highly productive shelf at the mouth of the Niagara River.

The fishing: The 20- to 30-foot depths hold incredible numbers of smallmouth bass and walleyes. Salmon (coho and king) stage here April through May and again in the fall just before launching their autumn spawning runs up the Niagara River. You know you're off the bar when you're over water 60 feet deep. On the deep end the bottom drops to over 200 feet, creating good year-round habitat for lake trout and salmon.

Directions: The bar reaches out into the lake for about 3.5 miles and stretches (east to west) from Fourmile Creek to Canada's Welland Shipping Canal.

12B. Niagara Pro-Am Artificial Reef *(see map on page 38)*

Description: Built to provide a spawning site for lake trout, this 205-foot-long reef's combination of red shale, concrete blocks, and 359 tons of limestone draws large numbers of all kinds of forage—which, in turn, attract predators. Yellow perch congregate here in spring and fall, smallmouth bass like it in summer, and lake trout spawn here in autumn.

Directions: The site is located 4.5 miles east of Wilson and 1.5 miles west of Olcott, in 25 to 35 feet of water.

12C. Point Breeze *(see map on page 55)*

Description: The water off the mouth of Lower Oak Orchard Creek (site 16) ranks as one of the best steelhead and landlocked salmon spots on the lake.

The fishing: The winning entries in the Lake Ontario Counties spring derbies of 1999 and 2000 were caught a couple hundred yards off Point Breeze. Troll for them at a quick clip, and stack your spoons in 5- to 10-foot increments through the water column. The state annually stocks about 20,000 landlocked Atlantic salmon fingerlings into Oak Orchard Creek. Survivors trickle back to spawn all summer long, and a few up to 15 pounds are taken by folks trolling crankbaits, spoons, and streamers off the mouth.

Directions: From Rochester, head west on Lake Ontario State Parkway for about 30 miles to the Point Breeze exit. Turn right on NY 98, follow it north for about 0.5 mile to the end, and turn left on Ontario Street.

Additional information: Orleans County Marine Park's boat launch and parking for about twenty rigs is at the end of Ontario Street.

12D. Rochester Area *(see map on page 58)*

Description: Lake Ontario's Rochester shoreline is rich in bays and ponds fed by fertile tributaries, including the Genesee River. In addition, the lake's floor slides quickly to depths over 100 feet. This combination of rich nutrients and a wide range of temperatures makes the waters around this major metropolitan area a veritable fish magnet.

The fishing: Coho, chinook, and landlocked Atlantic salmon and steelhead, brown, and lake trout hang out in the area all year long. Early spring's warming waters sees hoards of browns and steelhead cruising close to shore. Late summer calls humongous schools of salmon to stage off the mouth of the Genesee River—indeed, the mouths of all tributaries—where they actively feed, growing fatter and longer by the day while awaiting the urge to run upstream to spawn.

Directions: This fabulous fishery stretches for roughly 8 miles east (Ninemile Point) and 8 miles west (Lighthouse Point) of Rochester.

A pair of beautiful bronzebacks taken off Pultneyville (site 12E).

12E. Pultneyville *(see map on page 58)*

Description: Warmed by numerous tributaries, including the Genesee River and Salmon and Bear Creeks, and the discharge from the Ginna nuclear power plant, the near-shore water west of the hamlet ranks among the lake's warmest in early spring and late fall. Favorable temperatures combined with steep drops, bait-holding shoals, and boulder fields add icing to this angling paradise.

The fishing: In April brown trout hang out near shore, in 4 to 8 feet of water, from Hungerford Shoal (about 2 miles west of the harbor) to the Ginna power plant. Most are caught by flatlining Storm's original Junior ThunderSticks. Hungerford Shoal and nearby boulder fields hold incredible populations of smallmouths in the 12- to 20-inch range. Local guide Jim Tsepas's favorite technique is to cast a live minnow and when the line hits bottom, count to ten and set the hook.

Directions: Located halfway between Oswego and Rochester. Take CR 101 (the Seaway Trail) for about 13 miles west of Sodus Point.

Additional information: The harbor mouth is straddled by cribs that can ruin a motor. When entering the harbor, boaters are advised to follow a straight path set by lining up the two shore markers (white rectangles on poles with a green stripe running down the middle). Immediately after the 9/11 terrorist attacks, the Coast Guard slapped a 1,000-yard security zone around all nuclear power plants, including the nearby Ginna facility. Boats are prohibited from entering this restricted area. Contact the Coast Guard for further information.

12F. Nine Mile One and James A. Fitzpatrick Nuclear Plant Discharges *(see map on page 66)*

Description: Three nuclear power plants sit side by side on the beach about 6 miles east of the city of Oswego; the two oldest discharge hot water into the lake.

The fishing: From mid-October through May, the warmer water attracts walleyes, smallmouth bass, trout, and salmon. Troll crankbaits along the mile of shoreline out front in 40 to 50 feet of water for early- and late-season salmon, trout, and walleyes. Smallmouths hang out around nearby boulder fields and respond to drifted crayfish and minnows and to salted tubes and scented Carolina-rigged finesse worms dragged slowly on bottom.

Directions: Head east out of Oswego Harbor. Nine Mile Two's huge concrete cooling tower marks the spot.

Additional information: After the 9/11 terrorist attacks, the Coast Guard slapped a security zone around all nuclear power plants, and no craft are allowed within 1,000 yards of the facilities. Contact the Coast Guard for an update on the restricted area.

A 20-pound lake trout taken near the wall (site 121).

12G. Mexico Bay *(see map on page 78)*

Description: Stretching from Nine Mile Point to the mouth of the Salmon River, a distance of roughly 9 miles, this bay is blessed with several tributaries and a gently sloping floor that takes over a mile to reach 30 feet deep.

The fishing: This bay is a brown trout hot spot from April through May. They respond to minnow-imitating crankbaits flatlined off planer boards in 5 to 10 feet of water. Large lakers and chinooks hang out in the deep water, several miles out, all summer long and are taken mostly on cut bait trolled behind downriggers.

Directions: Take NY 3 south from Port Ontario for 4 miles. Turn west on NY 104B for 1 mile to Texas, then go north on CR 40 for about 0.5 mile.

Additional information: Mexico Point Boat Launch, a fee area located at the end of CR 40, offers a double-lane concrete ramp, parking for 150 rigs, shore-fishing access, and rest rooms. Campers at Selkirk Shores State Park (site 36A) are allowed to launch free. All others are charged a day-use fee from April through October. Free launching is allowed off-season until ice time.

12H. Henderson Trench *(see map on page 91)*

Description: Cut by a glacier during the last ice age—maybe even before that—the trench measures roughly 4 miles long by 1 mile wide. Its steep walls quickly drop 80 feet before hitting a gentler slope and sliding another 40 feet to an average depth of 120 feet.

The fishing: Containing summer's coldest and deepest water in the Black River Bay area, this spot holds salmonids all year long. The habitat is so good, in fact, the state stocks tens of thousands of lake trout, brown trout, rainbow trout, and chinook salmon directly into the trench. From August through mid-September, its cool waters turn into a liquid magnet, drawing and holding mature salmon who feast like pigs while milling around waiting for the biological signal that will cause them to stop feeding and ascend the Black River to spawn.

Directions: Head west out of Henderson Harbor. The trench is in the channel between Stony Point and Stony Island.

12I. The Wall *(see map on page 91)*

Description: Submerged under 60 feet of water in the main shipping channel, the wall is a clifflike structure between Galloo Island and Canada's Main Duck Island. Several contour lines squeeze together, creating a steep drop of about 100 feet stretching for about 1.5 miles from northeast to southwest.

The fishing: A strong current, deep water, and an abundance of bait keep lunker chinook salmon and lake trout here all summer long. For summer chinooks, troll black-and-silver Northern King 28 spoons tight to the wall in 90 to 125 feet of water. Lakers hang out 30 feet deeper and strike peanuts or Spin-N-Glos trolled behind Luhr-Jensen's Cowbells. Bill Saiff III, of Saiff Charters, a seven-boat family fleet boasting one of the best catch rates on the lake, says, "I've had days when my clients landed over fifty lake trout on these rigs, many over 15 pounds."

Directions: The middle of the wall is about 5 miles west of the southern tip of Galloo Island.

13. Wilson Harbor *(see map on page 38)*

Key species: Brown trout, steelhead, largemouth bass, northern pike, and panfish.

Description: Also called Tuscarora Bay, this relatively shallow 100-acre bay is fed by the east branch of Twelve Mile Creek (when it's running—it dries out most summers) and is separated from the lake by a narrow strip of land called the Island.

Tips: Vertically jig spoons like Kastmasters and Swedish Pimples through the ice for steelhead and brown trout.

The fishing: One of only a handful of bays on the western end of the lake, this place gets visited by salmonids in winter. Many are caught serendipitously through the ice on wax worms and minnows targeting panfish and pike. In the spring steelhead up to 15 pounds run up the east branch of Twelvemile Creek. They take egg sacs and Rooster Tails. The bay has good populations of warm-water species year-round. Largemouth bass range from 1.5 to 5 pounds, and northern pike mainly go from 22 to 30 inches. Both respond to minnows, spinnerbaits, and crankbaits. Perch averaging 10 inches and crappies running from 9 to 12 inches rule the slow, marsh-lined mouth of the east branch of Twelvemile Creek. They hit Beetle Spins in summer and small minnows and grubs through the ice. Bullheads ranging from 7 inches to 2 pounds swarm into the west side of the bay in April and respond to worms.

Directions: Located on the west side of the village of Wilson.

Additional information: Wilson-Tuscarora State Park, a fee area skirting the bay's west bank, offers a paved ramp, parking for thirty rigs, loads of shore-fishing access on the bay and the east branch of Twelvemile Creek, and rest rooms. A day-use fee is charged from May 1 to Labor Day.

Contact: New York State Department of Environmental Conservation Region 9 and Niagara County Tourism and Convention Corporation.

13A. Wilson East Pier

Description: This pier offers great shore-fishing access for seasonal runs of brown trout and steelhead. Yellow perch up to 14 inches are available from ice-out through April and respond to tiny minnows and lures. Post-spawn smallmouths load the channel for the first week or so of the season and hit minnows, worms, crankbaits, spoons, jigs—you name it.

Directions: At the end of Harbor Street in the village of Wilson.

14. Twelvemile Creek and East Branch *(see map on page 38)*

Key species: Chinook salmon, steelhead, bullhead, sunfish, and yellow perch.

Description: These skinny creeks are heavily influenced by runoff and all but dry up in summer and early fall.

Tips: Use yarn flies and egg imitations.

The fishing: Heavy autumn storms, winter thaws, and snowmelt swell these streams to ideal spawning size. Ripe chinooks up to 30 pounds run up both after September and October downpours. Steelhead up to 15 pounds pour in alongside them to feast on fresh caviar. Additional waves of steelhead flow in whenever water levels permit. The state tries ensuring the steelhead return by stocking roughly 37,000 fingerlings into the creeks annually. Chinooks are highly territorial and will savagely strike streamers, spoons, and fresh skein. The rainbows respond with relish to egg sacs and anything that looks like salmon eggs.

In the park, both creeks reach the same gradient as the lake and slow down to a crawl. Largely bordered by marsh, they load up with panfish, especially in spring and early summer. Bullheads can go 2 pounds, bluegills and pumpkinseeds reach the size of small frying pans, and yellow perch can stretch up to 14 inches. Each hits garden worms and red worms fished on bottom. The sunfish and perch will also hit pieces of night crawler floated below bobbers, 1-inch curly-tailed grubs, and wet flies.

Directions: These creeks straddle Wilson-Tuscarora State Park, located on NY 18 just west of the hamlet of Wilson.

Additional information: Wilson-Tuscarora State Park, a fee area, offers boat ramps, loads of shore-fishing access, handicapped ramps on both branches, picnic areas, and playgrounds. A day-use fee is charged from May 1 to Labor Day.

Contact: New York State Department of Environmental Conservation Region 9 and Niagara County Tourism and Convention Corporation.

14A. Public Fishing Rights

Description: Two miles of public fishing rights on Twelvemile Creek stretching upstream of Wilson-Tuscarora State Park.

Directions: Access from Wilson-Tuscarora State Park.

14B. Public Fishing Rights

Description: Shoulder parking and about 1 mile of public fishing rights on Twelvemile Creek stretching upstream of the bridge.

Directions: Head west out of Wilson on Youngstown Road for about 3 miles to the bridge.

14C. Public Fishing Rights *(see map on page 38)*

Description: Shoulder parking and roughly 2 miles of public fishing rights on the East Branch.

Directions: Youngstown Road parallels this stretch about 0.5 mile west of Wilson.

14D. Public Fishing Rights *(see map on page 38)*

Description: Shoulder parking and about 1 mile of public fishing rights along Daniels Road.

Directions: Head west out of Wilson on Youngstown Road for about 1.5 miles, then turn on Daniels Road and travel about 2 miles.

14E. Public Fishing Rights *(see map on page 38)*

Description: Shoulder parking and about 0.5 mile of public fishing rights downstream of the Braley Road bridge.

Directions: Head west out of Wilson on Youngstown Road for about 1.5 miles, turn on Daniels Road, and drive about 2.5 miles to the end, then turn east on Braley Road and continue a few hundred feet to the bridge.

15. Eighteenmile Creek (Niagara County) *(see map on page 38)*

Key species: Coho salmon, chinook salmon, brown trout, steelhead, northern pike, largemouth bass, yellow perch, sunfish, and brown bullhead.

Description: Named for its distance from the Niagara River, this gentle, angler-friendly stream offers about 2 miles of world-class seasonal salmonid fishing.

Tips: October sees all four species of salmonids enter the stream.

The fishing: This creek attracts runs of Lake Ontario salmonids each fall. In addition, steelhead overwinter, and fresh runs of ripe chromers enter in the spring. Each species hits fresh skein, egg sacs, and streamers in the fast water and spoons, spinners, and plugs in slow channels. Besides holding salmon and trout autumn through spring, the slow water near the mouth is a popular warm-water fishery. Northern pike up to 36 inches are targeted by locals with live minnows and spinnerbaits. Bucketmouths averaging 2.5 pounds thrive in the weeds and respond to bass bugs and poppers worked around lily pads and Texas-rigged worms worked along weed edges and windfalls. Yellow perch averaging 9 inches, sunfish up to 8 inches, and brown bullheads from 1 to 2 pounds are available in quantity and hit worms.

Directions: NY 78 parallels the stream from Burt to Olcott.

Contact: New York State Department of Environmental Conservation Region 9 and Niagara County Tourism and Convention Corporation.

Casting for early king salmon at Burt Dam Fishermen's Park (site 15A).

15A. Burt Dam Fishermen's Park

Description: This fee area offers parking for about fifty cars, toilets, and a gentle trail down to the fast-water portion of the river.

Directions: On NY 78, 1 mile south of the village of Olcott.

15B. Olcott Piers

Description: Two piers straddle the mouth of Eighteenmile Creek.

The fishing: These structures are highly popular local fishing spots year-round.

Directions: Located in the hamlet of Olcott. To get to the east pier, head north on Lockport Road to its end and turn west on Ontario Street. For the west pier, head north on Jackson Street to the parking lot at its end. If the lake's too rough to walk the beach to the pier, go to the road, turn left on Beach Street, then left again past the third house onto the fenced-in path leading to the pier.

15C. Golden Hill State Park

Description: This fee area, famous for its striking lighthouse, offers fifty campsites (some electric), hot showers, and a paved boat launch with parking for fifty rigs.

The campground is open from mid-April through mid-October. A day-use fee is charged noncampers in-season.

Directions: From Olcott, take NY 18 east for about 10 miles, turn north on Carmen Road, then east 1 mile later onto Lower Lake Road.

16. Lower Oak Orchard Creek (Oak Orchard River)

Key species: Coho salmon, chinook salmon, landlocked Atlantic salmon, steelhead, brown trout, northern pike, and yellow perch.

Description: Stretching from Lake Alice Dam to its mouth at Point Breeze, a distance of about 5 miles, this stream averages 100 yards wide and 2.5 feet deep. From autumn through spring, its water volume and temperature are perfect for seasonal runs of salmonids.

Tips: In autumn fly fish with egg-sucking leeches on a sinking line.

The fishing: The lower stretch of Oak Orchard Creek is world-class trophy salmonid water. It's made this way by the state annually stocking roughly 155,000 chinook fingerlings, 26,000 cohos averaging 5 inches, 20,000 6.5-inch Atlantic salmon, and 21,000 steelhead averaging 5 inches. It is especially noted for fall-run brown trout ranging from a paltry 3 pounds to over 20 pounds. Though none are stocked directly into the creek, it appeals to the species, and ripe browns from all over the lake converge on the place. They start trickling in by mid-September and stay as late as January. Chinook salmon up to 40 pounds and cohos up to 20 pounds run from early September through mid-November. Steelhead up to 20 pounds run in their wake, and many spend the winter, fattening up on all the red caviar washed out from under the rocks by ever-shifting currents. Spring runoff lures great numbers of ripe steelhead into the swollen rapids. The trout hit nymphs, streamers, egg sacs, and worms. The salmon strike streamers and raw salmon skein.

Directions: Head north out of Batavia on NY 98 for about 24 miles.

Contact: New York State Department of Environmental Conservation Region 8 and Orleans County Tourism.

16A. Park Avenue Extension Public Access

Description: This site offers shoulder parking for fifteen cars, a trail down to the river, and about 1 mile of river access.

The fishing: The trail down from the road ends at the point where the river's choicest fly-fishing water begins.

Directions: From I–90 exit 48 (Batavia), head north on NY 98 for about 18 miles and turn west on NY 279 (about 1 mile north of Albion). When NY 279 turns sharply west 4 miles later, continue straight on Park Avenue for 1.3 miles to Park Avenue Extension.

Lake Ontario: Point Breeze to Sandy Creek

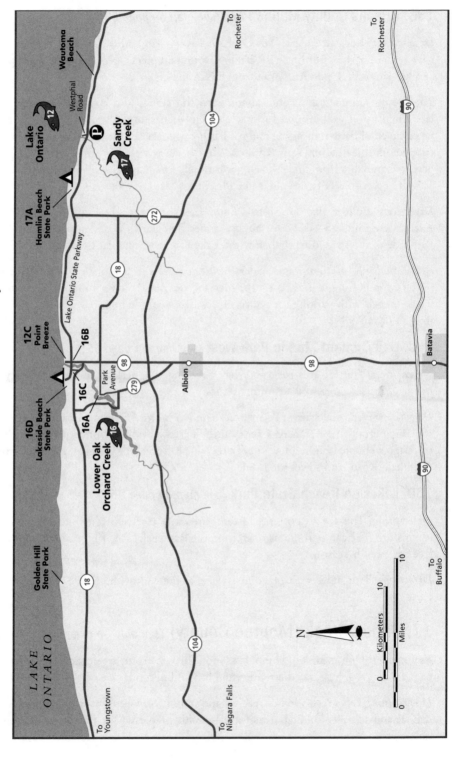

16B. Orleans County Marine Park *(see map on page 55)*

Description: Located in the Oak Orchard River Gorge, this safe harbor offers a paved ramp, parking for fifty rigs, fishing ramps and piers, seventy-one rental slips, and hot showers. Open April 15 through November 1.

The fishing: Chinook and coho salmon enter this slow and deep harbor as early as late August and mill around for a while before charging upstream. They can be taken on crankbaits and spoons and by drifting egg sacs and skein. Brown trout also enter about this time and respond to the same baits, as well as worms. Trophy steelhead are available from mid-November through April and take all the above baits, as well as Rooster Tails and plugs like Hot Shots and Lazy Ikes.

Directions: Follow the directions to site 16A, but instead of turning on Park Avenue, continue on NY 98 for about 2 miles. The park's main entrance is on the west side of the road, directly below the Lake Ontario State Parkway bridge.

Additional information: Bank anglers have thousands of feet of slow-water access in the 0.5-mile-long park and on the pier and jetty at the river's mouth. A no-fee paved launch with parking for ten rigs is located a couple hundred yards north, at the end of NY 98.

16C. Oak Orchard Marine Park West *(see map on page 55)*

Description: This fee area has a four-bay paved launch, parking for about twenty-five rigs, a picnic area, and a comfort station.

Directions: Head south from Point Breeze on NY 98 for 1.5 miles. Turn right at the stop sign, cross Oak Orchard Creek on the narrow bridge, then turn right at the stop sign a couple hundred feet later onto NY 18. Travel for 0.2 mile, turn right on Archibald Road, and travel for 1 mile.

16D. Lakeside Beach State Park *(see map on page 55)*

Description: This fee area offers 274 campsites with electricity, hot showers, and a camp store. The campground is open from the last week in April through October; free day use off-season.

Directions: Two miles west of Point Breeze, at the end of the Lake Ontario State Parkway.

17. Sandy Creek (Monroe County) *(see map on page 55)*

Key species: Coho salmon, chinook salmon, brown trout, steelhead, smallmouth bass, largemouth bass, northern pike, and brown bullhead.

Description: This creek's lower reaches and mouth contain dynamite warm-water habitat and serve as holding areas for salmonids preparing for their seasonal runs upstream.

Tips: Tip spinnerbaits with trailers and work them through holes.

The fishing: The state stocks roughly 26,000 5.5-inch cohos, 108,000 fingerling chinooks, and 20,000 steelhead averaging 5 inches here each year. Seasonal returns are good. Early autumn sees runs of chinook salmon averaging 25 pounds, coho salmon ranging from 6 to 10 pounds, and brown trout up to 15 pounds. The salmon aren't into feeding, but the spawning urge makes them macho, and they'll strike lures, streamers, and clumps of raw skein. The browns don't shut down as utterly as the salmon, but their appetites are suppressed by the spawn they're carrying. Still, they'll hit pieces of worm, egg sacs, and nymphs. Steelhead up to 20 pounds run from November through March and take egg sacs and small plugs like Hot Shots. Largemouth bass ranging from 2 to 5 pounds hang out in weeds and other cover, where they grab Texas-rigged worms. Pikesauruses up to 10 pounds lurk in the creek's holes and channels between the weeds, where they take minnows and spinnerbaits. Smallmouth bass invade the place every spring to spawn and usually stick around for at least a week after the season opens. Famished after making whoopie, the fish only range between 1 and 2 pounds, but they're scrappy and will hit just about any lure that crosses their path. Brown bullheads up to 16 inches swarm in around mid-April, stick around into May, and gobble up every worm they can find.

Directions: From Rochester, take Lake Ontario State Parkway west for about 15 miles to the Westphal Road exit and follow the signs to the fishing access site.

Additional information: One of the newer public access sites on the lake, the Westphal Road facility offers shore fishing, a paved ramp, parking for about fifty rigs, and a portable toilet.

Contact: New York State Department of Environmental Conservation Region 8 and Greater Rochester Visitors Association.

17A. Hamlin Beach State Park

Description: This 1,100-acre fee area offers 264 campsites with electric hookups, hot showers, playgrounds, and a fishing pier. In addition, Yanty Creek on its east side draws seasonal runs of brown trout, steelhead, and salmon, and bullheads and panfish enter the marsh in the spring.

Directions: Off Lake Ontario State Parkway, about 3 miles west of site 17.

18. Braddock Bay *(see map on page 58)*

Key species: Northern pike, largemouth bass, yellow perch, black crappie, sunfish, rock bass, and brown bullhead.

Description: Fed by Salmon and Buttonwood Creeks, this 250-acre bay boasts an incredible collection of warm-water habitat. Its wide, shallow mouth sports countless old pilings. Inside, the bay offers a menu of weed beds, undercut cattail edges, rock fields, new and abandoned docks, bridge abutments—you name it.

Lake Ontario: Wautoma Beach to Pultneyville and Nearby Ponds and Tributaries

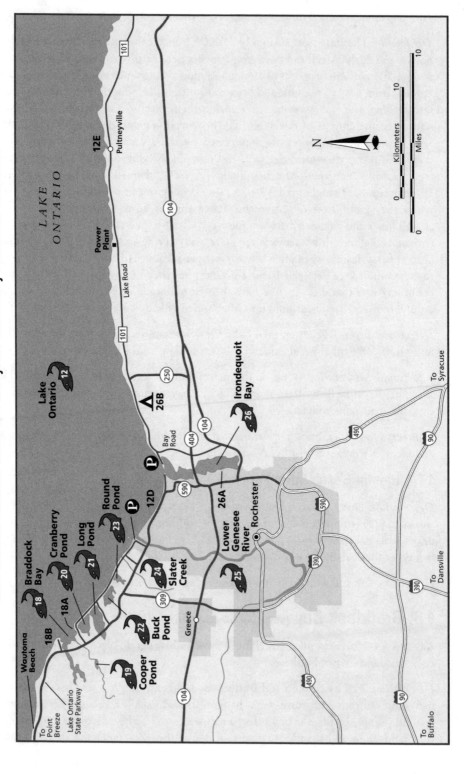

Tips: On calm days, fish for largemouth bass and northern pike by working surface baits like MirrOlure Prop Baits and surface popper/divers.

The fishing: Largemouth bass are normally in the 2- to 4-pound range, but heavier hawgs are caught regularly. Drag Texas-rigged worms along weed lines, cattails, and other structure. Cast crankbaits for northern pike from 20 to 28 inches long, but be prepared for brutes up to 36 inches. A highly productive nursery for everything from minnows and tadpoles to aquatic insects, Braddock Bay is the year-round home to good populations of yellow perch in the 8- to 12-inch range and crappies ranging from 9 to 12 inches. They have a taste for small minnows, jigs, and 2-inch Exude grubs. Bluegills and pumpkinseeds reach mind-boggling size—many go over a pound—on all the insects, tadpoles, and stuff. Go for them with spikes, mousies, and wax worms through the ice; garden worms and spikes in early spring; and worms, tiny poppers, and 1-inch Exude Curly Tail Grubs late spring through fall. Spawn-heavy rock bass up to 2 pounds swarm into the east side of the bay in May and take minnows, small jigs, and worms. Bullheads invade the bay from ice-out into May and hit worms fished on bottom, particularly at night.

Directions: Take Lake Ontario State Parkway west out of Rochester for about 5 miles.

Additional information: The shallow mouth is littered with pilings and sandbars. If you come in from the lake, follow the channel marked by the beacons.

Contact: New York State Department of Environmental Conservation Region 8 and Greater Rochester Visitors Association.

18A. Town of Greece Braddock Bay Park & Marina

Description: This fee area, a cooperative effort of government and private enterprise, offers complete marina services (three mechanics on-site), a ship-and-shore store, a paved boat launch, parking for fifty rigs, picnic tables, and rest rooms that are heated in winter for the comfort of ice fishers. The launch ramp is open from ice-out (April) to the end of November.

Directions: From Rochester, take Lake Ontario State Parkway west for about 7 miles, then go north on East Manitou Road a few hundred yards.

18B. Public Access

Description: The bottleneck of Salmon Creek just below the Lake Ontario State Parkway bridge is a popular bank-fishing spot for perch and bullheads.

Directions: The parking lot is at the end of the Manitou Beach Road transition, off Lake Ontario State Parkway about 8 miles west of Rochester.

19. Cooper Pond

Key species: Largemouth bass, northern pike, black crappie, bluegill, and yellow perch.

Description: Only about 3 acres, this partially man-made pond on Buttonwood Creek averages 3 feet deep and drops to a maximum depth of 10 feet.

Tips: Tip a tiny marabou jig with a wax worm or minnow and work it below a pencil bobber.

The fishing: Largemouth bass range from 2 to 6 pounds and have a taste for 7- to 10-inch plastic worms worked weightless over submerged weeds. Northerns up to 10 pounds are present and respond to large minnows suspended below bobbers and to buzzbaits ripped over submerged weeds. This pond is a local hot spot for black crappies up to 16 inches, bluegills bigger than a large man's hand, and yellow perch up to 12 inches. Crappies are partial to jigs tipped with minnows and 2-inch scented tubes and curly-tailed grubs rigged on spinner forms; the sunfish like worms and 1-inch scented curly-tailed grubs; and both love wax worms, spikes, and other maggots. Yellow perch love all the baits the sunnies and crappies like.

Directions: Head up weedy Buttonwood Creek, Braddock Bay's eastern tributary. The pond is on the east side, just upstream of the Lake Ontario State Parkway bridge.

Additional information: The pond is accessible only by boat.

Contact: New York State Department of Environmental Conservation Region 8 and Greater Rochester Visitors Association.

20. Cranberry Pond (see map on page 58)

Key species: Largemouth bass, northern pike, yellow perch, black crappie, and sunfish.

Description: Connected to Long Pond by a channel, this 250-acre pond is a superb warm-water fishery.

Tips: Fly fish with bass bugs on windless days.

The fishing: Largemouth bass in the 2- to 3-pound range and northern pike in the 2- to 4-pound range occupy the weed edges and readily take spinnerbaits and soft plastic jerkbaits. Come winter, the place is popular with ice anglers looking for northern pike, crappie, and perch dinners. Large minnows fished off bottom on tipups catch most of the northerns, including pikeasauruses over 10 pounds. Insect larvae and small minnows work for the perch ranging from 8 to 13 inches and crappies ranging from 9 to 12 inches.

Directions: From Rochester, head west for about 5 miles on Lake Ontario State Parkway. Take East Manitou Road north for about 0.5 mile to its end, turn right on Edgemere Drive, and travel a few hundred yards.

Additional information: Shore-fishing access, a beach launch for cartop craft, and parking for twenty cars is at the corner of Edgemere and Cranberry Drives.

Contact: New York State Department of Environmental Conservation Region 8 and Greater Rochester Visitors Association.

21. Long Pond *(see map on page 58)*

Key species: Northern pike, largemouth bass, yellow perch, black crappie, rock bass, and sunfish.

Description: Heavily developed on three sides and surrounded by weed beds, this 397-acre pond averages 5 feet deep and has a 100-acre hole in the middle that drops to a depth of 9 feet.

Tips: In spring fish with worms on bottom for bullheads.

The fishing: This is a great warm-water fishery. Largemouths typically range from 13 to 16 inches, with a lot of bigger ones present. Fish for them along weed edges with floating worms. Northern pike between 22 and 26 inches are commonly taken in summer on buzzbaits and jerkbaits, but many 30-plus-inchers are caught each year through the ice on large shiners. There's a good population of 8- to 11-inch yellow perch, which are mostly caught through the ice on minnows. Rock bass, crappies, and sunfish normally run from 0.5 to 0.75 pound, providing exciting action on wet flies and poppers, especially in early summer.

Directions: Take Lake Ontario State Parkway west out of Rochester for about 3 miles, turn north on Long Pond Road and continue for 0.75 mile, then turn west on Edgemere Drive.

Additional information: There is no public access from shore. However, the channel connecting Long Pond to Cranberry Pond is navigable by canoe or similar low craft that can go under a bridge with a 3-foot clearance.

Contact: New York State Department of Environmental Conservation Region 8 and Greater Rochester Visitors Association.

22. Buck Pond *(see map on page 58)*

Key species: Largemouth bass, northern pike, bluegill, black crappie, and yellow perch.

Description: Averaging 6 feet deep, surrounded by marsh, and smelling like a fresh fish, average folks consider this place a backwater suitable only for ducks and mosquitoes—which is another way of saying it's a dynamite fishing hole.

Tips: Work surface walkers like Zara Spooks in the holes between water lilies.

The fishing: Bucketmouths reach 6-plus pounds and northerns more than 30 inches on the pond's cornucopia of ducklings, baby muskrats, minnows, and frogs. Both species respond best to large minnows. The biggest northerns are caught through the ice. The place is also a great ice-fishing spot for bluegills and crappies ranging from 0.5 to 0.75 pound and perch ranging from 8 to 14 inches. They are normally targeted with teardrop jigs baited with grubs or minnows.

Directions: Head west out of Rochester on Beach Avenue. When it dips south, continue straight on Edgemere Drive for about 1.5 miles.

Additional information: Buck Pond's public access site has parking for ten cars.

Contact: New York State Department of Environmental Conservation Region 8 and Greater Rochester Visitors Association.

23. Round Pond (see map on page 58)

Key species: Largemouth bass, northern pike, sunfish, brown bullhead, and carp.

Description: This 38-acre pond is the shallowest and smallest of the four Greece—not grease—ponds just west of Rochester. Averaging 3 feet deep, full of weeds, and skirted on the west bank by cattails and marsh, this pond's muddy wakes and vocabulary of splashes and sucking sounds (made by monster carp) are enough to give normal people nightmares.

Tips: Cast small plugs and spinners for white perch and rock bass in the spring.

The fishing: Largemouth bass up to 4 pounds live under the slop and respond to jig-'n'-pigs. Northern pike between 20 and 26 inches find the place tolerable and can be taken when the weeds are down a bit—spring and fall—on buzzbaits ripped over holes in the weeds and on spinnerbaits and crankbaits worked along cattail mats. Carp up to 40 pounds thrive in the place. Fish for them with corn, bread balls, or pieces of boiled potato. Sunfish the size of small frying pans are also present and are especially cooperative in spring, when they can't resist garden worms fished on bottom or spikes hooked onto ice jigs and dangled from bobbers. There's a good run of 10- to 14-inch bullheads in the spring. Fish for them on bottom with worms.

Directions: A couple hundred feet west of the corner of Dewey Avenue and Edgemere Drive, just west of Rochester's city limits.

Additional information: Shoulder parking is prohibited; however, locals park in the undeveloped lot on the east side of the outlet bridge—enter at the end of the guardrail.

Contact: New York State Department of Environmental Conservation Region 8 and Greater Rochester Visitors Association.

24. Slater Creek (see map on page 58)

Key species: Steelhead.

Description: This short stream bubbles out of a residential area on the west side of Rochester.

Tips: Work baits in and around the discharge plume in winter.

The fishing: This creek is primarily known for the warm-water discharge from the power plant a couple hundred yards downstream of its mouth. The warm water reaches out almost 0.5 mile into the lake, drawing bait in cold weather, which lures salmon and trout.

Directions: From NY 104 in Rochester, head north on Lake Avenue. Travel to its end, turn west on Beach Avenue, and continue for a little under 0.5 mile.

Additional information: The public fishing access site on Beach Avenue has parking for about twenty-five cars and offers access to the stream from the power plant to its mouth.

Contact: New York State Department of Environmental Conservation Region 8 and Greater Rochester Visitors Association.

25. Lower Genesee River *(see map on page 58)*

Key species: Coho salmon, chinook salmon, brown trout, steelhead, smallmouth bass, walleye, channel catfish, freshwater drum, yellow perch, and white perch.

Description: This shallow, roily stream flows right through Rochester, the third largest city in New York. It offers about 0.75 mile of fast water below the lower falls, followed by a long stretch of flat water all the way to the lake.

Tips: From May through mid-July, walk the piers and canal walls near the mouth and jig bucktails, scented curly-tailed grubs, or tubes for walleyes, smallmouth bass, and sheepshead.

The fishing: Major runs of brown trout averaging 6 pounds, coho salmon up to 15 pounds, chinook salmon averaging 25 pounds, and steelhead up to 18 pounds enter the river September through November. The steelhead return in February and March. Trolling near the mouth with plugs and spoons is the technique favored by boat owners, while shore fishers casting off the piers and anglers wading the fast water below the lower falls take an equal number on egg sacs, skein, streamers, yarn flies, and in-line spinners. In summer the piers at the mouth are popular local spots for casting crankbaits and soft plastics for smallmouths up to 2 pounds. Walleyes, some over 5 pounds, are taken incidentally, and with increasing frequency, by bass enthusiasts casting crankbaits and working jigs on bottom. Still-fishers catch a lot of bronzebacks, perch up to 14 inches, and sheepshead up to 10 pounds on crayfish. While their numbers are down lately, the river's white perch population is notorious. Averaging 6 inches, they are targeted with worms and small lures like Bill Lewis' Tiny Traps fished with ultralight tackle. Catfish from 2 to 4 pounds are plentiful and are especially active in fast water in June, when they hit worms. Larger ones, some up to 15 pounds, hang out in holes and strike cut bait, shrimp, and gobs of worms.

Directions: Lake Avenue parallels the stream in Rochester.

Additional information: Monroe County's Ontario Beach Park occupies the last few hundred yards of the river's west bank, offering shore-fishing access, toilets, a paved ramp with parking for about a hundred rigs, and unlimited parking for shore anglers. A fishing access to the lower gorge's rapids is located at the corner of Seth Green Drive and St. Paul Street. Open only from 6:00 A.M. to 7:00 P.M., it offers limited parking, but street parking is nearby.

Contact: New York State Department of Environmental Conservation Region 8 and Greater Rochester Visitors Association.

26. Irondequoit Bay *(see map on page 58)*

Key species: Brown trout, steelhead, coho salmon, northern pike, walleye, and black bass.

Description: Located on the east side of Rochester, this 1,800-acre bay is fed by Irondequoit Creek. Bluffs, scarred by the elements, loom over its southeastern and southwestern shores, spawning such place names as Inspiration Point and Point Lookout. A deep trench runs down the center. In summer anaerobic degradation of organic material on the floor drastically lowers oxygen levels below 18 feet.

Tips: Work the drop-off around German Village (west bank, 0.5 mile inside the bay) with scented tubes and curly-tailed grubs on jigheads for smallmouths.

The fishing: This is the Rochester area's likeliest bay to save the day when the winds whip Lake Ontario into a frightful latticework of whitecaps and swells. This is especially true in early spring, when football-size brown trout averaging 6 pounds, a smattering of steelhead ranging from 4 to 10 pounds, and coho salmon from 3 to 10 pounds move in to pig out on the alewives basking in the bay's warmer waters. They hit minnows, small spoons, and minnow-imitating crankbaits flatlined off planer boards. The bay's best-kept secret is its black bass fishery. Bucketmouths up to 6 pounds rule the weed beds in the southern and northern basins and can be lured out with Texas-rigged worms worked along the edges and holes. Good numbers of 2- to 4-pound bronzebacks are present. Vertically jig for them with bladebaits and soft plastics around abutments, docks, and other structure in about 15 feet of water. The state has been stocking walleyes with good results. Five-pounders are common, with 8-pounders possible. In spring fish for them at night by casting or flatlining small silver crankbaits like C29 Spot Minnows and C.C. Shads. By July go deeper with larger (3 to 5 inch) crankbaits. Northern pike, many over 10 pounds, prowl the weed edges in 5 to 15 feet of water, just waiting for the chance to ambush noisy crankbaits like Rat-L-Traps. The two piers at the mouth are local hot spots for folks casting spoons, stickbaits, and egg sacs for autumn-running brown trout, steelhead, and coho and king salmon, then again in the spring for steelhead and browns.

Directions: NY 590 parallels the west bank; Bay Road parallels the east shore.

Additional information: Irondequoit Bay Marine Park, a fee area at the intersection of NY 590 and Lake Road, has a paved ramp, parking for thirty rigs, shore- and pier-fishing access, and toilets.

Contact: New York State Department of Environmental Conservation Region 8 and Greater Rochester Visitors Association.

26A. Irondequoit Bay County Park West

Description: This park offers a beach launch for cartop craft and parking for five cars.

Directions: Off South Glen Road in Rochester.

26B. Webster Park

Description: This 6,500-acre Monroe County park offers forty campsites with electric hookups, hot showers, picnic facilities, lake fishing from a pier, and access to Mill Creek, which gets seasonal runs of salmon and steelhead. The campground is open May 15 through October 15. The beach parking lot at the mouth of Mill Creek has room for thirty cars and is open year-round.

Directions: Take Lake Road east out of Rochester for about 4 miles.

Contact: Monroe County Parks.

27. Maxwell Creek (Salmon Creek) *(see map on page 66)*

Key species: Steelhead, sunfish, yellow perch, and brown bullhead.

Description: Shallow and narrow most of the year, runoff swells this stream into a super steelhead fishery each spring.

Tips: Work the holes and channel near the mouth with $\frac{1}{16}$- and $\frac{1}{32}$-ounce marabou and bucktail jigs suspended about 2 feet below tiny bobbers.

The fishing: This stream gets stocked with about 20,000 fingerling steelhead annually. They return each spring, making this Wayne County's best skinny water for trophy spring chromers. Typically ranging from 4 to 12 pounds, 15-pounders are possible. They hit egg sacs, worms, and small lures. In addition, good numbers of frying-pan-size bullheads, yellow perch, and sunfish can be caught in the marshy mouth throughout spring. The sunfish and bullheads are partial to worms; the perch like them, too, but they'll also hit a more active bait like a 2-inch curly-tailed grub or a Mepps Aglia streamer.

Directions: Head west out of the hamlet of Sodus Point on Lake Road (CR 101) for about 2 miles.

Additional information: A public fishing access site, with parking for about twenty-five cars, is on Lake Road.

Lake Ontario: Maxwell Creek to the Lower Oswego River

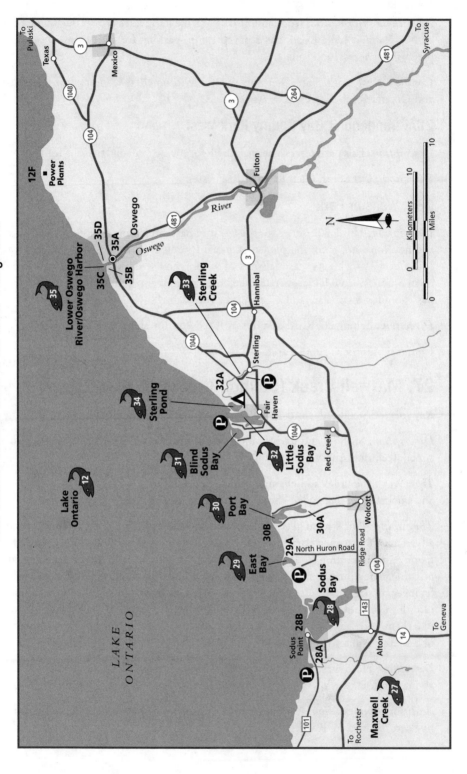

Contact: New York State Department of Environmental Conservation Region 8 and Wayne County Office of Tourism/History.

28. Sodus Bay

Key species: Northern pike, largemouth bass, coho salmon, chinook salmon, brown trout, steelhead, yellow perch, and black crappie.

Description: Covering about 3,700 acres, this bay's shoreline is heavily developed. It has three islands (from east to west: Leroy, Eagle, and Newark); a vast, shallow south end (the mouth of Sodus Creek); numerous creek mouths; and a generally shallow, weedy shoreline. It averages 25 feet deep and drops to a maximum of 40 feet. Two piers, one with a metal lighthouse, straddle its mouth.

Tips: Early in the morning and at dusk, flatline rattling crankbaits like MirrOlure Lipped 52Ms and Smithwick Rogues along the edges of weedy flats hugging break-lines.

The fishing: Northern pike between 5 and 8 pounds are so plentiful, misguided locals consider them a nuisance. A good number of fish twice that size is also available. Cast spinnerbaits over submerged vegetation and diving crankbaits along the edges of weeds and drop-offs. Largemouth bass in the 2- to 4-pound range are also common, and 6-plus-pounders are available. Drag Texas-rigged worms around cribs and under docks—be sure to hit the uprights with your sinker every now and then to wake the fish up. Roughly 100,000 fingerling chinooks and 26,000 fingerling cohos are stocked here each year. Early in the fall, cohos between 4 and 7 pounds and chinooks from 15 to 25 pounds mill around in the bay before ascending tributaries to spawn. Invariably, they're joined by brown trout up to 15 pounds and steelhead averaging 7 pounds. Highly aggressive, these fish respond to trolled spoons and stickbaits, especially in the deep channel separating Newark and Eagle Islands from the mainland. Yellow perch and crappies are plentiful around the islands, especially the east sides, and in the southern basin's shallows. The most popular method for taking them is with flathead or buckeye minnows fished below tiny floats in spring and fall and with jigs tipped with grubs through the ice. Good spring runs of bullheads, with some fish reaching 16 inches, occur in the bay. They are particularly abundant in the south end, where anglers fish for them off the Ridge Road (CR 143) bridge with worms.

Directions: The north end of NY 14 parallels the bay.

Additional information: There is no public camping on the bay; however, there are motels and commercial campgrounds in the area.

Contact: New York State Department of Environmental Conservation Region 8 and Wayne County Office of Tourism/History.

Sunday on the pier at Sodus Point Park (site 28B)

28A. Harriman Park Boat Launch *(see map on page 66)*

Description: This town park has a paved two-lane ramp and parking for about fifty rigs. It is marked with a square brown sign with yellow lettering saying HELP PROTECT WATER QUALITY on top and NYS DEPARTMENT OF ENVIRONMENTAL CONSERVATION on the bottom.

Directions: Located at the NY 14/Margaretta Road intersection, less than 1 mile south of the hamlet of Sodus Point. Parking is across the street on Margaretta Road.

28B. Sodus Point Park *(see map on page 66)*

Description: This large park offers a paved two-lane boat launch (next to the Coast Guard station) and parking for about a hundred cars. Fishing from the concrete pier is permitted year-round, but bank fishing in other areas of the park is prohibited in summer.

Directions: Take Greig Street to First Street in the hamlet of Sodus Point.

29. East Bay *(see map on page 66)*

Key species: Largemouth bass, northern pike, sunfish, and brown bullhead.

Description: Covering only 100 acres, this shallow bay's floor is carpeted with weeds. At the mouth, waves often pile cobblestones to within a couple inches of the channel's surface, and getting a boat in from the lake can be tricky, sometimes impossible.

Tips: Head up the bay's arms and tributaries and work floating soft plastic jerkbaits like Culprit's Jerkworm in the holes and along timber and undercut banks for huge largemouth bass.

The fishing: This bay is known for its hawg largemouths averaging 3 pounds and northern pike ranging from 4 to 6 pounds. Both take minnows, 7-inch worms tipped on bucktail jigs, and buzzbaits. Bluegills and pumpkinseeds up to 0.75 pound are plentiful and respond to spikes and mousies fished through the ice and to worms suspended below floats or fished on bottom in warm weather. From ice-out through the second week in May, bullheads swarm into the bay. Nocturnal anglers target them off the barrier beach by fishing worms on bottom under Coleman lanterns.

Directions: From the hamlet of Wolcott, take Main Street (Ridge Road) west for about 3 miles to North Huron Road (CR 156). Head north for 2.8 miles and turn west on Slaght Road.

Additional information: A gravel small-craft launch, with parking for three rigs, is 1.2 miles down Slaght Road. There is no public camping on the bay, but commercial campgrounds are in the area.

Contact: New York State Department of Enviornmental Conservation Region 8 and Wayne County Office of Tourism/History.

29A. Public Access

Description: Parking for six cars and access to the bay's barrier beach.

Directions: Follow the directions to site 29, but instead of turning left on Slaght Road, continue straight on North Huron Road for another 2.3 miles to its end. Park in the designated lot on the left, and take the access road on the south end of the lot to the beach. No unauthorized vehicles are allowed, so you'll have to walk about 0.3 mile down a steep grade.

30. Port Bay (see map on page 66)

Key species: Brown trout, largemouth bass, northern pike, walleye, black crappie, yellow perch, sunfish, and brown bullhead.

Description: Spread over 520 acres, this bay averages 20 feet deep and has a maximum depth of 29 feet. It is fed by two creeks, and its west and south sides are weedy. The shoreline is heavily developed with private residences.

Tips: From late April through May, fish live minnows or cast their imitations from the wall at the bay's mouth for brown trout.

King salmon caught off the Port Bay channel (site 30).

The fishing: Port Bay is famed for bucketmouths in the 4- to 6-pound range. Fish for them over deep weed beds with rattling jerkbaits, by working soft jerkbaits around submerged structure, and by casting floating Rat-L-Traps or walking Zara Spooks around timber and lily pads. Northern pike range from 22 to 36 inches and take buzzbaits ripped along weed lines and spinnerbaits bounced on bottom along drop-offs. Target walleyes averaging 4 pounds by deep-drifting worms along drop-offs. Cast small jigheads tipped with curly-tailed grubs and tubes in weed openings, along weed edges, and over breaks for perch ranging from 8 to 10 inches and around brush and timber for black crappies that can go over 1 pound. The entire south basin is hot in the spring for bullheads, which love worms fished on bottom at night or on rainy days. Weedy areas are loaded with bluegills and pumpkinseeds up to 0.75 pound. Work ½₂-ounce Hula Poppers over holes in vegetation and along weed edges.

Directions: From Main Street (Ridge Road) in the village of Wolcott, head north on West Port Bay Road for about 4 miles for the west bank; go the same distance on East Port Bay Road for the east bank.

Contact: New York State Department of Environmental Conservation Region 8 and Wayne County Office of Tourism/History.

30A. Public Access *(see map on page 66)*

Description: This site has a paved ramp, parking for fifty rigs, a handicapped fishing ramp, and a portable toilet.

Directions: In Wolcott, head north on West Port Bay Road for 4 miles and turn right on the dirt road.

30B. West Barrier Public Access *(see map on page 66)*

Description: This site is at the bay's mouth and has a paved ramp, parking for twenty-five rigs, and hundreds of yards of shore-fishing access on the bay, its mouth, and Lake Ontario.

Directions: Head north on West Port Bay Road out of Wolcott for about 6 miles to its end.

31. Blind Sodus Bay *(see map on page 66)*

Key species: Largemouth bass, northern pike, walleye, and panfish.

Description: This 240-acre bay averages 14 feet deep and has a maximum depth of 24 feet. Its shoreline is roughly half private residences, half bottomland forest.

Tips: Cast diving crankbaits along the inside of the barrier beach.

The fishing: Generally shallow and weedy, this bay supports an extraordinary warm-water fishery. Largemouth bass up to 5 pounds are common, with hawgs to 8 pounds possible. Work jig-'n'-pigs and spinnerbaits tipped with trailers against weed edges and submerged timber. Northern pike generally go 22 to 26 inches, but 15-pounders are also present. Big or small, they can't seem to keep their mouths shut when a Rat-L-Trap or spinnerbait swims by. Walleyes can be found year-round in the deep water off the barrier beach. Fish the deep weed edges with bucktail jigs tipped with worms or minnows or with plain jigheads tipped with scented curly-tailed grubs or tubes. Pumpkinseeds and bluegills ranging from 0.5 to 0.75 pound are plentiful. Some crappies up to 1 pound and perch from 8 to 12 inches are also available. Wet flies, fished at a dead drift suspended below tiny bubble floats or retrieved slowly with fly-fishing tackle, work great in summer for all panfish.

Directions: Take NY 104A west out of Fair Haven for about 1 mile. Turn north on Blind Sodus Bay Road and continue for a couple miles.

Additional information: There is no public access. Most anglers motor in from Little Sodus Bay (site 32).

Contact: New York State Department of Environmental Conservation Region 8 and Wayne County Office of Tourism/History.

32. Little Sodus Bay (see map on page 66)

Key species: Black bass, northern pike, walleye, yellow perch, sunfish, and black crappie.

Description: Sprawling over 750 acres, averaging 25 feet deep, and having a maximum depth of 36 feet, this bay's shoreline is almost totally developed with summer cottages and year-round homes.

Tips: From opening day through the first week of July, drag Carolina-rigged 4-inch rubber worms along the drop-offs on the northeastern corner for smallmouth bass.

The fishing: Smallmouth bass pour into the bay to spawn, and some stick around for the first couple weeks of the season. Typically ranging from 1 to 3 pounds, they can be taken on crayfish and minnows worked along drop-offs and weed lines. Largemouth bass from 2 to 5 pounds can be found in the weeds and under docks. The greatest number, however, is in the weedy, shallow southern basin. They respond to jig-'n'-pigs, Texas-rigged worms, and 4-inch worms tipping bucktail jigs. Northern pike averaging 7 pounds can be found on drop-offs and respond to large minnows and spinnerbaits. Walleyes typically go from 2 to 5 pounds and are taken in daylight by trolling minnowbaits like ThunderSticks in 20 to 30 feet of water and at night by casting Rat-L-Traps and Slapsticks near shore. Bluegills up to 0.75 pound and black crappies up to 1 pound are found in the southern basin. They are mostly taken through the ice on tiny jigs tipped with grubs and fished in 5 to 10 feet of water. Perch averaging 12 inches crowd into the bay in winter and are taken through the ice in the deep water on the northeastern corner with minnows and jigs.

Directions: West Bay Road parallels the west bank in the village of Fair Haven.

Additional information: West Barrier Bar Park, located at the end of West Bay Road, has loads of shore-fishing access, including off the mouth's western pier.

Contact: New York State Department of Environmental Conservation Region 7 and Cayuga County Tourism.

32A. Fair Haven Beach State Park

Description: This 865-acre fee area offers 191 campsites (44 electric), 32 cabins, hot showers, paved ramps on Little Sodus Bay with parking for 50 rigs, rowboat rentals, and fishing in Sterling Pond (site 34). The park's breakwall and three old Lake Ontario piers offer great casting platforms for brown trout and steelhead up to 15 pounds, autumn through spring.

Directions: On the east side of the village of Fair Haven.

33. Sterling Creek (see map on page 66)

Key species: Chinook salmon and steelhead.

Description: This tributary feeds Sterling Pond in Fair Haven Beach State Park.

Tips: Use egg sacs for a couple weeks after ice-out.

The fishing: This skinny creek gets stocked with 100,000 3-inch kings annually. When they return in autumn, they average 25 pounds and can be taken with streamers and raw roe. Fingerling steelhead are stocked to the tune of 18,000 annually, and they also return in autumn weighing up to 15 pounds. However, the greatest number of chromers enters the creek to spawn, from ice-out until mid-April. They respond to egg sacs, bead-head nymphs, and worms.

Directions: Head west out of Oswego for about 3.5 miles on NY 104, turn west on NY 104A (Sterling Valley Road), and travel for about 6.5 miles to the village of Sterling.

Additional information: Limited parking is available at the playground adjacent to the village barn on Williams Road (west side of the NY 104A bridge) and at the village offices a couple hundred yards west of the bridge. Additional informal access, on a slow, marshy stretch close to the mouth, is available on Old State Road.

Contact: New York State Department of Environmental Conservation Region 7 and Cayuga County Tourism.

34. Sterling Pond *(see map on page 66)*

(see map on page 66)

Key species: Northern pike, largemouth bass, sunfish, and brown bullhead.

Description: Averaging 4 feet deep and dropping to a maximum depth of 10 feet, this 83-acre pond is totally within Fair Haven Beach State Park.

Tips: Monster bluegills and pumpkinseeds up to a pound or more invade the place from late May through mid-July.

The fishing: Its heavy carpet of weeds makes this natural pond a remarkable, though challenging, warm-water fishery. Northern pike generally go 22 to 30 inches. The best time to get them is in the spring by suspending large minnows below bobbers and casting them into weed openings and along the edge of the old creek channel. While largemouth bass can reach 8 pounds, the average bucketmouth is 4 pounds. They respond to jig-'n'-pigs worked in slop, slugs run parallel to weed edges, and surface poppers and walkers worked over submerged vegetation. A decent resident population of bluegills and pumpkinseeds is available year-round; however, the greatest number of big fish is present during the early-summer spawn. They'll hit anything from wet flies and poppers to garden worms, red worms, and spikes. In spring brown bullheads up to 14 inches swarm into the pond and eagerly hit worms fished on bottom.

Directions: On the east side of the village of Fair Haven.

Additional information: Fair Haven Beach State Park, an 865-acre fee area, offers a paved ramp on Sterling Pond with parking for 25 rigs, rowboat rentals, several piers jutting into Lake Ontario (great casting platforms for spring brown trout and steelhead), 191 campsites (44 electric), 32 cabins, a swimming beach, playing fields, and hiking trails. Free day use is allowed off-season, roughly from Labor Day to Memorial Day.

Contact: New York State Department of Environmental Conservation Region 7 and Cayuga County Tourism.

35. Lower Oswego River/Oswego Harbor *(see map on page 66)*

Key species: Chinook salmon, brown trout, steelhead, walleye, smallmouth bass, largemouth bass, northern pike, channel catfish, freshwater drum, yellow perch, sunfish, rock bass, black crappie, and brown bullhead.

Description: Lake Ontario's second largest tributary, this river drains the Oneida Lake and Finger Lakes watersheds. Dropping roughly 125 feet in its 23.7-mile existence, its last dam is in downtown Oswego, the oldest port city on the Great Lakes. Its mouth is kept from roaming by jetties.

Tips: From opening day through May, flatline crankbaits at night, from the NY 104 bridge to the mouth, for huge walleyes.

The fishing: The lower leg up to the first dam (there are two in the city, about 1,000 yards apart) boasts good populations of resident warm-water species, as well as seasonal runs of salmonids and Lake Ontario's warm-water residents. Locals joke that in the fall lake-run fish are so thick, the river's water level rises about a foot. The state stocks roughly 127,000 fingerling kings annually into the downtown area. While mature stragglers return as early as late August, the main runs begin around the last week of September and continue through October. The fish range from precocious two-year-olds averaging 6 pounds to fully grown 40-pounders. Most are caught with egg sacs, skein, or gobs of colored sponge and mesh cast from the walls of the linear park running both sides of the river. One traveling angler described the setting as "the most comfortable and convenient chinook fishing I've ever done."

Brown trout up to 20 pounds start running the river in mid-September. Many stay the entire winter in the relatively warm waters. They hit worms and egg sacs. The state stocks about 20,000 steelhead each year. Chromers ranging from 4 to 15 pounds begin trickling in along with the kings. By mid-October their numbers are great enough to specifically target with egg sacs, yarn flies, and pieces of tinsel or other sparkling material. Enough steelhead overwinter to attract a dedicated following, who goes after them with egg sacs, wax worms, and pieces of night crawler fished on bottom or suspended a couple inches off the floor with a pencil bobber. Come March, great quantities of steelies run the river to spawn. These aggressive fish will strike in-line spinners and small plugs like Hot Shots and Lazy Ikes. Huge lake walleyes up to 15 pounds migrate into the rapids to spawn right behind the steelies and hang out in the harbor for most of May, fattening up on alewives and perch. They respond to crankbaits and night crawlers still-fished on bottom.

Lake-run smallmouth bass in the 1- to 3-pound range spawn in the harbor, often remaining there for the first couple weeks of the season. Afterwards they move out into the lake but return to the breakwalls during the calm following a few days of heavy winds. They take crayfish and minnows drifted parallel to structure and jigs and crankbaits cast toward shore and worked into deep water. Resident bucketmouths ranging from 2 to 4 pounds and northern pike up to 36 inches occupy the weedy areas in the harbor's turning basin. Both take large minnows, spinnerbaits, buzzbaits, and crankbaits like Bomber Long "A"s. Sheepshead from 1 to 10 pounds can be found virtually anywhere. These powerful fighters are particularly fond of crayfish but will also hit worms and lures. Weedy areas in the turning basin are thick year-round with bluegills and pumpkinseeds up to 1 pound, black crappies averaging 11 inches, and yellow perch from 6 to 14 inches. Massive quantities of lake-run rock bass the size of a small plate and brown bullheads up to 2 pounds migrate into this area in the spring to spawn. The sunfish, perch, rock bass, and bullheads like worms. Black crappies, rock bass, and yellow perch like minnows, spikes, small streamers, and wet flies.

Directions: The river runs through the heart of the city of Oswego and is paralleled by NY 481.

Additional information: West Linear Park, a family-friendly river walk complete with railings, has several parking lots with space for hundreds of cars and offers shore-fishing access to 70 percent of the west bank. East Linear Park offers free parking and shore access to about 50 percent of the east shore. Oswego has numerous motels, several right on the water.

Contact: New York State Department of Environmental Conservation Region 7 and Oswego County Promotion & Tourism.

35A. Leto Island

Description: This lock island is partly owned by the state. There is some free shore-fishing access but no free parking.

The fishing: Anglers park on the shoulder and walk the lock service road to access the old riverbed and the holes at the base of the falls. During low water you can wade the old riverbed to the middle wall and the deep hole below the powerhouse turbines.

Directions: Off East First Street (NY 481) in the city of Oswego.

Additional information: The Oswego River is big water whose levels are regulated by nature. If you decide to wade out to the middle wall or the ledge across from the powerhouse, keep an eye on the dam. Head for shore the moment you see water steadily streaming over it.

35B. Wrights Landing *(see map on page 66)*

Description: Protected by the harbor's breakwalls, this city-run fee area offers a six-lane paved ramp, 166 seasonal slips, 57 transient slips, a 1-ton boat hoist, showers, a fish cleaning station, and parking for about 150 rigs and 50 cars. Open April through October.

The fishing: In autumn the shipping channel in front of Wrights Landing and the turning basin to the west often load up with ripe salmon. Frustrated and angry over their inability to go over the dam, they strike at spoons and streamers. Steelhead can be found in this channel from autumn through late spring and take spinners and plugs like Hot Shots and Flatfish. For much of May monster walleyes are taken in the channel by trolling crankbaits like ThunderSticks and worms on spinner harnesses. In summer the south shore grows the only meaningful weed beds in the area, becoming a bucketmouth and pikeasaurus hot spot for anglers throwing everything from soft plastics to hard jerkbaits and crankbaits.

Directions: Head north on West First Street to Lake Street.

Additional information: Bank fishing, with free parking, is permitted off the marina's concrete walls but not off the docks.

35C. West Breakwall *(see map on page 66)*

Description: This jetty is a combination of decaying concrete pier and limestone blocks. Beginning right below the steam plant's obsolete discharge tunnels, the wall runs along the north side of the shipping channel, then banks north and runs for about another 0.5 mile to the lighthouse.

The fishing: This is a local hot spot for shore anglers targeting salmon in autumn with spoons, crankbaits, and streamers. In early spring steelhead mill around the turning basin and respond to egg sacs, small spoons, and Rooster Tails. In May walleyes follow in the wakes of the chromers and strike crankbaits like Red Fins.

Directions: In Oswego, take Bridge Street (NY 104) west to George Washington Boulevard. Turn right a couple blocks later onto Sixth Street and follow it to the end.

Additional information: The landing at the end of Sixth Street has parking for about ten cars.

35D. Drift Boat Launch *(see map on page 66)*

Description: This site has a paved ramp and street parking for ten rigs.

Directions: Below the east side of the NY 104 bridge, on East Canal View Drive.

36. Grindstone Creek *(see map on page 78)*

Key species: Brook trout and steelhead.

One down, two to go at the west breakwall (site 35C) near the N.R.G. Steam Plant.

Lake Ontario: Mexico Bay to Deer Creek Marsh

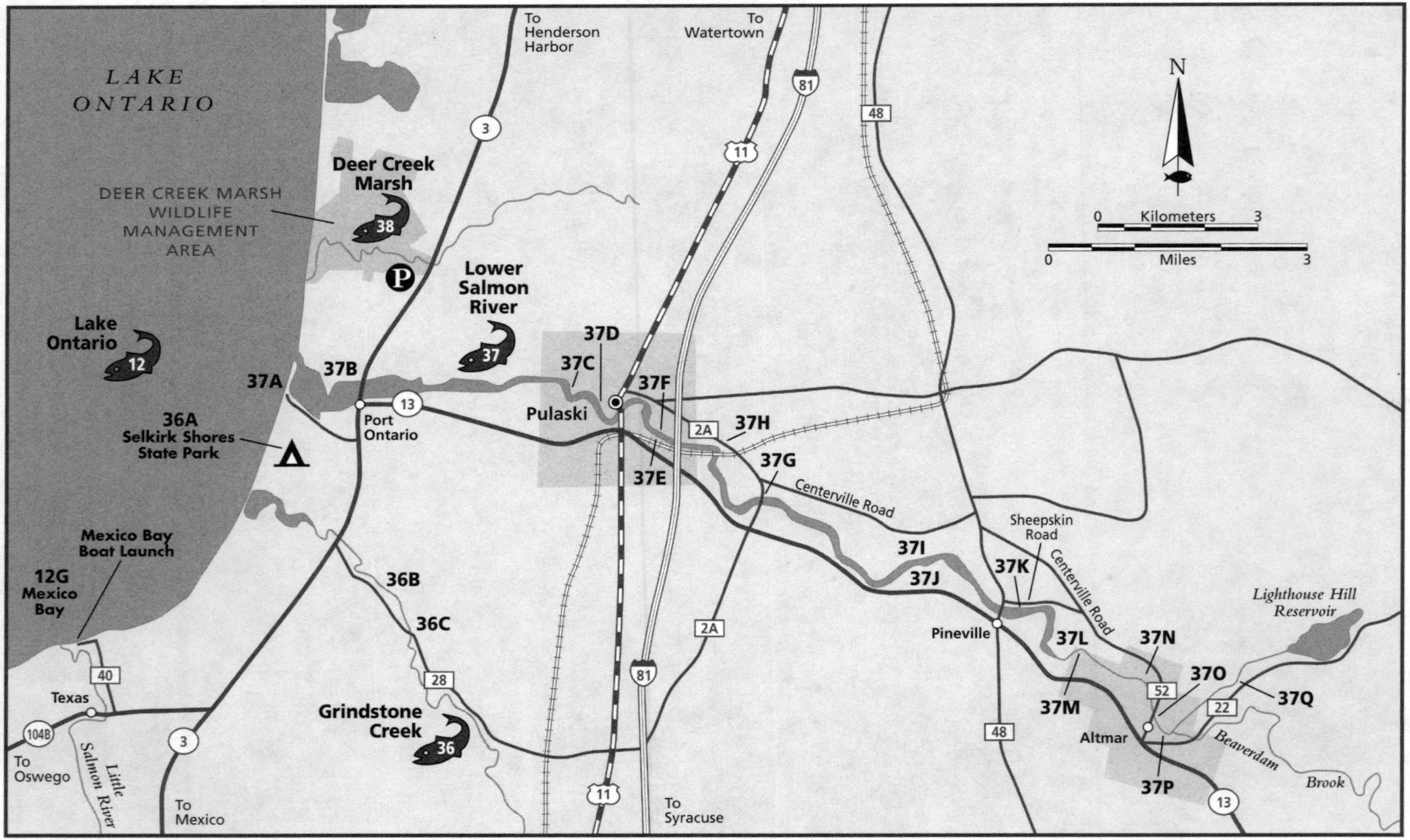

LAKE ONTARIO

Deer Creek Marsh 38

DEER CREEK MARSH WILDLIFE MANAGEMENT AREA

Lake Ontario 12

Lower Salmon River 37

To Henderson Harbor

To Watertown

Pulaski

37D
37C
37F
37E
37B
37A

Port Ontario

Selkirk Shores State Park

Mexico Bay Boat Launch

12G Mexico Bay

Texas

Little Salmon River

To Oswego

To Mexico

Grindstone Creek 36

36A
36B
36C

To Syracuse

Pineville

Altmar

Lighthouse Hill Reservoir

Beaverdam Brook

37G
37H
37I
37J
37K
37L
37M
37N
37O
37P
37Q

Centerville Road

Sheepskin Road

N

Kilometers

Miles

Description: A skinny creek by anyone's standard, it meanders for about 20 miles, finally swelling to fishable levels a couple miles before pouring into Lake Ontario at Selkirk Shores State Park.

Tips: For spring brook trout, drift garden worms and red worms tight to logs, stream banks, and boulders.

The fishing: Upstream of NY 3 the state annually stocks 2,000 4-inch brook trout. Their voracious appetites lead to exciting fishing for purists out to fill their memories with vivid images of colorful brookies caught on flies under scenic conditions. Meat anglers using worms and salted minnows manage to catch enough brookies from 6 to 10 inches to make their trips worthwhile. The state also stocks 5,000 fingerling steelhead annually. Many return fall through spring and are taken on egg sacs and worms, primarily by anglers fishing the last 100 yards upstream of the mouth in Selkirk Shores State Park.

Directions: CR 28 parallels much of the stream.

Contact: New York State Department of Environmental Conservation Region 7 and Oswego County Promotion & Tourism.

36A. Selkirk Shores State Park

Description: This site offers parking for about a hundred cars at the mouth, the creek's most productive stretch for steelhead.

Directions: From the NY 13/NY 3 intersection in Port Ontario, head south on NY 3 for about 1.5 miles.

Additional information: This 980-acre forested park offers 148 campsites (88 electric), 24 rustic cabins, picnic facilities, hot showers, a swimming beach, playing fields, and hiking trails. Noncampers are charged a day-use fee from Memorial Day through Labor Day.

36B. Public Access

Description: This site has parking for five cars.

Directions: Head south out of Port Ontario on NY 3 for about 1.5 miles, turn left onto CR 28 (just past the Selkirk Shores State Park entrance, site 36A), and continue for about 1 mile.

36C. Public Access

Description: This site has parking for five cars.

Directions: From site 36B, travel 0.5 mile further east on CR 28.

A keeper caught on the Lower Salmon River (site 37).

37. Lower Salmon River (see map on page 78)

Key species: Coho salmon, chinook salmon, landlocked Atlantic salmon, brown trout, steelhead, northern pike, black bass, and channel catfish.

Description: Shallow and fast, this section of the river runs from the Lower Reservoir dam to its mouth on Lake Ontario, a distance of about 13 miles.

Tips: Wear Cabela's boot chains or swim.

The fishing: This is the best trophy salmonid stream in the Northeast—and it's made that way by massive human intervention. The state hatchery at Altmar, just upstream of Beaverdam Brook's mouth, annually stocks roughly 193,000 6-inch steelhead, 105,000 cohos, 350,000 fingerling kings, and 30,000 7.5-inch Atlantic salmon into the river or its tiny tributaries. In addition, over 600,000 yearling brown trout are released each year into Lake Ontario near the river's mouth. Autumn runs of Pacific salmon are unequaled in the lower forty-eight states. Cohos over 30 pounds and chinooks over 40 pounds are caught each year. Massive runs of brown trout weighing up to 15 pounds enter the river in the fall along with the salmon, and many spend the winter. Steelhead up to 25 pounds enter en masse in mid-October to pig out on salmon eggs. Many overwinter, too. In addition, spawning runs of steelies enter the river from ice-out straight through April. The best baits for these fish are egg sacs, skein, worms, yarn flies, Hot Shots, Flatfish, and Aglia streamers. Summer sees runs of skamania (hatchery fish that have a fin clipped) averaging 10 pounds and landlocked Atlantic salmon averaging 8 pounds. These fish are mostly sought by fly fishers casting streamers and wet flies. However, they will take worms, especially in a drizzle or after a storm.

From opening day through summer, smallmouth bass up to 4 pounds can be found in holes and runs all the way to Altmar and respond to streamers and crayfish imitations. Lake bronzebacks from 1.5 to 5 pounds—some even bigger—hang out near the mouth and take minnows, crayfish, and Carolina-rigged finesse worms. Largemouth bass ranging from 2 to 6 pounds are available in the marshy area—locals call it the estuary—upstream of the mouth. They hit a litany of soft plastic baits worked on Texas and Carolina rigs, as well as surface baits like Hula Poppers and Zara Spooks. Northern pike up to 15 pounds share range with the bucketmouths but are especially fond of the river channel. They'll take spinnerbaits, jerkbaits, crankbaits, and minnows. Catfish averaging 6 pounds hang out in the channel from the mouth up to the lighthouse and take cut bait and shrimp.

Directions: NY 13 parallels the south bank from Port Ontario all the way to Altmar.

Additional information: This stream has more bait shops, guide services, campgrounds, and motels than some third-world countries, mostly on NY 13 and US 11 in the village of Pulaski. The state-of-the-art Salmon River Hatchery, open for self-guided tours, is located on CR 22 in Altmar. The river upstream of the bridge in Altmar is set aside for catch-and-release fly fishing only (fly fishers can use the whole river; bait fishers can't fish here) and catch-and-release. Camping is available at Selkirk Shores State Park (site 36A).

Contact: New York State Department of Environmental Conservation Region 7 and Oswego County Promotion & Tourism.

37A. Pine Grove Public Boat Launch

Description: This fee area is part of Selkirk Shores State Park (site 36A) and is located a couple hundred yards upstream of the Salmon River's mouth. It has a paved ramp and parking for fifty rigs. Open from April 1 through the end of October.

Directions: Head west out of Pulaski on NY 13 for 4 miles. Turn south on NY 3, then right 0.5 mile later, and travel several hundred yards.

37B. Port Ontario Public Access

Description: This site has an elevated handicapped platform and parking for nine cars.

Directions: Take NY 13 north out of Pulaski for 4 miles, turn north on NY 3, and cross the bridge.

37C. Black Hole *(see map on page 78)*

Description: The deepest pool on the river, it always has fish, including monster smallmouths in summer. There's a drift boat launch and parking for about a hundred cars; during salmon season, a fee is charged to park. The southern bank is part of the Douglaston Salmon Run, a private fishing preserve.

Directions: On Riverview Drive (off Bridge Street) in Pulaski.

37D. Pulaski Chamber of Commerce Boat Launch *(see map on page 78)*

Description: A drift boat launch on the "Staircase" and parking for twenty cars.

Directions: On Forest Drive (take Jefferson Street to James Street) in Pulaski.

37E. Dunbar Field–Clamshed Pool *(see map on page 78)*

Description: A drift boat launch and parking for about a hundred cars. The Short Bridge Pool (aka Village Pool) and Long Bridge Pools are downstream; the 81 Hole and Trooper Holes are upstream.

Directions: From the NY 13 railroad crossing in Pulaski, turn north onto Lewis Street and proceed for a couple hundred yards.

37F. Haldane Community Center *(see map on page 78)*

Description: Parking for one hundred cars across the river from the Clamshed Pool.

Directions: From the northernmost NY 11 traffic light in Pulaski, head east on Maple Avenue for a few hundred yards to the curve and bear right on Maple Avenue Extension.

37G. Compactor Pool Access *(see map on page 78)*

Description: A paved drift boat ramp, parking for about twenty-five cars, and a portable toilet.

Directions: Take NY 13 south out of Pulaski for about 1 mile, turn north on CR 2A, and cross the bridge.

37H. Paper Hole and Lower Paper Hole Access *(see map on page 78)*

Description: Parking for about ten cars and access to railroad tracks leading to these holes. The Paper Hole is upstream of the trestle.

Directions: From site 37G, continue straight on CR 2A for about 0.5 mile and park in the informal lot just across the railroad tracks.

37I. Sportsman's Pool North Access *(see map on page 78)*

Description: This site has parking for about fifty cars and a trail to the river's longest pool.

Directions: From site 37G, follow CR 2A for about 0.1 mile north, turn east on Centerville Road, and travel for 2.3 miles.

37J. Sportsman's Pool South Access *(see map on page 78)*

Description: This site has parking for fifty cars, a toilet, and a long path to the pool.

Directions: Take NY 13 south out of Pulaski for about 3 miles.

37K. Pineville Pool Access *(see map on page 78)*

Description: This site has parking for about a hundred cars and a drift boat launch.

Directions: Take NY 13 south out of Pulaski for about 4 miles to Pineville, turn left on CR 48, cross the bridge, and turn right on Sheepskin Road.

37L. Trestle Pool North Access *(see map on page 78)*

Description: This site has parking for about fifty cars.

Directions: Take Sheepskin Road (see site 37K) out of Pineville for about 0.5 mile, turn right on the gravel road, and continue for about 0.5 mile.

37M. Trestle Hole South Access *(see map on page 78)*

Description: This site has parking for about twenty-five cars.

Directions: About 1 mile from Pineville on NY 13 south.

37N. Ellis Cove Access *(see map on page 78)*

Description: This site has parking for about thirty cars.

Direction: Head north out of Altmar on CR 52 for about 1 mile.

37O. Altmar North Parking Area and Lower Fly-Fishing-Only Section *(see map on page 78)*

Description: This site has parking for about twenty-five cars.

Directions: Located on the north side of the CR 52 bridge in downtown Altmar.

Additional information: Upstream of this bridge, the river is set aside for catch-and-release fly fishing only; flea flicking (a local term for fly fishing) is allowed on the whole stream, but bait and lure folks can't fish here. Check the state *Fishing Regulations Guide* for fishing season, times, and terminal-tackle restrictions.

37P. Altmar Drift Boat Launch *(see map on page 78)*

Description: This site, restricted to vehicles with trailers, has a paved ramp and parking for about twenty rigs.

Directions: At the southeast corner of the CR 52 bridge in Altmar.

Deer Creek among the dunes.

37Q. Upper Fly-Fishing-Only Section Access *(see map on page 78)*

Description: This site has a trail leading to the last leg of the special fly-fishing, catch-and-release set-aside in the Salmon River Gorge. It has parking for about twenty cars. Closed December through March to protect wintering bald eagles.

Directions: About 1 mile east of Altmar on CR 22.

Additional information: See the state *Fishing Regulations Guide* for season, fishing times, and terminal-tackle restrictions.

38. Deer Creek Marsh *(see map on page 78)*

Key species: Largemouth bass, northern pike, sunfish, and yellow perch.

Description: On the last leg of its journey to Lake Ontario, Deer Creek meanders through the Deer Creek Marsh Wildlife Management Area. It moves so slowly in summer, the ground absorbs it at the lake's edge, turning it into a scenic barrier pond nestled in towering sand dunes, with a sandy isthmus only a few yards wide separating it from the lake.

Tips: Flip soft plastic worms into the openings and edges of vegetation.

The fishing: Largemouth bass in the 1.5- to 3-pound range hide under the mats of vegetation lining the creek channel. Gently drop floating baits on lily pads and exposed timber for a moment, then hop them into the water. Northern pike tend to be small, averaging 3 pounds. They prowl the edges of vegetation, violently striking any mouth-size critter, from mice and ducklings to snakes and frogs. Use lures imitating these life forms. Sunfish and yellow perch ranging from 5 to 10 inches are plentiful and find it all but impossible to pass up a fat, juicy worm or wet fly.

Directions: Head north out of Port Ontario for 2 miles on NY 3.

Additional information: The access site on NY 3 has a beach launch for cartop craft and parking for about ten cars.

Contact: New York State Department of Environmental Conservation Region 7.

39. Little Sandy Creek

Key species: Steelhead.

Description: This creek averages about 15 feet wide and flows into North Sandy Pond.

Lake Ontario: North Sandy Pond and Nearby Creeks

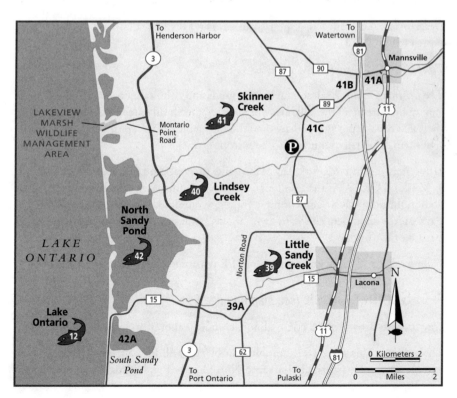

Tips: Drift a single plastic egg through pools and runs and under windfalls.

The fishing: Late fall through March, steelhead enter during high water, reaching all the way to the hamlet of Sandy Creek. They take egg sacs and egg patterns. The best time to fish is when the creek is murky and too high to wade across.

Directions: CR 15 parallels the stream.

Additional information: The village of Sandy Creek has several informal access sites.

Contact: New York State Department of Environmental Conservation Region 7 and Oswego County Promotion & Tourism.

39A. Norton Road Public Access *(see map on page 85)*

Description: This state site offers parking for about thirty cars and about 0.5 mile of public fishing rights above and below the bridge.

Directions: Take North Street (CR 62) out of Pulaski for about 3.5 miles. At the stop sign, continue straight on CR 15 east for 0.5 mile and turn left on Norton Road.

40. Lindsey Creek *(see map on page 85)*

Key species: Chinook salmon, coho salmon, and steelhead.

Description: This tiny creek pours out of Tug Hill Plateau's west side and feeds North Sandy Pond.

Tips: Use gobs of raw salmon roe.

The fishing: Chinook salmon up to 20 pounds and coho salmon averaging 8 pounds run up this stream in the fall during high water. Steelhead enter along with them, but they also run during winter thaws and the spring melt. Each species hits egg sacs and raw skein. The daily limit for rainbow trout is one.

Directions: From I–81 exit 39 at Mannsville, turn west on CR 90, then immediately south on CR 89. At the terminus a little over 1 mile later, turn left, then immediately right onto CR 87 and continue for a few hundred yards to the second bridge. Park on the shoulder. The state owns about 2 miles of public fishing rights downstream of the bridge.

Contact: New York State Department of Environmental Conservation Region 6.

41. Skinner Creek *(see map on page 85)*

Key species: Brown trout, coho salmon, chinook salmon, and steelhead.

Description: This small creek tumbles out of Tug Hill Plateau; winds through pasture, forest, and marsh; and pours into North Sandy Pond. Usually too low to hold trout larger than stockies, its lower portion draws small runs of Pacific salmon in autumn and decent groups of steelies during the spring thaw.

Tips: Salmon run best after an autumn rain.

The fishing: The state annually stocks 400 8-inch brown trout downstream of the dam in the village of Mannsville. They reach up to 14 inches and hit worms and nymphs. In early autumn chinook salmon up to 20 pounds and some coho salmon averaging 8 pounds enter this creek when water levels permit. However, even during dry years reluctant stragglers, propelled by their unwinding biological clocks, stage small runs. They hit single eggs, fresh skein, and streamers. Steelhead enter the stream during high water, autumn through spring, and hit egg sacs, wax worms, and garden worms. The daily limit for rainbow trout is one.

Directions: The creek skirts the south side of Mannsville.

Contact: New York State Department of Environmental Conservation Region 6.

41A. Public Access

Description: This site has parking for five cars.

Directions: On Brown Road in Mannsville.

41B. Public Access

Description: This site has parking for five cars.

Directions: From I–81 exit 39 in Mannsville, turn west on CR 90, then immediately south on CR 89, and travel for about 1 mile.

41C. Public Access

Description: This site has parking for five cars.

Directions: From site 41B, continue on CR 89 for about 1 mile to its end. Turn left and then immediately right onto CR 87, continue for a few hundred feet, cross the creek, and park in the small lot on the left.

42. North Sandy Pond *(see map on page 85)*

Key species: Northern pike, largemouth bass, black crappie, yellow perch, and sunfish.

Description: The biggest pond in the Eastern Lake Ontario Dune and Wetland Area, it covers 2,400 acres, averages 8 feet deep, and has a maximum depth of 13 feet. A popular summer destination, its shore is heavily developed with camps, year-round homes, and private marinas.

Tips: Ice fishing with tiny minnows is productive for yellow perch.

The fishing: Northern pike average 5 pounds, but monsters estimated at over 20 pounds are reported lost each year by ice anglers who claim the things were too big to squeeze through the hole. In summer most are taken on large minnows fished below bobbers along weed edges, early in the morning or late in the evening when boat traffic dies down. Largemouth bass rule the pond's weed beds, especially on the north end, and are partial to scented worms worked on the surface or along weed edges on Texas rigs. Crappies up to 12 inches and sunfish averaging 6 inches hang around vegetation, too, and take tiny $\frac{1}{16}$- to $\frac{1}{32}$-ounce marabou jigs. For a while, perch numbers plummeted, probably because of alewife predation of their fry (stomach analysis shows adult alewives can consume up to 300 perch fry daily). They're coming back, though, and batches in the 8- to 10-inch range are commonly caught through the ice on spikes and mousy grubs and in summer on 2-inch Berkley Power Grubs fished on bare or spinner-rigged jigheads.

Directions: Take NY 3 north from Port Ontario for about 4 miles to the flashing yellow light, turn left on CR 15, and continue for about 1 mile.

Additional information: Sandy Island Beach Park (at the end of CR 15) allows launching cartop craft. Several commercial operations with launch ramps ring the pond.

Contact: New York State Department of Environmental Conservation Region 7 and Oswego County Promotion & Tourism.

42A. South Sandy Pond *(see map on page 85)*

Description: Spilling over 360 acres, this pond's average depth is 14 feet, and its maximum depth is 25 feet. Bowl-shaped, its shallow shoreline steadily drops to a deep center, making it ideal habitat for the same warm-water species found in North Sandy Pond.

Directions: There is no public shore access. The only way to get in is through the shallow channel on the southwestern corner of North Sandy Pond.

43. Lakeview Marsh Wildlife Management Area Ponds (Lakeview, Floodwood, Goose, North Colwell, and South Colwell Ponds)

Key species: Northern pike, largemouth bass, black crappie, yellow perch, and sunfish.

Description: This 3,461-acre wildlife management area is the largest undeveloped parcel within the Eastern Lake Ontario Dune and Wetland Area, a 17-mile stretch of barrier beach with the tallest sand dunes between Lake Michigan and Cape Cod. Its five ponds are connected by channels navigable by canoe during years of normal rainfall.

Tips: Ice fish for crappies around dusk and dawn with tiny jigs tipped with grubs.

Lakeview Marsh Wildlife Management Area Ponds

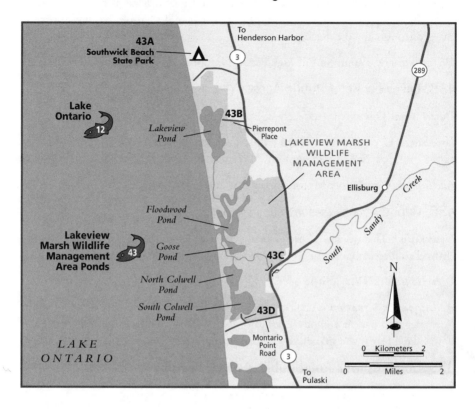

The fishing: Northern pike are present, but they're seldom longer than 24 inches. On the other hand, largemouth bass over 6 pounds are caught every year. Both of these predators react with extreme prejudice to soft and hard jerkbaits worked sloppily and quickly over openings in weeds and along weed edges. Drifting with worms is a productive way to take perch and sunfish. Crappies range between 0.5 and 0.75 pound but are known to go twice that. Fish for them in brush and timber with 2-inch scented curly-tailed grubs tipped on jigheads and worked on spinner forms. From mid-April through May, bullheads in the 8- to 14-inch range invade the ponds, gobbling up every worm they can find.

Directions: NY 3 hugs the wildlife management area from Montario Point Road to Southwick Beach State Park.

Additional information: Motors over ten horsepower are prohibited on the ponds.

Contact: New York State Department of Environmental Conservation Region 6.

43A. Southwick Beach State Park

Description: Covering 500 acres, this fee area borders the northern boundary of the

Lakeview Marsh Wildlife Management Area. It offers 112 campsites (44 with electricity), hot showers, playgrounds, a sand beach, and a launch ramp for hand-carried craft. The campground is open mid-May through mid-October. A day-use fee is charged from mid-June through Labor Day.

Directions: Head south out of Henderson Harbor on NY 3 for about 7 miles.

43B. Lakeview Pond Public Access *(see map on page 89)*

Description: This site has a beach launch and parking for fifteen rigs.

Directions: Head south on NY 3 from Southwick Beach State Park (site 43A) for about 1 mile on NY 3, turn west on Pierrepont Place, and travel 0.5 mile.

Additional information: Motors larger than ten horsepower are prohibited.

43C. Public Access *(see map on page 89)*

Description: This site has a beach launch on South Sandy Creek, upstream from the channel connecting Goose and Floodwood Ponds, and parking for about twenty cars.

Directions: On NY 3, a little over 2 miles south of site 43B.

Additional information: A short, steep drop prevents launching trailered craft. You'll have to paddle roughly 2 miles of scenic flat water, lazily winding through bottomland forest and marsh, to get to the pond.

43D. South Colwell Pond Public Access *(see map on page 89)*

Description: This site has a beach launch and parking for ten rigs.

The fishing: The clearing around the launch is a good spot for spring bullheads.

Directions: Head south about 1 mile on NY 3 from site 43C, turn west on Montario Point Road, and continue for about 0.5 mile.

Additional information: Motors exceeding ten horsepower are prohibited.

44. South Sandy Creek

Key species: Chinook salmon and steelhead.

Description: This stream has it all—undercut banks, deep pools, fast runs—and ends in a slow, quiet mile-long channel feeding Goose Pond.

Tips: The most productive public stretch is upstream of the NY 3 bridge.

The fishing: The state annually stocks this creek with roughly 28,750 fingerling steelhead and 100,000 3-inch chinooks. From mid-September through October, runoff from heavy rains draws spawn-minded chinook salmon in the 5- to 30-pound range into the stream. Steelhead up to 15 pounds follow to feast on salmon eggs, staying until ice starts forming. Both species will take streamers and egg sacs.

Lake Ontario: South Sandy Creek to Chaumont Bay

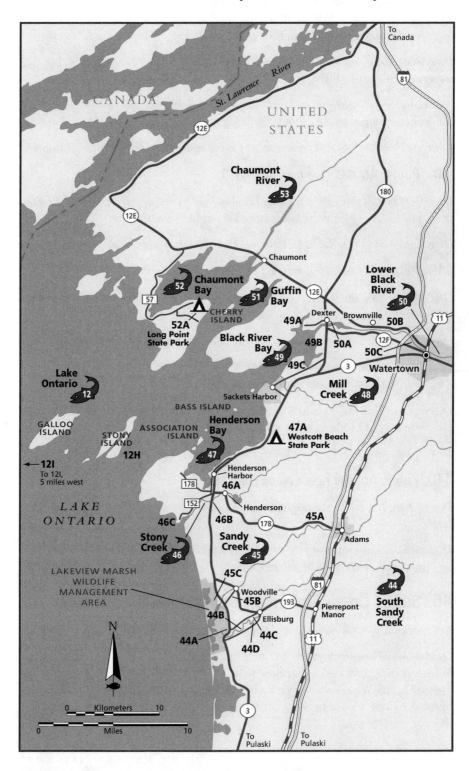

Steelies return immediately after ice-out and stick around for most of March—sometimes April, water levels permitting. Their stomachs full of spawn, they're not into large meals but snack on dime-size egg sacs and $\frac{1}{16}$- to $\frac{1}{8}$-ounce white in-line spinners. The daily limit for rainbow trout is one.

Directions: Take exit 40 (Pierrepont Manor) from I–81 and head west on NY 193 for about 4 miles to Ellisburg.

Additional information: Loads of public access is available in the hamlet of Ellisburg on both sides of the NY 193 bridge.

Contact: New York State Department of Environmental Conservation Region 6.

44A. Public Access *(see map on page 91)*

Description: This site offers parking for about fifty cars, a beach launch for cartop craft, a handicapped fishing platform, and creekside benches.

Directions: On NY 3, about 10 miles south of Henderson Harbor.

44B. Public Access *(see map on page 91)*

Description: This site leads to a deep, slow-moving section of stream and has parking for about fifteen cars.

Directions: Take South Landing Road (off NY 3, just north of site 44A) east for 0.3 mile.

44C. Public Access *(see map on page 91)*

Description: This site leads to a fast-flowing strip of water loaded with pools, runs, and undercut banks. Parking for about twelve cars.

Directions: On South Landing Road, about 0.5 mile east of site 44B.

44D. Public Access *(see map on page 91)*

Description: Access on the opposite side of site 44C. Parking for about twenty-five cars.

Directions: Head south on NY 3 from site 44A for a few hundred yards, turn east on Nash Road, and continue about 1 mile.

45. Sandy Creek (Jefferson County) *(see map on page 91)*

Key species: Chinook salmon, steelhead, brown trout, and brook trout.

Description: This small creek has multiple personalities. Its headwaters contain holes and runs separated by shallow riffs. Downstream of Adams it becomes flat water. Around Woodville it enters a low gorge and slides down a clean, gentle 2-mile-long slope whose broken floor creates violent backwashes, slicks, shallow

Autumn chinook caught at Sandy Creek (site 45).

pools, and runs. It feeds Lakeview Marsh Wildlife Management Area's Floodwood Pond.

Tips: Wear cleats for traction while wading.

The fishing: Each year the state stocks over 1,000 brown trout and several hundred brook trout averaging 8 inches and 350 two-year-old browns averaging 14 inches in the village of Adams. They take worms during high water and nymphs when it is low. The creek's major draw are seasonal runs of chinook salmon reaching 35 pounds and steelhead up to 15 pounds. While they have been known to reach as far as Adams during years of heavy rainfall, on average they normally don't get past Woodville. In autumn both species react violently to egg-sucking leeches and Woolly Buggers. Come spring, spawning steelies move in and take egg sacs and single plastic eggs bounced on bottom. The daily limit for rainbow trout is one.

Directions: Take exit 40 (Pierrepont Manor) from I–81 and head west on NY 193 for about 6 miles to Woodville.

Additional information: This stream is also called North Sandy Creek.

Contact: New York State Department of Environmental Conservation Region 6 and 1000 Islands International Tourism Council.

45A. NY 178 Access *(see map on page 91)*

Description: Sandy Creek flows through Adams and clings to the shoulder of NY 178 for about 1 mile downstream of town. This is all private property, but most owners don't seem to mind anglers in the stream. However, don't go where there are posted signs. Everywhere else, be polite to anyone who may challenge you.

Directions: Adams is located at I–81 exit 41, about 10 miles south of Watertown.

45B. Public Access *(see map on page 91)*

Description: The state owns public fishing rights to several sections of Sandy Creek. The longest stretch is from Woodville (shoulder parking in the village) downstream to just shy of the NY 3 bridge. A fishing access site with parking for about twenty cars is located on CR 120 (North Landing Road).

Directions: Take NY 3 south for about 6 miles from Henderson Harbor and turn left on CR 120. The access site will be on the left, 1.2 miles later. You'll have to walk through the field for about 250 yards to the creek.

45C. Public Access *(see map on page 91)*

Description: This site has parking for about thirty cars.

Directions: From Henderson Harbor, take NY 3 south for about 8 miles to the bridge.

46. Stony Creek *(see map on page 91)*

Key species: Chinook salmon, steelhead, largemouth bass, and northern pike.

Description: This relatively small, shallow creek flows through a tight gorge before feeding Lake Ontario on the south side of Sawyer Point.

Tips: Fish this stream in early spring with egg-pattern flies for steelhead.

The fishing: Roughly 201,000 fingerling steelhead are stocked into this creek annually. While the upper reaches flow through private property and access is tough, the state owns fishing access rights on some of its most productive water, about 0.5 mile above and below the NY 3 bridge. From mid-September through October, chinook salmon up to 30 pounds and steelhead up to 15 pounds enter the creek after heavy rains and will strike gobs of fresh salmon roe or egg sacs. From ice-out through March, steelhead ranging from 5 to 15 pounds run upstream to spawn. They hit egg sacs and pieces of worm. Largemouth bass up to 6 pounds and northern pike averaging 28 inches thrive in the mouth and take large minnows. The daily limit for rainbow trout is one.

Directions: The NY 3 bridge is less than 1 mile south of Henderson Harbor.

Contact: New York State Department of Environmental Conservation Region 6.

46A. Public Access

Description: A popular area with locals is the pool below the falls in the village of Henderson. Located at the foot of a dam, this hole often holds a salmonid or two in the morning. Shoulder parking is available.

Directions: Head east out of Henderson Harbor on NY 178 for about 1 mile. The site is behind the Henderson post office.

46B. Public Access

Description: This site is right at the NY 3 bridge and has parking for five cars.

Directions: Head south out of Henderson Harbor on NY 3 for about 500 yards.

46C. Stony Creek Public Access

Description: This site has a triple-wide paved ramp, parking for at least a hundred rigs, picnic tables, grills, shore fishing with a handicapped ramp, and toilets.

The fishing: The creek comes to a slow stop about 100 yards above the ramp. Lined with reeds and cattails, its gently caressing flow holds largemouth bass from 2 to 6 pounds and northern pike from 22 to 30 inches. Both take large shiners, crankbaits, and spinnerbaits fished during periods of low boat activity.

Directions: Take Harbor Road (CR 123) south out of Henderson Harbor. After crossing Military Road, turn right on Danley Road (CR 152). At the stop sign 1.9 miles later, turn right on Nutting Road and travel for 0.2 mile.

47. Henderson Bay *(see map on page 91)*

Key species: Black bass and northern pike.

Description: Averaging 30 feet deep and dropping to a maximum of 40 feet, this bay is the gateway to the Golden Crescent, a group of of embayments cut into the northeastern corner of Lake Ontario like a moose antler. This fabulous fishery contains habitats ranging from weed beds and deep boulder fields to muddy flats, river mouths, islands, and rocky shoals.

Tips: Snowshoe Bay, on the east side of the cut between the mainland and Hoveys Island (connected to the south end of Association Island), always holds bass: Largemouths rule the weed beds, and smallmouths claim the drop-offs.

The fishing: Northern pike up to 20 pounds and largemouth bass up to 7 pounds can be taken in the weed beds carpeting all coves and bays on large minnows, spinnerbaits, and buzzbaits. The biggest pike are caught through the ice on large minnows. Smallmouth bass between 1.5 and 3 pounds thrive on the rocky drop-offs around the islands and shoals and respond to live bait, crankbaits, and YUM Wooly Curltails dragged on bottom in 15 to 25 feet of water.

Directions: NY 3 parallels the bay from Sackets Harbor to Henderson Harbor.

Additional information: Coming in from the lake, the entrance to the bay is loaded with shallow shoals. A couple of the safest ways to get in are through the cut between the mainland and Hoveys Island and the channel between Bass and Horse Islands. A paved four-lane ramp, with parking for eighty-five rigs, is located on the west end of Henderson Harbor, off Military Road (CR 178).

Contact: New York State Department of Environmental Conservation Region 6 and Henderson Harbor Chamber of Commerce.

47A. Westcott Beach State Park *(see map on page 91)*

Description: This 318-acre fee area offers 168 campsites without hookups and 83 with electricity, a paved launch ramp, parking for 10 rigs, fishing access on a couple of jetties, hot showers, a swimming beach, and hiking trails.

Directions: On NY 3, about 4 miles north of Henderson Harbor.

48. Mill Creek (Jefferson County) *(see map on page 91)*

Key species: Coho salmon, chinook salmon, and steelhead.

Description: Possessing a relatively small volume of water, this creek slides over a wide, relatively flat riverbed and all but dries up in summer. However, autumn's rains and snowmelt give it bursts of life.

Tips: Fish yarn flies in the mouth for spring steelhead.

The fishing: Coho salmon averaging 8 pounds and chinook salmon up to 25 pounds try running the creek each fall. Often frustrated by the low water, they mill around in the pool at the mouth for a while, viciously attacking crankbaits and streamers that get in their way. Winter thaws and spring runoff attract steelhead ranging from 3 to 10 pounds. The best fishing is in the mouth and in the pools and runs a couple hundred feet upstream. Egg sacs and Rooster Tails are effective baits. The daily limit for rainbow trout is one.

Directions: On the north side of the village of Sackets Harbor.

Additional information: Mill Creek flows along the north edge of Madison Barracks, one of America's oldest army forts. It's said the first shot of the War of 1812 was fired here. Brigadier General Zebulon Pike, discoverer of Pike's Peak, is buried in the cemetery. The fence around the graveyard once circled Buckingham Palace and was given to America in compensation for British forces burning down the White House during the War of 1812. This was Ulysses S. Grant's first duty station upon graduating from West Point, and his quarters are now part of the Old

Stone Row Country Inn. Though some of the old buildings are in a terrible state of disrepair, most have been restored, making this historic ground one of the country's greatest living museums of military architecture.

Contact: New York State Department of Environmental Conservation Region 6 and 1000 Islands International Tourism Council.

49. Black River Bay *(see map on page 91)*

Key species: Walleye, northern pike, largemouth bass, smallmouth bass, channel catfish, burbot, carp, sunfish, bullhead, and American eel.

Description: Five miles long and up to 3 miles wide, this bay is one of the lake's most productive fisheries. You name the habitat and it's here: islands, shoals, sprawling weed beds, steep drops, deep holes, and channels.

Tips: In late spring flatline ThunderSticks off planer boards (use keel sinkers to get down 15 to 20 feet) along the north shore for walleyes averaging 8 pounds.

The fishing: Many local guides consider walleye the bay's top bread-and-butter fish. Twelve-pounders are taken in spring and fall by trolling crankbaits and worms on spinner harnesses and by casting bladebaits, Rat-L-Traps, and jigs along the edges of shoals. Coming in at a close second are smallmouth bass ranging from 1 to 3 pounds. They're mostly caught by fishing crayfish on bottom along drop-offs and breaklines. Largemouth bass aren't as commonly sought, but they have dedicated followers who pursue them on the surface in weedy areas with plugs like Zara Spooks or go deeper with Texas-rigged plastic worms. Monster channel catfish over 20 pounds are present in the holes below the Black River's last island and can be caught on large gobs of cut bait, strips of salmon milt, or shrimp. Burbot averaging 3 pounds are here year-round but are mostly taken in winter on minnows targeting pike. Carp from 20 to 30 pounds find the weed beds and mud flats hospitable and strike worms, bread balls, and corn. Huge numbers of bluegills and pumpkinseeds occupy weedy shallows, where, on a good day, even kids fishing with bobbers and worms catch enough 5- to 10-inchers to feed the whole family. Lake-run bullheads carpet shallow, muddy areas from ice-out through mid-May. They like worms still-fished on bottom. Although their numbers have been down recently, American eels find the bay to their liking and are often taken serendipitously on worms, shrimp, and minnows fished on bottom at night.

Directions: The bay is about 0.5 mile downstream from the village of Dexter.

Additional information: The village of Dexter operates a free boat launch with parking for about twenty-five rigs below the NY 180 bridge on the north side of the river.

Contact: New York State Department of Environmental Conservation Region 6 and 1000 Islands International Tourism Council.

49A. Dexter Marsh Public Access *(see map on page 91)*

Description: This site offers a beach launch suitable for small trailered craft and parking for ten cars.

The fishing: After ice-out the Perch River submerges this marsh in 2 to 3 feet of water, drawing one of the lake's greatest runs of spring bullheads. Ranging from 10 to 14 inches, they hit worms, especially at night and on overcast days.

Directions: From Dexter, take Lakeview Drive (the sign says Pillar Point) for about 0.5 mile, turn left onto Doane Road (CR 59), and travel for about 1 mile.

49B. Muskellunge Bay Public Access *(see map on page 91)*

Description: This site has a beach launch and parking for about fifteen rigs.

The fishing: Located across Black River Bay from Dexter Marsh, this marshy area also gets great runs of spring bullheads.

Directions: On NY 180, about 1.5 miles south of Dexter.

49C. Black River Bay Public Access *(see map on page 91)*

Description: This site offers a small-craft launch and parking for about thirty rigs.

Directions: Take NY 180 for about 2 miles south of Dexter, turn west on Military Road, and continue for a little over 1 mile.

50. Lower Black River *(see map on page 91)*

Key species: Walleye, smallmouth bass, largemouth bass, chinook salmon, land-locked Atlantic salmon, brown trout, steelhead, channel catfish, and panfish.

Description: This section of the Black River runs from the Mill Street Dam in Watertown (the first barrier impassable by Lake Ontario's salmonids) to the mouth. Habitats range from shallow ripples and raging rapids to long stretches of flat water, deep pools, shoals, islands, ledges, steep drop-offs, gentle slopes, weed beds, lily pads—you name it.

Tips: Catfish the size of miniature Minotaurs hang out in the holes.

The fishing: From Watertown downstream to its mouth, this river only rests twice, both times above dams. The state stocks almost 1,900 two-year-old brown trout in the city of Watertown. Urban anglers take them with worms, in-line spinners, and flies deep into summer. The stretch below Dexter is one of Lake Ontario's most productive fisheries. The major reason is the state's massive intervention. Upwards of 25,000 Atlantic salmon averaging 7 inches, 50,000 chinook salmon fry, and 72,000 fingerling steelhead are released each year. Autumn salmon ranging from 3 to 8 pounds trickle into the river in summer. They respond to crankbaits, streamers, and worms. Chinook salmon weighing up to 45 pounds and some coho salmon averaging 8 pounds run the river from mid-September through October. They hit egg sacs, raw roe, and lures. Around October steelhead in the 5- to 15-pound range move in to feast on salmon eggs. Many overwinter and are joined in the spring by spawn-heavy steelies up to 22 pounds. They respond to egg sacs, worms, and crankbaits like Hot Shots.

Post-spawn walleyes up to 12 pounds can be caught in the channels, holes, and rapids by trolling crankbaits, particularly Rapalas and Bomber Long "A"s. Monster catfish up to 25 pounds—fish so big, you'll feel like jumping on their backs and riding them—carpet the river's deep holes in the fall and are targeted with raw skein, strips of milt, and pieces of salmon. Smallmouth bass ranging from 1 to 3 pounds prowl the river's shoals and rocky shelves. They have a taste for crayfish and minnows. Post-spawn largemouth bass up to 7 pounds can be found in the marshy areas around the river's mouth. They viciously attack jig-'n'-pigs and Texas-rigged worms violating their space. From mid-May through the first week of June, massive schools of spawn-minded panfish—everything from white perch and sunfish to bullheads, yellow perch, and rock bass—mill around the dams in Dexter in such quantities, locals drop everything and stand shoulder-to-shoulder fishing for them with worms, minnows, and small spinners.

A word on suckers: From late April through May, the rapids in Dexter teem with spawning suckers of every type. Most folks take the runs in stride. However, a few incompetent sour grapes targeting steelhead take out their frustration on the "French trout" by snagging them, then leaving them on shore to die. This atrocious behavior is not only unsportsmanlike, it's illegal (no fish or parts can be discarded on shore) and hurts the overall fishery by reducing the number of adults (bottom feeders, they're the lake's most efficient vacuum cleaners) and baby suckers (a primary forage base).

Up to the impassable waterfalls in Watertown, the daily creel limit for rainbow trout is one.

Directions: NY 12F parallels the river from Watertown to Dexter.

Additional information: The village of Dexter offers ample shore-fishing access and a boat launch with parking for thirty rigs right at the NY 180 bridge. Informal shore-fishing access with shoulder parking is on Lee Road (south side of the river, at the foot of the dam) and off Lock Street. The state operates two fish ladders, one at Dexter and the other at the Glen Park Hydro Project. Fishing is prohibited within 100 yards of these devices.

Contact: New York State Department of Environmental Conservation Region 6 and 1000 Islands International Tourism Council.

50A. Fish Island Public Access

Description: Located just above the dams in Dexter, this site has a paved ramp, parking for one hundred rigs, and shore-fishing access. The river here is slow and wide, punctuated with islands. About 0.5 mile upstream, it begins narrowing and

Fishing the Black River at Dexter (site 50A).

picking up speed as it enters a scenic gorge stretching to Watertown. From Brownville to Watertown the river contains the state's only year-round, adventure-class white water.

The fishing: This stretch is warm-water habitat and has good populations of northern pike running from 22 to 36 inches, largemouth bass up to 5 pounds, walleyes up to 27 inches, and smallmouth bass averaging 1.5 pounds. Salmon and steelhead run through here in the fall, and steelhead pass through again on their way back to the lake in the spring.

Directions: Off Canal Street in Dexter.

50B. Public Access *(see map on page 91)*

Description: Situated below the Glen Park Power Project Dam, this site has parking for ten cars.

The fishing: This stretch gets seasonal runs of salmon and steelhead.

Directions: About 2 miles east of Brownville on NY 12E. From the lot, cross the power canal, walk the edge on the other side, and follow the arrows down to the river.

Additional information: There is a fish ladder below the dam, and fishing is prohibited within 100 yards of the device, including the pool at its end.

50C. Public Access *(see map on page 91)*

Description: This site has parking for ten cars and shore-fishing access on both sides of the river. Frank Flack, senior fisheries biologist with Region 6, calls this the best, safest fishing spot between Dexter and Watertown.

The fishing: This is where the state stocks roughly 2,000 browns averaging 14 inches each May. They take worms, minnows, and flies.

Directions: At the Vanduzee Street bridge in Watertown.

51. Guffin Bay *(see map on page 91)*

Key species: Walleye, smallmouth bass, yellow perch, black crappie, and bullhead.

Description: This bay has the Golden Crescent's largest island.

Tips: In May flatline crankbaits along the breaks ringing the shoreline for walleyes.

The fishing: Like the rest of the Golden Crescent, trophy walleyes have become the bread-and-butter fish for some charter captains. Most flatline for them with ThunderSticks and Bomber Long "A"s from opening day through early June and again in October and November. Jigs tipped with minnows and worms also catch "eyes." Post-spawn smallmouths roam the bay until mid-July looking to fatten up after their ordeal. Work crayfish, minnows, scented tubes, and fat-bodied, deep-diving crankbaits in 15 to 20 feet of water, especially on the south end of Cherry Island. Bullheads from 10 to 16 inches, yellow perch from 8 to 12 inches, and black crappies up to 1.5 pounds move into the northwestern shallows immediately after ice-out. Fish worms on bottom for bullheads, and suspend minnows on tiny bobbers, 3 inches to 1 foot off bottom, in 3 to 6 feet of water for crappies and perch.

Directions: Between Black River Bay and Chaumont Bay.

Contact: New York State Department of Environmental Conservation Region 6 and 1000 Islands International Tourism Council.

52. Chaumont Bay *(see map on page 91)*

Key species: Northern pike, walleye, black bass, and yellow perch.

Description: Covering 9,000 acres, this bay is the biggest in the Golden Crescent. The isthmus connecting Point Peninsula to the mainland is so low and narrow, some folks won't drive over it on windy days for fear their cars will be swept into the bay.

Tips: In autumn troll stickbaits tight to shoreline vegetation for large northern pike.

An angler with a Chaumont Bay bronzeback (site 52).

The fishing: Ideal spawning habitat for warm-water species, the bay is a magnet for game fish. Largemouth bass, some over 6 pounds, and northern pike averaging 8 pounds hang out year-round in the weedy shallows and on the gently sloping south-western basin. Both species viciously attack loud crankbaits like Rat-L-Traps and ThunderSticks and jerkbaits like Slap-Stiks and Slug-Gos. For most of May walleyes from 6 to 12 pounds can be picked up by flatlining crankbaits like ThunderSticks and Bomber Long "A"s along the relatively steep drop-off paralleling the south shore. When the walleyes move out in June, spawned-out smallmouth bass ranging from 1 to 3 pounds move in and stick around until mid-July. Fish for them on bottom with live crayfish and minnows. There are so many perch ranging from 8 to 12 inches that the state allows some commercial netting. They hit 2-inch scented grubs.

Directions: From Dexter, head north on NY 180 for about 2 miles. Turn left on NY 12E and travel about 4 miles.

Additional information: The state launch on NY 12E, 2 miles west of the village of Chaumont, offers a paved ramp and parking for one hundred rigs.

Contact: New York State Department of Environmental Conservation Region 6 and 1000 Islands International Tourism Council.

52A. Long Point State Park *(see map on page 91)*

Description: This 22-acre fee area offers eighty-six tent and trailer sites (sixteen with electricity), a paved launch and marina, shore-fishing access on Chaumont Bay, showers, picnic areas, and playgrounds. Open May 1 through September; a day-use fee is charged to noncampers in-season.

Directions: From the hamlet of Chaumont, head west on NY 12E for about 5 miles. Turn left onto CR 57 (North Shore Road), cross the isthmus about 5 miles later, and head straight on State Park Road when CR 57 bears right.

53. Chaumont River *(see map on page 91)*

Key species: Largemouth bass, channel catfish, and brown bullhead.

Description: The river's mouth is shallow and bordered by marsh.

Tips: Fish on bottom in the deep holes in the river channel and at the mouth with large minnows and cut bait for trophy catfish, some over 20 pounds.

The fishing: Largemouth bass in the 2- to 5-pound range thrive among the lower river's thick cattails, reeds, and weeds. Rip floating worms quickly over holes in weed beds or flip Texas-rigged 7- to 10-inch worms along the edges of emergent vegetation and windfalls. Massive schools of bullheads ranging from 10 to 14 inches move in to spawn in the spring, creating a carnival-like atmosphere among the anglers who fish for them at night with worms.

Directions: From I-81 exit 46 in Watertown, take NY 12F west 5.2 miles to Dexter, then turn right onto NY 180 north. Two miles later turn left on 12E and follow it for about 7 miles to the village of Chaumont.

Contact: New York State Department of Environmental Conservation Region 6 and 1000 Islands International Tourism Council.

54. St. Lawrence River *(see maps on pages 104, 108, and 114)*

Key species: Muskellunge, black bass, northern pike, walleye, carp, yellow perch, black crappie, sunfish, rock bass, and brown bullhead.

Description: Draining the entire Great Lakes system (the world's greatest freshwater reservoirs, combined they cover fully 1 percent of the planet's land mass), the St.

St. Lawrence River: Cape Vincent to Clayton

Lawrence is the world's fourteenth largest river. Its New York section stretches for over 100 miles, from Cape Vincent to the St. Regis Mohawk Indian Reservation east of Massena.

Tips: Muskies are biggest and hungriest in autumn.

The fishing: This is trophy water. Arthur Lawton's 69-pound-15-ounce muskie—a fish that held the world record until being dethroned in the 1990s on a technicality (by an only slightly less controversial fish, incidentally)—came out of this river. Their numbers nose-dived in the 1960s and 1970s, but catch-and-release practices, along with increased minimum lengths, allowed muskellunge to bounce back. Currently 20-pounders are common, 40-pounders are very possible, and 50-pounders are caught each year. Most are taken by trolling large crankbaits like Cisco Kids, Swim Wizzes, Buchertail Depth Raiders, and MirrOlure 111MRs. A good number is also taken on top-water lures like Jitterbugs and buzzbaits.

Northern pike average 4 pounds and there are enough in the 10- to 15-pound range to make targeting them reasonable. While a skillful guide can still get his clients twenty-five pike a day, their numbers are down significantly from twenty years ago. Scientists trace the problem to the construction of the Seaway Trail, whose flow regime prevents extreme fluctuations in river levels, destroying marshes northerns need for spawning. Others blame the drop in pike numbers on shrinking weed beds, the result of strict antipollution laws that reduce nutrients discharged into the river by municipalities and industry. The remaining pike are larger, healthier, and a lot more challenging to catch. Captain Myrle Bauer—a Clayton guide known for leading clients to trophy muskies in the morning, followed by twenty or more northerns in the afternoon—says enhanced water clarity "requires you fish further from the boat." The largest pikeasauruses are most successfully targeted with live minnows. However, scrappy northerns in the 22- to 26-inch range love buzzbaits, spinnerbaits, and jigheads tipped with minnow/tube combinations.

There's a great population of largemouth bass in the 3- to 6-pound range. Crayfish, minnows, crankbaits, Texas- and Carolina-rigged worms, and loud surface baits all produce. The river is loaded with roving schools of smallmouth bass averaging 1.5 pounds. Find a school and you can catch them till your arms hurt. They respond to crayfish, shiners, spinnerbaits, crankbaits, and Carolina-rigged worms and craws dragged on bottom. Walleyes weighing over 10 pounds are caught so frequently, they rarely raise an eyebrow anymore. Troll for them with Krocodile spoons and crankbaits like Red Fins, Rapalas, and MirrOlure Lipped 52Ms or bounce jigs tipped with worms, minnows, or 3-inch YUM Walleye Grubs on bottom in deep water.

The state's greatest concentration of really huge carp, ranging from 20 to 50 pounds, is found here. Most are taken by bow-fishing. However, anglers are learning the thrill of monster carp on light tackle and are increasingly going after them with kernel corn, bread balls, and baked potato. Yellow perch ranging from 7 to 12 inches, sunfish 5 to 7 inches, and rock bass up to 0.5 pound can be found anywhere, anytime. Black crappies up to 1.5 pounds roam around the bays. Perch, crappies, and rock bass love small minnows, wet flies, and 2-inch curly-tailed grubs and tubes. All but the crappies have a taste for worms. Sunfish and rock bass provide explosive summertime action on 1/32-ounce Hula Poppers. In spring bullheads ranging from 8 to 16 inches congregate on muddy bottoms in bays and are taken by still-fishing with worms on bottom.

The St. Lawrence River is governed by the special Great Lakes regulations found in the *New York State Department of Environmental Conservation Fishing Regulations Guide*. The minimum length for muskies is 48 inches, and the daily limit is one. Minimum length for northern pike is 22 inches, and the daily limit is five. Minimum length for walleyes is 18 inches, and the daily limit is three.

Directions: Take I–81 north out of Watertown for approximately 30 miles to exit 50. NY 12 and NY 37 parallel the east half of the river, and NY 12, NY 12E, and CR 6 parallel its west half.

Additional information: All river villages offer municipal docks and boat launches. The north half of the river is Canadian, and you need a Province of Ontario license to fish there. Many fishing derbies are held here annually, including qualifying events for major tournaments (check tourism offices for details).

Contact: 1000 Islands International Tourism Council, St. Lawrence County Chamber of Commerce, and New York State Department of Environmental Conservation Region 6.

54A. Cape Vincent Fisheries Research Station Aquarium and Visitor Center *(see map on page 104)*

Description: Located about 3 miles east of the source of the St. Lawrence River, this state facility offers free transient docking for up to two nights in a sheltered harbor, picnic tables, shore-fishing access, an aquarium, and toilets.

The fishing: Large muskies prowl the outside edges of deep weed beds from late summer till season's end. Walleyes averaging 7 pounds can be taken on the drop-offs and rocky flats. The weed bed out front holds year-round populations of northern pike ranging from 3 to 5 pounds, 6- to 10-inch yellow perch, and smallmouth bass averaging 1.5 pounds.

Directions: From Watertown, head north on NY 12 for 18 miles into Clayton and turn west on NY 12E. Travel for 14 miles into the village of Cape Vincent. The facility is at 541 East Broadway.

54B. Cape Vincent Village Park *(see map on page 104)*

Description: This strip park offers a couple hundred yards of shore-fishing access and parking. The east end has a launch with two paved ramps, parking for about twenty rigs, and toilets.

The fishing: This park's benches serve as the ideal venue for folks still-fishing for anything that bites. Further out, in a diagonal line from the launch to the head of

Carlton Island, rests Feather Bed Shoal, a legendary muskie hot spot. Troll over the deep weed line. Smallmouths can be taken over shoals and drop-offs. In early summer and fall, walleyes come up on the shoals at night.

Directions: Head west out of Clayton on NY 12E for about 14 miles.

54C. Burnham Point State Park *(see map on page 104)*

Description: This 12-acre fee area offers forty-eight campsites (eighteen with electric hookups), showers, a picnic area, swing sets, a gravel launch ramp with parking for ten rigs, and dockage. The campground is open mid-May through mid-September. Free day use is permitted off-season.

The fishing: From the park east to the third bay, the shoreline drops off quickly to a shelf that is 20 feet deep. Northern pike and smallmouth bass hold here year-round. Carlton Island, due north, is an internationally famous hot spot for walleyes. They range from 4 to 10 pounds and take bucktail jigs tipped with minnows or night crawlers. Many are also taken in daytime by trolling spoons like Krocodiles off downriggers and at night by flatlining floater/divers and deep-diving crankbaits.

Directions: Located 9 miles west of Clayton on NY 12E.

54D. Cedar Point State Park *(see map on page 104)*

Description: Covering 46 acres, this fee area offers 172 campsites (55 with electric and 33 with full hookups), hot showers, a boat launch, and a marina with docks, gas, and boating supplies. In addition, this family-oriented place boasts a kids' playground, a ball field, horseshoe pits, a swimming beach, and shore fishing. The campground is open from early May through Columbus Day weekend, and free day use is allowed off-season.

The fishing: Steep drop-offs hug the shoreline for miles in both directions. Smallmouth bass are plentiful on the shelves, where they take crayfish and Carolina-rigged finesse worms. Northern pike and an occasional muskie prowl the weed edges at the mouths of bays and deep weed lines.

Directions: On NY 12E, 6 miles west of Clayton.

54E. Clayton Launch Ramp and Village Dock *(see map on page 108)*

Description: This fee area offers a paved ramp and parking for about forty rigs.

The fishing: Deep in the Thousand Islands region, the village of Clayton has a long tradition of launching memorable fishing adventures. The municipal launch is right on French Creek Bay, one of the hottest largemouth bass and northern pike spots on the river. Both species can be found prowling just about any habitat in the creek and its bay. In addition, they occupy the weed edges and openings in the massive weed beds around nearby islands and bays. Pike also cruise the weeds and the edges of shoals. Walleyes and smallmouths occupy the deep drops. Yellow perch and rock bass know no bounds and can show up anywhere.

St. Lawrence River: Clayton to Morristown

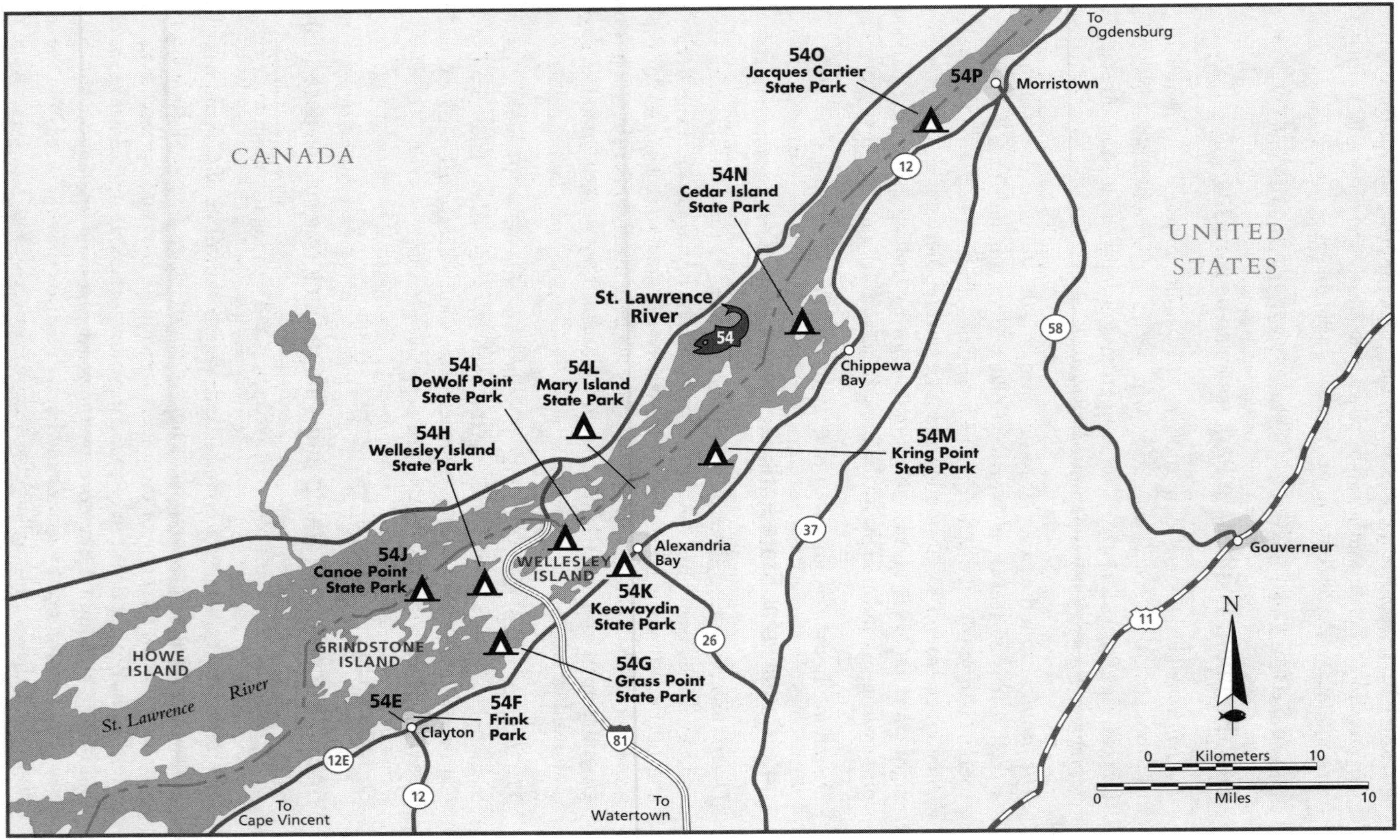

Directions: Located at the end of Mary Street on French Creek Bay.

54F. Frink Park

Description: Downtown Clayton occupies a squared peninsula, and this park is on the east side of the waterfront's commercial district. Sitting on a huge slab of flat granite, on the site of the village's old railroad station and coal docks, the water right at the foot of the park wall is 20 feet deep and quickly drops to over 30 feet.

The fishing: Just about every species in the drink comes to the park at one time or another. Safe, scenic, easily accessible, and punctuated with benches, this spot is popular from spring through fall with family groups dunking worms and crayfish primarily for perch, rock bass, catfish, and smallmouth bass. Northern pike stray from the weedy bay due east, and a few walleyes come up from the deep to prowl the adjacent cribs.

Directions: Located on Riverside Drive in Clayton.

54G. Grass Point State Park

Description: This 60-plus-acre fee area offers seventy-six campsites (twenty with electric hookups), hot showers, dockage with thirty-two slips, a paved double-wide ramp, parking for ten rigs, and picnic areas. The campground is open from mid-May through mid-September. Free day use is allowed off-season.

The fishing: The bay in front of the park holds massive numbers of small northern pike up to 24 inches, largemouth bass from 2 to 6 pounds, and swarms of sunfish and perch. The weed lines on the outside edges of nearby islands hold larger northern pike and smallmouth bass averaging 1.5 pounds. In June channel catfish averaging 8 pounds converge on the mouth of the bay on the west side of Reed Point (due west of Grass Point) and are taken with gobs of worms, large minnows, and fish bellies. The shelves along the canyon walls of the shipping channel hold walleyes. Mid-October sees muskies cruising the drop-off stretching from Reed Point to Round Island.

Directions: From Clayton, take NY 12 east for 5 miles.

54H. Wellesley Island State Park

Description: Covering 2,636 acres, this park contains the largest parcel of undeveloped land in the Thousand Islands. Its campground, open from the last Friday in April through October 15, offers 429 tent sites, 74 trailer sites with electricity, 57 trailer sites with full hookups, showers, a sandy beach, picnic facilities, 4 boat launches (one with 2 paved ramps) with combined parking for over 100 rigs, and miles of shore-fishing access. In addition, there are ten cabins and twelve cottages available year-round. The park is open all year, but a day-use fee is only charged from Memorial Day through Labor Day.

The fishing: Boasting several miles of shoreline, this park offers bank-fishing access to most of Eel Bay, a shallow, weedy area loaded with northern pike and yellow perch. The 600-acre Minna Anthony Common Nature Center, on the bay's south shore, is especially popular with family groups fishing for perch, bullheads, and rock bass from shore with worms. Northern pike ranging from 22 to 26 inches prowl the narrow strip of open water between shore and the bay's massive weed bed. Smallmouths hold around the two small islands on the bay's north side, the drop-offs along the nature center's granite slopes, and the "Narrows," the natural cut between Wellesley Island and Murray Isle.

Continuing south from the Narrows, South Bay is a bullhead hot spot in May and holds perch and northerns year-round. The park's north shore is only about 100 yards from the Canadian border. If you cast from the bank, you'll be all right. If you go out in a boat, however, it's good to have a Canadian fishing license. The deep Canadian Middle Channel is loaded with smallmouths and walleyes. They come up on the American shelf on cloudy days and at night.

Directions: Head north out of Watertown on I–81 for about 30 miles, cross the American Narrows on the Thousand Islands Bridge, and take exit 51. Turn right on CR 191, then right again about 0.25 mile later onto CR 100. Travel for a few hundred yards, take the next right onto Cross Island Road, and continue for about 2 miles.

Additional information: A $2.00 toll is charged to cross the Thousand Islands Bridge. Discount books are available at the tollbooths.

54I. DeWolf Point State Park *(see map on page 108)*

Description: This 12-acre park offers fourteen campsites, fourteen cabins, a paved launch, parking for ten rigs, and hot showers. The campground is open from mid-May to Labor Day; free day use off-season.

The fishing: Located on Lake of the Isles, the bad news about this lake is that its largemouth bass fishing has deteriorated tremendously since the tournament anglers got wind of it. The good news is that bucketmouth numbers are creeping back, and fish ranging from 2 to 4 pounds are fairly common again, with 6-pounders possible. They like Texas-rigged worms tossed into timber, jig-'n'-pigs, and spinnerbaits worked in weed openings. Northern pike from 2 to 5 pounds are very common and respond to 3-inch scented curly-tailed grubs and jig-rigged tubes tipped with minnows. Bluegills from 5 to 8 inches, black crappies up to 14 inches, and yellow perch averaging 10 inches are plentiful. These panfish are mostly taken by ice anglers using teardrop jigs tipped with insect larvae. Locals first chum the holes with crushed egg shells to attract attention.

Directions: At I–81 exit 51 (see site 54H), head north on CR 191 for about 2 miles.

Additional information: The international border runs down the middle of the two channels connecting the Lake of the Isles to the river.

54J. Canoe Point State Park *(see map on page 108)*

Description: Located on the easternmost tip of Grindstone Island, this fee area overlooks the Canadian channel and is accessible by boat only. It offers thirty-five campsites, six cabins, a shelter, potable water, and toilets. Open from Memorial Day through Labor Day.

The fishing: The waters around Grindstone Island contain habitats ranging from massive weed beds to deep rifts. The channels off its east bank separating it from Picton Island are loaded with northerns and smallmouths. Pike are plentiful along Grindstone's entire south shore year-round and rule the flats and shallow bays up until July. As summer progresses they move into deeper water off the mouths of bays, along shoals and drop-offs. Schools of smallmouths compete with the northerns in these habitats. By mid-October a few muskies move into the channel between Picton and Grindstone for the winter.

Directions: On the northeastern tip of Grindstone Island, due west from the northwestern point of Wellesley Island.

54K. Keewaydin State Park *(see map on page 108)*

Description: This 241-acre fee area offers 41 campsites, a marina with a paved ramp and 110 slips, parking for 50 rigs, picnic facilities, a swimming pool, and shore-fishing access on paved paths skirting the park's steep slopes. Camping is allowed from mid-May through Labor Day. Free day use is permitted off-season.

The fishing: The drop-offs along the main channel and off the countless nearby islands are loaded with smallmouths. Northerns can be found off the narrow weed lines clinging to shelves near shore. A productive technique for taking them here is to work a Dardevle spoon by jigging it so it darts and flutters. The marina is a popular ice-fishing spot. Locals catch large perch, northerns, and an occasional walleye by jigging minnows rigged a few inches below attractors like C.C. Spoons.

Directions: Take NY 12 west out of Alexandria Bay for about 2 miles.

Additional information: Part of this park is atop a granite outcrop towering over the American Narrows. A couple of antique gazebos are on the cliff, offering views of river traffic, including large ocean freighters that look like they are coming right out of Comfort Island.

54L. Mary Island State Park *(see map on page 108)*

Description: Accessible by boat only, this fee area is perched atop a high, heavily wooded 12-acre island overlooking the Canadian Middle Channel. It offers twelve campsites, picnic facilities, potable water, and toilets during camping season, mid-May through Labor Day. Free day use is permitted off-season.

The fishing: The island's north shore quickly drops 50 feet. Smallmouths and northerns are attracted here by the cool, safe depths in close proximity to the productive shallows on the island's other three sides. The international boundary is only a few hundred feet north.

Directions: Cross the American Narrows from Keewaydin State Park and head east along Wellesley Island. Mary Island is separated from Wellesley's eastern tip by a channel so narrow, you can jump it.

54M. Kring Point State Park *(see map on page 108)*

Description: This 56-acre fee area is on a peninsula and offers eight cabins, fifty-eight tent sites without hookups, twenty-eight sites with electricity, a paved boat launch, parking for ten rigs, two docks, a swimming beach, shore-fishing access, hot showers, and microwave oven rentals for use in the cabins. The campground is open the first Saturday in May through Columbus Day. A day-use fee is charged from Memorial Day through Labor Day.

The fishing: Northern pike ranging from 22 to 36 inches can be found in the mouths of bays, in channels, and over the submerged weed beds. Smallmouth bass up to 3 pounds lurk along the drop-offs. Goose Bay, on the peninsula's south side, loads up with bullheads in the spring. Come summer, its weed beds are a magnet for largemouth bass, yellow perch, and sunfish. When water temperatures reach the upper 40s in autumn, the weeds lay down and northerns move into the bay to overwinter.

Directions: Head north out of Alexandria Bay on NY 12 for about 5 miles, turn west on Kring Point Road, and continue for about 1.5 miles.

54N. Cedar Island State Park *(see map on page 108)*

Description: This park is on an island that is half private and half state owned. The public property has been made into a fee area boasting day-use and camping sections. The day-use area offers a pavilion, picnic facilities, hiking trails, and shore-fishing. The campground has eighteen lightly wooded sites, toilets, and two floating docks.

The fishing: Chippewa Bay is a traditional hot spot for northern pike ranging from 22 to 36 inches. They can be found virtually anywhere in the bay from October through spring, around tributaries in May, and at the drop-offs around Cedar Island all summer long. The channel running the length of the bay's mouth is a productive trolling area for muskies in autumn. Largemouth bass up to 6 pounds thrive in the bay's massive weed beds. Smallmouth bass averaging 1.5 pounds always mill around Chippewa Point and the numerous rocky shoals surrounding it. Brown bullheads up to 14 inches literally invade the bay from April through May. Yellow perch ranging from 7 to 11 inches, black crappies up to 14 inches, and rock bass, pumpkin-seeds, and bluegills from 5 to 10 inches live in the bay year-round.

Directions: Head northeast out of Kring Point (site 54M) for about 4 miles. Cedar is the large island in the mouth of Chippewa Bay, midway between Chippewa Point and Oak Island.

54O. Jacques Cartier State Park *(see map on page 108)*

Description: This 463-acre fee area offers ninety-two campsites (twenty-six with electric hookups), a flat rock launch ramp with parking for ten rigs, a swimming beach, hot showers, and picnic facilities. The campground is open from mid-May through Columbus Day. A day-use fee is charged from Memorial Day through Labor Day.

The fishing: This section of the St. Lawrence River gives up numerous muskies in the 20- to 30-pound range and several 40-pounders every year. The local hot spot is around American Island, about 1 mile upstream of the park. Northern pike range from 22 to 30 inches and occupy the outside edges of weedy bays, tributary mouths, island drop-offs, and deep weed beds out in the main river. Walleyes ranging from 6 to 10 pounds hang out on rocky shelves at the heads and tails of islands and along drop-offs. Locals go for them by flatlining diving lures or by drifting worms and minnows. Smallmouth bass ranging from 1 to 2.5 pounds are plentiful off points from opening day through the second week of July and around rocky shoals for the remainder of the season. They like live minnows fished on bottom or free-lined. Yellow perch generally run from 7 to 11 inches and are found in weeds, on shoals, at drop-offs—you name it. They respond to minnows, grubs, worms, and tiny jigs.

Directions: Off NY 12, 2 miles west of Morristown.

54P. Morristown Municipal Boat Ramp and Dock *(see map on page 108)*

Description: This facility offers a paved ramp, parking for ten rigs, overnight docking for a fee, and ice-fishing access.

The fishing: The islands out in front of the village hold good numbers of northern pike in the 22- to 28-inch range. They like tube jigs tipped with minnows. Area shoals and drop-offs are prime smallmouth habitat and contain good numbers of bronzebacks in the 1.5- to 2.5-pound class. They like live crayfish and their imitations. Yellow perch from 6 to 12 inches can be found anywhere there are rocks or weeds and respond to 2-inch scented YUM Wooly Curltails.

Directions: On Water Street in Morristown.

54Q. Ogdensburg Municipal Boat Launch *(see map on page 114)*

Description: This site has two double-lane paved ramps, parking for thirty rigs plus overflow parking, and a long stretch of shore-fishing access.

St. Lawrence River: Ogdensburg to Massena

The fishing: Drift worms, minnows, or crayfish over the sandbar located due north of the boat launch for yellow perch from 8 to 12 inches. Northern pike in the 22- to 36-inch range are taken by trolling Ripplin' Red Fins and ThunderSticks around the mouth of the Oswegatchie River. Smallmouth bass ranging from 12 to 16 inches are so plentiful around shoals, folks fishing on bottom with crayfish or minnows expect fifty-fish days. The rocky shoal just upstream of the international bridge draws schools of bronzebacks. Walleyes ranging from 5 to 10 pounds also like this shoal and respond to crankbaits like Bomber "A"s and ThunderSticks. The deep water between the red-and-white buoys directly in front of the boat launch is a traditional muskie spot. Some claim this is where Arthur Lawton caught his 69-pound-15-ounce world record. Most are taken on large crankbaits trolled against the flow. Wheathouse Bay, just downstream from the launch, is a popular ice-fishing spot for yellow perch, northerns, and walleyes.

Directions: At the end of Paterson Street in the city of Ogdensburg.

54R. Public Access

Description: This parklike site has a double-wide paved ramp, parking for about ten rigs, picnic facilities, and shore-fishing access.

Directions: Riverside Avenue in Ogdensburg.

54S. Waddington Boat Launch

Description: Open year-round, this facility offers a double-wide paved ramp and parking for twenty-five rigs. Overflow parking is available in the adjacent park.

The fishing: The bay here holds perch ranging from 6 to 10 inches, largemouth bass up to 6 pounds, and northern pike in the 22- to 27-inch range. Smallmouths up to 2.5 pounds thrive in the weed lines and drop-offs. They all take minnows and jigs. Walleyes up to 12 pounds are taken by flatlining deep-diving crankbaits like Heddon Hellbenders over the shelves skirting the drop-off paralleling the north side of Ogden Island (the big island due north).

Directions: Head north on NY 37 out of Ogdensburg for about 15 miles to Waddington. The launch is on Pine Street.

54T. Brandy Brook Boat Launch

Description: This site offers a hard-surface ramp and parking for ten rigs.

Directions: The launch is about 3 miles east of Waddington on NY 37.

Additional information: Immediately after the September 11, 2001, terrorist attacks, the government imposed a security zone around structures such as dams and nuclear power plants. Individuals and crafts are prohibited from entering within a 1,000-yard radius of the Iroquois Dam, about 4 miles upstream of Waddington.

Contact the U.S. Coast Guard Marine Safety Office for an update on the safety zone's status.

54U. Coles Creek State Park *(see map on page 114)*

Description: This 1,800-acre fee facility offers 228 primitive campsites, 147 campsites with electricity, hot showers, picnic facilities, a swimming beach, and shore-fishing access. The campground is open from mid-May through Labor Day. A day-use fee is charged from Memorial Day through Labor Day.

The fishing: The park is on the shores of Lake St. Lawrence, the massive impoundment created by the Robert Moses Power Dam. The weedy shallows in Coles Creek's mouth and the area's countless weedy bays hold largemouth bass ranging from 2 to 6 pounds and yellow perch from 8 to 12 inches year-round. In the spring northerns up to 40 inches come around. Drop-offs paralleling the main river channel and the outer edges of islands hold smallmouth bass ranging from 1 to 3 pounds and walleyes up to 10 pounds.

Directions: Take NY 37 north from Waddington for about 3 miles.

54V. Wilson Hill Public Access *(see map on page 114)*

Description: This site offers a paved launch ramp and parking for fifteen rigs.

The fishing: The site is located on the eastern border of the Wilson Hill State Wildlife Management Area. Northern pike from 22 to 40 inches and largemouth bass over 6 pounds rule the weedy bays, growing big and fat on a generous supply of perch and sunfish. Smallmouth bass from 1 to 2 pounds and walleyes up to 8 pounds lurk along the drop-offs and shelves hugging the ancient river channel. This is the best spot on the river for trophy carp over 40 pounds. Fishing is prohibited in the wildlife management area.

Directions: About 5 miles west of Massena on NY 131.

54W. Robert Moses State Park *(see map on page 114)*

Description: An arm of the St. Lawrence River runs through this 2,322-acre fee area. Built half on the mainland and half on Barnhart Island (constructed from river rubble brought up during construction of the St. Lawrence–FDR Power Project), this park offers 130 campsites without hookups, 38 campsites with electricity, 2 boat launches with paved ramps, miles of shore-fishing access, a marina with 42 slips, hot showers, picnic areas, playgrounds, hiking trails, and a pump-out station. The park is open year-round, and camping is allowed from mid-May through Columbus Day. A day-use fee is charged from mid-June through Labor Day.

The fishing: The dams here block muskie and walleye migrations. The fish find the pickings pretty good below the barriers and always stick around for a while before heading back downstream. Muskies ranging from 20 to 40 pounds are commonly taken in autumn by trolling crankbaits through the heavy current. Walleyes ranging from 3 to 12 pounds share this habitat with the muskies; however, they also run up the southern arm of the river below the Long Sault Spillway Dam. They respond to crankbaits. Smallmouths up to 3 pounds can be taken in the fast water on crayfish, jigs, and crankbaits.

Directions: Take NY 37 east out of Massena for about 2 miles. Turn north on NY 131 for about 1 mile, then continue north on Barnhart Island Road for 0.5 mile to the park.

Additional information: Barnhart Island Road goes under the Eisenhower Lock, and ocean freighters are often visible in the channel above the road. Since the September 11, 2001, terrorist attacks, authorities have imposed a security zone within a 1,000-yard radius of the Robert Moses Power Dam. Contact the U.S. Coast Guard's Marine Safety Office for an update on the restricted area.

55. Lake of the Isles *(see map on page 118)*

Key species: Largemouth bass, northern pike, yellow perch, black crappie, and sunfish.

Description: Set into the east end of Wellesley Island, this 2,500-acre lake averages 6 feet deep and has a maximum depth of 20 feet. Two navigable channels connect it to the St. Lawrence River: the Rift, located on the northeastern end of the island, and the unnamed channel on its eastern tip. Besides having the international border running down their centers, the channels separate Wellesley Island from Canada's Hill Island.

Tips: Fish the deep pools and channels of the Rift with wet flies on a sinking line for huge bluegills and pumpkinseeds.

The fishing: This is considered the best spot in the Thousand Islands for bucketmouths. The average size is 3 pounds, but many tipping the scale at more than 5 pounds are caught annually. Northerns averaging 24 inches are plentiful and respond enthusiastically to free-lined minnows and bucktail jigs tipped with trailers like Cabela's Livin' Eye baits. They like soft plastic slugs jerked over submerged weeds, Texas-rigged 7- and 10-inch worms jigged slowly over deep breaks, and jig-'n'-pigs pitched into slop. Yellow perch and black crappies up to 14 inches hungrily respond to dot jigs tipped with grubs during ice season. From spring through fall, they like minnows and curly-tailed grubs retrieved steadily through the water column on spinner forms. Sunfish up to 0.5 pound are plentiful and respond to worms and flies.

Directions: Head east out of Clayton on NY 12 for about 5 miles. Get on I–81 north, cross the Thousand Islands Bridge ($2.00 toll), and take the first exit (exit 51). Turn left on CR 191 and travel for about 2 miles.

Lake of the Isles

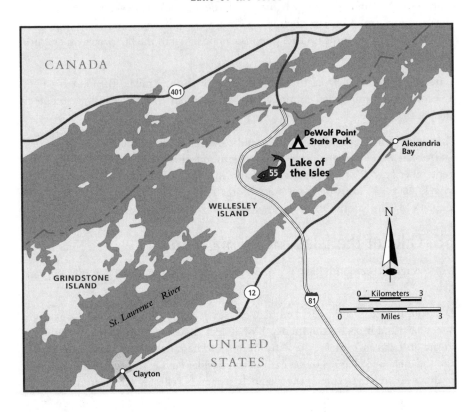

Additional information: Covering 12 acres of choice waterfront, DeWolf Point State Park (located on CR 191) offers fourteen campsites, fourteen cabins, a paved launch, parking for ten rigs, and hot showers. The campground is open from mid-May through Labor Day; free day use off-season. A Canadian license is required to fish that nation's waters, in the channels and at the northeastern corner of the lake.

Contact: New York State Department of Environmental Conservation Region 6 and 1000 Islands International Tourism Council.

WESTERN NEW YORK REGION: INLAND WATERS

This section deals with inland waters whose fisheries are independent of the Great Lakes. Some, like the Genesee River, drain into the system but have barriers near their mouths, making them inland fisheries. On the other hand, the Allegheny River (fed by Oswayo and Conewango Creeks) flows into the Ohio River.

56. Findley Lake (see map on page 120)

Key species: Tiger muskie, northern pike, walleye, black bass, black crappie, yellow perch, and sunfish.

Description: Created by a War of 1812 veteran to generate water power for his mill, this 292-acre impoundment averages 11 feet deep and has a maximum depth of 37 feet.

Tips: Fly fish with wet flies and tiny poppers for memorable panfish action.

The fishing: A long, winding shoreline, small islands, and large weed beds make this lake a super warm-water fishery. The state stocks about 600 9-inch tiger muskies each year. They grow up to 40 inches and take large minnows, crankbaits, and bucktail spinners. The authorities also stock walleyes occasionally, most recently in 2002 when 5,500 4-inchers were released. They like crankbaits like Bomber Long "A"s. Northern pike are the lake's baddest natural predator. Reaching up to 30 inches, they hit large minnows, spinnerbaits, and Rat-L-Traps. Largemouth and smallmouth bass typically range from 10 to 14 inches, but larger ones are present. They respond to top-water lures, spinnerbaits, and plastic worms. Yellow perch ranging from 6 to 9 inches, black crappies from too small to 11 inches, and pumpkinseeds and bluegills between 0.25 and 0.5 pound are common. Perch and crappies are partial to small minnows, 1-inch scented curly-tailed grubs, streamers, and flies. The sunfish like worms, poppers, and wet flies. In late summer oxygen levels in depths greater than 14 feet are too low to support fish. The minimum size for walleyes is 18 inches, and the daily limit is three.

Directions: Head west out of Jamestown on I–86 for about 27 miles to exit 4, turn south on NY 426 and travel about 1 mile, then turn east on NY 430.

Additional information: Two boat launches straddle the dam on NY 430. The state fishing access site on the east side has a beach launch for cartop craft and parking for ten cars. The Findley Lake Association launch on the west side has a paved ramp but no parking, and it is only open to the public on weekdays. The entire north

Chautauqua Lake and Nearby Lakes · Chadakoin River

Triple-header from Findley Lake (site 56).

shore is open to bank fishing, and additional shore access, with picnic tables, is available at the parking area 1 mile south of Findley Lake village on NY 426. The state publishes a free *Findley Lake Fishing Guide and Map.*

Contact: New York State Department of Environmental Conservation Region 9 and Chautauqua County Visitors Bureau.

57. Upper Chautauqua Creek (see map on page 122)

Key species: Brown trout and rainbow trout.

Description: This stretch flows north for about 15 miles through Chautauqua County, ending at the barrier at Westfield Waterworks. It is classified as a landlocked/inland trout stream and has no connection with Chautauqua Lake.

Tips: This creek is easiest to fish in May.

The fishing: The state annually stocks several hundred 8-inch brown trout into the headwaters west of Summerdale. Most are taken by June on worms and salted minnows. This stream's midsection is popular with purists due to the wild browns and rainbows that thrive in the rugged, remote stretch called the Gulf. These wild fish average 10 inches and are partial to nymphs and worms.

Upper Chautauqua Creek

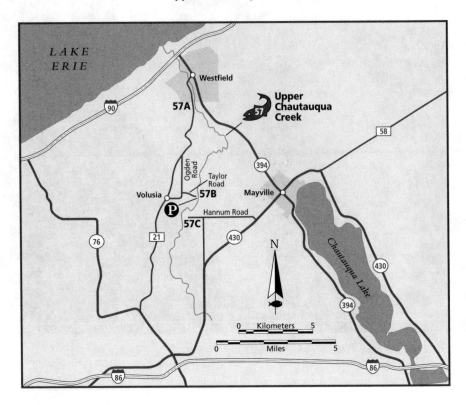

Directions: CR 21 parallels the stream.

Additional information: Primitive camping is allowed in Chautauqua Gorge State Forest.

Contact: New York State Department of Environmental Conservation Region 9.

57A. Public Fishing Rights

Description: Shoulder parking and a mile-long section of public fishing.

Directions: Upstream of the South Gale Street bridge in the hamlet of Westfield.

57B. Public Fishing Rights

Description: State-owned fishing rights to about 2 miles of stream.

Directions: Head east out of the hamlet of Volusia on Pigeon Road for about 0.5 mile to its end, turn north onto Ogden Road, and then east a couple hundred yards later on Taylor Road. Drive about 0.5 mile to the end, park, and walk the path a few hundred yards down to the creek.

57C. Chautauqua Gorge State Forest

Description: This scenic gorge's walls tower up to 300 feet above the creek. The forest contains the south end of the public fishing rights section described in site 57B.

Directions: Head west out of the village of Mayville on NY 430 for about 1.5 miles, turn right on Hannum Road, and follow it for about 2 miles.

Additional information: Hannum Road dead-ends in the forest. Several trails head west to the creek.

58. Chautauqua Lake *(see map on page 120)*

Key species: Muskellunge, walleye, black bass, yellow perch, and black crappie.

Description: Stretching for almost 18 miles, this 13,156-acre lake is divided into two basins of similar size. The south basin averages 11 feet deep, with a maximum depth of 19 feet, and its bottom is generally soft and weedy. The north basin averages 25 feet deep, drops to a maximum depth of 75 feet, and is rocky.

Tips: Jig bladebaits along drop-offs and over boulder fields.

The fishing: This lake has its own strain of muskie. While a naturally reproduced population exists, the state intervenes by stocking roughly 10,000 youngsters averaging 9.5 inches annually. They do well, typically growing to 40 to 50 inches. Most are caught by trolling large minnow imitations along the south basin's weed edges. Walleyes ranging from 18 to 23 inches thrive in the north basin. They take bucktail jigs and worms drifted or trolled on spinner harnesses. Largemouth bass outnumber smallmouths two to one, but you have a better chance of catching a trophy bronzeback, probably because they are not fished for as much as bucketmouths. This is one of the few places in the state where you can reasonably expect to catch a 5- to 6-pound smallie. The largemouth fishery is good, with most fish in the 14- to 16-inch range, but many reach 4 to 5 pounds. Both species take minnows and crayfish. Yellow perch mostly range from 7 to 9 inches and respond to minnows and 2-inch curly-tailed grubs. Most crappies just barely make the 9-inch minimum length; however, enough keepers are around to attract a dedicated following. They take grubs through the ice and small minnows and marabou jigs cast into windfalls and submerged timber during warm weather.

The minimum length for muskellunge is 40 inches.

Directions: The lake brushes the west side of Jamestown. NY 430 parallels most of the east shore; NY 394 parallels the west bank.

Additional information: The state publishes a free *Fishing Chautauqua Lake Official Map and Guide.* Another free brochure, *Chautauqua Lake Hot Spots,* is available at most local bait shops and marinas and through the county visitors bureau. The lake is surrounded by numerous commercial campgrounds.

Contact: New York State Department of Environmental Conservation Region 9 and Chautauqua County Visitors Bureau.

58A. Mayville Residential Boat Launch *(see map on page 120)*

Description: This site has a paved ramp and parking for about ten rigs. During summer nonresidents are asked to make a donation.

Directions: Off NY 394 in the village of Mayville's Lakeside Park.

58B. Pendergast Point Public Access *(see map on page 120)*

Description: This site has a double-lane concrete launch, parking for fifty rigs, and toilets.

Directions: Located on NY 394, 1.5 miles south of the traffic light at the entrance to Chautauqua Institute. Turn at the CHAUTAUQUA LAKE FISH HATCHERY sign.

58C. Lakewood Community Park *(see map on page 120)*

Description: This facility offers a double-lane paved ramp and parking for twenty-five rigs.

Directions: Take NY 394 west out of Jamestown for about 4 miles, turn right on Fairdale Avenue (across from Wal-Mart) and travel to the end, then turn right.

58D. Lucille Ball Memorial Park *(see map on page 120)*

Description: This park has a paved ramp, parking for twenty-five rigs, a playground, rest rooms, and picnic areas.

Directions: Head west on NY 394 out of Jamestown for about 2.5 miles to Celeron, turn north on Dunham Avenue, and travel to the end.

Additional information: Folks from Celeron claim actress Lucille Ball was born and raised here—Jamestown residents claim she's from their city.

58E. Bemus Point Public Access *(see map on page 120)*

Description: This site has a double-lane concrete ramp, loading ramps, and parking for about fifty rigs.

Directions: Head west out of Jamestown on I–86 for about 8 miles to exit 9, then take NY 430 north for about 1 mile to Bemus Point. Turn left on Lincoln Road, then take the second right onto Elm Street.

58F. Long Point State Park *(see map on page 120)*

Description: This 320-acre fee area offers a concrete ramp, loading docks, parking for about a hundred rigs, a swimming beach, picnic facilities, rest rooms, and hundreds of feet of shore-fishing access.

Directions: On NY 430, 2 miles north of Bemus Point (site 58E).

59. Chadakoin River *(see map on page 120)*

Key species: Largemouth bass, smallmouth bass, and bluegill.

Description: The outlet of Chautauqua Lake, this river flows for a little over 5 miles, largely through an urban/industrial setting, goes over a falls in downtown Jamestown, and feeds Cassadaga Creek on the outskirts of Falconer.

Tips: If you have to use a motor, keep it small.

The fishing: Decades of industrial and municipal pollution all but turned this river into a cesspool in the last century. Environmental awareness stopped the abuse. The river is coming back nicely and currently offers decent bass fishing. Largemouths up to 5 pounds are present and respond well to soft jerkbaits worked around structure and to spinnerbaits worked along weed edges and yo-yoed down channel drop-offs. Smallmouths ranging from 0.75 to 1.5 pounds are plentiful and hit Rat-L-Traps, ThunderSticks, and tube jigs. Bluegills go 5 to 8 inches and like worms, grubs, and tiny poppers.

Directions: NY 394 parallels the river.

Additional information: McCrea Point Park, off Jones and Gifford Avenue on the western outskirts of Jamestown, offers a paved launch and parking for ten rigs.

Contact: New York State Department of Environmental Conservation Region 9 and Chautauqua County Visitors Bureau.

60. Bear Lake *(see map on page 120)*

Key species: Muskellunge, northern pike, black bass, yellow perch, walleye, black crappie, bluegill, pumpkinseed, and brown bullhead.

Description: Formed after the last ice age, when the huge chunk of glacial ice sitting on the site finally melted, this 141-acre body of water is classified a kettle lake. Its average depth is around 7 feet, and its deepest spot drops to 35 feet. Roughly three-quarters of the shoreline is wetland.

Tips: Drift and cast Mepps bucktail spinners or MirrOlure Minnows.

The fishing: This lake is loaded with cover, and predators grow big quickly on all the small stuff in the aquatic cornucopia. Muskies reach about 30 inches, and so do the pikeasauruses. Largemouth and smallmouth bass ranging from 12 to 15 inches are common, and a lot grow up to 20-something inches. All of these predators take minnows, crankbaits, spinnerbaits, and jerkbaits. In 1997 the state stocked walleyes, and fish over 20 inches are being reported with increasing frequency. They like bucktail jigs and worms. The small stuff gets big, too. Black crappies reach 12 inches, perch run 7 to 12 inches, bluegills and pumpkinseeds grow to 10 inches, and bullheads stretch the tape to 14 inches. Crappies and perch take small minnows and lures, and the sunfish and bullheads like worms. All but the bullheads hit grubs fished through the ice.

The minimum length for walleyes is 18 inches, and the daily limit is three. In summer the lake suffers oxygen depletion below 15 feet.

Directions: Head east out of Mayville on NY 430 for about 2 miles to Hatfield. Continue east on CR 58 for 7 miles to Stockton, then take CR 380 north for 1.6 miles. When it bears left, continue straight on Kelly Hill Road for 0.5 mile. Turn left at the stop sign onto Bear Lake Road and travel for 0.25 mile.

Additional information: The public fishing access site on Bear Road has parking for about five cars and shore-fishing access. The state publishes a free *Bear Lake Fishing Guide and Map.*

Contact: New York State Department of Environmental Conservation Region 9 and Chautauqua County Visitors Bureau.

61. Cassadaga Lakes (see map on page 120)

Key species: Largemouth bass, northern pike, muskellunge (Ohio River strain), bluegill, and black crappie.

Description: A series of three interconnected kettle lakes (formed after the last ice age when three huge chunks of ice finally melted), locals call them the upper, middle, and lower lakes. The mean depth is 8 feet, and the maximum is 50 feet. More than half the collective shoreline is undeveloped marsh.

Tips: Work weightless plastic worms along marsh brush.

The fishing: These lakes contain some of the best bass habitat in the western side of the state. The authorities are trying to enhance the trophy fishery by imposing a special slot limit in which bass between 12 and 15 inches must be released. This has resulted in the lake being blessed with an extraordinary number of bucketmouths over 3 pounds, and 6-plus-pounders are caught regularly on plastic worms, jig-'n'-pigs, and frog, mouse, and snake imitations. Northern pike reach over 30 inches and respond to minnows, spinnerbaits, and Dardevle spoons. The state stocks purebred muskies, which have been known to exceed 40 inches. They are normally targeted by trolling large crankbaits. Black crappies ranging from 9 to 11 inches and bluegills averaging 0.5 pound are available. They are mostly targeted with grubs by ice anglers.

Possession of black bass between 12 and 15 inches is prohibited—every other size is fair game. In summer these lakes suffer oxygen depletion below 15 feet.

Directions: The village of Cassadaga skirts the lower lake's south end.

Additional information: A public access site on Dale Drive has a hard-surface ramp and parking for about twenty rigs. The state publishes a free *Cassadaga Lakes Fishing Guide.*

Lily Dale, the world's largest spiritualist community, is located here. The facility offers up to thirty registered mediums for consultation with the dearly departed, a research library, a healing temple, and daily events all summer long, including Monday-night circles.

Contact: New York State Department of Environmental Conservation Region 9 and Chautauqua County Visitors Bureau.

62. Cassadaga Creek (see map on page 128)

Key species: Brown trout, muskellunge, northern pike, walleye, smallmouth bass, and white sucker.

Description: The outlet of Cassadaga Lakes, this creek has many faces. Starting out as warm-water habitat, it meanders for a couple miles, picks up a couple tributaries and springs, and cools down to good trout habitat. Several miles later it slows down, flattens out, and warms up into a shallow, riverlike environment, providing 28 miles of challenging warm-water habitat before pouring into Conewango Creek. Averaging 3 feet deep, it has holes that drop to 12 feet.

Tips: Fish the flat stretches from a craft light enough to carry around logjams.

The fishing: Each year the state stocks the creek a couple miles south of its source with 1,400 8.5-inch brown trout and 200 two-year-olds. Most are taken early in the season on worms and salted minnows. Veterans can be taken the rest of the season on nymphs and in-line spinners. When the creek turns warm-water again, it's a mediocre fishery set in splendid natural surroundings. The state stocks massive quantities of muskellunge; the figures change each year. In 2002 the numbers were 19,200 1-inchers and 29,000 0.5-inchers. Survival is less than desirable, but anglers report taking 30-plus-inch keepers occasionally on minnows and crankbaits intended for other species. Northern pike typically range from 18 to 24 inches, but bigger ones are available. They respond to minnows, spinnerbaits, and jerkbaits. Walleyes typically go from 15 to 18 inches and take jigs tipped with minnows or 3-inch Berkley Power Grubs worked in deep holes. Smallmouth bass average 12 inches and take worms, spinners, and crankbaits. Besides being valuable forage, white and redhorse suckers in the 15- to 18-inch range are plentiful, and fishing for them on bottom with worms is a popular local rite of spring.

Directions: NY 60 parallels the stream from its source downstream to Kimball Stand; CR 65 and CR 55 parallel its last leg.

Additional information: The flat-water section has been developed into the western arm of the Marden E. Cobb Waterway Trail, a popular 50-plus-mile-long canoe route; the visitors bureau publishes a brochure containing maps. In addition to being extremely rain sensitive, capable of violent turbulence after most any storm, old black willows are constantly falling down and blocking the waterway, making carries necessary until county crews clear the trees out.

Cassadaga Creek · Conewango Creek

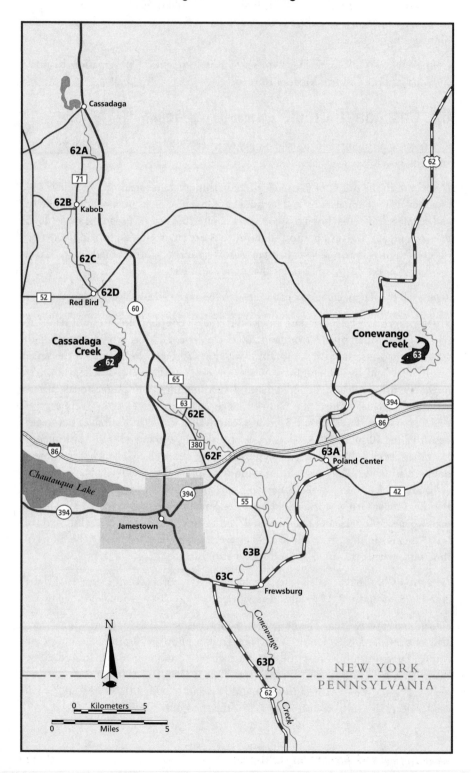

Contact: New York State Department of Environmental Conservation Region 9 and Chautauqua County Visitors Bureau.

62A. Public Fishing Rights

Description: Shoulder parking and access to the creek.

Directions: Head south on NY 60 out of the village of Cassadaga for a couple of miles and turn west on Luce Road.

Additional information: The state owns fishing rights to about 1,000 yards upstream and almost 1 mile downstream of the bridge.

62B. Public Fishing Rights

Description: Shoulder parking and access to the creek.

Directions: From site 62A, continue west on Luce Road for a couple hundred yards, turn south on CR 71 and travel almost 2 miles through the hamlet of Kabob, then turn west on Waterman Road and continue for a couple hundred yards to the bridge.

Additional information: The state owns 1,000 feet of public fishing rights directly upstream of the bridge. In addition, over 1 mile of public fishing rights are downstream, but the first few hundred feet below the bridge is private property. At press time it wasn't posted.

62C. Public Access

Description: This site has parking for five cars and a beach launch.

Directions: On CR 71, a few hundred feet north of the hamlet of South Stockton.

62D. Public Access

Description: Parking for ten cars and steps down to the creek.

Directions: On CR 52, just upstream of the bridge in the hamlet of Red Bird.

62E. Public Access

Description: Parking for eight cars and a beach launch.

Directions: In the hamlet of Ross Mills at the CR 63 bridge.

Additional information: Two lean-tos are located 1 mile upstream (north). They are available free, on a first-come, first-served basis. Camping is limited to one night.

62F. Public Access

Description: This site, located at the creek's confluence with the Chadakoin River (the outlet of Chautauqua Lake), offers parking for twenty cars and a launch below a stairway cut into the south bank.

Directions: In the hamlet of Lavant, about 90 yards upstream of the CR 65 bridge.

Additional information: The site has a picnic area and an iron railroad bridge dating back to 1883.

63. Conewango Creek *(see map on page 128)*

Key species: Muskellunge, northern pike, walleye, smallmouth bass, and white sucker.

Description: This slow-moving, murky stream spreads out to 40 feet wide in spots, averages 4 feet deep, and has numerous holes up to 12 feet deep and a few that go 30 feet deep.

Tips: Jig tube/minnow combinations around timber.

The fishing: Each year the state stocks hundreds of thousands of fry muskellunge and several thousand 8-inchers. Survival is so-so, and anglers report it takes a lot of hard fishing to catch a keeper—30 inches. They react violently to crankbaits and bucktail spinners worked around cover, under logjams, and along steep undercut banks. Northern pike in the 18- to 24-inch range are present and hit free-lined minnows and silver spoons. Walleyes aren't too plentiful, but there's enough around in the 15- to 18-inch range to keep anglers hoping they nailed one whenever they get a hit on a jig intended for smallmouths. They take worms drifted on harnesses and bucktail jigs fished plain or tipped with a worm, minnow, or scented curly-tailed grub. Smallmouths average 13 inches and take crayfish, minnows, and spinnerbaits. White and redhorse suckers are the primary forage. Reaching up to 20 inches, they can be caught with worms.

Directions: The creek is paralleled by NY 394 and US 62.

Additional information: Each year huge, old black willows fall into the drink, making portages necessary to get around them—until the county clears them away. The 25-mile stretch from the Cattaraugus County line to the Pennsylvania border forms the eastern arm of the Marden E. Cobb Waterway, a popular 50-plus-mile-long canoe route; the visitors bureau publishes a brochure containing maps.

Contact: New York State Department of Environmental Conservation Region 9 and Chautauqua County Visitors Bureau.

63A. Public Access

Description: This site has shoulder parking and steps down to the beach launch.

Directions: On CR 42, a few hundred yards east of the hamlet of Poland Center.

63B. Public Access

Description: This access is 11 miles downstream of site 63A and has parking for four cars.

Directions: Head north out of Frewsburg on CR 55 for a few hundred yards. The launch is on the east bank, downstream of the bridge.

63C. Public Access

Description: This scenic, gently sloping, grassy area is 2 miles downstream from site 63B and has parking for ten cars.

Directions: At the US 62 bridge, just west of Frewsburg.

Additional information: A dock and two lean-tos are located on a county-owned island roughly 3.5 miles downstream.

63D. Public Access

Description: This access is about 4 miles downstream of site 63C and has a dock and parking for about ten cars.

Directions: Head south out of Frewsburg on US 62 for about 5 miles, to just before the New York–Pennsylvania border.

64. New Albion Lake *(see map on page 132)*

Key species: Brown trout, rainbow trout, brook trout, largemouth bass, white crappie, pumpkinseed, bluegill, yellow perch, and brown bullhead.

Description: This 50-acre flood-control impoundment averages 6 feet deep and has a maximum depth of 14 feet.

Tips: Cast flies that imitate food pellets.

The fishing: The state's stocking policies for this lake change constantly. In 2002 the figures were 2,700 9-inch rainbows, 100 15.5-inchers, and 95 23-inch breeders; 200 browns averaging 13.5 inches and 2,800 averaging 9 inches; 1,000 two-year-old brook trout averaging 12.5 inches, 25 surplus brookie breeders averaging 15 inches, and 35 spent breeders averaging 23 inches. The trout take worms, minnows, commercial trout baits, kernel corn, and miniature marshmallows. Largemouth bass average 14 inches and take minnows, crayfish, and spinnerbaits. White crappies from 9 to 12 inches and yellow perch averaging 8 inches are plentiful and respond to minnows and 2-inch tubes. Pumpkinseeds and bluegills range from 5 to 10 inches and take worms and 1-inch curly-tailed grubs. Trout can be taken year-round.

Directions: From Salamanca exit 20 of I–86, head east on NY 417 for about 0.5 mile and turn north on NY 353. Travel for about 8 miles, then bear west on CR 5 for about 5.5 miles.

Additional information: A cartop launch with parking for about five cars is on the north end near the dam. No gas motors allowed.

New Albion Lake

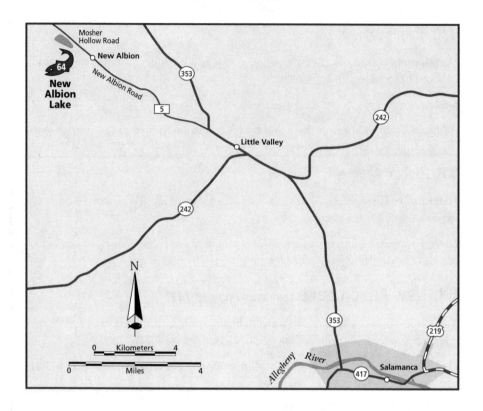

Contact: New York State Department of Environmental Conservation Region 9 and Cattaraugus County Department of Economic Development, Planning, and Tourism.

65. Little Genesee Creek *(see map on page 133)*

Key species: Brown trout.

Description: This freestone stream starts in the rolling hills of southern Allegany County, flows for about 10 scenic, historic miles (it cuts through the state's oil country), and pours into Oswayo Creek in Pennsylvania.

Tips: In autumn work egg-sucking leeches in pools and runs.

The fishing: The state annually stocks about 3,700 8-inch brown trout and 200 two-year-olds averaging 14 inches. Those that aren't caught during the first few weeks of the season find the pickings decent and gain a couple inches by season's end. They respond to worms and salted minnows bounced on bottom in spring, terrestrials and nymphs in summer, and worms, Exude Roe, Berkley Power Wigglers, and streamers in fall.

Little Genesee Creek · Oswayo Creek

Directions: Head east out of Olean on NY 417 for about 9 miles. The highway parallels the creek from here to Bolivar.

Additional information: The state publishes a free map showing public fishing rights. There are numerous working oil wells in the area.

Contact: New York State Department of Environmental Conservation Region 9 and Allegany County Tourism.

65A. Public Access (see map on page 133)

Description: This site has parking for ten cars.

Directions: Liberty Street in the village of Bolivar.

65B. Public Fishing Rights (see map on page 133)

Description: Shoulder parking and stream access.

Directions: Head south out of Bolivar on NY 417 for about 1 mile, turn west on Forman Hollow Road, and drive to the end.

Additional information: The state owns public fishing rights from just upstream of the Forman Hollow Road terminus to downstream for a little over 0.5 mile.

65C. Public Fishing Rights (see map on page 133)

Description: Shoulder parking and stream access.

Directions: Head south out of Bolivar on NY 417 for about 3 miles, turn west on CR 5C, and travel several hundred yards to the bridge.

Additional information: The state owns public fishing rights on the section of stream flowing between the CR 5C bridge downstream almost 1 mile to the CR 5 bridge.

65D. Public Fishing Rights (see map on page 133)

Description: Shoulder parking and stream access.

Directions: Head south out of the hamlet of Little Genesee on NY 417 for a few hundred yards and turn west on Wells Road.

Additional information: The state owns about 1 mile of public fishing rights stretching from 1,000 yards upstream of the first Wells Road bridge to roughly 300 yards downstream of the Foster Brook Road bridge.

65E. Public Access (see map on page 133)

Description: This site has parking for five cars.

Directions: Head south out of Little Genesee on NY 417 for a little over 1 mile, turn west on Sanford Hollow Road, and travel for about 0.5 mile.

Additional information: The state owns public fishing rights for several hundred yards upstream and downstream of the bridge.

66. Oswayo Creek *(see map on page 133)*

Key species: Muskellunge, northern pike, smallmouth bass, and carp.

Description: Tracing its roots to Pennsylvania, this tributary of the Allegheny River doesn't spend much time in New York. However, while here it carves an extremely scenic 3-mile course laced with exceptional warm-water habitat.

Tips: Cast large streamers.

The fishing: Gallon for gallon, this creek is the state's hottest spot for fly fishing for muskies in a creek environment. Divided almost equally into shallow ripples, shaded pools, and undercut runs, all littered with boulders and fallen timber, this perfect stream is ideal for ambushing prey. Its warm-water predators behave like trout— striking first, asking questions later. Historically muskies claim the highest rung on the food chain. They typically range from 2 to 3 feet and respond well to streamers, spinners, and crankbaits. Lately, however, northern pike from Kinzua Reservoir have discovered the place, found it to their liking, and settled in. Averaging about 25 inches, they take the same baits the muskies do. Smallmouth bass tend to be small, but some up to 18 inches are available. They like crayfish and minnows worked in ripples and drifted through pools. Carp ranging from 2 to 20 pounds are plentiful. Most locals still-fish for them in pools with dough balls, corn, or potato. Increasingly anglers are discovering the thrill of sight-fishing for these "freshwater bonefish" with small garden worms on light fly-fishing tackle.

Directions: NY 417 parallels the stream about 7 miles southeast of the city of Olean.

Additional information: This creek is best fished from a canoe. Launch at road crossings.

Contact: New York State Department of Environment Conservation Region 9.

67. Ischua Creek *(see map on page 136)*

Key species: Brown trout.

Description: Slowly slicing through a relatively flat valley in fertile farm country, this deep, silt-bottomed stream flows for about 20 scenic miles, under a backdrop of rolling Allegheny foothills, and feeds Olean Creek, a tributary of the Allegheny River.

Tips: Use live crayfish.

The fishing: Each year the state stocks this stream heavily with brown trout of varying sizes. In 2001 the figures were (these numbers are pretty consistent from year to year) 10,000 fry averaging 3.5 inches, 11,050 yearlings ranging from 8 to 9 inches,

Ischua Creek

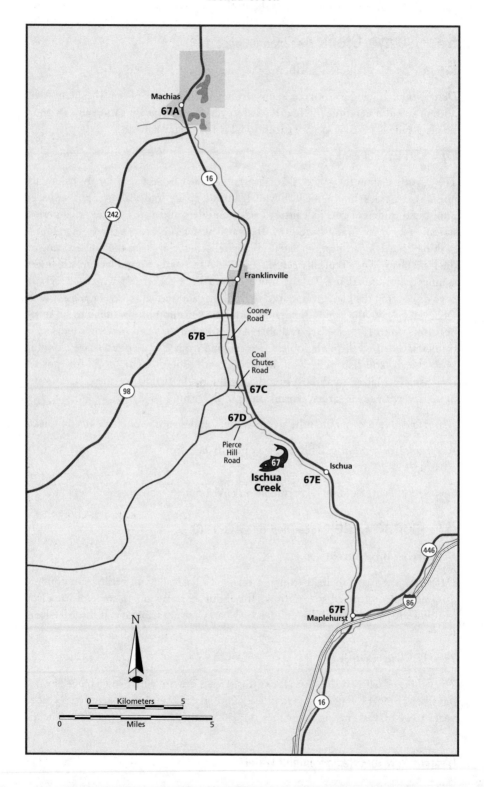

1,200 14-inch two-year-olds, and 600 15-inchers. The trout grow well dining on the plentiful minnows and crayfish living in the creek's deep pools and runs. State fisheries biologist Joe Evans says, "This creek is like one long pool, which makes it ideal for casting in-line spinners and working crayfish on bottom. The stream gets little fishing pressure after mid-May, and the browns, especially wild ones, can go 20 inches or better."

Directions: NY 16 parallels the creek for its entire length.

Contact: New York State Department of Environmental Conservation Region 9 and Cattaraugus County Department of Economic Development, Planning, and Tourism.

67A. Public Fishing Rights

Description: Shoulder parking.

Directions: Head south on NY 16 out of the hamlet of Machias for about 1 mile.

Additional information: The state owns public fishing rights for about 1,000 feet upstream of the bridge.

67B. Public Access

Description: Parking for about five cars.

Directions: Head south out of the village of Franklinville on NY 16 for about 2 miles, turn west on Cooney Road, and drive to the end.

Additional information: The state owns public fishing rights stretching for about 3 miles upstream to 1 mile downstream.

67C. Public Fishing Rights

Description: Shoulder parking.

Directions: Head south out of the village of Franklinville on NY 16 for about 3 miles, turn west on Coal Chutes Road (CR 18), and travel a few hundred feet.

Additional information: The state owns public fishing rights to about 1 mile upstream of the bridge.

67D. Public Fishing Rights

Description: Shoulder parking.

Directions: Head south out of Franklinville on NY 16 for about 4 miles, turn west on Pierce Hill Road, and travel a few hundred feet.

Additional information: The state owns public fishing rights from the bridge downstream for about 2 miles.

67E. Public Fishing Rights *(see map on page 136)*

Description: Shoulder parking.

Directions: Head south on NY 16 out of the hamlet of Ischua for a few hundred yards, turn right on Dutch Hill Road, and travel for a few hundred yards.

Additional information: The state owns public fishing rights from the bridge downstream for about 1.5 miles.

67F. Public Fishing Rights *(see map on page 136)*

Description: Shoulder parking.

Directions: In the hamlet of Maplehurst.

Additional information: The state owns public fishing rights from Maplehurst downstream for about 3 miles.

68. Allegheny River

Key species: Muskellunge, northern pike, walleye, smallmouth bass, channel catfish, bluegill, and rock bass.

Description: Rising in Pennsylvania's Potter County, the Allegheny River comes up to New York as a wide, slow-moving stream averaging 4 feet deep, punctuated with holes up to 12 feet deep. Only running through New York for about 40 miles, totally within Cattaraugus County, it slices through two cities and ends its tour of the state on Seneca Allegany Indian Territory as the Allegheny (Kinzua) Reservoir. In Pittsburgh, Pennsylvania, it joins the Monongahela River to form the mighty Ohio River.

Tips: Tip jigs with worms and work them on bottom for walleyes and smallmouths.

The fishing: State fisheries biologist Scott Cornett says muskellunge are indigenous to the Allegheny drainage, but spawning habitat is sparse above Kinzua Dam. The state maintains their presence through heavy stocking—nearly 11,000 4.5-inch fingerlings and 1,850 8-inchers in 2001. Survival to the 30-inch legal size is good, and some make it to over 30 pounds. Most are taken by trolling large crankbaits like Smithwick Rogues and Rebel Minnows. Northern pike typically range from 20 to 25 inches, but 20-pounders are reported occasionally. They like live suckers drifted or fished below a bobber and spinnerbaits fished plain or tipped with YUM Samurai Shads. One of the Kinzua Reservoir's most important walleye spawning grounds, most of the hanky-panky is done by the time the season opens and the majority has returned to the lake. However, many stay—some up to 10 pounds. They can be taken year-round by casting jigs, crankbaits, and spinnerbaits in the deep water near bridge abutments and bends in the river. Smallmouths range from 12 to 20 inches and respond well to in-line spinners, scented tubes, crayfish, and live 3-inch shiners. Channel catfish typically go 14 to 20 inches, but trophies up to 15 pounds are available. Average cats like

Allegheny River

worms, chicken livers, shrimp, and minnows. The trophies are partial to live minnows and cut bait fished in deep holes. Although not extraordinarily plentiful, bluegills and rock bass the size of a big man's hand are available and hit worms, small poppers, and Exude grubs.

Just east of the village of Vandalia, the river enters the Seneca Allegany Indian Territory, and a tribal license is needed to fish this stretch.

Directions: I–86 and NY 417 parallel most of the river. (*NOTE:* I–86, the former NY 17, is still called NY 17 in spots that have not yet been converted.)

Additional information: This river is highly rain sensitive and can turn into a torrent after a heavy storm. Most anglers access the river at bridges or the shoulder of the road.

Contact: New York State Department of Environmental Conservation Region 9; Cattaraugus County Department of Economic Development, Planning, and Tourism; and the Seneca Nation of Indians.

68A. Public Access (see map on page 139)

Description: This site is suitable for hand-launching cartop craft only and has parking for nine cars.

Directions: On CR 60 (West River Road), south of the village of Allegany.

69. Allegheny Reservoir (Kinzua Reservoir)

Key species: Walleye, northern pike, muskellunge, smallmouth bass, brown trout, rainbow trout, and channel catfish.

Description: Set in the Allegheny foothills, this Army Corps of Engineers flood-control project on the Allegheny River covers anywhere from 21,180 acres during the spring thaw down to 12,080 acres at summer pool. Roughly 25 percent of it is in New York, and 90 percent of that is on the Seneca Allegany Indian Territory, one of the six tribes in the Iroquois Confederacy. The shoreline is mostly forested.

Tips: Jig worms or minnows along breaks.

The fishing: In addition to keeping weed growth at a minimum, wild fluctuations in water levels sometime destroy entire generations of shallow spawners like sunfish and northern pike. Stream and deep-water spawners, however, are relatively immune to this meteorological form of birth control. Indeed, the reservoir's unpredictable character, combined with a floor carpeted mostly with boulders, pebbles, and mud, makes for ideal walleye habitat. The state record, a 16-pound-7-ounce monster, was caught here in May 1994. Numerous 10- and 12-pounders are caught each year on everything from minnows and worms to bladebaits, spinnerbaits, and crankbaits. The best times to fish are in the first month of the season and in late fall when they're in the tributary bays in 5 to 20 feet of water. The Ohio River strain of muskie is king of the reservoir. Smaller (seldom exceeding 30 pounds), darker, and

Allegheny Reservoir (Kinzua Reservoir)

more likely to have stripes than the Great Lakes variety, they're naturally bred so there aren't too many of them, but specialty anglers target them with large minnows and crankbaits. Smallmouths in the 1- to 3-pound range are plentiful and respond to live minnows and crayfish drifted off points early in the season and along the old riverbed in summer. Northern pike occupy the bays year-round and respond to large minnows and jerkbaits. Huge channel catfish roam the floor. They hit live minnows and cut bait fished on bottom in the lower holes of feeder creeks in late spring and early summer, and in the deep holes off tributary mouths from mid-July through October.

The reservoir's population of trout spends most of the time in the deeper waters of Pennsylvania. Spring sees rainbows and autumn sees browns migrate into streams to spawn, where they will take worms, streamers, and nymphs. In addition, the larger tributaries are stocked with trout, offering decent stream fishing all summer long. Since the turn of this century, the state has been stocking paddlefish to see if they can be restored to this former haunt. If they take, the reservoir will be the only water in the state to have the weird-looking filter-feeders, which can reach over 100 pounds.

Directions: Head west out of Salamanca on I–86 (former NY 17) for about 7 miles to exit 18 and turn south on NY 280, which parallels the reservoir.

Additional information: A reservation fishing license, available at all Seneca Nation One Stops and the Clerk's Office (see the appendix), is needed to fish on Indian territory (most of the open water). A New York license is required to fish the inside halves of large bays and all tributaries.

Contact: Seneca Nation of Indians; Cattaraugus County Department of Economic Development, Planning, and Tourism; and New York State Department of Environmental Conservation Region 9.

69A. High Banks Campground *(see map on page 141)*

Description: An enterprise of the Seneca Nation of Indians, this fee area offers over 200 campsites (some with electricity and water), 50 winterized cabins, showers, a hard-surface launch ramp, and a country store that sells Seneca Nation of Indians fishing licenses. The campground is open May 1 through October 12.

Directions: Off Onoville Road, about 3 miles south of Steamburg (I–86 exit 17).

69B. Onoville Marina *(see map on page 141)*

Description: This county-owned fee area boasts 365 slips for boats up to 40 feet long, a paved launch ramp, boat rentals, camping, shore fishing, and showers.

Directions: On Onoville Road, about 2 miles south of site 69A.

69C. Allegany State Park *(see maps on pages 141 and 143)*

Description: Covering 65,000 acres (97 square miles), this fee area offers 300 campsites, 377 cabins (150 winterized), a paved ramp on Allegheny Reservoir with parking

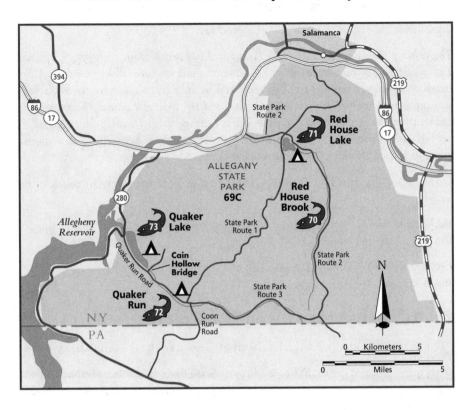

for 20 rigs, 2 big lakes, boat rentals, hiking trails, and hot showers. The campgrounds are open April through mid-December; winterized cabins are available year-round.

The fishing: The park's two major lakes, Red House (site 71) and Quaker (site 73), are productive enough to deserve their own listings. Science Lake, a tiny pond along Quaker Run Road, is stocked annually with 460 brook trout averaging 9.5 inches — they like in-line spinners and small spoons. In addition, according to state fisheries biologist Joe Evans, the streams running through the park all contain wild brook trout, particularly in remote areas.

Directions: The park has entrances off three I–86 exits: exit 20 in the village of Salamanca and exits 18 and 19 west of the village.

70. Red House Brook

Key species: Brook trout and rainbow trout.

Description: Pouring from the side of a hill, this stream slices through 6 miles of Allegany State Park before feeding Red House Lake. Along the way, beavers dam it countless times, prompting one old-timer to quip, "This creek looks like a string of shimmering jewels running through the woods."

Tips: Trout are easiest to catch in April and May.

The fishing: The state annually stocks roughly 2,500 brook trout averaging 9.5 inches and about 800 9-inch rainbow trout. Since the stream runs alongside a road for much of its length, most of the fish are taken in the first couple months of the season on worms and minnows. And that's good because in summer the numerous beaver ponds warm the flow to temperatures inhospitable to trout. Still, enough fish are left over to provide summer pickings for energetic fly fishers willing to walk the creek in search of spring holes and shaded pools.

Directions: Allegany State Park Route 2 runs alongside the creek for much of its length.

Additional information: The surrounding state park, a fee area, offers 300 campsites and 377 cabins (see site 69C).

Contact: New York State Department of Environmental Conservation Region 9 and Allegany State Park.

71. Red House Lake *(see map on page 143)*

Key species: Largemouth bass, rainbow trout, brown trout, and brook trout.

Description: Part of the 65,000-acre Allegany State Park, this 90-acre impoundment averages 7 feet deep and has a maximum depth of 20 feet. Most of its shoreline is mowed, making for easy bank fishing.

Tips: In deep summer fish hang out in the old creek channels etching the lake's floor.

The fishing: A relatively shallow lake with lots of weed beds, Red House is a decent largemouth bass fishery. While bucketmouths typically range from 12 to 18 inches, 20-plus-inchers are available. They take Cabela's Livin' Eye Minnows, Slug-Gos, and soft plastic baits like Yamasenkos worked in weed openings and along weed lines. The state annually stocks roughly 2,700 9-inch brown trout and 700 two-year-olds averaging 14 inches. Most are caught in the spring on worms and minnows. The most warm-water-tolerant of the salmonids, some of the spring releases manage to survive into summer, providing decent brown trout action for folks fishing with Berkley's Trout Bait or working worms through tributary mouths after a rain.

Each autumn the state releases some of its surplus and spent breeders. In 2002 the figures were 325 15-inch brook trout, 100 rainbow trout averaging 15.5 inches, and 105 rainbows stretching the tape to over 30 inches. Terribly naive, they're fairly easy to catch on everything from commercial trout baits, streamers, and worms to dot jigs tipped with wax worms and fished through the ice. Trout can be taken year-round

Directions: Head west out of Salamanca on I–86 (former NY 17) for about 5 miles to exit 19. Get on Allegany State Park Route 2 for a couple miles, then hook a right at the four corners onto Allegany State Park Route 1.

Additional information: The lake's cartop launch has parking for five cars. Gas motors are prohibited on the water. One of the park's three campgrounds hugs the lake, offering 100 no-frills campsites (half with electricity), 147 cabins, a general store, a laundry, and hot showers.

Contact: New York State Department of Environmental Conservation Region 9 and Allegany State Park.

72. Quaker Run *(see map on page 143)*

Key species: Brook trout and rainbow trout.

Description: This creek traces its roots to the New York–Pennsylvania state line, flows west through scenic Allegany State Park, and feeds Quaker Lake.

Tips: In the spring fish beaver ponds with a small minnow suspended below a bubble bobber.

The fishing: Each year the state stocks roughly 2,200 9-inch brook trout and about 850 rainbow trout averaging 9.5 inches. State fisheries biologist Joe Evans says its numerous beaver ponds warm the water early in the season, making the trout cooperative earlier than in most creeks. This, combined with easy accessibility, makes the stream a popular early-season magnet for locals, who quickly remove the majority of stockies with worms and minnows. Come summer, the trout that survived the spring campaign are scattered far and wide. Savvy veterans, they occupy cool runs and spring pools, providing challenging sport to ambitious anglers who walk the stream quietly while casting streamers and nymphs.

From the Cain Hollow Bridge at the run's mouth upstream to Coon Run Road, bait is restricted to artificial lures only. In addition, the Allegany State Park Commission is working with the state Department of Environmental Conservation to implement a delayed harvest program that would prohibit the killing of any fish taken in this stretch from April 1 to May 15. It's hoped that the program will be in effect for the 2004 season. Check park regulations for details.

Directions: Quaker Run Road (Allegany State Park Route 3) parallels the stream.

Additional information: The surrounding state park, a fee area, offers 300 campsites and 377 cabins (see site 69C).

Contact: New York State Department of Environmental Conservation Region 9 and Allegany State Park.

73. Quaker Lake *(see map on page 143)*

Key species: Brown trout, rainbow trout, brook trout, northern pike, black bass, bluegill, yellow perch, and brown bullhead.

Description: This 270-acre man-made lake is totally surrounded by Allegany State Park. Its average depth is 15 feet, and it drops to a maximum depth of 40 feet. The floor is very rocky.

Tips: Fish from a belly boat.

The fishing: As a rule, the state annually stocks this place with about 4,800 browns averaging 9.5 inches, 400 two-year-old browns up to 14 inches, 3,900 rainbows averaging 9 inches, and 225 15.5-inch "bows." Come fall, whopper surplus and spent breeders are also released. In 2002 the numbers were 50 rainbows averaging 23 inches, 75 rainbows over 30 inches, 108 15-inch brook trout, and 142 brookies stretching over 19 inches. They take worms, minnows, Krocodile spoons, Exude Erupt paste, and Exude Corn Niblets. Some invariably make it to winter, when they're taken through the hard water on ice jigs tipped with wax worms, mousies, or spikes. Trout can be taken year-round.

Its dam only about 0.25 mile from Allegheny Reservoir, Quaker Lake is subject to informal stocking of warm-water species by anglers who catch them in the big impoundment, show them off in the park's campgrounds, then release them into the lake. Finding the pickings good, the deportees thrive and multiply. Northern pike range from 18 to 25 inches and take minnows, Dardevles, and spinnerbaits. Largemouth bass go anywhere from 12 to 20 inches and attack bass bugs, buzzbaits, jig-'n'-pigs, and jerkbaits. Smallmouths between 12 and 16 inches are plentiful and are targeted mostly by free-lining minnows, drifting with crayfish and worms, or by dragging jigs tipped with minnows and soft plastics. Bluegills generally run from 4 to 8 inches, bullheads average 12 inches, and yellow perch go from 5 to 10 inches. All of these panfish take worms, and the perch and sunfish hit wet flies, Exude Trout Worms, and Exude Curly Tail Grubs.

Additional information: The lake's cartop launch has parking for ten cars. Gas motors are prohibited on the lake. One of Allegany State Park's campgrounds (100 sites) and its largest cabin colony (230 cabins) are within a stone's throw of shore.

Directions: From Salamanca, head west on I–86 (former NY 17) for about 10 miles to exit 18. Travel south on NY 280 for about 5 miles to the park entrance.

Contact: New York State Department of Environmental Conservation Region 9 and Allegany State Park.

74. Lime Lake

Key species: Largemouth bass, walleye, and tiger muskie.

Description: Mainly fed by springs, this 154-acre impoundment's average depth is 15 feet, and the maximum is 50 feet. The shoreline is almost totally ringed with summer cottages.

Tips: Minnow-imitating crankbaits and soft plastic jerkbaits worked alongside and under docks work great for largemouth bass and an occasional muskie.

Springville, Hinsdale, and Caneadea Triangle

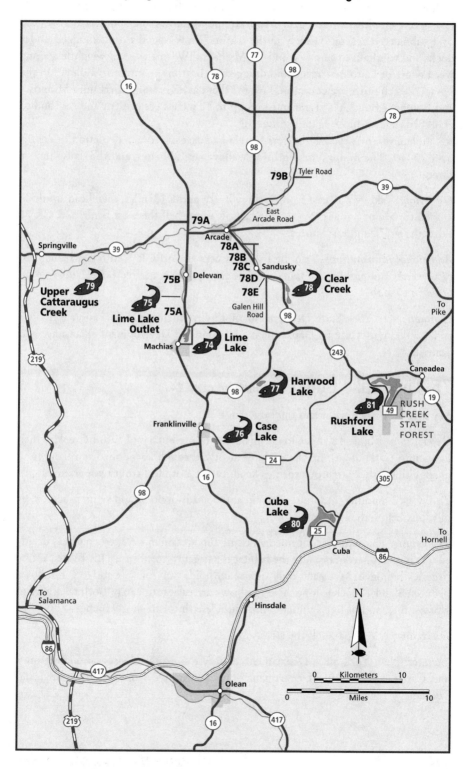

To Pike

Tyler Road

79B

East Arcade Road

79A

Arcade

Springville

Delevan

78A
78B
78C Sandusky
78D
78E

Galen Hill Road

Upper Cattaraugus Creek 79

75B

75

75A

Lime Lake Outlet

Machias

Clear Creek 78

Lime Lake 74

243

Caneadea

Harwood Lake 77

81 **Rushford Lake**

49

19

RUSH CREEK STATE FOREST

Franklinville

Case Lake 76

24

305

Cuba Lake 80

25

Cuba

To Hornell

To Salamanca

Hinsdale

N

Olean

0   Kilometers   10

0   Miles   10

The fishing: This lake is known for its largemouth bass. Most are in the 12- to 14-inch range, but a lot of 15- to 20-inch fish are available. They have a taste for shallow-diving crankbaits like Lazer Eye Extreme Minnows and spinnerbaits worked over submerged vegetation early in the season, Texas-rigged worms dragged under docks and windfalls in summer, and YUM Shakin' Worms worked weightless along weed edges or Carolina-rigged and dragged on bottom in autumn. Walleyes in the 18- to 22-inch range are common. Fish for them at night with MirrOlure Minnows and Bomber Long "A"s. Tiger muskies up to 40 inches are present and respond to crankbaits and in-line bucktail spinners.

In late summer the lake suffers from a bad case of oxygen depletion in depths over 20 feet. The minimum length for walleyes is 18 inches, and the daily limit is three.

Directions: Take NY 39 east from Springville for about 10 miles, then head south on NY 16 for about 7 miles. NY 16 runs along about half the west bank, and CR 70 skirts the south and east shores.

Additional information: A public fishing access site off CR 70 offers a launch for cartop craft and parking for five cars. The state publishes a free *Lime Lake Fishing Guide and Map.*

Contact: New York State Department of Environmental Conservation Region 9 and Cattaraugus County Department of Economic Development, Planning, and Tourism.

75. Lime Lake Outlet *(see map on page 147)*

Key species: Brown trout and rainbow trout.

Description: About 4.5 miles long, this creek is a tributary of Elton Creek, which flows into Cattaraugus Creek. Snaking mostly through abandoned farmland, it is lined with brush. Numerous springs keep its water at ideal trout temperatures.

Tips: Cast a muddler minnow upstream at the heads of pools and swim it back rapidly, just below the surface.

The fishing: The state discontinued stocking this stream in 1993, when it was decided that it didn't need it because the habitat is perfect for wild trout. Joe Evans, a state fisheries biologist, says each mile of stream holds 800 browns and 100 rainbows between 8 and 12 inches long. The rainbows are easiest to catch. Both take garden worms, flies, and in-line spinners. Minimum length for trout is 9 inches.

Directions: NY 16 parallels the stream.

Contact: New York State Department of Environmental Conservation Region 9 and Cattaraugus County Department of Economic Development, Planning, and Tourism.

75A. Public Access

Description: Parking for five cars and access to roughly 0.5 mile of public fishing rights, upstream and downstream.

Directions: On NY 16, about 3 miles south of Delevan.

75B. Public Access

Description: Parking for five cars and access to 0.75 mile of public fishing rights.

Directions: On West Street in Delevan.

76. Case Lake *(see map on page 147)*

Key species: Brown trout, rainbow trout, largemouth bass, black crappie, brown bullhead, bluegill, and pumpkinseed.

Description: This 80-acre flood-control impoundment averages 10 feet deep and drops to a maximum depth of 32 feet.

Tips: In summer drift minnows 15 to 20 feet deep.

The fishing: This lake offers a lot of public access and is very popular. The state makes sure there's enough fish for everyone by stocking it with massive quantities of trout. Brown trout are the main species. Each year the state generally stocks roughly 3,300 browns averaging 9.5 inches and 350 14-inch two-year-olds. Rainbows are also stocked annually to the tune of 1,600 averaging 9 inches. This is another one of the lakes in Region 9 that gets surplus and spent breeders each fall. In 2002 the numbers were 100 browns averaging 25 inches and 65 19.5-inchers, and 50 rainbows averaging 23 inches and 35 15.5-inchers. Both species hit worms, minnows, and crayfish during warm weather and spikes and wax worms through the ice. In summer they respond to white dry flies cast over the old creek channel on the south end at dusk and dawn. Trout season is open year-round.

Largemouth bass ranging from 1 to 6 pounds hang out in the weedy southern end, where they're partial to Zara Spooks, Hula Poppers, and worms rigged whacky-style and fished along weed lines and other structure. Black crappies run 9 to 11 inches and respond to minnows, tiny jigs and tubes, and Beetle Spins. Brown bullheads averaging 8 inches are suckers for worms fished over muddy bottoms, especially in the rain or at night. Bluegills and pumpkinseeds up to 10 inches hit pretty well on worms, flies, and poppers but just can't resist a mousie or spike.

Directions: Head north on NY 16 out of Hinsdale (I–86 exit 27) for about 12 miles to Franklinville, turn east on CR 24, and continue for 1.5 miles.

Additional information: A small park on the east shore boasts a cartop launch, parking for fifty cars, and a picnic area. Only electric motors are permitted on the lake.

Contact: New York Department of Environmental Conservation Region 9.

77. Harwood Lake *(see map on page 147)*

Key species: Brook trout, rainbow trout, brown trout, largemouth bass, yellow perch, white crappie, sunfish, and brown bullhead.

Description: Located on the northwestern border of the 300-acre Harwood Lake Multiple Use Area, this flood-control impoundment covers 35 acres, averages 8 feet deep, and has a maximum depth of 12 feet.

Tips: Cast Panther Martins around the inlet in the morning and evening.

The fishing: The state annually stocks the place with around 1,800 brookies and 1,900 rainbows averaging 9 inches, 1,500 browns running 9.5 inches, and 300 two-year-old browns averaging 14 inches. In addition, surplus and spent breeders are often released in autumn. The 2002 figures were 120 brookies over 19 inches and 180 15-inchers. The trout take worms, minnows, crayfish, and commercial trout baits. Largemouth bass go from 12 to 20 inches and are targeted along weed lines and weed openings with Texas-rigged worms and by ripping slugs across the surface. Boasting easy access, including a handicapped ramp, this spot's panfish get a lot of pressure. Still, white crappies reaching up to 12 inches and yellow perch ranging from 6 to 10 inches are available and hit minnows and 1- and 2-inch curly-tailed grubs and tubes. Pumpkinseeds and bluegills averaging 7 inches and brown bullheads up to 14 inches are also present and can be taken on worms.

Trout season is open year-round.

Directions: Head north out of Franklinville on NY 98 for about 10 miles.

Additional information: No gas motors allowed. Camping is prohibited in the 300-acre multiple use area around the lake but is permitted in the adjoining 2,809-acre Bush Hill State Forest. The state fishing access site offers a cartop launch, parking for about twenty rigs, handicapped access, and hundreds of feet of shore fishing.

Contact: New York State Department of Environmental Conservation Region 9.

78. Clear Creek *(see map on page 147)*

Key species: Brown trout and rainbow trout.

Description: Originating in the northwestern corner of Allegany County, at 2,000 feet above sea level, this 11-mile-long creek drops 645 feet before feeding Cattaraugus Creek in Arcade.

Tips: Fish weighted nymphs in the pockets.

The fishing: State fisheries biologist Joe Evans says his office stopped stocking this stream in 1992. Still, it's loaded with wild fish ranging from 7 to 12 inches. Evans says, "Wild brown trout average about 600 to 800 trout per mile . . . and rainbows average 450 trout per mile. Clear Creek has the highest wild rainbow trout population of any stream in Region 9." Both species hit worms, minnows, and flies. Minimum length for trout is 9 inches.

Directions: NY 98 parallels the stream.

Contact: New York State Department of Environmental Conservation Region 9.

78A. Public Access

Description: Parking for about five cars.

Directions: Take NY 98 about 0.5 mile south from Arcade and turn east on Bray Road.

78B. Public Access

Description: Parking for five cars.

Directions: Take NY 98 south from Arcade for about 1.5 miles and turn east on Sparks Road.

78C. Public Access

Description: Parking for five cars.

Directions: Take NY 98 south from Arcade for about 2 miles and turn east on Jones Road.

78D. Public Access

Description: Parking for about five cars.

Directions: On NY 98, 0.5 mile south of Sandusky.

78E. Public Access

Description: Parking for five cars.

Directions: Take NY 98 south from Sandusky for 1 mile and turn south on Galen Hill Road.

79. Upper Cattaraugus Creek *(see map on page 147)*

Key species: Brown trout and rainbow trout.

Description: This stretch snakes for roughly 30 miles, from its source east of the village of Arcade to the dam in Springville.

Tips: Cast small Panther Martins upstream, especially along undercut banks, and work them back faster than the current.

The fishing: This half of the creek is stocked annually with about 6,400 brown trout averaging 8 inches and about 1,300 two-year-olds averaging 14 inches. It also has a good population of wild browns and a smattering of wild rainbow trout. All respond to salted minnows, worms, and flies.

Directions: NY 39 and East Arcade Road parallel the stream.

Additional information: The state owns about 6 miles of public fishing rights stretching from about 2 miles east of Arcade upstream.

Contact: New York State Department of Environmental Conservation Region 9.

79A. Public Access *(see map on page 147)*

Description: Parking for about twenty cars.

Directions: On NY 39/NY 16, about 2 miles west of Arcade.

79B. Public Access *(see map on page 147)*

Description: Parking for five cars.

Directions: From Arcade, head east on NY 98 for about 2 miles, turn east on East Arcade Road, and travel for a little over 2 miles to the site across from the terminus of Tyler Road.

80. Cuba Lake *(see map on page 147)*

Key species: Northern pike, walleye, black bass, yellow perch, black crappie, white crappie, rock bass, and sunfish.

Description: Impounded in 1858 to supply water for the Genesee Valley Canal System, this 445-acre lake averages 20 feet deep and has a maximum depth of 46 feet.

Tips: Black or purple worms with chartreuse tails work best for bass.

The fishing: Northern pike somehow made it into the lake in the 1990s and found the habitat good. Many reach 30-something inches and hit large minnows fished below bobbers. Walleyes range from 16 to 20 inches and take worms, Rat-L-Traps, and ThunderSticks. Bucketmouths reach up to 6 pounds and are caught regularly on 7- to 12-inch rubber worms. Smallmouth bass average a couple pounds and take crayfish and jigs. Yellow perch, locally called jacks, reach up to 14 inches and are mostly caught through the ice on small minnows or Swedish Pimples tipped with a perch eye. In the spring locals catch black and white crappies ranging from 9 to 12 inches on small minnows and tiny purple rubber worms fished below a pencil bobber and retrieved slowly. Rock bass and sunfish range from 5 to 7 inches and take worms and tiny poppers. During summer oxygen depletion plagues depths exceeding 15 feet.

Directions: Head east out of Olean on I–86 for about 12 miles to exit 28 (Cuba). Take NY 305 north for 2 miles and turn west on CR 25 (South Shore Road).

Additional information: A public boat launch with a hard-surface ramp and parking for twelve rigs is on South Shore Road. If that's full, there's a small-craft launch on West Shore Road. The Cuba Lake Bass Tournament is held every opening day. The state publishes a free *Cuba Lake Fishing Guide and Map.*

Contact: New York State Department of Environmental Conservation Region 9 and Allegany County Tourism.

81. Rushford Lake *(see map on page 147)*

Key species: Rainbow trout, brown trout, smallmouth bass, and walleye.

Description: Built in 1929 by Rochester Gas and Electric, this 585-acre lake has an average depth of 50 feet and a maximum depth of 115 feet. Owned by an association of lakefront property owners who bought it in 1981, the lake is drawn down 15 to 20 feet in winter.

Tips: In the early season cast Panther Martin spinners in brown-and-yellow combinations parallel to the shoreline for both species of trout.

The fishing: Normally this place is stocked annually with about 3,400 9-inch rainbows, 2,800 browns averaging 9.5 inches, and 300 two-year-old browns over 13 inches. In 2002 the state threw in an additional 40,000 brown trout fry. Difficult to reach in the deep water, quite a few grow to the ripe old age of 20-something inches. Deep-trolling with ThunderSticks and silver Dardevles is productive in summer. The lake's steep drop-offs are super smallmouth bass habitat, and fish in the 14- to 16-inch range are plentiful. Drifting with crayfish and live minnows always seems to work. Walleyes aren't very numerous, but they grow huge. Eight- to 10-pound fish are taken regularly. They respond best during periods of low light and at night to minnow-imitating crankbaits such as Mann's Wally-Tracs and Loudmouth jerkbaits worked parallel to shore and to worms drifted on harnesses or trolled on spinner rigs.

Trout season runs from April 1 to November 30. Ice fishing is prohibited.

Directions: From the village of Cuba (see directions to site 80), head north on NY 305 for about 11 miles, turn north on NY 19 for 4.5 miles, then turn west on NY 243. Continue for 3 miles and turn south on Balcom Beach Road.

Additional information: Rushford Lake Recreation District offers a boat launch with parking for ten rigs on Balcom Beach Road. Only fishing boats are allowed to launch free—everyone else is charged a fee. Shore-fishing access is at the end of Dam Road, off NY 243, less than 1 mile east of the launch. Primitive camping is allowed in Rush Creek State Forest, across CR 49, on the south end of the lake.

Contact: New York State Department of Environmental Conservation Region 9 and Allegany County Tourism.

82. Allen Lake

Key species: Brown trout, brook trout, rainbow trout, and largemouth bass.

Description: Covering 58 acres, averaging 8 feet deep, and dropping to a maximum depth of 19 feet, this man-made lake is located in the northeastern corner of the 2,421-acre Allen Lake State Forest.

Tips: Still-fish a scented floating trout bait about 18 inches off bottom.

The fishing: State fisheries biologist Joe Evans says, "Historically this lake was managed as a trout fishery. That idea was shelved when it was realized the habitat was more suited for warm-water species." Largemouth bass were stocked in 1995 to control runaway populations of panfish, which grew to such numbers, they were stunted. Still, trout proved very popular and are now stocked on a put-and-take basis. In 2002 the lake got roughly 2,000 brookies and 2,600 rainbows averaging 9 inches. In addition, 180 brookies averaging 15 inches and 120 19.5-inchers were released. Most of these fish are caught early in the season on worms, minnows, and commercial trout baits. The largemouth bass do well, ranging from 12 to 22 inches. They take crankbaits, spinnerbaits, and bass bugs.

Allen Lake

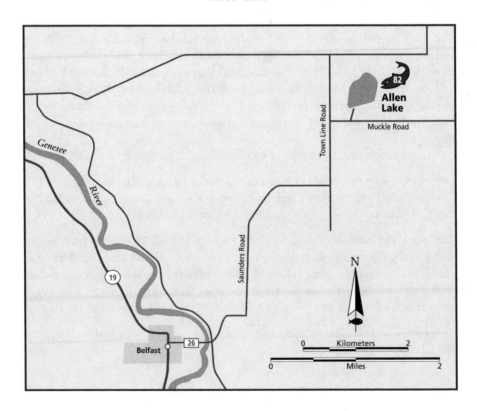

Trout can be taken year-round. The minimum size for bass is 15 inches, and the daily limit is three.

Directions: Take CR 26 east out of Belfast for about 0.25 mile and turn north on Saunders Road. Continue for about 1.5 miles and turn left on Town Line Road. Proceed for roughly 0.5 mile, turn right on Muckle Road (Vincent Hill Road), then turn left a couple hundred yards later on the gravel road.

Additional information: A cartop launch, parking for five cars, and a privy are at the end of the dirt road. Gas motors are not allowed. Camping is prohibited around the lake but is allowed in the state forest south of Muckle Road and west of Town Line Road. The state publishes a free map of the area.

Contact: New York State Department of Environmental Conservation Region 9.

83. East Branch Cazenovia Creek

Key species: Brown trout.

Description: This scenic stream flows north for about 12 miles and joins the West Branch to form the main stem of Cazenovia Creek in East Aurora.

East Branch Cazenovia Creek

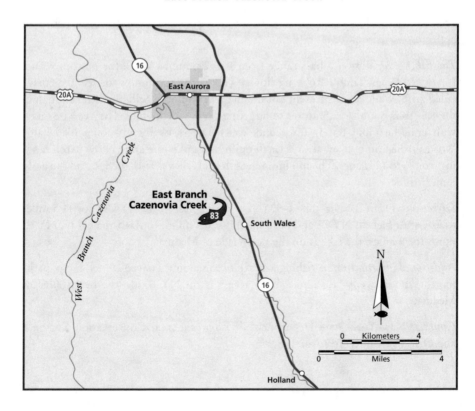

Tips: Cast 1- and 2-inch Exude Curly Tail Grubs upstream in riffles and runs, then reel them back as fast as you can.

The fishing: The state annually stocks the roughly 7-mile stretch from South Wales to Holland with about 4,250 brown trout averaging 9 inches and 300 14-inch two-year-olds. They respond to worms, minnows, nymphs, and in-line spinners.

Directions: NY 16 parallels the stream.

Additional information: The state doesn't own any public fishing rights to this stream. Landowners are mainly fisher-friendly, however, and posted signs are rare along its length. Locals access the stream from the shoulder or at bridges.

Contact: New York State Department of Environmental Conservation Region 9 and Buffalo Niagara Convention and Visitors Bureau.

84. Glenwood Lake

Key species: Smallmouth bass, walleye, yellow perch, white perch, and brown bullhead.

Description: This power reservoir is fed and drained by Oak Orchard Creek. It covers 93 acres, averages 25 feet deep, and has a maximum depth of 46 feet. Its bank is largely lined with ragged boulders.

Tips: In May walleyes hang out near shore and can be caught with worms fished on bottom.

The fishing: Smallmouth bass range from 1 to 2 pounds. Work the bottom with a Lindy No-Snagg Timb'r Rock Jig tipped with a worm, minnow, or scented curly-tailed grub. Walleyes are present but not in great numbers. Still, there are enough in the 1.5- to 3-pound range to make targeting them worthwhile. They can be taken with crankbits like Rat-L-Traps and Wally Divers or by yo-yoing bladebaits. Worms fished on bottom always catch bullheads and white and yellow perch ranging from 6 to 12 inches. The minimum length for walleyes is 18 inches, and the daily limit is three.

Directions: From Batavia, take I–90 (New York State Thruway) west for 11.5 miles to exit 48A. Get on NY 77 and head north for 6.5 miles. In Alabama get on NY 63 north for 9 miles; the lake is on the north side of Medina.

Additional information: A fishing access site containing a paved launch ramp, parking for about twenty rigs, and shore access is on NY 63 on the north edge of Medina.

Contact: New York State Department of Environmental Conservation Region 8 and Orleans County Tourism.

Glenwood Lake · Waterport Pond (Lake Alice)

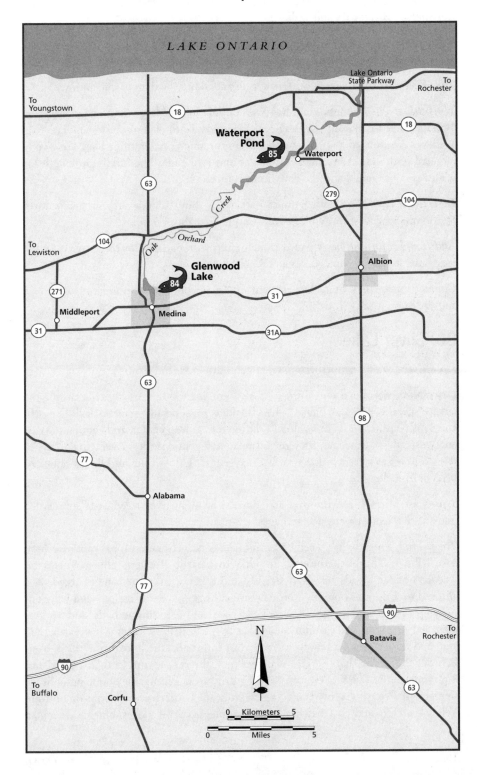

85. Waterport Pond (Lake Alice) *(see map on page 157)*

Key species: Black bass and walleye.

Description: This reservoir is fed and drained by Oak Orchard Creek. Covering 125 acres, it averages 30 feet deep and drops to a maximum of 60 feet.

Tips: Fish near the river's mouth in spring and along the dam in midsummer.

The fishing: The impoundment has good populations of largemouth bass averaging 3 pounds and smallmouths averaging 1.5 pounds. Both take minnows and crayfish. Walleyes are stocked annually by the local sportsmen's federation. They are mostly targeted with crankbaits such as Rapalas and Red Fins. The minimum length for walleyes is 18 inches, and the daily limit is three.

Directions: Take NY 98 north out of Batavia for about 17 miles. About 1 mile north of Albion, bear west on NY 279 and continue for about 5 miles.

Additional information: A paved launch ramp with parking for three rigs is on the west side, just after you cross the NY 279 bridge.

Contact: New York State Department of Environmental Conservation Region 8 and Orleans County Tourism.

86. Silver Lake

Key species: Walleye, northern pike, largemouth bass, and panfish.

Description: Scrubbed out of the hills of Wyoming County by a glacier during the last ice age, this 836-acre banana-shaped lake is wonderfully symmetrical. Its north and south basins are shallow, slowly sliding into a deep center, and though the east and west sides are steeper, they're still relatively gentle slopes. Averaging about 20 feet deep, it has a trench that's 35 feet deep running down the middle for about 70 percent of its length.

Tips: Cast MirrOlure Minnows and Rapalas at night over weed beds submerged under 2 to 6 feet of water for walleyes.

The fishing: Ringed with weed beds, this lake is rich largemouth bass and northern pike habitat. The bucketmouths respond to Charlie Brewer's Slider Worms on weedless Slider Heads retrieved steadily and quickly over the tops of weeds and allowed to drop into openings. Northerns get huge—over 36 inches—and hang out in deep weeds and along their edges. They ambush spinnerbaits and spoons retrieved in a stop-and-go motion so that they alternately swim a few yards then stop and flutter down a few feet. Keep your fingers on the line during the descent in order to feel the slightest tap. Walleyes typically range from 15 to 23 inches, but 8-pounders are available. Go for them by drifting worm rigs or bouncing jigheads tipped with live bait, scented curly-tailed grubs, or 4-inch finesse worms on bottom. Yellow perch from 7 to 10 inches, black crappies up to 14 inches, bluegills from 0.3

Silver Lake · Wiscoy Creek · East Koy Creek

to 0.75 pound, and bullheads averaging 10 inches are plentiful. In summer the crappies and perch hit minnows and spinner-rigged jigheads tipped with 2-inch scented curly-tailed grubs and tubes. The sunfish like worms and poppers, and the bullheads take worms. In winter the crappies and perch like minnows and grubs, and the sunfish go for grubs.

Directions: Head west on US 20A out of Geneseo for about 6 miles. Turn southwest on NY 39 and travel about 4 miles to the hamlet of Perry, which brushes the northeast shore.

Additional information: From July through September oxygen levels in depths below 20 feet are too low to support fish. Silver Lake State Park, off West Lake Road on the south shore, has a fishing access site with a concrete ramp, parking for forty rigs, and toilets. Camping is not allowed in the park, but Letchworth State Park, only 3 miles east, has several campgrounds (see site 91). The state publishes a free *Silver Lake Fishing Guide and Map.*

Contact: New York State Department of Environmental Conservation Region 9 and Wyoming County Tourism Promotion Agency.

87. Wiscoy Creek *(see map on page 159)*

Key species: Brown trout and brook trout.

Description: This tributary of the Genesee River flows through gently rolling countryside crowned with a patchwork of forests and farms. Steeped in the sounds and beauty of nature, Wiscoy Creek is the ideal location for peaceful solitude, broken periodically by exciting encounters with wild trout.

Tips: Green drake spinners are effective in late May and early June.

The fishing: Cutting through fertile, well-aerated soil and kept at comfortable temperatures by numerous springs, this is one of the state's most productive wild trout streams. Joe Evans, a state fisheries biologist, says, "On average there's 150 pounds of wild brown trout per surface acre of water." Furthermore, Evans claims, "The stream hasn't been stocked in over twenty years, and the fishing keeps getting better every year." The minimum length for trout is 10 inches, and the daily limit is three.

Directions: The stream is paralleled by NY 39 and NY 19.

Additional information: The stretch 0.5 mile upstream and 0.5 mile downstream of the East Hill Road bridge (off NY 39, about 0.5 mile east of Bliss) is a no-kill/artificial-lures-only section that is open year-round. There are no public campgrounds on the stream, but several private campgrounds are nearby.

Contact: New York State Department of Environmental Conservation Region 9 and Wyoming County Tourism Promotion Agency.

87A. Beardsley Park Rest Area Public Access

Description: Parking for about ten cars right on the stream.

Directions: On NY 39, about 2 miles west of the hamlet of Pike.

87B. Main Street Public Access

Description: Street parking with access to the stream.

Directions: Main Street (NY 19) runs through the heart of Pike. Access is by the library.

87C. East Koy Road Public Access

Description: This road has four marked public access points for the 2 miles it skirts the creek.

Directions: East Koy Road heads east off NY 19 in the village of Pike.

88. East Koy Creek *(see map on page 159)*

Key species: Brown trout.

Description: This large stream runs through farmland and woods and feeds Wiscoy Creek.

Tips: Work streamers in the heads and tails of spring pools at night, all summer long, for brown trout ranging from 14 to 20 inches.

The fishing: Unlike the Wiscoy, the East Koy depends on runoff to cool it off after summer's heat spells. As a result, much of it isn't capable of holding trout year-round. The state compensates for warm-weather casualties by stocking over 10,000 brown trout each spring—1,200 of them 13 inches or better. Still, large brown trout exist in spring holes, and smaller fish move into nearby pocket water and runs. With nothing in much of the creek during summer to feed on its minnows, crayfish, and abundant insects, an abundance of food sweeps into its patches of cold spots, thus the East Koy contains more large trout gallon per gallon than comparably sized streams with more suitable habitat.

Directions: Shearing Road parallels the stream southeast of Hermitage to Gainesville, and Lamont Road parallels it for most of its length downstream of Gainesville.

Contact: New York State Department of Environmental Conservation Region 9 and Wyoming County Tourism Promotion Agency.

88A. Public Access

Description: Parking for about five cars.

Directions: NY 78 bridge in Hermitage.

88B. Public Access *(see map on page 159)*

Description: Parking for about five cars.

Directions: Hardy's Road (Lincoln Avenue) bridge, southeast of NY 78, in Hermitage.

88C. Public Access *(see map on page 159)*

Description: Parking for about five cars.

Directions: Head east on NY 78 out of Hermitage for about 1 mile, then go south on Green Bay Road for about 0.5 mile.

88D. Public Access *(see map on page 159)*

Description: Roadside parking and access along railroad tracks up to NY 19.

Directions: Head south from the Green Bay Road access (site 88C) for about 0.5 mile, then go east on Shearing Road.

88E. Public Access *(see map on page 159)*

Description: Fishing access just north of the village of Lamont with parking for about ten cars.

Directions: Head north out of Lamont on Lamont Road for about 0.5 mile and turn east onto Murphy Road.

89. Oatka Creek

Key species: Brown trout.

Description: From its source in the gentle hills just south of the village of Wyoming, this freestone stream winds for about 25 miles, slicing through pastures, agricultural fields, and woodlots in three counties before feeding the Genesee River near Scottsville.

Tips: Light cahills at dusk catch trout all summer long.

The fishing: The state annually stocks almost 10,000 browns averaging 9 inches and 1,600 two-year-olds ranging from 12 to 15 inches. They are mostly taken on worms and salted minnows early in the season and on flies in summer and autumn.

Directions: The Oatka Trail and NY 383 parallel the stretch containing some of the best trout water and most of the easily accessible public fishing rights.

Additional information: Trout fishing in the Genesee County portion of this creek is permitted year-round. The state and Brite Fox Flyfishers publish a free pamphlet titled *Oatka Creek Fishing Facts.*

Oatka Creek

Contact: New York State Department of Environmental Conservation Region 8 and Genesee County Chamber of Commerce.

89A. Public Access *(see map on page 163)*

Description: This site offers parking for five cars.

Directions: On the Oatka Trail, about 1 mile east of Fort Hill.

89B. Oatka Creek Park *(see map on page 163)*

Description: This Monroe County park offers access to the 1.7-mile-long special section set aside for catch-and-release fishing with artificial lures only.

Directions: Take NY 383 west for about 2 miles out of Scottsville and turn south on Union Street in the hamlet of Garbutt.

89C. Public Access *(see map on page 163)*

Description: Shoulder parking and access to the creek.

Directions: Head south on Union Street from site 89B for 0.5 mile, turn on Stewart Road, and travel about 1 mile.

90. Beaver Lake (Alma Pond)

Key species: Largemouth bass, northern pike, bluegill, and brown bullhead.

Description: An old beaver pond on which someone built a permanent dam, this exceptionally scenic 50-acre impoundment averages 4 feet deep and has a maximum depth of 7 feet.

Tips: Much of this pond suffers oxygen depletion in late summer.

The fishing: Largemouth bass average about 2.5 pounds, but fish more than twice that size are taken each year. Walk-the-dog-type lures, weightless worms ripped across the surface, and finesse worms hooked on a jig and bounced or dragged on bottom work equally well. Northern pike can reach up to 36 inches and take minnows and spinnerbaits. This is a popular site for local families to bring the kids for a day of worm-fishing for bluegills and brown bullheads. Palm-size sunfish are common, and bullheads can reach 14 inches.

Directions: Head south out of Wellsville on NY 19 for about 5 miles, turn west on CR 29 and travel for 2.5 miles, then turn west on CR 38 (Four Mile Road) and continue for 2 miles.

Additional information: The state's beach launch on CR 38 has parking for five cars.

Contact: New York State Department of Environmental Conservation Region 9.

Beaver Lake (Alma Pond)

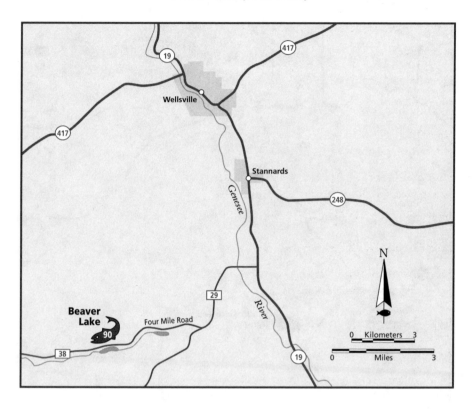

91. Upper Genesee River *(see maps on pages 166 and 167)*

Key species: Brown trout, rainbow trout, smallmouth bass, northern pike, walleye, bluegill, rock bass, and bullhead.

Description: The size of a large trout stream, this stretch of the river runs north for over 100 miles, from Pennsylvania to its lower falls in Rochester.

Tips: In May fish whole night crawlers on bottom for walleye.

The fishing: This stream is mostly known for its cold water stretching from the Pennsylvania border downstream for about 16 miles to the Belmont Dam. Each year the state stocks about 5,400 rainbows averaging 9 inches, 20,000 browns averaging 8.5 inches, and about 2,500 two-year-old browns averaging 13.5 inches into this stretch. Worms, salted minnows, and small spoons and spinners catch most fish early in the season, while flies work best in summer.

The vast majority of the river is warm-water habitat, populated primarily by smallmouths ranging from too small to 16 inches. Fly fishers target them with

Upper Genesee River: Shongo to Letchworth State Park

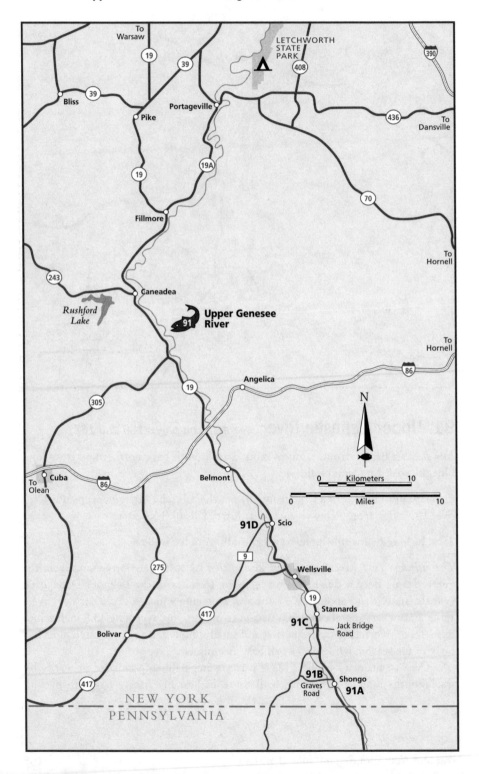

Upper Genesee River: Letchworth State Park to Rochester

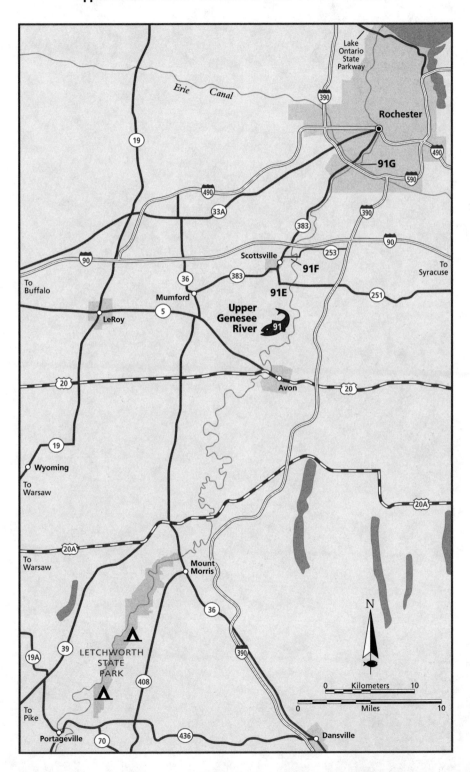

*Upper Genesee River in
Letchworth State Park (site 91).*

streamers, poppers, and flies (dry, wet, nymphs, worm and crayfish imitations). Walleyes ranging from 15 to 22 inches and northerns up to 28 inches are available from Mount Morris to Rochester, and they hit jigs and crankbaits. Bluegills and rock bass averaging 7 inches and bullheads up to 12 inches respond to worms.

Directions: Heading north from the Pennsylvania border, NY 19, NY 19A, NY 39, and NY 383 parallel the river, respectively.

Additional information: From Portageville to Mount Morris, the river flows through 18-mile-long Letchworth State Park, whose cliffs tower 500 feet above the water. This fee area offers 270 campsites with electricity, 82 cabins (18 winterized), a fully furnished three-bedroom lodge, 3 waterfalls, hiking trails, playgrounds, and hot showers.

Contact: New York State Department of Environmental Conservation Regions 8 and 9, Allegany County Tourism, Wyoming County Tourism Promotion Agency, Livingston County Chamber of Commerce, and Greater Rochester Visitors Association.

91A. Public Access *(see map on page 166)*

Description: This site has parking for ten cars and marks the beginning of the special 2.5-mile-long catch-and-release/artificial-lures-only section that's open year-round for trout fishing.

Directions: At the NY 19 bridge in the hamlet of Shongo.

91B. Public Access *(see map on page 166)*

Description: Parking for five cars.

Directions: Take NY 19 for about 0.5 mile north of Shongo and turn west on Graves Road.

91C. Public Access *(see map on page 166)*

Description: Parking for five cars.

Directions: On Jack Bridge Road, 0.5 mile south of the hamlet of Stannards.

91D. Public Access *(see map on page 166)*

Description: Parking for five cars.

Directions: Knight Creek Road bridge (CR 9) in Scio.

91E. Public Access *(see map on page 167)*

Description: This site has a launch for cartop craft and parking for seven cars.

Directions: Take NY 251 south out of Scottsville for 2 miles.

91F. Browns Bridge Public Access *(see map on page 167)*

Description: This site has a launch for cartop craft and parking for twelve cars.

Directions: On NY 253, about 1 mile east of Scottsville.

91G. Genesee Valley Park *(see map on page 167)*

Description: The river crosses the Erie Canal here. Fairly wide, murky, and running with a steady current, it can get pretty fast and dangerous, especially when swollen with snowmelt and after a heavy rain. A dam downstream at the I–490 bridge makes this the last part of the upper river that is navigable. The park rents canoes on weekends in summer. A pedestrian bridge crosses the river, and there is shore-fishing access on both sides. The park has picnic facilities, shelters, rest rooms, and several parking lots.

The fishing: This stretch teems with smallmouth bass averaging 13 inches, which provide moderately thrilling action for anglers casting Dardevles and Rooster Tails. Northern pike ranging from 18 to 25 inches and walleyes running from 1 to 3 pounds readily take jigs tipped with 3-inch scented grubs fished plain or rigged on spinner forms and worked deep. Sunfish and rock bass running from 4 to 7 inches and bullheads averaging 1 pound are enthusiastically targeted by urban kids fishing from shore with worms.

Directions: Off Scottsville Road (NY 383) in Rochester.

FINGER LAKES REGION

ccording to Iroquois legend, the Finger Lakes were created when the great spirit Manitou held the Earth to bless it. His benediction was so passionate, the squeeze so intense, that when he let go, eleven lakes were etched into the heart of Iroquois League (the Seneca, Cayuga, Onondaga, Oneida, Mohawk, and Tuscarora tribes) territory. Today the region is famed worldwide for its splendid wines, rolling hills, scenic glens, 1,000 waterfalls, and clear, cool lakes.

While many lakes are in this area, only eleven are considered true Finger Lakes: Conesus, Hemlock, Canadice, Honeoye, Canandaigua, Keuka, Seneca, Cayuga, Owasco, Skaneateles, and Otisco. These are governed by special fishing regulations, including an extended catch-and-release bass season in some. Check the special Finger Lakes regulations in the state's *Fishing Regulations Guide*.

Besides the Finger Lakes regulations, a special daily limit for trout applies to all waters in New York State Department of Environmental Conservation Regions 7 and 8. Of the five trout allowed, only two can be 12 inches or longer. An additional five brook trout less than 8 inches long can be kept daily as well.

92. Conesus Lake (see map on page 172)

Key species: Black bass, northern pike, walleye, tiger muskie, black crappie, yellow perch, sunfish, and brown bullhead.

Description: The westernmost Finger Lake, 3,420-acre Conesus Lake averages 40 feet deep and has a maximum depth of 66 feet.

Tips: Cast jig-'n'-pigs into weed openings, slop, and timber for bucketmouths.

The fishing: This lake is a terrific warm-water fishery. The shallow, weedy areas are loaded with largemouth bass in the 2- to 4-pound range, and 5-pounders are common. Early in the morning and evening, when the wind is down, work surface baits like Jitterbugs and floating/diving crankbaits like Slapsticks for what one native describes as "bass with mouths the size of miniature steam shovels." When the lake is rough, work spinnerbaits tipped with YUM Houdini Worms along weed edges and breaks. Schools of smallmouths hang out on the drop-offs. Ranging from 1.5 to 3 pounds, they respond to ⅛- and ¼-ounce bucktail jigs—fished plain or tipped with minnows—bounced or dragged on bottom in 10 to 20 feet of water. The state annually stocks around 9,500 9-inch norlunge. Most of these tigers end up ranging from 8 to 10 pounds and are caught regularly on large bucktail spinners. The lake is famous for monster northern pike in the 15-pound category. Most are caught in autumn on large minnows and by trolling or casting large red-and-white Dardevles and crankbaits like MirrOlure Lipped 52Ms.

Conesus Lake · Hemlock Lake · Canadice Lake · Honeoye Lake

Walleyes were the local favorite until alewives almost wiped them out in the 1980s by feeding on their fry. (Ironically, according to popular theory, the alewives were introduced illegally by anglers as forage for the walleyes.) The state wants them back and is intervening on a massive scale—first by stocking tiger muskies, a species with a taste for sawbellies (the local name for alewives), and following through a few years later by releasing great quantities of walleyes. For example, in 2002 the numbers were 65,000 walleye fry and 32,500 5-inchers. The program seems to be paying off. "Eyes" in the 2- to 5-pound range are plentiful enough to attract a following, who goes after them by trolling worms on spinner harnesses and by drifting worms, minnows, or leeches. Yellow perch and black crappies running up to 12 inches are targeted primarily by ice anglers using minnows or tiny jigs baited with grubs. Bluegills and pumpkinseeds generally go from 0.3 to 0.75 pound and are also caught through the ice on grubs and in summer on worms and wet flies. After ice-out bullheads up to 14 inches swarm into the southern basin and are caught on worms fished on bottom.

Directions: Head east out of Geneseo on US 20A for about 5 miles.

Additional information: In summer oxygen levels in depths below 35 feet are too low to support fish. Ice-fishing shelters are prohibited. The state publishes a free brochure containing fishing tips and a map.

Contact: New York State Department of Environmental Conservation Region 8 and Finger Lakes Visitors Connection.

92A. Vitale Park

Description: This community park is great for launching cartop craft and has parking for forty-five cars and about 1,000 yards of shore-fishing access on the lake and both sides of the outlet—the west side is accessible via a pedestrian bridge.

Directions: On US 20A in the north shore village of Lakeville.

Additional information: Vitale Park has picnic areas, gazebos, a group shelter, heated rest rooms, and a playground.

92B. Pebble Beach Public Access

Description: Cartop launch and parking for 120 cars.

Directions: On Pebble Beach Road at the northwest corner of the lake.

92C. Conesus Lake Boat Launch

Description: This site offers a hard-surface ramp and parking for about forty-five rigs.

Directions: Head south out of Lakeville on East Lake Road for 4 miles.

92D. Conesus Inlet Public Access *(see map on page 172)*

Description: This site has a hard-surface ramp (for cartop craft only), parking for forty cars, and a couple hundred feet of shore-fishing access.

Directions: Off NY 256 on the south end of the lake.

Additional information: Fishing is prohibited in part of the inlet from March 1 to the first Saturday in May to protect spawning walleyes and northerns. The restricted area stretches from the lake south to the dam but, according to the state fishing guide, doesn't include "the canal west of Conesus Inlet and that portion of the inlet north of the canal; North McMillian Creek."

93. Hemlock Lake *(see map on page 172)*

Key species: Lake trout, rainbow trout, brown trout, landlocked Atlantic salmon, black bass, chain pickerel, yellow perch, and black crappie.

Description: Set in the gently rolling hills south of Rochester, this 1,800-acre lake is an integral part of the city's water supply and remains totally undeveloped. Seven miles long, it averages 40 feet deep and has a maximum depth of 91 feet.

Tips: Work surface lures over submerged weed beds and along weed edges for monster pickerel.

The fishing: While some natural reproduction takes place, this lake's splendid salmonid fishery is maintained through massive state intervention. Every year roughly 3,200 9-inch lake trout and 8,200 averaging 6 inches are stocked. They grow rapidly to range from 5 to 8 pounds on the habitat's abundant smelt and alewives and are commonly targeted by trolling flutter spoons through the thermocline and by jigging spoons on bottom. Another popular laker technique is to hang a lantern over the side of the boat at night and fish live minnows below slip bobbers about 40 feet deep. Two thousand six-inch rainbows and 5,000 9-inch browns are stocked annually, too. They end up averaging 3 pounds and hit minnows and their imitations. Finally, 4,100 landlocked salmon running about 6.5 inches are released each year. They end up averaging 18 inches and are taken by flatlining Bomber Long "A"s near shore off planer boards in early spring and by trolling spoons through the thermocline in summer. The rainbows and salmon like a fast-moving bait, so crank up your engine speed a couple notches, especially in the summer. Many trout and salmon are also taken with minnows fished deep with slip bobbers.

Smallmouths range from 1 to 3 pounds and hang out along drop-offs, where they can't seem to resist a salted or scented tube dragged on bottom. A small number of largemouth bass in the 2- to 4-pound range rule the south tip of the lake and its weed lines. Fish for them with Texas-rigged worms and surface plugs. Pickerel grow to over 30 inches. They love fast-moving Dardevles, Rooster Tails, and soft rubber worms and jerkbaits ripped over windfalls and weed beds and along weed edges. While most ice anglers go for trout, many rig a tip-up or two for black crappies and yellow perch.

Stretching up to 12 inches or better, these delicious panfish hit minnows, grubs, and Swedish Pimples tipped with a perch eye or spike.

Directions: Head south out of the hamlet of Lima on NY 15A for about 9 miles.

Additional information: Recreational activity on this lake is limited to fishing and boating by permit. Permits can be obtained from the self-service kiosk in Hemlock Lake Park, on the north end of the lake off NY 15A (see site 93A), or can be downloaded on-line at www.cityofrochester.gov/watershedpermit.htm. Boats may not exceed 16 feet in length or be powered by motors greater than ten horsepower. The state publishes a free brochure containing fishing information and a map.

Contact: New York State Department of Environmental Conservation Region 8 and Finger Lakes Visitors Connection.

93A. Public Access

Description: This site offers a gravel launch and parking for twenty rigs.

Directions: Head south out of the hamlet of Hemlock on NY 15A for about 1 mile, turn right on Rix Hill Road, then immediately left on Boat Launch Road and travel 1.2 miles.

Additional information: Boat Launch Road is mostly unpaved and gets sloppy and slippery in the spring. The self-service kiosk containing access permits is about 100 yards down Rix Hill Road. Access to the waters north of the launch, for any reason, is prohibited.

93B. Public Access

Description: This site has a hard-surface launch and shoulder parking.

Directions: Off NY 15A on the south end of the lake.

94. Canadice Lake *(see map on page 172)*

Key species: Lake trout, brown trout, rainbow trout, black bass, chain pickerel, and panfish.

Description: Covering 649 acres, averaging 50 feet deep, and dropping to a maximum of 95 feet deep, this is the smallest Finger Lake. Its shoreline is undeveloped.

Tips: Fish live minnows directly on bottom in water 5- to 15-feet deep for rainbows and browns in the spring and fall. Use a slip sinker and allow the trout to run a few feet before setting the hook.

The fishing: The cold-water fishery is completely maintained with annual stockings of three trout species. The numbers are 5,100 lakers averaging 8 inches, 2,500 9-inch browns, and 2,500 rainbows averaging 8.5 inches. Occasionally surplus landlocked Atlantic salmon from a nearby hatchery are thrown in for diversity. The trout range from too small to keep to decent 20-plus-inchers. Lakers are taken by trolling silver spoons like Dardevles and Suttons on Seth Green rigs. Browns and rainbows are taken by trolling the same spoons over deep water above the thermocline. Landlocked salmon will take the spoons, too, but respond best to flatlined streamers.

Smallmouth bass ranging from 0.5 to 2 pounds are abundant and are taken on minnows and crayfish worked 15 to 20 feet deep. Largemouths go between 12 and 18 inches. They like spinnerbaits, jerkbaits, and top-water lures worked above submerged vegetation and through emergent vegetation and timber. Chain pickerel in the 15- to 25-inch range are plentiful and react violently to Cabela's Livin' Eye Glass Minnows jerked around vegetation, Bill Lewis' Slapsticks worked on the surface, and worms swum on spinner harnesses. Still-fishing with worms for bullheads running up to 2 pounds is a rite of spring among locals. Bluegills and pumpkinseeds ranging from 6 to 10 inches and yellow perch up to 14 inches are popularly targeted by ice anglers jigging with grubs.

Directions: Head south out of Lima on NY 15A for about 12.5 miles, turn east on Purcell Hill Road and travel 1.3 miles, then turn south on Canadice Lake Road and continue for 1.4 miles.

Additional information: A public access site on Canadice Lake Road has a hard-surface gravel launch—park on the shoulder of Canadice Lake Road. The maximum length for boats is 16 feet, and motors cannot exceed ten horsepower. You need a permit to fish this lake. They are available for free at the self-service kiosk in Hemlock Lake Park, on the north end of neighboring Hemlock Lake (take NY 15A to Rix Hill Road).

Contact: New York State Department of Environmental Conservation Region 8 and Finger Lakes Visitors Connection.

95. Honeoye Lake (see map on page 172)

Key species: Walleye, chain pickerel, black bass, black crappie, yellow perch, rock bass, and sunfish.

Description: Named after the Iroquois word for "finger lying," this 1,772-acre lake averages 13 feet deep and has a maximum depth of 30 feet. Its banks are lined with private residences.

Tips: Work Road Runners in the southern basin for black crappies.

The fishing: An above average warm-water fishery, Honeoye has good populations of largemouths running from 2 to 4 pounds and smallmouths ranging from 1.5 to 3 pounds. The lake is the preferred practice site of Rochester-area pros honing their bass-fishing techniques. The fish get stuck so often, they develop a savvy that's legendary in these parts. Still, largemouths can be fooled with YUM Samurai Shads, jig-'n'-pigs, and worms fished whacky-style. Smallmouths like Carolina-rigged lizards, YUM Shakin' Worms, and YUM Wooly Curltails. The state has stocked millions of walleye fry. Growth is good, and "eyes" ranging from 15 inches to 8 pounds are available. They hit leeches, crankbaits such as C.C. Shads and Bomber Long "A"s, and worms trolled and drifted on harnesses, plain or spinner-rigged. This is the only Finger Lake where the minimum length for walleyes is 15 inches.

Locals count on pickerel ranging from 15 to 25 inches to save the day when largemouths have lockjaw. They'll hit anything bite-sized that's worked quickly in shallow, weedy areas, especially worms on spinner harnesses and Slug-Gos. Yellow perch and crappies running up to 14 inches, rock bass averaging 8 inches, and bluegills and pumpkinseeds between 6 and 10 inches are plentiful. In summer the perch, rock bass, and crappies like 2-inch curly-tailed grubs, small crankbaits, and spinnerbaits. The sunnies like worms. These panfish are actively targeted through the ice with live grubs.

This is the only Finger Lake where the minimum length for walleyes is 15 inches.

Directions: Take CR 36 for about 12 miles north of the village of Naples.

Contact: New York State Department of Environmental Conservation Region 8 and Finger Lakes Visitors Connection.

95A. Sandy Bottom Beach

Description: This site has a beach launch suitable for small trailered craft and parking for six cars, along with street parking. It's closed from June 15 to Labor Day.

Directions: On Sandy Bottom Road off CR 36 in Honeoye.

95B. Honeoye Lake Public Boat Launch

Description: This fee area offers a hard-surface ramp and parking for about thirty rigs. A fee is charged mid-April through September. It's plowed in winter for ice anglers.

Directions: Off East Lake Road on the southeast corner of the lake.

96. Naples Creek *(see map on page 179)*

Key species: Rainbow trout.

Description: Canandaigua Lake's major tributary, this stream was world famous for its spring runs of rainbows until Lake Ontario took the limelight in the 1970s.

Tips: The first week of April is most productive.

The fishing: Now that the crowds concentrate on the tiniest Great Lake's tributaries, opening day on Naples Creek is better than ever, offering elbow room and loads of wild rainbow trout in the 2- to 5-pound range. Egg sacs are the most popular bait, but worms, salted minnows, and tiny Rooster Tails also work. The minimum length for trout is 15 inches, and the daily limit is three.

Opening day on Naples Creek (site 96).

Directions: NY 21 parallels much of the creek.

Additional information: Each April 1 the Rotary Club sponsors the Naples Creek Rainbow Trout Derby. The 42nd annual, held in 2003, saw 650 fish brought in, the largest weighing 8 pounds, 4 ounces. Sutton Company, maker of world-famous hand-crafted, Sutton spoons, operates out of a colorful—and smoky—old-time sporting goods store located on the main drag in the village of Naples. The state owns 9.5 miles of public fishing rights on the stream, plus an additional 3 miles on its tributaries: Grimes, Reservoir, and Tannery Creeks.

Contact: New York State Department of Environmental Conservation Region 8 and Finger Lakes Visitors Connection.

96A. Parish Road Public Access

Description: The creek's northernmost access site, the flow here is slow and deep. Parking for about twenty cars.

Directions: Head north on NY 21 for about 2 miles out of Naples and turn right on Parish Road.

Naples Creek · Canandaigua Lake

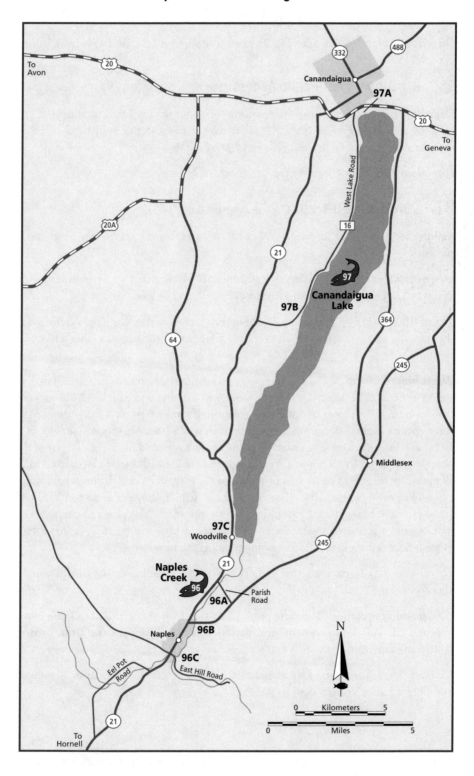

96B. Public Access *(see map on page 179)*

Description: Parking for about twenty-five cars.

Directions: From Naples, take NY 21 north for about a 0.5 mile and turn right on NY 245.

96C. Big Dipper Pool Public Access *(see map on page 179)*

Description: Two access sites, with parking for about ten cars each, at the junction of Reservoir and Naples Creeks. It is so named because the pool used to be a favorite swimming hole in the 1920s and 1930s.

Directions: On Mark Circle on the south side of Naples.

97. Canandaigua Lake *(see map on page 179)*

Key species: Lake trout, brown trout, rainbow trout, black bass, yellow perch, and sunfish.

Description: Set in a high valley, this 10,558-acre lake is just short of 16 miles long, averages 125 feet deep, and has a maximum depth of 276 feet.

Tips: Fish at night by anchoring in about 100 feet of water, hanging a light over the side, and staggering live alewives spaced 8 feet apart, the lowest a couple feet off bottom.

The fishing: Close to Rochester, this place gets pounded heavily. The state annually stocks about 30,000 lake trout ranging from 5 to 9 inches and roughly 8,000 brown trout averaging 9.5 inches. A natural population of rainbow trout is also present. All three species average 3 pounds and take minnows and Sutton spoons (see site 96, additional information). The shallows in the north basin hold numerous largemouth bass ranging from 1 to 5 pounds. Fish for them at night with surface lures like Hula Poppers. Bronzebacks run 1 to 3 pounds and are plentiful along drops, where they respond to diving crankbaits, minnows, and crayfish. Yellow perch up to 12 inches and 0.5-pound bluegills and pumpkinseeds are abundant. The perch like minnows, worms, and streamers in summer and minnows, grubs, and perch eyes in winter. Sunfish hit worms and wet flies in summer and grubs in winter.

Directions: NY 21 parallels the lake. The city of Canandaigua sits on the north shore.

Additional information: The state publishes a free *Canandaigua Lake Guide* containing a lake map and pertinent information. The Canandaigua Lake Trout Derby is held annually during the first full weekend in June.

Contact: New York State Department of Environmental Conservation Region 8 and Finger Lakes Visitors Connection.

97A. Canandaigua Lake State Marine Park

Description: This site offers multiple paved ramps, parking for 110 rigs, toilets, and pump-out facilities. A fee is charged during peak season.

Directions: Off US 20 in Canandaigua.

97B. Onanda Park

Description: This site, open to winter launching only, offers a concrete ramp and parking for twenty-five rigs.

Directions: On West Lake Road (CR 16), 6.5 miles south of Canandaigua.

97C. Woodville Public Access

Description: This site offers a concrete ramp and parking for eighty rigs.

Directions: Off NY 21, 3 miles north of Naples.

98. Cold Brook *(see map on page 182)*

Key species: Rainbow trout, brown trout, and landlocked Atlantic salmon.

Description: Only about 4 miles long, this stream averages 6 feet wide.

Tips: Fish eggs sacs on bottom in April for rainbow trout.

The fishing: This is Keuka Lake's best spawning ground for salmonids. Spring sees runs of rainbows in the 1.5- to 5-pound range. They hit worms and egg sacs. In autumn brown trout up to 15 pounds and landlocked Atlantic salmon ranging from 2 to 5 pounds run the creek and respond to worms and egg-sucking leeches. The minimum length for trout and salmon is 15 inches, and the daily limit is three in any combination.

Directions: NY 54 parallels the stream.

Additional information: The deepest, slowest stretch crawls through Hammondsport.

Contact: New York State Department of Environmental Conservation Region 8 and Steuben County Conference and Visitors Bureau.

98A. Public Access

Description: This informal site has shoulder parking for about ten cars.

The fishing: Although the creek here is too shallow and narrow to hold anything larger than minnows most of the time, it's worth investigating during high water.

Directions: Head south on NY 54 from Hammondsport for about 4 miles, turn right on Hatchery Road, and follow it for 1.5 miles.

Cold Brook · Keuka Lake · Keuka Lake Outlet

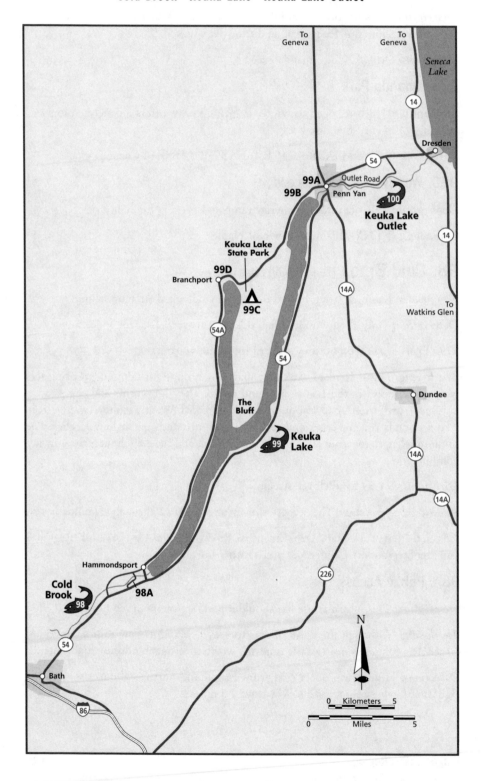

99. Keuka Lake

Key species: Rainbow trout, lake trout, brown trout, landlocked Atlantic salmon, black bass, northern pike, chain pickerel, and yellow perch.

Description: This is the only Finger Lake that is forked, prompting feminists to call it the Lady of the Lakes. Male chauvinist pigs retort Manitou, the great spirit who created the lakes when he held the Earth in blessing, had a double thumb. Whatever. This 11,584-acre lake averages 100 feet deep and has a maximum depth of 183 feet. A bluff spreads its arms—or legs.

Tips: Troll Sutton spoons on Seth Green rigs in the wide water south of the bluff.

The fishing: Keuka's most popular salmonid is its naturally occurring lake trout. Ranging from 3 to 10 pounds, locals go after them the old-fashioned way, with Seth Green rigs (a 20-ounce sinker is used to hold down a main line bearing multiple leaders, spaced about 8 feet apart and baited with spoons or minnows) trolled slowly through 100 feet or so of water. Rainbows are also self-sustaining and run from 1 to 3 pounds. Troll spoons or minnow-imitating crankbaits just above the thermocline. Each year the state stocks about 20,000 brown trout ranging from 4.5 to 9.5 inches, and many survive to average 4 pounds. They are commonly targeted with live minnows fished 30 to 50 feet deep on slip bobbers. Roughly 30,000 Atlantic salmon yearlings are stocked annually as well. They end up averaging 20 inches and respond to crankbaits, metallic silver Rooster Tail spinners, and flatlined streamers, especially around tributary mouths in autumn.

Smallmouth bass in the 1.5- to 3-pound range prowl the breaklines. Spinnerbaits are the favorite local lure, but many are also taken by swimming jigheads tipped with minnows, scented plastic worms, or curly-tailed grubs or by dragging them on bottom. Northerns up to 15 pounds hang out in the relatively shallow north and south ends, where they share range with hawg largemouths weighing up to 6 pounds. Both take minnow-imitating crankbaits, 3- and 4-inch tubes, and jerkbaits. Chain pickerel up to 5 pounds rule the weed lines and clumps clinging to the east and west banks and can be taken on everything from ThunderSticks and white Rooster Tails to Slug-Gos and worms on spinner harnesses. In autumn 8- to 12-inch yellow perch gather off points in 30 to 50 feet of water and hit minnows, jigs, and worms.

Directions: The village of Penn Yan sits on the tip of the northeastern arm. NY 54 parallels the east shore, and NY 54A runs along the west shore.

Additional information: The south shore village of Hammondsport offers hundreds of feet of prime shore-fishing access in the village park on Water Street. U.S. fish commissioner Seth Green, father of American fish culture, felt Keuka Lake was the best fishery in the country. The state publishes a free *Keuka Lake Guide* containing a map and fishing tips.

Contact: New York State Department of Environmental Conservation Region 8 and Yates County Chamber of Commerce.

99A. Village of Penn Yan Public Access *(see map on page 182)*

Description: This site has multiple paved ramps, docks, and parking for 120 rigs.

Directions: Off NY 14A in Penn Yan.

99B. Indian Pines Park *(see map on page 182)*

Description: This site is for ice-fishing access only and has parking for twenty cars.

Directions: Old Pines Trail Road, off NY 54A in Penn Yan.

99C. Keuka Lake State Park *(see map on page 182)*

Description: This 621-acre fee area offers 150 campsites (53 electric), a paved launch ramp with parking for 15 rigs, and 10 docks. The campground is open mid-May through mid-October. Free day use off-season.

Directions: Take NY 54A south out of Penn Yan for about 6 miles.

99D. Guyanoga (Sugar) Creek Public Access *(see map on page 182)*

Description: Located about 250 yards upstream of the mouth of Guyanoga Creek, this site has a gravel launch suitable for small trailered craft and parking for about ten cars.

The fishing: Also called Sugar Creek, this stream gets seasonal runs of trout and salmon.

Directions: At the NY 54A bridge in Branchport.

100. Keuka Lake Outlet *(see map on page 182)*

Key species: Brown trout and rainbow trout.

Description: Formerly called Minnesetah River, this stream starts out mildly in Penn Yan and picks up speed as it drops 300 feet on its 6-mile trek to Seneca Lake.

Tips: In autumn work streamers like egg-sucking leeches for lake-run brown trout.

The fishing: After a hiatus of nearly ten years, the state started annually stocking the stream again in 1999 with about 1,000 browns ranging from 8 to 13.5 inches. However, most anglers go up this creek searching for lake-run fish ranging from 3 to 10 pounds. Seneca Lake browns, mixed with a few landlocked salmon, start running around November and can be found all the way up to Cascade Mills, the first waterfall impassable by fish. Rainbows about the same size run the same stretch in early April. Both species hit worms, egg sacs, streamers, silver Dardevle spoons, and

Father and daughters angling at the Keuka Lake outlet (site 100).

white Rooster Tail spinners. From the mouth to Cascade Mills, the minimum length for salmon and trout is 15 inches, and the daily limit is three in any combination.

Directions: Outlet Road skirts the outlet from Penn Yan for half its length.

Additional information: The Outlet Trail, a footpath built on the old towpath of the Crooked Lake Canal, runs along 95 percent of the stream and is accessible off Penn Yan's Outlet Road. Additional access is in Dresden: behind the ice-cream stand on the northeastern corner of the NY 14 bridge, at the railroad crossing on Seneca Street, and at the bridge in the heart of the village.

Contact: New York State Department of Environmental Conservation Region 8 and Yates County Chamber of Commerce.

101. Catharine Creek *(see map on page 186)*

Key species: Rainbow trout and white sucker.

Description: This creek is Seneca Lake's major tributary and has a long history as a world-class trout stream. Indeed, it was one of the top ten trout streams in the state until Lake Ontario tributaries dethroned it in the 1970s.

Catharine Creek · Seneca Lake

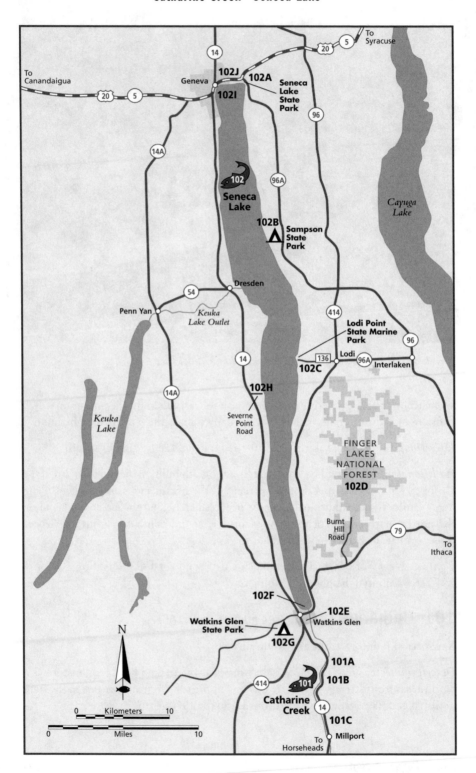

Tips: Fish with streamers and nymphs in late fall.

The fishing: While this creek gets small runs of brown trout and landlocked salmon each fall, its main draw is its runs of wild Seneca Lake rainbows. Spring draws spawners ranging from 2 to 8 pounds. Autumn sees young, restless males in the 2- to 4-pound range ascending in search of salmon and brown trout eggs. They can be found from Watkins Glen to Pine Valley, but the best water is upstream of Montour Falls. Egg sacs, salted minnows, worms, silver Dardevles, and white Rooster Tails all catch fish. White suckers up to 20 inches long swarm into the creek to spawn in May. They hit worms.

Directions: NY 14 parallels the stream.

Additional information: Late in the last century, heavy storms changed this stream's course. Property owners didn't cotton to the modification, and the state sent in bulldozers to put it back in line—and a straight one at that. It'll take years for the channel to look natural again.

Contact: New York State Department of Environmental Conservation Region 8 and Schuyler County Chamber of Commerce.

101A. Public Access

Description: This site has parking for about twenty cars and a portable toilet.

Directions: On NY 14, 3.2 miles south of Watkins Glen.

101B. Public Access

Description: This site has parking for fifteen cars and a portable toilet.

Directions: On NY 14, 4.3 miles south of Watkins Glen.

101C. Public Access

Description: This site has parking for fifteen cars and a portable toilet.

Directions: On NY 14, 6.3 miles south of Watkins Glen.

102. Seneca Lake

Key species: Lake trout, brown trout, rainbow trout, landlocked Atlantic salmon, black bass, northern pike, and yellow perch.

Description: While locals disagree on which is the biggest Finger Lake, Seneca holds the most water, over four trillion gallons. Covering 43,343 acres and up to 3 miles wide and 35 miles long, this lake's average depth is just under 300 feet, and its maximum depth is 618 feet—deep enough for the military to keep a couple of deep-water research barges out in the middle year-round. Half the shoreline is developed and includes the city of Geneva and the village of Watkins Glen, cradle of the

American Grand Prix and current home of the Watkins Glen International of NASCAR fame.

Tips: In spring fish live minnows below slip bobbers or cast spoons from the Watkins Glen pier and adjacent breakwall.

The fishing: Seneca's bread-and-butter fish is lake trout. Around 60,000 ranging from 6.5 to 9 inches are stocked annually. Survival is good, and most make it to between 3 and 6 pounds. You name the technique and it works, from fishing live bait and jigging spoons on cooper line to trolling peanuts (Worden's Wobble Troll) off downriggers and Sutton spoons off Seth Green rigs. The state also releases an equal number of brown trout about the same size. They grow to average 3.5 pounds. About 24,000 6.5-inch Atlantic salmon are stocked yearly as well. They run between 1.5 to 5 pounds. The browns and salmon are mostly caught by flatlining minnow-imitating crankbaits such as Bomber "A"s and MirrOlure Minnows parallel to shore in spring and autumn. In summer both species are targeted by trolling the same lures off downriggers in water ranging from 56 to 59 degrees Fahrenheit. The lake's rainbows are naturally occurring, averaging about 20 inches. In summer most are caught by trolling just above the thermocline at a relatively quick clip. In spring and autumn "bows" gather around the villages of Watkins Glen and Dresden waiting for snowmelt or a good rain to send them into Catharine Creek and Keuka Outlet.

Smallmouth bass in the 16- to 20-inch range can be caught along any steep drop or shelf. Their bait of choice is crayfish, but plastic tubes and grubs also produce. Largemouth bass ranging from 2 to 5 pounds occupy all weedy areas and react violently to any jig-'n'-pig or Texas-rigged worm that kicks mud in their faces. Although the number of 20-pound northern pike has decreased dramatically over the last couple of decades, fish ranging from 6 to 12 pounds are still plentiful. Drift live minnows or cast spinnerbaits anywhere you find weeds. During the heat of summer, troll red-and-white Dardevles and long crankbaits such as Cotton Cordell's Jointed Red Fins a few feet above bottom in 20 to 30 feet of water. This lake is famous for huge yellow perch. Locally called elephant perch, they range from 1 to 2 pounds and like minnows, crayfish, bucktail jigs, and curly-tailed grubs jigged along deep weed edges, especially on the southeastern end of the lake.

Lamprey eels continue to plague the lake. The state keeps them under control by chemically treating Catharine Creek and Keuka Outlet every three years.

Directions: The lake abuts the city of Geneva's east side. NY 14 runs along the west bank of the lake and NY 96A and NY 414 run along the opposite shore.

Additional information: The state publishes a free *Seneca Lake Guide* containing a map and fishing tips. The National Lake Trout Derby is held every Memorial Day weekend. Don't tie off on the military barges out in the middle because men bearing guns may appear.

Contact: New York State Department of Environmental Conservation Region 8, Finger Lakes Visitors Connection, Schuyler County Chamber of Commerce, Seneca County Tourism, and Yates County Chamber of Commerce.

The Watkins Glen Pier (site 102F).

102A. Seneca Lake State Park (see map on page 186)

Description: Located on the northeastern corner of the lake at its outlet, the Seneca River, this fee area offers a paved double-lane ramp, parking for over a hundred rigs, a marina with transient slips, shore-fishing access, picnic facilities, and rest rooms. The park is open year-round, but a day-use fee is charged from May through October.

Directions: Located about 1 mile east of Geneva on US 20/NY 5.

102B. Sampson State Park (see map on page 186)

Description: This 1,852-acre fee area offers a paved four-lane ramp (open year-round), 285 campsites (245 with electricity), a marina with numerous slips, showers, playgrounds, playing fields, a swimming beach, and shore fishing. A day-use fee is charged noncampers from mid-April through October.

Directions: From Geneva, take US 20/NY 5 east for about 2 miles, then head south on NY 96A for about 10 miles.

Additional information: Set on a gentle slope dipping into the eastern shore of Seneca Lake, this park occupies the grounds of the former Samson Naval Station, the country's second largest naval training base during World War II. Now part of the state park system, all that remains of the military presence is a statue dedicated to sailors, a couple decorative naval guns, and a naval museum (open Wednesday through Sunday from Memorial Day through Labor Day).

102C. Lodi Point State Marine Park (see map on page 186)

Description: This fee area offers a four-lane paved ramp, parking for sixty-eight rigs, picnic tables, rest rooms, a few docks, and some dynamite shore-fishing access.

The fishing: The only point for miles around, it draws lake trout (April through June), smallmouth bass (mid-October through November), and yellow perch (autumn and spring) within range of bank anglers.

Directions: From Lodi, take CR 136 west for about 2 miles.

102D. Finger Lakes National Forest (see map on page 186)

Description: Primitive camping is allowed on this 13,232-acre national forest, the only one in the state.

Directions: Head north on NY 414 from Watkins Glen. About 1 mile later, bear east on NY 79 and turn left (north) about 3 miles later onto Burnt Hill Road.

102E. Watkins Glen Boat Launch (see map on page 186)

Description: This fee area is on the canal portion of Catharine Creek and offers a paved ramp and parking for about forty rigs. No fee charged off-season (mid-fall through spring).

*Watkins Glen State Park
(site 102G).*

Directions: On Fourth Street in Watkins Glen.

102F. Watkins Glen Pier *(see map on page 186)*

Description: This pier and its adjacent breakwall are popular shore-fishing sites.

Directions: Located at the interface of downtown Watkins Glen and the lake, at the intersection of NY 14 and Lincoln Drive.

102G. Watkins Glen State Park Wonderland and Campground *(see map on page 186)*

Description: Called the Eighth Wonder of the World by natives, this 1,000-acre fee area is internationally famous for its staircase of waterfalls. It offers 305 campsites, a 50-meter swimming pool, a bathhouse, showers, and miles of developed trails that skirt its spellbinding waterworks and the rim high above. The park is closed in winter.

Directions: Located in downtown Watkins Glen.

102H. Severne Point Public Access *(see map on page 186)*

Description: This site offers a concrete ramp and parking for twelve rigs. It's plowed for winter use.

Directions: Head south from Dresden on NY 14 for 8 miles and turn east on Severne Point Road.

102I. Geneva Lakefront Park *(see map on page 186)*

Description: This site has a paved ramp, parking for fifty rigs, and a breakwall that is popular with shore anglers.

Directions: Off US 20/NY 5 at the Lake Street intersection in Geneva.

102J. Geneva Pier *(see map on page 186)*

Description: This 100-yard-long concrete pier is a popular shore-fishing site. Parking is limited to about six cars, so many anglers park in Lakefront Park (site 102I) and walk over.

The fishing: In spring and fall lakers cruise within casting distance and can be taken with Krocodiles, Cotton Cordell's Red Fins, and live bait.

Directions: Located at the US 20/NY 5 intersection with East Washington Street.

103. Lake Como

Key species: Tiger muskie, largemouth bass, chain pickerel, bluegill, black crappie, yellow perch, and bullhead.

Description: This lake covers 64 acres, averages 15 feet deep, and has a maximum depth of 22 feet. Its shoreline is heavily developed with cottages.

Lake Como · Upper Fall Creek

Branch Road
Lake Como
103
104A
Como Road
104B
Hinman Road
Groton City
Upper Fall Creek
104
Groton City Road
Groton
Homer
Cortland
Freeville
Dryden
Ithaca
Cayuga Lake
38
90
41
41A
81
281
13
222
215
366
392
79
N
0 Kilometers 5
0 Miles 5

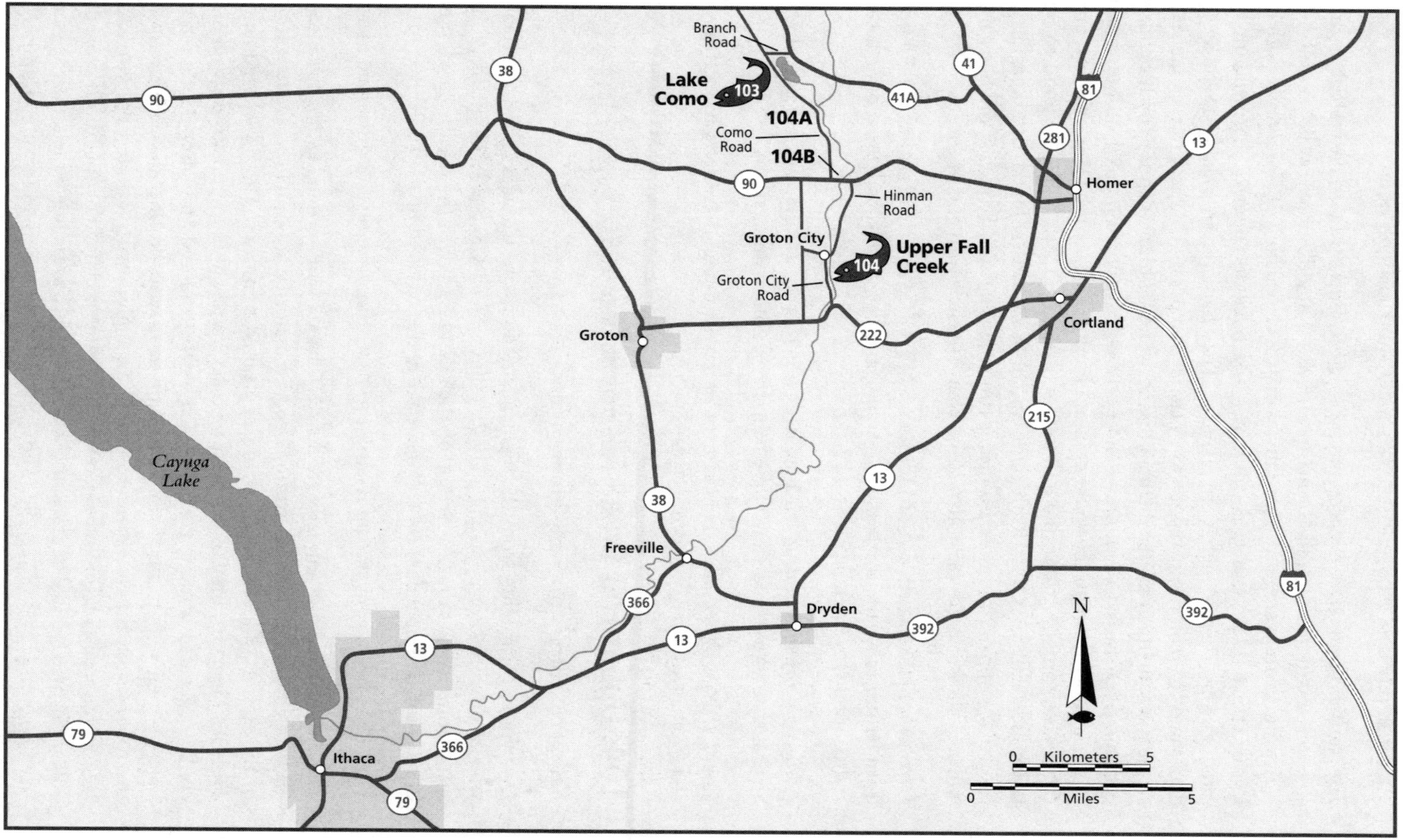

Tips: Fish bite best on overcast days when the boats aren't out.

The fishing: Senior state fisheries biologist Jeff Robins says the lake is stocked annually with a couple hundred 10-inch norlunge. "They do pretty well," says Robins, "growing to an average of 8 pounds, with a few reaching 30-something pounds." Locals target them with large minnows and bucktail spinners. Largemouth bass ranging from 12 to 20 inches are plentiful. They hang out in weed beds and around docks and strike jigs tipped with soft plastics and pork. Pickerel up to 25 inches are so plentiful, many consider them a nuisance. They'll hit just about any lure but are particularly attracted to spinners and curly-tailed grubs bounced on bottom and swum steadily through the water column. Panfish thrive in the lake's shallow areas. Crappies averaging 0.5 pound and yellow perch up to 12 inches respond to minnows and small lures like Beetle Spins and Spot Minnows. Hand-size bluegills prefer grubs, poppers, and flies. Bullheads run between 6 and 14 inches and like garden worms fished at night on bottom, especially on the south end of the lake.

Directions: Head north out of Homer on NY 41 (I–81 exit 12) for about 3.5 miles. Turn left on NY 41A north and travel for 4.6 miles, then turn left on Branch Road and continue for 0.2 mile.

Additional information: A hard-surface launch ramp and parking are available for a fee at the Lake Como Inn. There is no free public fishing access.

Contact: New York State Department of Environmental Conservation Region 7 and Cayuga County Tourism.

104. Upper Fall Creek *(see map on page 193)*

Key species: Brook trout and brown trout.

Description: Springing from the highlands of southern Cayuga County, this creek wiggles downhill for approximately 25 miles to feed Cayuga Lake in Ithaca. This section only covers the headwaters on the inland stretch of the stream. The last mile or so is totally dependant on Cayuga Lake and is covered in site 107E.

Tips: The brook trout section is easiest to fish from opening day through mid-May.

The fishing: The state annually stocks 2,000 brook trout averaging 9 inches into the Cayuga County section of stream. The vast majority are caught in the first month of the season by locals using worms and salted minnows. Those lucky enough to settle into logjams, undercut banks, or holes inaccessible to humans do well in the cool, oxygenated water and easily reach between 12 and 16 inches. These veterans invariably move back upstream in autumn to spawn and find ideal habitat close to the road, where they overwinter, providing anglers with wonderful surprises the following spring. In Tompkins County the water warms to temperatures more suitable for brown trout. The state stocks around 8,500 averaging 8 inches in the stretch from Groton City to Freeville. Those that survive opening month end up ranging from 9 to 20 inches and respond well to flies and in-line spinners all summer long.

Directions: Lake Como Road and Hinman Road both parallel the creek in Cayuga County and NY 366 runs alongside it in Tompkins County.

Additional information: The stretch running through Tompkins County has no official public access, and most anglers enter it at bridges. In Ithaca, Fall Creek enters Cornell University and becomes creative, carving a spectacular gorge through the heart of the campus.

Contact: New York State Department of Environmental Conservation Region 7.

104A. Public Access

Description: Parking for about five cars.

Directions: From the NY 90/NY 281 intersection in Homer, take NY 90 north for 5 miles, then turn right on Como Road and travel for 1.8 miles.

104B. Public Access

Description: Parking for five cars.

Directions: From the NY 90/NY 281 intersection in Homer, take NY 90 north for 4.8 miles.

105. Cayuga Inlet *(see map on page 196)*

Key species: Rainbow trout and brown trout.

Description: This stream gathers numerous tributaries rolling down from the hills towering above Ithaca and then feeds into Cayuga Lake on the city's west side.

Tips: Use egg sacs in April for lake-run rainbow trout.

The fishing: The state stocks about 15,000 yearling rainbows annually. Most migrate into the lake and return in the fall and spring. Autumn-run fish are relatively young 1 to 3 pounders, looking for adventure and salmon and brown trout caviar. Spring is spawning time, and the rainbows reach 8 pounds, even bigger. They hit egg sacs, yarn flies, worms, and in-line spinners. Brown trout—and a few brookies—in the 8-inch category are in the creek year-round. Come fall, lake-run browns ranging from 2 to 6 pounds and some landlocked salmon up to twice that size enter the fast water, primarily in the section between the mouths of Enfield and Buttermilk Creeks. They'll take worms and nymphs for nourishment but act with extreme prejudice to streamers like egg-sucking leeches. The minimum length for landlocked salmon is 18 inches.

Directions: NY 13 parallels the most productive stretch.

Contact: New York State Department of Environmental Conservation Region 7 and Ithaca/Tompkins County Convention & Visitors Bureau.

Cayuga Inlet · Lower Salmon Creek · Cayuga Lake · Cayuga-Seneca Canal (Seneca River)

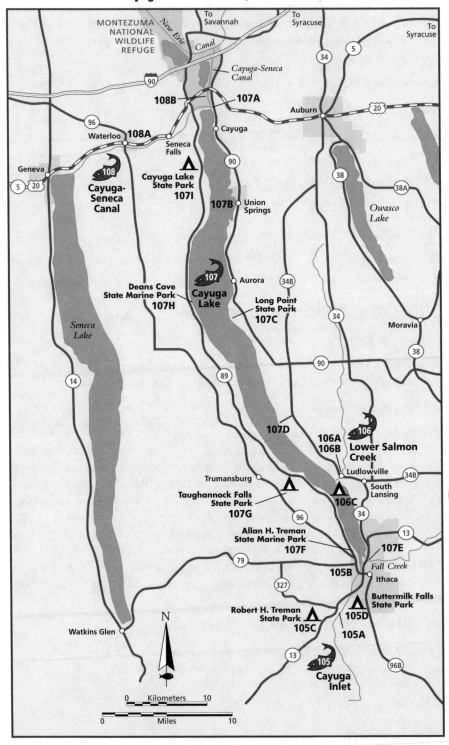

105A. Public Access

Description: This is an informal site with parking for about five cars.

Directions: At the NY 13 bridge, about 3.5 miles south of Ithaca.

105B. Coreorgonel State Historic Site

Description: The site of an old Indian village destroyed by Sullivan's Army, this historic ground has parking for about ten cars.

Directions: Head south out of Ithaca on NY 13 for a little over 0.5 mile.

105C. Robert H. Treman State Park

Description: This 1,025-acre fee area offers seventy-two campsites (eleven electric), fourteen cabins, hot showers, playgrounds, trails along spectacular Enfield Glen (home of scenic Lucifer Falls), and swimming in the pool below the lower falls. The park is open year-round, and the campground operates from mid-May through November. A day-use fee is charged noncampers from Memorial Day through Labor Day.

The fishing: The state annually stocks about 1,600 brown trout averaging 8 inches into Enfield Creek, which runs through the park and feeds Cayuga Inlet. They take nymphs and worms. Below the first falls impassable by fish, this creek is governed by Finger Lakes tributary regulations.

Directions: Head south out of Ithaca on NY 13 for about 3 miles, then turn right on NY 327. The lower entrance is a few hundred feet down the road, and the upper entrance is a couple miles farther.

Additional information: Enfield Creek's mouth is about 0.5 mile east of Park Road.

105D. Buttermilk Falls State Park

Description: This 750-acre fee area offers sixty no-frills campsites, seven cabins, hot showers, playgrounds, a nature trail along the creek's spectacular gorge, and swimming in the pool below Buttermilk Falls. The park is open year-round, and the campground operates from mid-May through October. A day-use fee is charged noncampers from Memorial Day through Labor Day.

The fishing: The state annually stocks 500 9-inch brown trout into Buttermilk Creek, a tributary of Cayuga Inlet. They take nymphs and worms. Below the falls the stream is governed by Finger Lakes tributary regulations.

Directions: On NY 13 south, just beyond Ithaca's city line.

106. Lower Salmon Creek

Key species: Rainbow trout and brown trout.

Description: After diving off the falls in Ludlowville, this scenic stream runs through a slate gorge for about 2 miles before feeding Cayuga Lake.

Tips: Use egg sacs in the pools for spring-run rainbow trout.

The fishing: This creek holds some rainbows between 6 and 12 inches year-round. Most anglers are drawn here, however, by its seasonal runs of brown trout (autumn) and rainbow trout (spring). Typically ranging from 2 to 6 pounds, both species hit egg sacs, worms, streamers, and nymphs.

Directions: Head north out of Ithaca on NY 34 for about 5 miles. In South Lansing, continue north on NY 34B for a little under 2 miles to Myers and turn east on Ludlowville Road. The creek runs between the two villages.

Contact: New York State Department of Environmental Conservation Region 7 and Ithaca/Tompkins County Convention & Visitors Bureau.

106A. Public Access *(see map on page 196)*

Description: Parking for about twenty cars.

Directions: On Ludlowville Road in the village of Ludlowville.

106B. Public Access *(see map on page 196)*

Description: Parking for about twenty cars.

Directions: On Mill Road in Ludlowville.

106C. Lansing Park (Myers Park) *(see map on page 196)*

Description: This fee area offers twenty-five campsites; showers; a picnic area; shore access to Salmon Creek, its mouth, and Cayuga Lake; a paved ramp; and parking for about forty rigs. A day-use fee is charged noncampers in-season, mid-May through Columbus Day.

Directions: On Myers Road in the village of Myers.

107. Cayuga Lake *(see map on page 196)*

Key species: Black bass, northern pike, chain pickerel, black crappie, yellow perch, lake trout, rainbow trout, brown trout, and landlocked Atlantic salmon.

Description: The longest (38 miles) digit in the system, this 42,000-acre lake averages 180 feet deep and has a maximum depth of 435 feet. The city of Ithaca and numerous villages hug half the shore; the other half is steep, forested hills and sheer cliffs.

Tips: When deep-trolling in summer, high-line a minnow-imitating crankbait for salmon and rainbows.

The fishing: This lake is known for huge largemouth bass. Most run 3 to 6 pounds, but 9-pounders are available. The shallow northern basin, from Mud Lock to

Hibiscus Point, is loaded with them. They hang out in the weedy shallow water in early summer and late fall and in the channel running down the center during hot weather. Northern pike up to 15 pounds and chain pickerel up to 4 pounds share this fertile range. Lately pickerel have become far more numerous than northerns. All three species hit live bait, spinnerbaits, twitchbaits, and minnow-imitating crankbaits worked along weed edges, over submerged weed beds, and around structure. In spring schools of crappies move into the bays and coves around the north pond and into the mouth of the canal. Use small minnows, Beetle Spins, and Road Runners. The steep, rocky drop-offs on the east and west banks are home to small-mouths up to 4 pounds and yellow perch ranging from 6 to 14 inches. Both take worms, live crayfish, and minnows. In addition, the smallmouths have a taste for diving crankbaits and 3-inch scented curly-tailed grubs and tubes bounced or dragged on bottom. Unlike most of the other Finger Lakes, bass season is the same as the regular state season.

The central portion of the lake is deep and cold, ideal habitat for salmonids. Each year the state stocks tremendous quantities. For instance, 2002 saw 43,000 yearling landlocked salmon, 15,000 6-inch rainbows, 30,000 9.5-inch browns, and 60,000 lakers averaging 8 inches. Brown, rainbow, and lake trout range from 3 to 6 pounds, with many caught each year double that. Most landlocked salmon range from 18 to 22 inches. Salmonids hang out close enough to shore from fall through spring to be within range of bank anglers still-fishing with live bait or tossing spoons and crankbaits. Flatlining crankbaits and spoons off tributary mouths and along drops-offs is also productive during cool and cold weather. Come summer, salmonids head for deep, open water, where they are targeted with spoons, crankbaits, or cut baits trolled off downriggers. The minimum length for landlocked Atlantic salmon in the lake and its tributaries is 18 inches.

This lake has a minor lamprey eel problem. Les Wedge, a retired state senior aquatic biologist, says the authorities combat serious infestation with "integrated pest control." Under this system, adult eels are annually trapped and exterminated at the fish ladder on Cayuga Inlet, and chemicals are used as needed, every seven years or so.

Directions: NY 90 and NY 34B parallel the east shore, and NY 89 parallels the west shore.

Additional information: Frontinac Island in Union Springs is the only island in the Finger Lakes.

Contact: New York State Department of Environmental Conservation Region 7, Cayuga County Tourism, Ithaca/Tompkins County Convention & Visitors Bureau, and Seneca County Tourism.

107A. Mud Lock Public Access

Description: This facility offers a paved ramp, hundreds of feet of shore-fishing access above and below Cayuga-Seneca Canal Lock 1 and in the fast water at the foot of the dam, parking for about thirty rigs, picnic tables, and a toilet.

Directions: Take US 20/NY 5 west from Auburn for about 8 miles. A couple hundred feet beyond the traffic light at NY 90, turn left onto River Road (before the bridge) and continue for about 1 mile.

107B. Union Springs Municipal Boat Launch *(see map on page 196)*

Description: Located in Frontinac Park, this site has a concrete ramp, parking for fifty rigs, toilets, a swimming beach, a playground, a shelter, picnic tables, and shore fishing. There is no formal fee, but a donation is requested.

Directions: At the end of Chapel Street in Union Springs.

107C. Long Point State Park *(see map on page 196)*

Description: This fee area offers a protected harbor, a four-lane paved ramp, parking for thirty rigs, toilets, picnic facilities, and shore-fishing access into one of the deepest canyons in the lake. A day-use fee is charged from Memorial Day through Labor Day.

Directions: On Lake Road, about 1.5 miles south of Aurora.

107D. Cayuga Station Public Access *(see map on page 196)*

Description: Formerly known as Milliken Station, this site is currently owned by AES Eastern Energy L.P. and offers parking for about fifteen cars.

The fishing: During cold weather the power company's warm-water discharge draws brown trout and landlocked salmon to within casting distance of surf anglers.

Directions: Head north out of Ithaca on NY 34 for 6.5 miles to South Lansing, turn north on NY 34B and travel for 7.8 miles, then turn west on Cayuga Drive. About 0.5 mile later, turn left at the fork and travel for 0.7 mile, then take a right into the gravel driveway just above the railroad tracks. Park in the lot, backtrack to the road, cross the tracks, and take the fenced-in trail running north along the edge of the lake.

107E. Ithaca Falls (Lower Fall Creek) *(see map on page 196)*

Description: Set in the deep valley at the southern tip of Cayuga Lake, the city of Ithaca, home of Cornell University and Ithaca College, has about as many waterfalls per square foot as it has academics. Its greatest cataract is Ithaca Falls.

The fishing: Less than 2 miles upstream of Fall Creek's mouth, opening week finds the holes below this barrier loaded with post-spawn smallmouth bass. From late October through December, a steady stream of lake-run brown trout averaging 2 pounds and landlocked salmon up to 10 pounds hang out in the rapids and pools below the falls. Rainbow trout averaging 3 pounds take their turn in the spring. Opening day usually finds good numbers of rainbow trout already here, and latecomers trickle in throughout the month of April. These fish all hit worms, egg sacs, and streamers.

A leisurely day angling at
Ithaca Falls (site 107E).

Directions: In Ithaca, take NY 13 north to Dey Street (the last light in town) and turn right. Take an immediate left onto Lincoln Street and follow it for about 6 blocks to its end. The parking lot will be right in front of you, across the road. Follow the path to the falls.

107F. Allan H. Treman State Marine Park *(see map on page 196)*

Description: This fee area offers a paved ramp, parking for 100 rigs, 370 seasonal slips, 30 transient slips, showers, and picnic facilities. The season runs from the first of May through the third Monday in October.

Directions: Located on Taughannock Boulevard (NY 89) in Ithaca.

107G. Taughannock Falls State Park *(see map on page 196)*

Description: This 783-acre fee area offers seventy-six campsites (sixteen electric), sixteen cabins, hot showers, a paved boat launch, docks, picnic areas, hiking trails, a bathhouse, a swimming beach, and hundreds of feet of shore-fishing access. The camping season is from April through mid-October. A day-use fee is charged non-campers from Memorial Day through Labor Day.

The fishing: Fall through spring, perch move onto the shallow shelf clinging to shore and trout and salmon mill around the steep drop-off—all within reach of shore anglers. The perch are targeted with worms and minnows. Salmonids are taken by suspending alewives 10 to 30 feet below slip bobbers and on trout pastes, egg sacs, and bare fluorescent floating jigheads suspended 6 inches to 3 feet off bottom. The park provides shacks on shore to protect anglers from the biting winds and bubblers keep the launch area open for winter use.

Directions: Located 8 miles north of Ithaca on NY 89.

Additional information: One of the most beautiful parks in the state system, Taughannock's greatest claim to fame is its 215-foot-high falls, the tallest free-falling cataract in the state.

107H. Deans Cove State Marine Park *(see map on page 196)*

Description: This site has a paved ramp and parking for fifty rigs.

Directions: Located off NY 89, about 15 miles south of the US 20/NY 5 intersection.

107I. Cayuga Lake State Park *(see map on page 196)*

Description: This 141-acre fee area offers 286 campsites (36 electric), 14 cabins, hot showers, a paved ramp, parking for 50 rigs, shore-fishing access, a swimming beach, a playground, and playing fields. The park is open year-round, and the camping season is from the last weekend in April through the last weekend in October. A day-use fee is charged noncampers from Memorial Day through Labor Day.

Directions: Head west out of Auburn on US 20/NY 5 for about 10 miles, turn south on NY 89, and travel for about 2 miles.

108. Cayuga-Seneca Canal (Seneca River) *(see map on page 196)*

Key species: Largemouth bass, smallmouth bass, northern pike, walleye, channel catfish, freshwater drum, carp, yellow perch, black crappie, sunfish, white bass, and white perch.

Description: Also known as the Seneca River, this canal starts as the outlet of Seneca Lake, picks up the outflow of Cayuga Lake about 10 miles later, and flows north for a couple more miles to join the New Erie Canal. Its channel averages 12 feet deep.

Tips: One or more gates open at the Cayuga Lake Dam draw walleyes to the pool below.

The fishing: Largemouth bass in the 1- to 4-pound range and northern pike from 18 to 36 inches rule the bays, backwaters, canal shelves, and tributary mouths. They hit minnows, Rat-L-Traps, ThunderSticks, and spinnerbaits. Smallmouths from 0.75 to 3 pounds like the canal's drop-offs, channel, discharges below locks, and the pools and rapids below dams. They have a taste for minnows, crayfish, scented plastic minnows on drop-shot rigs, and Carolina-rigged finesse worms dragged on bottom. Walleyes are rare above Cayuga Lake's dam but very common downstream. Ranging from 1 to 6 pounds, they hit worms and minnows drifted along drop-offs, worms slow-trolled on spinner harnesses, bladebaits, minnow-imitating crankbaits, and jigs. Channel catfish up to 10 pounds hug bottom in the deepest water they can find and take worms, minnows, shrimp, and cut bait. Sheepshead in the 12- to 20-inch range can show up anywhere but are especially fond of fast water. Average-size drum are most likely to hit crayfish and worms, but those over 5 pounds will take crankbaits and jigs, too.

Palm-size bluegills, pumpkinseeds, and rock bass and yellow perch averaging 8 inches are plentiful in shallow, quiet areas thick with weed beds, lily pads, and timber. They take worms, 1-inch Berkley Power Grubs, and Power Wigglers. Silver bass running from 4 to 10 inches prefer current and have a taste for worms and in-line spinners. Black crappies up to 12 inches are plentiful around root systems and windfalls, at the base of locks, and along riprap crowned with brush. They hit small minnows and lures like Stump Jumpers and Crappie Thunders. Carp averaging 10 pounds are everywhere. They hit canned corn, bread balls, and baked potato fished on bottom.

Directions: US 20/NY 5 parallels the canal from its source on Seneca Lake to the highway's intersection with NY 90.

Additional information: Cayuga-Seneca Canal can be accessed at the marina of Seneca Lake State Park (site 102A).

Contact: New York State Department of Environmental Conservation Regions 7 and 8 and Seneca County Tourism.

Elizabeth Cady Stanton, Amelia Jenks Bloomer, and Susan B. Anthony, champions of women's rights, are immortalized by statues overlooking the Cayuga-Seneca Canal at Seneca Falls (site 108).

108A. Waterloo Community Center Launch *(see map on page 196)*

Description: This site has a paved ramp, parking for ten rigs, several docks, shore-fishing access on the canal and Oak Island's backwater, picnic tables, and toilets.

Directions: On Oak Street in the village of Waterloo.

108B. Seneca River Public Access *(see map on page 196)*

Description: This site offers a paved launch, parking for about forty rigs, 100 feet of bank access, and toilets.

Directions: Take US 20/NY 5 west from Auburn for about 8 miles. Cross the bridge over the canal and take a left at the sign, a couple hundred yards later.

109. Clyde River

Key species: Largemouth bass, smallmouth bass, northern pike, walleye, pumpkin-seed, bluegill, black crappie, silver bass, brown bullhead, channel catfish, and carp.

Clyde River

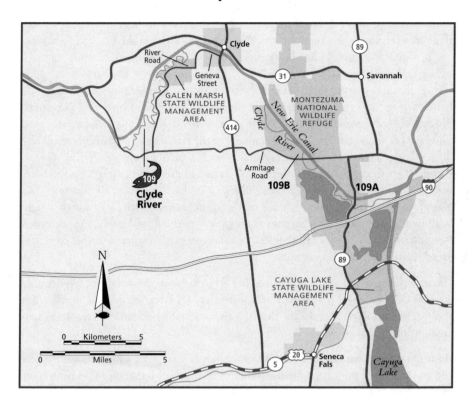

Description: Formerly a large tributary of the Seneca River, its sources (Garnagua Creek and Canandaigua Outlet) were diverted in the early twentieth century to feed the Barge Canal (currently the New Erie Canal), leaving its upper section a shallow, serpentine backwater resembling a southern bayou. Stagnant, stump-ridden, and twisting and turning through the Galen Marsh State Wildlife Management Area, it presents a prehistoric setting steeped in the hair-raising sounds of its amazing array of waterfowl and wildlife. Downstream of the village of Clyde, the stream was mostly incorporated into the canal, but its original oxbows still weave in and out.

Tips: In spring and fall cast jigs and crankbaits in the fast water at Mays Point.

The fishing: The still upper reaches are ideal warm-water habitat. Largemouth bass up to 6 pounds are regularly taken on deer-hair and cork-bodied bugs cast along lily pads, jerkbaits and crankbaits run along the edges of channels, and Texas-rigged worms worked around stumps, windfalls, and undercut banks. Smallmouth bass ranging from 0.75 to 3 pounds are plentiful at the mouth of the upper river, in the channels of midstream oxbows, and in the fast water at Mays Point. They respond well to spinnerbaits, jigs, and free-lined minnows. The canal's northern pike, some over 15 pounds, spawn in swampy reaches. Afterwards they have a deep hunger and are especially fond of large minnows and strange-acting lures like Flatfish. Walleyes typically go between 15 and 25 inches and are mostly caught early in the season from the dam at Mays Point all the way to the mouth on the Seneca River. They like night crawlers dragged along bottom, Bomber "A"–type crankbaits, and jigs.

Bluegills and pumpkinseeds ranging from 4 to 7 inches, black crappies up to 14 inches, and bullheads up to 10 inches thrive in the upper river. The sunfish like poppers, grubs, and worms; crappies take small minnows, Beetle Spins, 2.5-inch Exude Trout Worms, and tiny jigs. The bullheads like worms fished on muddy bottoms. Although their numbers have recently gone down dramatically, white perch and white bass in the 4- to 7-inch range hang out in the fast water at Mays Point and bite all day long on worms, streamers, and 1- and 2-inch Exude Curly Tail Grubs. Channel catfish typically go from 12 to 20 inches, but monsters up to 15 pounds are available. The smaller fish pack into the rapids and holes at Mays Point from late May through June. They like worms cast into the current with just enough weight to allow them to bounce on bottom as they go with the flow. Carp are everywhere. Ranging from 3 to 30 pounds, they can be taken on garden worms, kernel corn, and bread balls still-fished on bottom.

Directions: From the south side of the NY 414 bridge in the village of Clyde, head west on Geneva Street for about 1 mile, turn right on River Road, and continue for about 0.5 mile. River Road runs through the wildlife management area and skirts much of the upper river.

Additional information: The backwater stretch is a popular canoe route. Parking and launching are permitted off the shoulder of the road but camping is prohibited in the Galen Marsh State Wildlife Management Area.

Contact: New York State Department of Environmental Conservation Region 8 and Wayne County Office of Tourism/History.

109A. Mays Point Public Access *(see map on page 205)*

Description: Parking for about six cars and shore-fishing access above and below the dam.

Directions: Head east on US 20/NY 5 out of Seneca Falls for about 3 miles, turn left on NY 89 and travel 3.4 miles, then turn right on South Mays Point Road and go 0.2 mile to the access site on the right.

Additional information: This stretch of NY 89 skirts the 3,500-acre Montezuma National Wildlife Refuge. An observation tower overlooking Tschache Pool and North Spring Pool is about 0.5 mile west of the fishing access site. The pools are loaded with waterfowl during seasonal migrations. The rest of the year birds of every feather hang out here, everything from blue herons and bald eagles to kingfishers and red-winged black birds.

109B. Public Access *(see map on page 205)*

Description: This bridge offers shoulder parking and access onto public land at one of the river's original oxbows.

Directions: From site 109A, head north on NY 89 for 1.9 miles and turn left on Armitage Road. Cross the steel bridge over the New Erie Canal 1.5 miles later and continue for 0.3 mile to the second bridge.

110. Hemlock Creek *(see map on page 208)*

Key species: Rainbow trout.

Description: Only averaging about 6 feet in width, this skinny creek tumbles down one of the northernmost foothills of the Appalachian Plateau and feeds Owasco Inlet in the hamlet of Locke.

Tips: Very sensitive to runoff, this creek is most productive in April when it's still swollen by snowmelt.

The fishing: Owasco Lake rainbows spawn in this creek, primarily before the season opens. Still, stragglers, some over 10 pounds, trickle in after April showers— popular local outdoor writer Mike Kelly pulled a 10.5-pounder out of here. They hit egg sacs, garden worms, and egg-pattern flies drenched in cod liver oil or a commercial trout scent.

Directions: NY 90 parallels the lower half of the creek.

Additional information: A stretch of public fishing rights and parking for twenty-five cars is on NY 90 on the western edge of Locke. There are several informal pull-offs along the highway.

Contact: New York State Department of Environmental Conservation Region 7 and Cayuga County Tourism.

111. Decker Creek *(see map on page 208)*

Key species: Brown trout.

Description: This stream bubbles up in the high country between Skaneateles and Owasco Lakes and flows due south for about 6 miles. Its union with Dresserville Creek on the east side of Moravia spawns Mill Creek, a tributary of Owasco Inlet.

Tips: During low light and at night, work a streamer upstream of windfalls and log-jams so that the fly swings under the timber.

The fishing: This skinny creek has great quantities of native browns ranging from 9 to 14 inches. Savvy and skittish, they're extremely challenging to catch. Locals

Owasco Lake and Tributaries

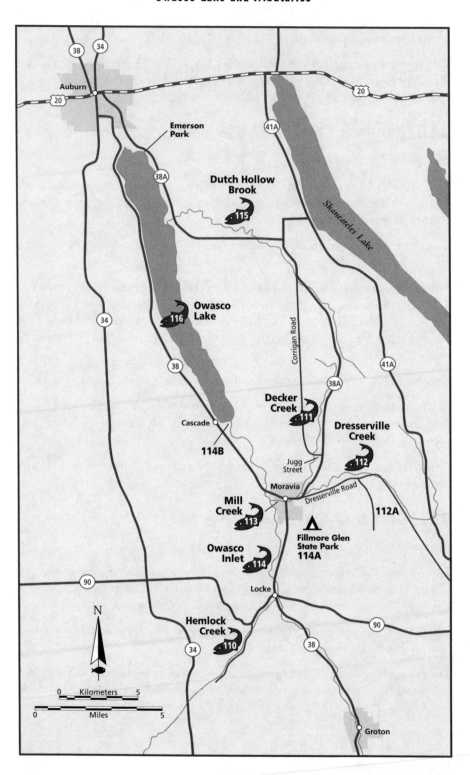

38 34

Auburn
20

Emerson
Park

41A

38A

Dutch Hollow
Brook
115

Skaneateles Lake

Owasco
Lake
116

34

Corrigan Road

41A

38

38A

Cascade

Decker
Creek
111

Dresserville
Creek
112

114B

Jugg
Street

Moravia

Dresserville Road

Mill
Creek
113

112A

Fillmore Glen
State Park
114A

Owasco
Inlet
114

90

Locke

N

90

Hemlock
Creek
34
110

38

0 — Kilometers — 5

0 — Miles — 5

Groton

take them in the spring on salted minnows and with worms after summer and autumn rains.

Directions: Head north out of Moravia on NY 38A for 2.5 miles, turn left on Jugg Street, and travel 0.3 mile to the bridge.

Additional information: The state owns fishing rights stretching from just a few yards upstream of the Jugg Street bridge to downstream for almost 3 miles.

Contact: New York State Department of Environmental Conservation Region 7 and Cayuga County Tourism.

112. Dresserville Creek

Key species: Brown trout and rainbow trout.

Description: This creek rises out of a meadow and cuts like a giant fishhook through the countryside. It joins Decker Creek just east of Moravia, forming Mill Creek, a tributary of Owasco Inlet.

Tips: In summer the rainbows like flies, and the browns like Phoebes.

The fishing: According to state fisheries biologist Jeff Robins, "this stream hasn't benefited from human intervention in at least twenty years. It's unique because it's the only creek in Central New York with wild rainbows." They average 10 inches and like nymphs, dry flies, and streamers. Wild browns ranging from 7 to 14 inches are also available. Endowed with conservative dietary habits, they respond best to live bait fished deep in high water and spinners skimmed downstream just under the surface, in the early evening and just after dawn during the dog days of summer.

Directions: From the NY 38/ NY 38A intersection in Moravia, head north on NY 38A for 0.9 mile, turn right on Dresserville Road, and continue for 2.7 miles to the bridge. Dresserville Road parallels the creek from the bridge upstream for a couple of miles.

Additional information: The state owns public fishing rights to 4.3 miles of this stream, most of it upstream of the first Dresserville Road crossing. There is no formal access site, and most anglers enter the stream from the shoulder of the road and at bridge crossings.

Contact: New York State Department of Environmental Conservation Region 7 and Cayuga County Tourism.

112A. Summerhill State Forest

Description: Primitive camping is allowed in this 4,377-acre state forest.

Directions: Head north out of Moravia on NY 38A for about 0.5 mile and turn right on Dresserville Road. Two miles later, turn right on Dumplin Hill Road, and state forest lands signs will appear on the trees about 0.5 mile later.

113. Mill Creek (Cayuga County) *(see map on page 208)*

Key species: Rainbow trout.

Description: This mile-long stream, created by the union of Dresserville Creek and Decker Creek, flows on a relatively straight path through the village of Moravia and feeds Owasco Inlet.

Tips: Wear camouflage and walk slowly.

The fishing: This creek, notorious for its vodka-clear water, gets spring runs of rainbow trout. They range anywhere from 2 to 8 pounds and respond to egg sacs and garden worms bounced on bottom. Incidentally, surplus landlocked salmon are stocked occasionally, most recently in 2002, when 1,000 2-inchers were released. They don't do very well in Owasco Lake, and those that manage to survive long enough to return in autumn to spawn are so few, they go unnoticed.

Directions: Aurora Street (off NY 38 in Moravia) parallels the creek.

Additional information: The state owns about 1,000 feet of public fishing rights from the mouth upstream. Get there by taking Aurora Street to the bridge over Owasco Inlet. Park on the shoulder and walk downstream a few hundred feet along the east side of the inlet, then upstream on Mill Creek.

Contact: New York State Department of Environmental Conservation Region 7 and Cayuga County Tourism.

114. Owasco Inlet *(see map on page 208)*

Key species: Brown trout, rainbow trout, brook trout, largemouth bass, black crappie, and bullhead.

Description: Springing from towering hill country, the geological signature of the southern Finger Lakes region, this stream meanders north for about 15 miles, picking up numerous tributaries before pouring into Owasco Lake.

Tips: Work garden worms on bottom at the heads of pools in April.

The fishing: The fast-flowing stretch of this stream south of Moravia gets stocked annually with roughly 5,600 browns averaging 8 inches and 32,500 fingerling rainbows. Most of these fish migrate to the lake. Even so, quite a few browns take up year-round residence here. Running anywhere from 8 to 16 inches, they hit worms, minnows, and nymphs. Lake-run browns reaching up to 10 pounds enter the stream in autumn to spawn and can be taken on worms and streamers. The rainbows invariably head for the lake but return in the spring, ranging anywhere from 2 to 10 pounds. Also, a few averaging 1.5 pounds run upstream in autumn in search of salmon and brown trout caviar. Regardless of the season, rainbows will take egg sacs, worms, in-line spinners, and streamers. Wild brook trout averaging 7 inches inhabit the headwaters south of Locke. They hit worms, salted minnows, and flies. The minimum length for trout is 9 inches.

In some years the state stocks surplus Atlantic salmon fingerlings, most recently in 2002 when 2,000 2-inchers were released. Although they don't do very well in Owasco Lake, a few do make it to maturity and run up the inlet in autumn looking for love. Averaging about 4 pounds, they are sometimes caught incidentally by anglers targeting trout with streamers and worms.

Good bass habitat exists in the swampy wood-choked lower reaches near the mouth. Bucketmouths up to 5 pounds can be taken all summer long on spinnerbaits and jerkbaits. Black crappies up to 14 inches find this gently flowing lower portion to their liking, too, especially in the spring and autumn. They respond to tiny minnows, marabou jigs, and 2- and 3-inch Berkley Power Grubs fished on spinner forms. Bullheads swarm into this swampy area from ice-out into mid-May and are targeted with worms fished on bottom.

Directions: NY 38 parallels the inlet from Moravia to Groton.

Additional information: Informal access to the stream is available where it touches or is crossed by NY 38. Landowners are generally willing to grant access across their property just for the asking.

Contact: New York State Department of Environmental Conservation Region 7 and Cayuga County Tourism.

114A. Fillmore Glen State Park

Description: This 938-acre fee area offers sixty campsites (ten with electricity), three rustic cabins, hot showers, nature trails, and swimming. The campground is open mid-May through mid-October. A day-use fee is charged noncampers when swimming is allowed, roughly June through August.

Directions: On NY 38, 1 mile south of Moravia.

114B. Owasco Flats Public Access

Description: This site is at the creek's mouth, along a stretch of murky water snaking through a lowland forest. Groomed trails strike off into the woods to clearings on the inlet and the south shore of Owasco Lake. There is parking for about thirty cars.

The fishing: Lowland habitat like this isn't exactly the kind of place average folks consider attractive. But minnows, frogs, ducklings, baby muskrats—you name it— think it's beautiful. Their presence draws bass, crappies, and a few northern pike.

Directions: Head north out of Moravia on NY 38 for about 5 miles to Cascade. Turn right onto Old Plank Road (Firelane 1) and continue a couple hundred feet past Christy's Lake House Restaurant. When the road takes a sharp left turn, continue straight onto the road marked with a Cayuga County Parks sign.

115. Dutch Hollow Brook (see map on page 208)

Key species: Rainbow trout.

Description: An important rainbow trout and walleye nursery, this brook tumbles out of the hills, runs on a serpentine course about 10 miles long, and feeds Owasco Lake.

Tips: Soak yarn flies in bait scents and work them on bottom.

The fishing: This stream gets good runs of spring rainbows ranging from 2 to 5 pounds. They take worms, egg sacs, egg-imitating flies, and in-line spinners. Sometimes the state stocks Atlantic salmon, most recently in 2002, when 960 6.5-inchers were released. Though returns have been paltry in the past, mature land-locks have been known to climb the brook in autumn, especially after a rain, and should take a worm or streamer.

Directions: NY 38A parallels the stream.

Additional information: Between March 16 and opening day of walleye season, fishing is prohibited from the mouth upstream to the first NY 38A bridge.

Contact: New York State Department of Environmental Conservation Region 7 and Cayuga County Tourism.

116. Owasco Lake (see map on page 208)

Key species: Black bass, northern pike, rainbow trout, brown trout, lake trout, walleye, yellow perch, and black crappie.

Description: The middle finger on the right hand of the Finger Lakes, this 6,781-acre body of water averages 96 feet deep and has a maximum depth of 177 feet. It is named after Osca (crossing place), an Indian village that stood on the site of riffs on the outlet, where the penitentiary stands now.

Tips: The best smallmouth habitat is tight to the east and west banks.

The fishing: This lake is a superb two-story fishery. Local bass enthusiasts claim Owasco is the best water in the Finger Lakes for trophy smallmouths. Most range from 2 to 3 pounds, but 5-pounders—and then some—are present. They respond to crayfish, minnows, and soft plastics ranging from unscented curly tails and finesse worms to flavored ones like Berkley Power Worms and YUM Samurai Shads. Largemouths up to 6 pounds and northerns between 4 and 8 pounds are common in the southern basin and are inclined to attack spinnerbaits, buzzbaits, and soft and hard jerkbaits. The biggest pike, up to 20 pounds, are taken through the ice on large minnows and by jigging spoons. Yellow perch reaching up to 14 inches hang out in the weedy southern basin and the weed lines clinging to the east and west banks. They hit worms, minnows, and 2-inch curly-tailed grubs. Black crappies up to 16 inches roam the southern basin, primarily in

Ice fishing at Owasco Lake (site 116) can result in a great catch, such as this northern pike.

and around the inlet. They take minnows and spinner-rigged 2-inch curly-tailed grubs and tubes.

Although natural reproduction occurs, this better-than-average cold-water fishery is maintained by massive state intervention. Besides stocking the tributaries, the authorities annually pump roughly 10,000 9.5-inch browns, 16,000 lakers averaging 7.5 inches, and 5,000 yearling rainbows directly into the lake. They do well in the rich habitat, growing to range from 2 to 10 pounds. All three are taken by flatlining Sutton and Dardevle spoons parallel to shore in spring and fall and by deep-trolling spoons and crankbaits in summer. In winter browns and rainbows are caught on sawbellies suspended a couple feet below the ice, and lakers are taken with minnows fished on bottom. Due to poor returns, the state's landlocked salmon stocking program was all but axed a few years back. Still, surplus salmon are often stocked. For instance, 13,000 yearlings averaging 6.5 inches were released in 2002, and some actually make it to maturity. In addition, surplus and spent breeders, many up to 26 inches long, are often retired here. Salmon ranging anywhere from 15 to 30 inches take minnows through the ice and worms drifted along drop-offs. The minimum length for rainbow and brown trout is 9 inches.

Over the past few years, the Owasco Anglers Association, in cooperation with the state, has been stocking thousands of walleyes. Fish up to 6 pounds have been caught as of 2002, mostly by drifting worms and casting crankbaits. That year the state actively pitched in by stocking 30,000 fry. Unfortunately this fishery is totally dependent on stocking, and, although the regional Department of Environmental Conservation office has submitted a stocking policy recommendation to headquarters, it faces uncertainty.

Directions: Head south out of Auburn for about 1 mile on NY 38A for the east bank and NY 38 for the west bank.

Additional information: The north shore's Emerson Park offers a paved ramp, parking for fifty rigs, rest rooms, a swimming beach, and hundreds of yards of shore-fishing access, including off a pier. Fillmore Glen State Park in Moravia (see site 114A) offers a campground and three rustic cabins.

Contact: New York State Department of Environmental Conservation Region 7 and Cayuga County Tourism.

117. Grout Brook *(see map on page 216)*

Key species: Rainbow trout, landlocked Atlantic salmon, and white sucker.

Description: Although this is Skaneateles Lake's largest tributary, it's so skinny and shallow, you can cross it in spots without getting your feet wet.

Tips: Use worms during the first couple of weeks of April.

The fishing: Lake-run rainbows ranging from 15 to 22 inches enter this stream throughout the month of April, especially after it rains. They respond best to garden worms and egg sacs. From mid-October through November, Atlantic salmon up to 20 inches are drawn here by the urge to spawn. They hit night crawlers. Suckers up to 20 inches pack the place from mid-April through early May, gathering so thickly in spots, the floor seems to breathe. Coming from one of the cleanest lakes in the state, the beasts are delicious and take worms fished on bottom. The minimum length for rainbow trout is 9 inches.

Directions: From Homer (I–81 exit 12), head north on US 11 for about 1 mile to NY 41. Turn left (west) and travel for a little over 6 miles to Scott, then turn west on Glen Haven Road, which parallels the creek, crossing it in several places.

Additional information: Posted signs punctuate much of this tiny stream. The state owns public fishing rights on several stretches off Glen Haven Road and provides fishing access sites with parking for about five cars each.

Contact: New York State Department of Environmental Conservation Region 7 and Cortland County Visitors Bureau.

117A. Bridge Access

Description: The pool below this culvert often holds a fish or two. Park at the shoulder.

Directions: From NY 41 in the hamlet of Scott, head west on Glen Haven Road. At the curve about 1 mile later, continue straight on Grinnell Road for a few hundred feet to the stop sign.

117B. Bear Swamp State Forest

Description: Named after a skinny creek that flows through it, this 3,280-acre forest towers 1,000 feet above Grout Brook's west bank. Primitive camping is allowed.

The fishing: Skaneateles Lake's second largest tributary, Bear Swamp Creek pours into the lake's west side about 4 miles north of Grout Brook. Wild brook trout ranging from 4 to 10 inches are present. They hit worms, nymphs, and terrestrials. The minimum length for rainbow trout, from the mouth to the first barrier impassable by fish, is 9 inches.

Directions: From NY 41 in the hamlet of Scott, head west on Glen Haven Road. At the curve about 1 mile later, continue straight on Grinnell Road for a few hundred feet. Bear right at the stop sign onto West Scott Road (which turns into Gulf Road) and travel for about 1 mile, turn right onto Iowa Road, then right again a few hundred yards later onto Bear Swamp Road.

118. Skaneateles Lake *(see map on page 216)*

Key species: Lake trout, rainbow trout, landlocked Atlantic salmon, cisco, smallmouth bass, and yellow perch.

Skaneateles, Otisco, Onondaga, and Cross Lakes and Drainages

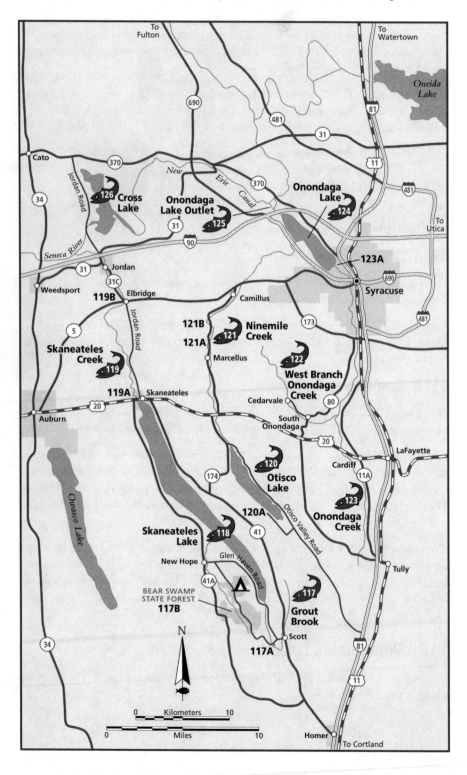

Description: Skaneateles is Iroquois for "long lake." The Indians said it slowly and solemnly: sken-ee-at-less. Contemporaries pronounce it skinny-atlas, like it's an anorexic version of the famous figure in Greek mythology. Almost exclusively spring fed, this 8,700-acre lake averages 145 feet deep and has a maximum depth of 300 feet.

Tips: Troll Baby ThunderSticks or Mystics over weed beds submerged in 30 to 45 feet of water.

The fishing: Pure enough to drink without treatment, lake trout are native to this pristine water. While 20-pounders are available, most of the fish are frying-pan-size 15- to 18-inchers. This is mainly because the lake's shallow thermocline (water temperatures stratify around 35 feet) makes them more easily accessible than in other places. They respond to small crankbaits trolled off downriggers. If you run your lures over structure in 30 to 50 feet of water, you'll pick up a lot of yellow perch, smallmouths, and lakers too small to trip the downrigger's release, so check your baits every twenty minutes or so to prevent drowning the little guys.

The state annually stocks about 27,000 rainbows ranging from 4 to 8 inches, and they easily grow to 12 to 18 inches. In spring and fall they cruise near shore and are taken by bank anglers still-fishing with worms and Berkley Trout Bait or by boats flatlining ⅛- to ¼-ounce perch-colored spoons parallel to shore in 5 to 15 feet of water. The state stocks Atlantic salmon regularly, though not necessarily annually. In 2002 the figures were 9,500 6.5-inchers and 228 8-inchers. Survival to the 15-inch limit is fair. The keepers seem partial to the southern basin, where quite a few are caught on small jigs targeting perch. Anglers who go for them specifically do so by flatlining streamers. Some natural reproduction occurs in Grout Brook, making the lake the best bet in the area to catch a wild salmon.

Cisco range from 1 to 2 pounds and can be taken on a small worm, minnow, or dry fly. Smallmouth bass are abundant but seldom grow bigger than 12 inches. Extraordinarily aggressive, they take worms, minnows, and just about any lure they can fit in their mouths. Perch range from 6 to 10 inches, and there are enough to attract a following who fish for them with 1/16-ounce jigs and worms in summer and through the ice with grubs.

The minimum size for rainbow trout is 9 inches. Black bass season is the same as the regular state season, and the minimum length for smallmouths is 10 inches.

Directions: From Syracuse, take I–81 south for about 6 miles to LaFayette (exit 15), then head west on US 20 for 16 miles to the village of Skaneateles.

Additional information: Primitive camping is allowed in Bear Swamp State Forest (see site 117B). A public access site with a paved ramp and parking for thirty rigs is on NY 41A, 3 miles south of Skaneateles—get there early.

Contact: New York State Department of Environmental Conservation Region 7.

119. Skaneateles Creek (see map on page 216)

Key species: Rainbow trout and brown trout.

Description: Skaneateles Creek breaks away from its namesake by pouring through a pipe at the dam on the lake's north end and tumbling north for about 11 wavy miles to feed the Seneca River (New Erie Canal) west of Jordan. Along the way it runs through a couple of large rural villages and tiny hamlets and squeezes through a scenic gorge.

Tips: In the beginning of April, use garden worms downstream of the Jordan Road bridge in the village of Jordan.

The fishing: This stream is stocked annually with about 2,000 10-inch rainbows and 300 browns averaging 11 inches. The rainbows have a taste for just about every fly imaginable and suck them down pretty carelessly all through May. Generally the water heats up unbearably by late June, sending the majority hightailing it out to the river in search of cooler environs. Not the browns, though. Far more warm-water tolerant than rainbows, this species has a history of growing larger than average in this stream, and since catch-and-release regulations were imposed late in the last century, there are more 18-inchers now than ever before. Most average 14 inches, however, and respond to Berkley Power Wigglers, Exude Trout Worms, in-line spinners, spoons, nymphs, and Wooly Worms. The biggest browns, on the other hand, didn't get that way by being stupid. They've developed discriminating palates and specialized feeding habits and are easiest (relatively speaking) to catch from dusk to dawn on streamers, large terrestrials, and patterns imitating food pellets.

Directions: Jordan Road parallels the creek from Skaneateles to Elbridge, and NY 31C parallels it from Elbridge to Jordan.

Additional information: Restrictions now limit popular access to Skaneateles Creek, one of Central New York's most scenic streams. Under pressure from special interests, the authorities have set aside 10.2 miles (almost its entire length, amounting to the longest set-aside in the state) for catch-and-release fishing with artificial lures only. This is good for elitist anglers; bad for average locals, especially kids. "We can't afford lures, let alone fly-fishing equipment," quipped a single mom, "and there's no place else within walking distance for the kids to fish."

Contact: New York State Department of Environmental Conservation Region 7 and Syracuse Convention and Visitors Bureau.

119A. Charlie Major Nature Trail

Description: This mile-long forested trail skirts the creek on an abandoned railroad grade, passing the ruins of several mills. Shoulder parking is available at the trailhead.

Directions: Head north out of Skaneateles on Fennel Road for a little over 1 mile to its end. At the stop sign at the intersection of Old Seneca Turnpike, cross the highway, enter Mill Road, and travel a few hundred feet.

119B. Public Access

Description: This village park has parking for ten cars and picnic tables.

Directions: On NY 31C in the village of Elbridge.

120. Otisco Lake *(see map on page 216)*

Key species: Tiger muskie, walleye, brown trout, black bass, and black crappie.

Description: The pinkie on the right hand of the system, this 2,213-acre lake averages 34 feet deep and has a maximum depth of 70 feet. More than half of its shoreline is developed with private residences, and a causeway, with a break to allow boats to pass, runs across its south end.

Tips: The best spot for tigers is the massive weed bed off the north side of the causeway.

The fishing: Gallon for gallon, Otisco spits out more trophy tiger muskies and walleyes than lakes twice its size. In the 1960s alewives were dumped into the lake, probably by anglers releasing bait, and slowly wiped out the native walleyes, a strain known for reaching trophy proportions, by feeding on their fry. The drop in walleyes led to an explosion of white perch—another alien. The authorities fought back by stocking norlunge and brown trout. The battle rages on, and the state annually releases about 7,500 9.5-inch muskies. They take to the place like minnows to water, earning the lake a reputation for 20-plus-pound tigers. They hit large minnows, Mepps bucktail spinners, and crankbaits like MirrOlure Minnows, Cotton Cordell's Red Fins, and Mann's jerkbaits. More than 6,000 brown trout ranging from 8.5 to 14.5 inches are stocked each year. They reach an average of 18 inches and respond to minnow-imitating crankbaits trolled off downriggers and to sawbellies suspended a couple feet below the ice. Smallmouth bass ranging from 1 to 2.5 pounds are common and are targeted with spinnerbaits and Carolina-rigged worms worked along the drop-offs on the east and west banks. Largemouths up to 6 pounds thrive in the weed beds circling the lake. They respond to Texas-rigged worms and curly-tailed grubs pitched into vegetation and under docks and to topwater lures like Zara Spooks worked over vegetation and along its edges. Black crappies typically run from 10 to 13 inches. They're mostly taken in spring on small minnows and through the ice on minnows and jigs tipped with spikes and mousies.

Back to the walleyes. The state tried reintroducing the species by stocking tens of thousands in the 1990s but stopped after the five-year management program expired. Private interests took over for a couple of years. Now the state is at it again, stocking 60,000 fry in 2002. Great numbers of trophy walleyes haven't made it on the evening news yet, but enough fish ranging from 18 to 23 inches are being caught to put the lake back on the map as a walleye hot spot. Locals troll for them with jointed crankbaits. From mid-May through mid-July, they come to shore at night to feed on alewives, and bank anglers take them by casting crankbaits like Bomber "A"s and Rat-L-Traps.

Directions: From Syracuse, take I-81 south for 6 miles to exit 15 (LaFayette). Head west on US 20 for about 13 miles, turn south onto NY 174, and continue for about 3 miles. At the dam NY 174 turns sharply west to skirt a large portion of that shore, while Otisco Valley Road heads south and hugs the east bank.

Additional information: Otisco Lake County Park, on Otisco Valley Road, offers parking for about seven cars and several hundred yards of shore fishing. Launching cartop craft is permitted. There isn't a public ramp suitable for launching trailered craft at the park, but a couple of commercial operations on Otisco Valley Road offer hard-surface ramps.

Contact: New York State Department of Environmental Conservation Region 7 and Syracuse Convention and Visitors Bureau.

120A. Public Access *(see map on page 216)*

Description: This site offers parking for fifteen cars and access to hundreds of feet of prime shore fishing at the causeway. It is suitable for beach-launching cartop craft.

Directions: From its junction with NY 174, head south on Otisco Valley Road for roughly 7 miles. Turn right on Sawmill Road, then right again 0.5 mile later onto West Valley Road, and follow it for about 2 miles.

121. Ninemile Creek *(see map on page 216)*

Key species: Brown trout, brook trout, and carp.

Description: This creek pours out of Otisco Lake and flows north for about 15 miles to feed Onondaga Lake. Fed by numerous springs along the way, it remains at an ideal temperature for trout year-round.

Tips: Fish bead-head nymphs in pocket water.

The fishing: The upper reach is a potluck angler's fantasy come true. The water close to the lake's dam holds everything from tiger muskies and bass to trout and carp, but it is only accessible by canoe. Access and trout habitat get better downstream, particularly between Marcellus and Camillus. In this popular stretch the creek tumbles over several dams and waterfalls and runs through a huge swamp, offering habitat for every temperament. Great quantities of trout are stocked annually, but the numbers vary wildly from year to year. In 2002 more than 7,000 browns ranging from 7 to 23 inches and 925 brookies running from 7 to 12 inches were released. In addition, a lot of hanky-panky goes on, so quite a few naturally produced fish are available. Both species take worms, salted minnows, Panther Martin spinners, and flies. Carp averaging 5 pounds can be found throughout the stream. They respond to garden worms.

Directions: NY 174 parallels most of the creek.

Contact: New York State Department of Environmental Conservation Region 7.

121A. Public Access

Description: This site has parking for about thirty-five cars.

Directions: Head north out of Marcellus on NY 174 for about 0.5 mile.

121B. Public Access

Description: This site has parking for about ten cars.

Directions: Continue north on NY 174 for about 500 yards from site 121A.

122. West Branch Onondaga Creek *(see map on page 216)*

Key species: Brown trout.

Description: Springing from rolling hills a few miles west of Syracuse, this small creek grows to fishable size just upstream of Cedarvale, enters a swamp east of the hamlet, and emerges a couple miles later in the village of South Onondaga. It joins Onondaga Creek right at the border of Onondaga Indian Nation territory.

Tips: Work bass bugs that resemble mice in the channel running through the South Onondaga swamp.

The fishing: The state stocks a little over 1,000 8-inch and 150 two-year-old browns annually. Most of the stockies are like average anglers, hanging out at the bridges, where they're caught relatively early in the year. Those that break away from the crowd avoid this fate and end up averaging a respectable 12 inches—with many growing between 16 and 20 inches—providing good sport for adventurous anglers who float or wade the difficult stretches of this challenging creek.

Directions: Head south out of Syracuse on I–81 for 6 miles to exit 15 (LaFayette). Turn west on US 20 and travel for about 6 miles, then turn north on NY 80 and travel a little over 1 mile to the bridge in South Onondaga. If you continue up the hill for a few hundred yards and turn west at the stop sign, you'll be on Cedarvale Road, which parallels the stream to Cedarvale.

Additional information: There are no official public access sites. Most anglers enter the stream at bridges in Cedarvale and South Onondaga.

Contact: New York State Department of Environmental Conservation Region 7 and Syracuse Convention and Visitors Bureau.

123. Onondaga Creek (see map on page 216)

Key species: Brown trout and carp.

Description: This creek starts a couple miles northwest of Tully, flows north for about 20 miles through Onondaga Indian Nation territory and Syracuse, and feeds Onondaga Lake at the city's inner harbor, under the shadow of Carousel Center Mall.

Tips: Don't fish on Onondaga Nation territory without permission.

The fishing: The state annually stocks about 2,250 8-inch browns and 250 two-year-olds averaging 14 inches in the town of LaFayette. Survival is good in this agricultural area, and fish ranging from 8 to 16 inches are available all season long. The stream is channelized for flood control beyond Onondaga Nation territory, but some trout manage to survive all the way to Ballantyne Road, primarily near tributary mouths. This is the valley section of Syracuse and the fish are generally skinny, average 14 inches, and are extremely savvy. They hit salted minnows in the spring, worms after a rain, and flies and small lures all summer long. Carp up to 25 pounds hang out in the mouth at Syracuse's inner harbor and upstream for about 1 mile. They hit worms and corn still-fished on bottom.

Directions: NY 11A parallels the stream south of Syracuse.

Additional information: Anglers who fish the creek for trout in Syracuse access the stream from the bridges on Dorwin Avenue and Seneca Turnpike.

Contact: New York State Department of Environmental Conservation Region 7, Syracuse Convention and Visitors Bureau, and Onondaga Nation of Indians.

123A. Inner Harbor Park

Description: This site offers fishing access to the creek's mouth and lower reaches, parking for about fifty cars, picnic facilities, and rest rooms.

Directions: Kirkpatrick Street in Syracuse.

124. Onondaga Lake (see map on page 216)

Key species: Walleyes, northern pike, largemouth bass, and smallmouth bass.

Description: This 2,942-acre body of water averages 39 feet deep and has a maximum depth of 67 feet. After being force-fed municipal and industrial sewage for over a hundred years, the lake went belly-up in the 1950s. The smell was so bad, Syracuse's west end was nicknamed Skunk City. By 1972 the authorities—concerned over what might emerge from the sticky, slimy waves—banned fishing and a massive clean-up was begun, including construction of a new sewage treatment plant in 1979. Within five years water quality improved so dramatically, game fish returned and prospered. Although the public's fishing rights were reinstated in 1986 and the health advisory against eating the fish lifted in 1999, this lake is still considered the country's filthiest and serves as the national poster child for the heartbreak of industrial pollution—and the joys of reclamation.

Tips: The lake gets nastier the closer you get to Syracuse.

The fishing: Smallmouth bass are the predominate predator. Ranging from 1 to 6 pounds, they take minnows, crayfish, and scented tubes and curly-tailed grubs dragged on bottom. Largemouth bass up to 7 pounds rule the weed lines and beds on the northern half. They respond to spinnerbaits and bass bugs. Walleyes up to 10 pounds hang out near the outlet and respond to minnows, worms drifted plain or on harnesses, and minnow-imitating crankbaits cast between an hour before dusk to an hour after dawn. Northerns up to 15 pounds lurk along the outsides of weed edges and in the north bays. They respond to large minnows, Rat-L-Traps, Rattlin' Red Fins, and Mepps bucktail spinners.

Directions: The lake abuts Syracuse's west side and is paralleled by I–690 and NY 370.

Additional information: Onondaga Lake Park, the county's most popular, occupies the lake's entire northern half, offering about 6 miles of shore access on the lake and about 2 miles on the outlet, a paved ramp, several huge parking lots, and free shuttle service during summer. The park closes at dark, and there are no camping facilities. In August 2001 the lake hosted the richest freshwater fishing tournament in history, the WTVH Ultimate Fishing Challenge, a derby in which fifty-two tagged fish were worth $5.5 million in cash and prizes. New York governor George Pataki and former Minnesota governor Jesse Ventura participated but didn't catch anything. However, eighteen bass wearing $200,000 worth of tags were caught. The tournament was also held in 2002 and 2003. No future tournaments had been scheduled as of press time.

Contact: New York State Department of Environmental Conservation Region 7, Onondaga County Parks, and Syracuse Convention and Visitors Bureau.

125. Onondaga Lake Outlet (see map on page 216)

Key species: Black bass, walleye, northern pike, black crappie, sunfish, and channel catfish.

Description: Connecting the lake with the Seneca River (New Erie Canal), the mile-long outlet averages 12 feet deep and boasts a couple of islands and the remnants of an Old Erie Canal–era lock.

Tips: Work buzzbaits around the islands and abandoned lock.

The fishing: Even when Onondaga Lake was closed to fishing, the outlet had a dedicated following of serious bass and pike anglers. Largemouths running between 1.5 and 6 pounds are found in the weedy shallows and respond to top-water baits.

Smallmouths up to 4 pounds and walleyes averaging 20 inches thrive in the channel and along drop-offs. Both take worms, minnows, C.C. Shads, Berkley Power Grubs, and YUM Wooly Curltails. Northerns ranging from 18 inches to 3 feet are plentiful and hit large minnows, Dardevles, and spinnerbaits. The thruway bridge is a local hot spot for black crappies ranging from too small to 10 inches, sunfish up to 10 inches, and channel catfish averaging 18 inches. The crappies respond to small jigs and minnows, and the sunfish and catfish like worms.

Directions: From Syracuse, take I–690 west for about 6 miles. Get on John Glen Boulevard and travel for about 2 miles to the second traffic light. Turn left (west) onto NY 370 and travel a couple hundred yards to the park entrance on the left.

Additional information: The outlet is almost entirely on Onondaga Lake County Park property. The park offers several parking lots with room for hundreds of cars, over 1 mile of shore-fishing access, picnic facilities, a snack bar, and rest rooms.

Contact: New York State Department of Environmental Conservation Region 7 and Syracuse Convention and Visitors Bureau.

126. Cross Lake (see map on page 216)

Key species: Northern pike, tiger muskie, black bass, and white perch.

Description: To some folks, Cross Lake sounds kind of spiritual. There's nothing holy about the place, though. Heck, some argue, since the Finger Lakes feed into it, it's handmade. Conjecture aside, this 1,920-acre lake averages 25 feet deep, drops to a maximum depth of 65 feet, and gets its name from the Seneca River flowing in and out of its south end like the horizontal beam on Saint Peter's cross.

Tips: Cast Rat-L-Traps in June and November for "log pikeasauruses."

The fishing: The lake has been one of the state's best spots for trophy pike for as long as anyone can remember. Each year fish over 15 pounds are caught on large minnows and Rat-L-Traps. The state has been annually stocking thousands of 9-inch tiger muskies for at least the past decade. Most migrate into the Seneca River. Those that stay range from too small to 38 inches and respond to large minnows, crankbaits, and bucktail spinners. Smallmouth bass averaging 2 pounds are common along drop-offs and the river channel. They're mostly targeted with live bait, jigs, and scented plastics tipped on Slider Heads and swum through the water column or dragged on bottom. Largemouth bass grow huge, with 5-pounders being common. They are mostly found in and around weeds and timber and under docks. They take Texas-rigged worms and bucktail jigs tipped with scented worms or craws. When fishing under docks, sound the dinner bell by hitting the upright with the lead. In summer rafts of white perch prowl the upper layer over deep water in such numbers, their fins dimple the surface. They seldom grow larger than 0.5 pound, but they strike small lures with such savagery, your heart will skip a beat each time.

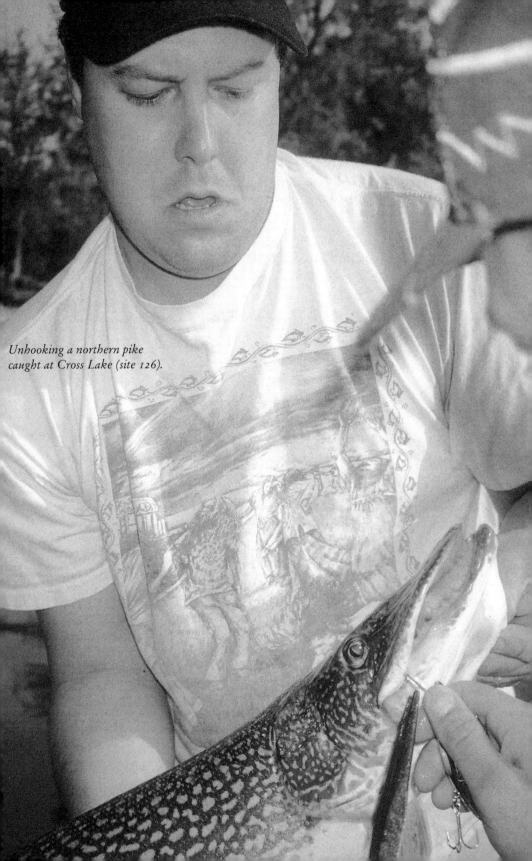

Unhooking a northern pike caught at Cross Lake (site 126).

The state is attempting to restore the lake's walleye fishery through heavy stocking. In 2002 84,500 1.5-inch fry were released. Whether they take or not won't be known for a couple of years. However, Seneca River walleye averaging 18 inches prowl the river channel, where they take worms, jigs, and crankbaits.

The minimum length for walleyes is 18 inches, and the daily limit is three. The minimum length for northerns is 22 inches.

Directions: From I–90 exit 40 (Weedsport) head south on NY 34 for about 0.5 mile, then turn east on NY 31 and travel for about 5 miles. After crossing the thruway bridge in Jordan, turn left onto River Road, which turns into Jordan Road and parallels the lake.

Additional information: There is no public access or camping on the lake. Most launch on the New Erie Canal (see sites 159D and 159E) and motor in. The lake's commercial marina on Jordan Road and a couple commercial campgrounds on the east shore have ramps.

Contact: New York State Department of Environmental Conservation Region 7 and Cayuga County Tourism.

127. Gillie Lake

Key species: Rainbow trout, largemouth bass, and bluegill.

Description: Built in the 1960s, this parklike 7-acre impoundment is spring fed, averages 7 feet deep, and has a maximum depth of about 18 feet.

Tips: Fish around the outlet pipe with Berkley Trout Bait.

The fishing: Roughly 4,000 fingerling rainbow trout have been stocked annually since around 1996. They reach an average of about 10 inches, and some have been known to make it to 16 inches. They are commonly taken on worms, flies, and commercial trout baits. This place has numerous largemouth bass ranging from 1 to 4 pounds. They react violently to streamers, bass bugs, and jerkbaits. Sunfish from 3 to 6 inches are plentiful and eagerly hit worms, tiny poppers, and 1-inch curly-tailed grubs.

Directions: Head north out of Camillus on Newport Road for about 2.5 miles. At the stop sign, go straight onto Canal Road and travel for 0.4 mile, turn left onto Breed Road, then 100 yards later turn right onto Sands Road and travel for 1 mile to the park entrance on the right.

Additional information: The centerpiece of the town of Camillus's 94-acre Veteran's Memorial Park at Gillie Lake, this site is wheelchair accessible and has picnic tables, grills, and a swimming beach. Camping, boating, and ice fishing are prohibited.

Contact: Town of Camillus Parks and Recreation.

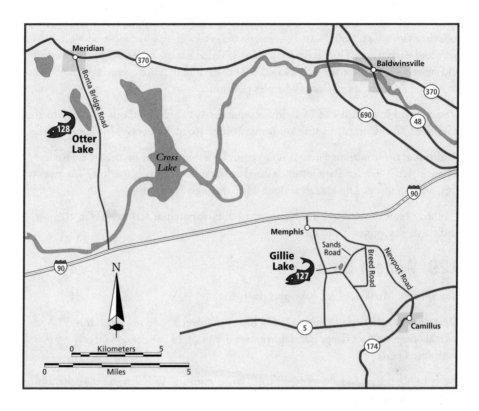

128. Otter Lake

Key species: Walleye, northern pike, largemouth bass, black crappie, and brown bullhead.

Description: This 282-acre lake averages 7 feet deep and drops to a maximum depth of 15 feet. Twenty percent of its shoreline is developed with private residences; protected wetland borders the rest.

Tips: Cast spinnerbaits in spring for walleyes and northerns.

The fishing: The state occasionally stocks surplus walleye fry, most recently in 2002, when 1,300,000 were released. The Weedsport Rod and Gun Club is a little more consistent, stocking an average of 2,000 4-inch walleyes annually. Many reach the 20- to 25-inch range typical for this lake. Locals catch them during the day by casting spinners and crankbaits like Husky Jerks over submerged weed beds. Northern pike aren't as plentiful as they were in the 1990s, but when you get one, chances are it'll be over 28 inches. They hit large minnows and the same baits the walleyes do.

Largemouth bass typically range from 3 to 5 pounds, and 8-pounders are available. They love making waves on calm days by taking buzzbaits, Jitterbugs, and Hula Poppers off the surface. The place is loaded with black crappie, but unfortunately most are too short. Still, 9- to 12-inchers are available and are most cooperative in May and early June. They'll hit 2-inch curly-tailed grubs, YUM Wooly Beavertails, and minnows. Bullheads reach 14 inches and are mostly taken with worms.

The lakewide speed limit is 5 miles per hour.

Directions: Head west out of Baldwinsville on NY 370 for about 10 miles to the hamlet of Meridian, turn south on Bonta Bridge Road, and travel for about 1 mile.

Additional information: There is no free public fishing access on the lake. However, Leisure Acres Trailer Park offers a hard-surface boat launch, parking for twenty rigs, and camping. The launch is open May through September.

Contact: New York State Department of Environmental Conservation Region 7 and Cayuga County Tourism.

129. Waneta Lake

Key species: Muskie, black bass, and panfish.

Description: Cradled in gently rolling hills 1,100 feet above sea level, this 812-acre lake averages 14 feet deep, has a maximum depth of 29 feet, and is largely carpeted with weed beds.

Tips: In October and November troll large minnow-imitating crankbaits along weed edges for trophy muskies.

The fishing: The state stocks several thousand 7-inch Chautauqua-strain muskies annually, and they grow to range between 15 and 40 pounds. Some claim the new state record lurks beneath this lovely lake's waves. While many trophies are caught incidentally by bass anglers in summer, the biggest are taken by a small group who targets the brutes with large minnows and by trolling plugs like Luhr Jensen's Javelins and Bomber Magnum Long "A"s and large spoons like Z-Rays (Sea-Zs) along weed lines. Largemouth bass range from 3 to 5 pounds, but fish approaching 10 pounds have been netted by biologists. Savvy locals go for the really big bass at night with surface lures like Hula Poppers and MirrOlure Top Dogs. Daylight anglers do well pitching Texas-rigged plastic worms into weed clearings, around timber, and under docks. Smallmouth bass range from 1 to 2 pounds. Fish for them in 10 to 20 feet of water with rattling crankbaits like MirrOlure Shad Rattlers. Yellow perch ranging from 6 to 12 inches, slab crappies up to 14 inches, and sunfish averaging 8 inches are sought year-round. The sunnies respond best to worms, while crappies and perch like small minnows, tiny jigs, and 2-inch scented curly-tailed grubs.

Waneta Lake · Lamoka Lake

Directions: Head south out of Penn Yan on NY 54 for about 13 miles, hook a left on NY 230 and head east for roughly 2 miles into Wayne, then turn south on CR 25 (Waneta Lake Road), which parallels the lake.

Additional information: A 0.7-mile-long channel connects Waneta to Lamoka Lake, but the culvert under CR 23 is too low to navigate. A paved boat launch is on the Waneta side, but you have to park in the Lamoka fishing access site lot across the road, which is large enough for about fifteen rigs. There is no public campground on the lake; however, primitive camping is permitted in Sugar Hill State Forest, located on CR 23 about 6 miles east of the boat launch.

Contact: New York State Department of Environmental Conservation Region 8 and Schuyler County Chamber of Commerce.

130. Lamoka Lake *(see map on page 229)*

Key species: Black bass, chain pickerel, muskie, yellow perch, black crappie, and sunfish.

Description: Its shoreline largely developed with summer cottages, this 590-acre lake averages 22 feet deep, drops to a maximum depth of 47 feet, and has an island on its northwest side.

Tips: Bucketmouths up to 7 pounds are always in the channel on the north end.

The fishing: Largemouth bass are the lake's bread-and-butter fish. They average 3 pounds, and 5-pounders are common. Biologists have netted many around 9 pounds. They take minnows, crayfish, and worms fished whacky-style. Smallmouth bass aren't as common. Ranging from 1 to 3 pounds, they generally like a clear bottom, but a surprising number prowl the weed lines. They take surface poppers and walkers, tubes and curly-tailed grubs dragged on bottom, and lipless crankbaits like Rat-L-Traps. Chain pickerel up to 5 pounds are plentiful. They hit jerkbaits and worms on spinner harnesses worked in and around weeds on hot summer days. Muskies come in from Waneta Lake. They reach 30-something pounds and respond to trolled crankbaits like Rapalas and Cotton Cordell's Red Fins. Perch and sunfish up to 1 pound and crappies ranging from 10 to 14 inches thrive in the southeastern bay and the weed line running along the west bank. The crappies like Road Runners, the perch can't resist 2-inch scented curly tails, and the pumpkinseeds and bluegills love wet flies and surface poppers.

Directions: Less than 1 mile due south of Waneta Lake (site 129). West Lake Road hugs the west bank.

Additional information: A fishing access site with a concrete ramp and parking for fifteen rigs is on CR 23. There are no public campgrounds, but primitive camping is allowed in Sugar Hill State Forest, on CR 23 about 6 miles east of the launch, and in Birdseye Hollow State Forest, off NY 226 3 miles south of the lake.

Contact: New York State Department of Environmental Conservation Region 8 and Schuyler County Chamber of Commerce.

131. Cayuta Lake *(see map on page 232)*

Key species: Walleye, tiger muskie, largemouth bass, and chain pickerel.

Description: Its shoreline only about half developed, this 518-acre lake averages 10 feet deep and has a maximum depth of 26 feet. It is very weedy, especially on its north and south ends.

Tips: Cast alewife imitations like Spot Minnows and Rat-L-Traps.

The fishing: This natural lake's alewife population has attracted the attention of Cornell University, which is experimenting with controlling their numbers by stocking walleyes. Apparently it's working, because in 2002 the state lent a hand by releasing 52,500 4-inchers. Well fed, the walleyes aren't easy to catch, but patient anglers are paid off with large fish, often exceeding 7 pounds. They like crankbaits and spinnerbaits. The state stocked 1,000 tiger muskies in 1998. Anglers have reported norlunge over 10 pounds, and a few fish up to 20 pounds should be available for much of this decade. They respond to jerkbaits and bucktail spinners. Largemouth bass average 4 pounds, and 8-pounders are available. They lurk in weeds, violently ambushing walk-the-dog-type surface baits, Texas-rigged plastic lizards, and night crawlers hooked in the head and tail to form a ring, then drifted weightless over submerged vegetation. Pickerel ranging from 20 to 25 inches are plentiful. They react with extreme prejudice to worms on spinner rigs and soft plastic jerkbaits like Cabela's Livin' Eye Minnows.
    The minimum length for walleyes is 18 inches, and the daily limit is three.

Directions: Head west out of Ithaca on NY 79 for 11 miles to Mecklenburg. Turn south on NY 228 and travel for 5.7 miles, turn left on Cayutaville Road, then right 0.1 mile later onto the public fishing access site road.

Additional information: The fishing access site has a hard-surface beach launch suitable for small motorized craft and parking for twenty rigs.

Contact: New York State Department of Environmental Conservation Region 8 and Schuyler County Chamber of Commerce.

132. Cayuta Creek *(see map on page 232)*

Key species: Brown trout.

Description: This Chemung River tributary drains Cayuta Lake. Starting off as a warm-water fishery, it quickly collects several springs and by the time it reaches the village of Alpine, cools down into a decent trout stream all the way to its mouth.

Tips: Trout habitat is best downstream of the village of Cayuta.

Cayuta Lake · Cayuta Creek · Park Station Lake (Beaver Pond)

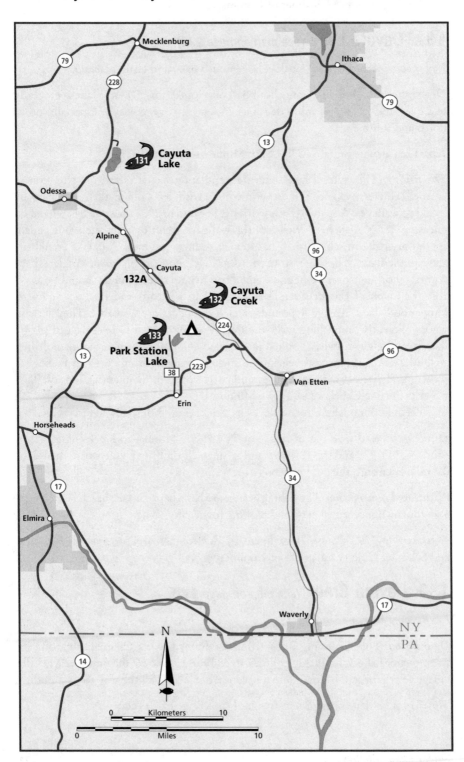

The fishing: The state stocks about 4,000 brown trout annually. Most are 9-inchers, but 20 percent are two-year-olds averaging 14 inches. Survival is good, and the stream boasts a better than average population of browns in the 16- to 20-inch class. They respond well to most nymphs in sizes 8 through 14. Larger nymphs work best in summer. Trout season is open year-round. The daily limit is five fish, with no more than two over 12 inches. Chemung County boasts a trophy artificial-lures-only section stretching for about 2 miles from the NY 223 bridge downstream to the Wyncoop Creek Road bridge. The minimum length for trout in this special section is 12 inches, and the daily limit is two.

Directions: NY 224 parallels the stream between the villages of Alpine and Van Etten, and NY 34 parallels it to Waverly.

Contact: New York State Department of Environmental Conservation Regions 7 and 8.

132A. Public Access

Description: This fishing access site has a paved lot and parking for about six cars.

Directions: At the NY 224 bridge, about 0.7 mile south of the hamlet of Cayuta.

133. Park Station Lake (Beaver Pond)

Key species: Rainbow trout, brown trout, largemouth bass, yellow perch, and bullhead.

Description: The crown jewel of Chemung County's 500-acre Park Station Recreation Area, this spring-fed 100-acre impoundment is almost completely surrounded by woods, averages 16 feet deep, and has a maximum depth of 36 feet. A 5-foot-wide trail, carpeted in wood chips, skirts the lake.

Tips: A special anglers' parking area off CR 38 (Laurel Hill Road) is just a couple hundred feet from the dam, the deepest part of the lake.

The fishing: Each year the state stocks roughly 2,000 rainbows and 400 browns averaging 9 inches and an additional 450 two-year-old browns. Survival is good, and anglers report decent catches of rainbows up to 14 inches and browns up to 16 inches. Most are taken on Berkley Trout Bait and night crawlers. Largemouth bass find the place to their liking. Ranging from 2 to 5 pounds, they hit surface lures like Zara Spooks and Hula Poppers, crankbaits like C.C. Rattlin' Shads and ThunderSticks, and weightless plastic lizards and worms. Yellow perch run a respectable 7 to 12 inches. Most are taken through the ice on flathead minnows. Brown and black bullheads ranging from 6 to 14 inches are plentiful and like worms fished on bottom. Park manager Jerry Jones, an avid fisherman, says a child caught a 29-pound channel catfish in the summer of 2002. He suspects it was one of the original fifteen channel cats that were stocked into the lake when it was built in the late 1970s.

Directions: Head north on NY 13 out of Horseheads for about 2 miles and turn east on NY 223. Travel roughly 5 miles to the west side of Erin, then turn north on CR 38 (Laurel Hill Road) and continue for a couple miles.

Additional information: Park Station Recreation Area charges a fee from Memorial Day through Labor Day. This facility boasts forty-one year-round campsites with electricity, a swimming beach, a small-craft launch, boat rentals, a picnic area, ball fields, and miles of groomed trails. Motors are not allowed on the lake, except for the electric motors the park rents to the physically disabled. Private rowboats are allowed but must be registered. The park is open from sunrise to sunset.

Contact: New York State Department of Environmental Conservation Region 8 and Park Station Recreation Center.

134. Alexander Lake

Key species: Largemouth bass and bluegill.

Description: Built in 1965 and currently owned by the Newark Valley School System, this 15-acre impoundment is completely surrounded by woods. Averaging 4 feet deep and dropping to a maximum of 15 feet, its floor is littered with tree stumps.

Tips: Fly fish with poppers.

The fishing: Don Alexander, the guy who built the place and for whom it's named, says he originally stocked it with brook trout. However, largemouth bass and bluegills from a neighboring pond swam in on runoff, ate all the brookies, and seeded Alexander Lake with their own kind. Largemouth bass average 3 pounds, and many larger ones are available. They like surface baits and soft plastics fished on bottom tight to tree stumps. Bluegills are larger than average—indeed, Alexander claims to have caught a half dozen one day that collectively weighed 4 pounds. They hit worms, grubs, and flies.

Directions: From NY 38 in the hamlet of Newark Valley, head west on Silk Street (Courtright Hill Road on most maps) for a little less than 1 mile and turn north on Dr. Knapp Road. Travel for about 1 mile and turn right on the gravel road to the pond.

Additional information: Alexander says consumptive activities like fishing used to be prohibited, and some no-fishing signs still remain on trees. However, fishing is currently allowed.

Contact: New York State Department of Environmental Conservation Region 7 and Tioga County Tourism.

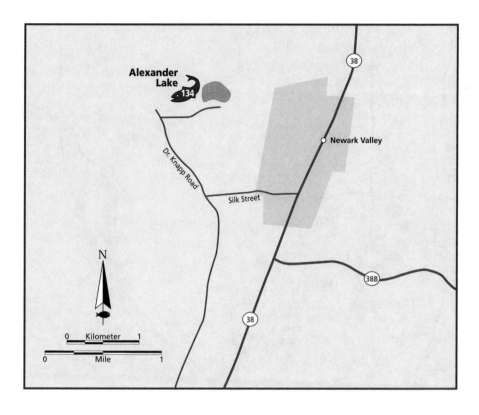

135. Loon Lake *(see map on page 236)*

Key species: Largemouth bass, chain pickerel, and yellow perch.

Description: This natural 141-acre lake averages 15 feet deep and has a maximum depth of 45 feet.

Tips: In late summer oxygen is sparse in depths below 25 feet.

The fishing: Largemouth bass usually run from 2 to 4 pounds, but larger ones are available. They respond to jig-'n'-pigs and whacky-rigged finesse worms worked along weed edges and to Bill Lewis' Slapsticks jerked around lily pads. Pickerel in the 15- to 25-inch range are also plentiful and react violently to just about any lure, especially flashy ones like Rooster Tail spinners. Yellow perch range from 6 to 12 inches and like worms, minnows, and 2-inch curly-tailed grubs.

Directions: Head north out of Bath on NY 415 for about 15 miles to the village of Cohocton. Turn west on CR 121 and travel 3.5 miles to its end, turn north on NY

Loon Lake · Cohocton, Canisteo, and Tioga Rivers

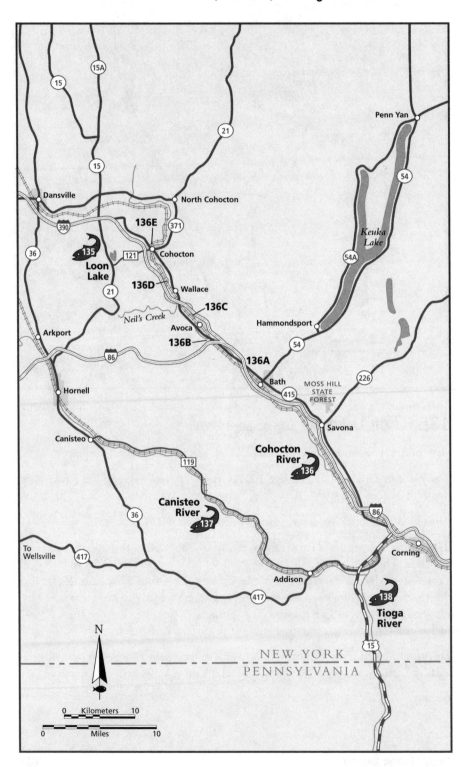

21 and continue for roughly 0.5 mile, then turn right on Laf-A-Lot Road and travel for about 100 yards to the Laf-A-Lot Inn.

Additional information: There is no free public access on the lake. However, the Laf-A-Lot Inn on the west bank offers access and a hard-surface ramp for a fee.

Contact: New York State Department of Environmental Conservation Region 8 and Steuben County Conference and Visitors Bureau.

136. Cohocton River

Key species: Brown trout.

Description: This river snakes for about 40 miles, slicing through farm country, swamps, and woodlots overshadowed by gentle hills that seem to roll on forever. Bath marks the transition from cold water (upstream) to warm water. Its union with the Tioga River in Painted Post forms the Chemung River. According to local lore, the original name was Conhocton, an Indian word meaning "log on the water," but a drunken painter left the first *n* out of a village sign, and the name stuck.

Tips: Rip Muddler Minnows across the surface.

The fishing: Each year the state stocks in excess of 8,000 brown trout averaging 9.5 inches and 2,800 two-year-olds averaging 13.5 inches. Winter survival is good, and 18-inch fish are relatively abundant. A few brook trout, migrants from the numerous tiny tributaries, are also present. Both take worms, minnows, and flies. Trout season is open year-round.

Directions: I–390 runs alongside the river from Cohocton to about 1 mile south of Avoca, and I–86 (former NY 17) follows it from there to its mouth.

Additional information: The state owns roughly 20 miles of public fishing rights; the longest stretch is between the village of North Cohocton and the city of Bath. NY 371 and NY 415 parallel most of this stretch, and there are many informal pull-offs. Two sections are restricted to artificial lures only (see sites 136A and 136C). Primitive camping is allowed in Moss Hill State Forest, which touches NY 415 3 miles south of Bath.

Contact: New York State Department of Environmental Conservation Region 8 and Steuben County Conference and Visitors Bureau.

136A. Knight Settlement Bridge Public Access

Description: Parking for about twenty cars.

Directions: Head north on NY 415 out of Bath for a little over 1 mile.

Additional information: This site is on the artificial-lures-only section stretching from the northern boundary of the Veterans Administration facility in Bath

Fly fishing on the Cohocton River (site 136).

upstream to the NY 415 bridge. The minimum length for trout is 12 inches, and the daily limit is three.

136B. Owens Road Public Access *(see map on page 236)*

Description: Parking for five cars.

Directions: Head south out of Avoca on NY 415 for 1 mile, turn left on Owens Road and travel for about 100 yards, then turn right into the parking area at the base of the bridge.

136C. Cross Road Public Access *(see map on page 236)*

Description: Cross Road dead-ends at the river. Shoulder parking for about five cars.

Directions: Head north out of Avoca on NY 415 for a little under 1 mile.

Additional information: This site is on the special artificial-lures-only section stretching from the northern boundary of Avoca to Neil's Creek. The minimum length for trout is 12 inches, and the daily limit is two.

136D. Wentworth Road Bridge Public Access *(see map on page 236)*

Description: Parking for four cars.

Directions: Take NY 415 north out of Avoca for about 3.5 miles.

136E. Cohocton Train Station Public Access *(see map on page 236)*

Description: Parking for about five cars at the old train station.

Directions: On Maple Avenue on the west side of the village of Cohocton.

137. Canisteo River *(see map on page 236)*

Key species: Brown trout, smallmouth bass, and walleye.

Description: This warm-water stream flows for about 50 miles, through a gently rolling countryside spotted with farms and woodlots, and feeds the Tioga River about 5 miles southwest of Corning.

Tips: Use minnows—live or salted.

The fishing: The headwaters in the township of Hornellsville are stocked annually with around 2,100 brown trout averaging 9.5 inches and 400 two-year-olds stretching the tape to about 14.5 inches. As planned by the state, most are caught before summer on worms, minnows, and flies. Those that survive only stick around until about July, when the water gets unbearably warm, then migrate downstream or into tributaries. However, some find spring pools and others manage to stay cool in the stretch between Hornell and Arkport, providing summer action for anglers who don't mind walking the creek, searching for the holes. Smallmouth bass ranging from 12 to 14 inches are present south of Hornell and respond to streamers and worms. Walleyes ranging from 15 to 20 inches are found in the mouth in spring and fall. They take worms and jigs.

Directions: NY 36 parallels the trout water from Arkport to Canisteo, and CR 119 skirts the rest, almost to its mouth.

Additional information: Most of the riverbank is privately owned; however, some areas are opened to public fishing and are blazed with LANDOWNER COOPERATIVE FISHING PERMITTED disks. According to Bill Abraham, formerly a senior fisheries biologist with the state, "These rivers [the Tioga and Canisteo] have very limited informal canoe access at bridge crossings. Formal access is in the process of being developed."

Contact: New York State Department of Environmental Conservation Region 8 and Steuben County Conference and Visitors Bureau.

138. Tioga River *(see map on page 236)*

Key species: Smallmouth bass, walleye, and channel catfish.

Description: Relatively deep and slow moving, this warm-water stream snakes up from Pennsylvania and runs north for about 10 miles. En route it picks up the Canisteo River. About 3 miles further it joins the Cohocton River, a union which forms the Chemung River.

Tips: Wear camouflage while drifting.

The fishing: Smallmouth bass up to 18 inches are available. They respond best to minnows and crayfish. Walleyes ranging from 15 to 23 inches occupy the deeper holes and undercut banks and take jigs worked on bottom and minnow-imitating crankbaits worked through the heads and tails of pools in the evening. Channel catfish typically run from 14 to 20 inches, but some real bruisers up to 12 pounds have been reported. They hang out in deep holes at bends and under windfalls and have a taste for meat: worms, shrimp, and cut bait.

Directions: US 15 parallels the river.

Additional information: According to Bill Abraham, formerly a senior fisheries biologist with the state, "These rivers [the Tioga and Canisteo] have very limited informal canoe access at bridge crossings. Formal access is in the process of being developed."

Contact: New York State Department of Environmental Conservation Region 8 and Steuben County Conference and Visitors Bureau.

139. Chemung River

Key species: Walleye, smallmouth bass, muskellunge, and channel catfish.

Description: Spawned by the union of the Cohocton and Tioga Rivers in Painted Post, this medium-size stream is typical of the other strands in the web of rivers flowing through southern New York: shallow riffles and flats one moment, fast skinny runs the next, and fishy-looking pools around the bends.

Tips: Use a dark jig below the dam in Elmira at night and on overcast days.

The fishing: This has always been a popular stream for scrappy smallmouth bass ranging from 0.75 to 1.5 pounds. They'll hit Mepps spinners worked through the heads of pools, Rapalas cranked through deep holes, and worms, crayfish, and minnows drifted along breaklines and around windfalls. Walleyes ranging from 15 to 22 inches are plentiful and respond to jigheads tipped with minnows, the bottom halves of night crawlers, or YUM Shakin' Worms. Crankbaits such as Rat-L-Traps and Cotton Cordell's Red Fins worked through pools will catch both species. The rivers biggest predators are muskies, Ohio River–strain purebreds and tigers. Both range from 30 to 40 inches and take large minnows, bucktail spinners, and minnow-imitating crankbaits like Bomber A-Salts. Channel catfish average 16 inches, with specimens over 20 inches common. Slowly drift cut bait or live minnows on bottom, along eddies, or anywhere else you find current over deep holes.

Chemung River

To Hornell

Cohocton River

Painted Post

To Binghamton

Van Etten

224

34

220

Waverly

86

427

139E

Wellsburg

427

14

Horseheads

14

Elmira

139D

139

Chemung River

Big Flats

139C

352

225

Steege Hill Road

139B

44

Corning

South Corning

414

139A

River

Tioga

15

15

NEW YORK

PENNSYLVANIA

N

Kilometers

10

Miles

10

0

0

Directions: I–86 and NY 352 parallel the river.

Additional information: Informal shore-fishing access is good along most of the river's route, including in the cities of Elmira and Corning.

Contact: New York State Department of Environmental Conservation Region 8.

139A. Kinsella Park Public Access (see map on page 241)

Description: This site, on the Cohocton River just upstream of its mouth, offers a beach launch for cartop craft and parking for twenty cars.

Directions: On Canada Road in Painted Post.

139B. Bottcher's Landing Public Access (see map on page 241)

Description: This site has a paved ramp and parking for fifteen rigs.

Directions: Head east out of Corning on River Road (CR 44) for about 3 miles. At the end, turn south on Steege Hill Road, then immediately east on Old River Road.

139C. Minier's Field Launch Public Access (see map on page 241)

Description: This site offers a paved ramp and parking for fifteen rigs.

Directions: Head south out of the village of Big Flats on NY 352 for about 1 mile.

139D. Dunn Field Public Access (see map on page 241)

Description: This site offers bank fishing, a cartop beach launch, and parking for twenty cars.

Directions: Located on Fair Street in Elmira.

139E. Toll Bridge Park Public Access (see map on page 241)

Description: This site offers shore-fishing access, a paved ramp, and parking for fifteen rigs.

Directions: Head east out of Elmira on NY 427 for about 4 miles to the CR 8 bridge at Wellsburg.

140. Dryden Lake

Key species: Largemouth bass, chain pickerel, yellow perch, black crappie, and bluegill.

Description: This 117-acre lake averages 4 feet deep and has a maximum depth of 12 feet.

Tips: Walk Zara Spooks over submerged timber and weed edges.

Dryden Lake

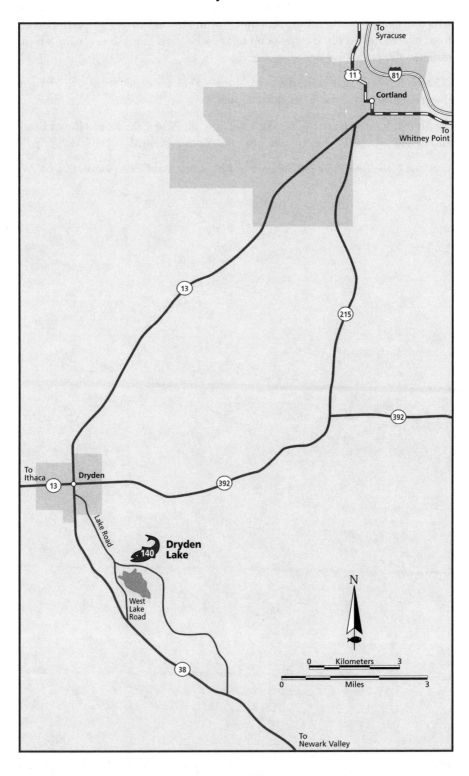

The fishing: The lake has largemouth bass up to 5 pounds and scrappy pickerel ranging from 15 to 26 inches. Both like jerkbaits and spinnerbaits worked around structure and cover. Ice fishing is popular for mixed bags of yellow perch ranging from 6 to 10 inches, black crappies up to 12 inches, and bluegills averaging 8 inches. They all like dot jigs tipped with grubs.

Directions: Head south out of Cortland on NY 13 for about 9 miles to Dryden, then take Lake Road south for about 2 miles.

Additional information: The fishing access site on West Lake Road offers a beach launch and parking for fifteen cars. Motors are not permitted on the lake.

Contact: New York State Department of Environmental Conservation Region 7.

CENTRAL NEW YORK

This section primarily covers the Oswego River and the Salmon and Oneida River drainages. All the waters listed, with the exception of the Fish Creek drainage (sites 152 through 156), are located within New York State Department of Environmental Conservation Region 7. A special rule applies to the five-trout daily limit: Only two of the trout can be 12 inches or longer. In addition, five brook trout under 8 inches can be taken. In brook trout habitats like Oswego County's Mad River (site 163), you are allowed to keep ten brookies daily: two 12 inches or longer, three from 8 to 11.9 inches, and five under 8 inches.

141. Glacier Lake *(see map on page 246)*

Key species: Chain pickerel, walleye, bluegill, and bullhead.

Description: The plunge pool of an ancient river, this scenic 10-acre lake is completely surrounded by forest, has sheer cliffs towering over half its shoreline, averages 45 feet deep, and has a maximum depth of 62 feet.

Tips: Half of the lake is bordered by marsh, and wearing hip boots will allow you to get beyond most obstacles. But don't venture out too far—the mud gets deep.

The fishing: Pickerel range from too small to over 25 inches. They react violently to scented plastic slugs ripped across the surface and spinnerbaits (in-line, buzzbaits, and offset). The state stocks thousands of walleye fry most years. The majority falls victim to pickerel or migrates out through the tiny outlet. Those that stay end up averaging 15 inches and take scented 3-inch curly-tailed grubs jigged on bottom or retrieved steadily through the water column. Sunfish average 4 inches, but palm-size whoppers are present. They like wet flies and surface poppers. Bullheads go anywhere from 6 to 14 inches and like worms fished on bottom.

Directions: Head east out of Syracuse on NY 173 (Seneca Turnpike) for about 4 miles.

Additional information: You'll have to climb down a 100-plus-foot-long stone staircase to the lake. Totally within Clark Reservation State Park, a day-use fee is charged from Memorial Day through Labor Day. The gate remains open, however, and anglers who arrive before 7:30 A.M. get in free. Boats are not allowed on the lake.

Contact: New York State Department of Environmental Conservation Region 7 and Clark Reservation State Park.

Glacier Lake · Butternut Creek · Jamesville Reservoir

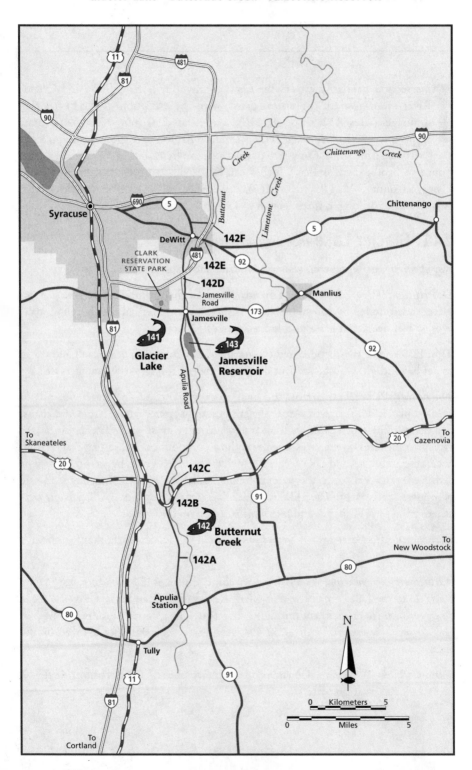

142. Butternut Creek

Key species: Brown trout, brook trout, and carp.

Description: Bubbling to the surface just south of Apulia Station, at the divide separating the Susquehanna and Oswego River drainages, this creek flows north for about 20 miles, fills and drains Jamesville Reservoir, and pours through a gorge before joining Limestone Creek in North Manlius.

Tips: Use brown nymphs.

The fishing: The state stocks this stream annually, but the figures are always different. In 2003, for instance, the statistics for brown trout were 2,200 8-inchers, 1,250 averaging 14 inches, and 500 over 15 inches. Seven hundred brookies averaging 8.5 inches were also released. In addition, quite a bit of natural reproduction occurs, especially in the gorge running through the village of Jamesville. Overall, trout average 10 inches, but 20-inchers are possible. The biggest fish are taken on worms. Carp ranging from 1 to 10 pounds thrive from DeWitt downstream to the mouth. They provide explosive action in summer for anglers sight-fishing for them with worms or still-fishing on bottom in deep pools with corn, dough balls, and baked potato.

Trout can be taken year-round downstream (north) of US 20.

Directions: Apulia Road parallels the stream from Apulia Station to Jamesville, and Jamesville Road parallels it to DeWitt.

Contact: New York State Department of Environmental Conservation Region 7 and Syracuse Convention and Visitors Bureau.

142A. Public Access

Description: Formal parking for three cars.

Directions: Take Apulia Road north out of Apulia Station for about 3.5 miles and turn east on Cascade Road.

142B. US 20 Public Access

Description: Shoulder parking for ten cars.

Directions: At the US 20 bridge, about 0.5 mile east of the US 20/Apulia Road intersection.

142C. Public Access

Description: Formal parking for about five cars.

Directions: Take Apulia Road about 1 mile north from its intersection with US 20. Turn east on Dodge Road.

Angler with winter brown trout caught in Butternut Creek (site 142).

142D. Public Access (see map on page 246)

Description: Formal parking for about ten cars.

Directions: Head north out of Jamesville on Jamesville Road for about 0.5 mile. The site hugs the I–481 North off-ramp.

142E. Public Access (see map on page 246)

Description: A clearing off the highway, this informal site has parking for ten cars.

The fishing: This downstream stretch of creek is good trout habitat from mid-fall through spring. In summer it's "carp city."

Directions: Take the I–481 North on-ramp across from site 142D, travel about 2 miles to the bridge, and park in the landing on the north side.

142F. Erie Canal State Park Public Access (see map on page 246)

Description: Parking for twenty cars right below the Old Erie Canal aqueduct.

The fishing: The pools hold huge carp, a few smallmouth bass, some bullheads, and sunfish.

Directions: From the Kinne Road/Erie Boulevard East intersection in Syracuse, head east on Kinne Road, cross I–481 about 1.5 miles later, turn left on Butternut Road, and travel about 100 yards to the parking lot.

143. Jamesville Reservoir (see map on page 246)

Key species: Walleye, black bass, tiger muskie, chain pickerel, perch, black crappie, rock bass, and sunfish.

Description: This 200-acre impoundment averages 22 feet deep and has a maximum depth of 35 feet. Local legend says the dam was built on the site of a haunted bridge, but the ghost hasn't been seen since.

Tips: In May and October wade out as far as you can in the county park and cast minnow-imitating crankbaits.

The fishing: This reservoir has always been known for large walleyes. You don't catch many, but when you get one there's a good chance it'll be over 5 pounds. The best time to fish for them is at night with lipless lures like Rat-L-Traps and floating/diving crankbaits like Smithwick Rogues. Smallmouth bass up to 3 pounds can be caught along the rocky drop-offs on fat-bodied crankbaits like the Poe's Super Cedar Series 300 and Worden's Timber Tiger DC 8. Hawg bucketmouths up to 8 pounds rule the weedy south end and respond well to surface lures like Hula Poppers, Jitterbugs, and Zara Spooks from dusk through dawn. The state stocks tiger muskies annually. Although those lucky enough to avoid being eaten their first year end up reaching up to 30 pounds, there aren't too many and they don't have a following. Still, several are serendipitously taken each year on crankbaits targeting bass and walleye. Pickerel up to 5 pounds are available and respond to worms worked on spinner rigs over deep weeds and along weed edges. Rock bass and yellow and white perch ranging between 6 and 10 inches and black crappies averaging 9 inches are plentiful and hit 2-inch tubes and curly-tailed grubs jigged on bottom or worked through the water column on spinner forms. Bluegills and pumpkinseeds up to 8 inches thrive in the weedy southern bays and hit worms, Berkley Power Wigglers, and 1-inch Power Grubs, poppers, and wet flies.

Directions: Head east out of Syracuse on Seneca Turnpike (NY 173) for about 3 miles to Jamesville, turn right on Apulia Road, and travel about 1 mile.

Additional information: Fishing is permitted on the east shore, off the shoulder of NY 91, but parking isn't and the police are quick to issue tickets. Public access with a beach launch for cartop craft and parking for hundreds of cars is available at Jamesville Beach County Park, a fee area on Apulia Road. The fee is only charged from mid-June through Labor Day. Toads Landing, a private operation on West Shore Manor Road (the left before the park), has a paved ramp and parking for about seven rigs. If no one is around, stick the $7.00 launch fee ($15.00 if you rent a canoe) into one of the envelopes provided at the door and drop it in the mail slot.

Contact: New York State Department of Environmental Conservation Region 7 and Onondaga County Parks.

144. Green Lake

Key species: Rainbow trout and northern pike.

Description: This 64-acre lake's beauty makes its park one of Central New York's most popular. Created by an ancient glacial waterfall, the lake was believed to be bottomless by Indians and early settlers alike, but recent measurements reveal it is only 195 feet deep.

Tips: Use a line with interchangeable tips, such as RIO's AquaLux VersiTip, to flat-line streamers, anywhere from 2 to 20 feet deep, behind one of the park's rental rowboats.

The fishing: Every year the Onondaga County hatchery stocks roughly 2,500 rainbow trout ranging from 10 to 15 inches, half before the season opens and half sometime in May. Many are caught early in the season from the boathouse docks on pieces of worms and small minnows suspended below tiny bobbers. Still-fishing with kernels of canned corn and Berkley Trout Bait suspended a few inches off bottom also works. Northern pike were introduced in the last century. There aren't many, but when you get one, chances are it'll be over 30 inches. They hit minnows, minnow-imitating crankbaits, and Dardevles.

Directions: Head east on NY 5 out of Fayetteville for about 1 mile.

Green, Cazenovia, and Tuscarora Lakes · DeRuyter Reservoir Drainages

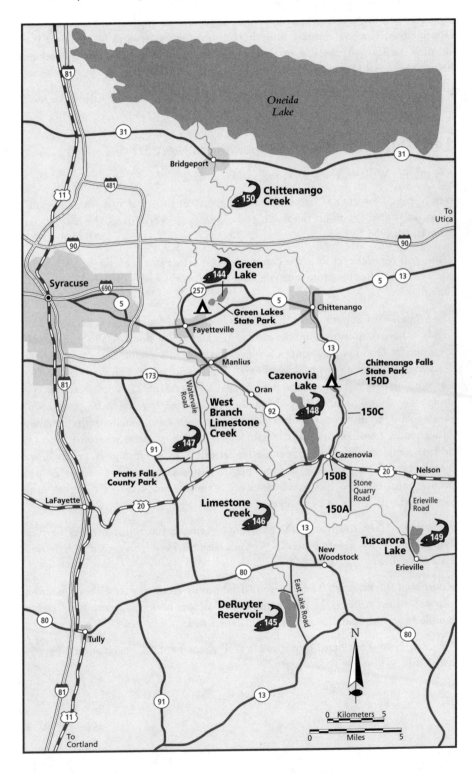

Additional information: Trout season is open until November 30. The lake is entirely within Green Lakes State Park, a 1,700-acre facility offering 137 campsites (42 electric), 7 cabins, an 18-hole golf course, a sandy swimming beach, picnic facilities, two shelters, rowboat rentals, and shore-fishing access from a recreational trail skirting the lake. A day-use fee is charged noncampers from the first weekend before Memorial Day through Labor Day.

Contact: New York State Department of Environmental Conservation Region 7 and Green Lakes State Park.

145. DeRuyter Reservoir (see map on page 251)

Key species: Walleye, black bass, and yellow perch.

Description: Covering 576 acres, the only section of shoreline that isn't someone's backyard is at the dam on the north end. Averaging 15 feet deep, the lake's maximum depth is 55 feet.

Tips: Drift for walleyes near the dam with two outfits: Bounce a jig-rigged scented curly-tailed grub off bottom with one, and drift a worm with a spinner harness with the other.

The fishing: This impoundment has always been famed for walleyes. Recently their numbers have diminished, and the state is helping out by stocking almost 3,000,000 fry annually. Good populations of walleyes in the 2- to 4-pound range are available. They take everything from Wally Divers and ThunderSticks to jigs and leeches. Largemouth bass running up to 5 pounds are also abundant. They respond to everything from floating worms ripped rapidly over emergent weeds to flipping jig-'n'-pigs into slop to dragging Carolina-rigged craws over mud. Smallmouths averaging 14 inches are common around the dam and other rocky areas, where they hit fat-bodied crankbaits like Poe's Super Cedar Series 1100s, live minnows, crayfish, and 3-inch scented curly-tailed grubs and plastic minnows worked on drop-shot rigs. Yellow perch in the 6- to 10-inch range are popularly targeted by ice anglers using jigs tipped with grubs or perch eyes.

Directions: Head south on NY 13 from Cazenovia for about 6 miles to New Woodstock. Hook a right onto NY 80 west, then turn south about 1 mile later onto East Lake Road.

Additional information: There is no official public access site, but shore fishing is allowed off the dam on the north end, with shoulder parking for about six cars. A couple of private launches are on South Lake Road.

Contact: New York State Department of Environmental Conservation Region 7 and Madison County Tourism.

146. Limestone Creek *(see map on page 251)*

Key species: Brown trout, brook trout, and carp.

Description: Spawned by DeRuyter Reservoir, this creek runs north for about 25 miles to join Butternut Creek.

Tips: The best trout water is from Fayetteville upstream.

The fishing: The state annually stocks about 6,500 browns ranging from 7 to 15.5 inches; 1,800 are longer than 13 inches. The county hatchery chips in with several thousand more. In addition, about 300 10-inch brookies are released. Most of the stockies are removed early in the season by anglers fishing with worms and minnows in the pools below bridges. Still, enough survive to offer live-bait and fly fishers decent sport for the rest of the season. Worms, salted minnows, and nymphs are the most popular baits. Carp are plentiful downstream of the dam in Fayetteville, providing exciting sight-fishing for stalking anglers using worms.

Trout can be taken year-round downstream (north) of US 20.

Directions: This stream flows through the villages of Oran, Manlius, and Fayetteville and is paralleled for much of its length by NY 92.

Additional information: Informal access is available at the US 20 bridge (shoulder parking), the NY 173 bridge and Mill Park (off Mill Street) in Manlius, and behind the village offices on Brooklea Drive in Fayetteville. Nearby Green Lakes State Park (see site 144) offers camping.

Contact: New York State Department of Environmental Conservation Region 7.

147. West Branch Limestone Creek *(see map on page 251)*

Key species: Brown trout.

Description: Springing just a couple miles east of Fabius Brook, right at the divide separating the Susquehanna River drainage from the Oswego River drainage, this tiny stream flows north for about 7 miles—through a patchwork of forests, pastures, farm fields, and backyards—and feeds Limestone Creek in the village of Manlius.

Tips: The first couple weeks of the season are your best bet for nailing holdover Limestone Creek browns that migrated into the West Branch the previous fall to spawn.

The fishing: This creek has a couple of waterfalls that are over 50 feet high. The first, Brickyard Falls, located about 1.5 miles from the mouth, stops Limestone Creek trout from migrating further upstream. However, Onondaga County's Carpenter's Brook fish hatchery annually stocks the Pratts Falls County Park section with about 700 browns averaging 7.5 inches and 250 two-year-olds up to 14 inches long. The fish are placed above and below the falls. They respond to worms and nymphs fished in pockets.

Directions: Watervale Road parallels the stream from Manlius to US 20.

Additional information: Pratts Falls County Park, a fee area run on the honor system, offers a 1-acre mill pond above the falls and trails skirting the creek downstream of the cataract. Informal access is available at the NY 173 bridge in Manlius.

Contact: New York State Department of Environmental Conservation Region 7 and Onondaga County Parks.

148. Cazenovia Lake *(see map on page 251)*

Key species: Largemouth bass, chain pickerel, yellow perch, sunfish, and black crappie.

Description: This 1,184-acre lake averages 15 feet deep, has a maximum depth of 48 feet, and is almost completely surrounded by private residences.

Tips: Ice fish on the north end at night for slab crappies.

The fishing: This lake is loaded with largemouth bass ranging from 12 to 15 inches. For explosive surface action, fly fish for them with $\frac{1}{16}$- and $\frac{1}{24}$-ounce Hula Poppers. Pickerel ranging from 15 to 25 inches are plentiful and hit Rooster Tail spinners worked along weed edges and Flukes jerked around lily pads. Cazenovia's massive weed beds are a panfish factory. Indeed, its name is Indian for "lake where the yellow perch swim." Bluegills, pumpkinseeds, and crappies average better than 0.5 pound. Most yellow perch range from 7 to 12 inches, but 14-inchers are present. The perch and crappies hit small minnows and Beetle Spins, especially on the north end. The sunfish love $\frac{1}{32}$-ounce Hula Poppers, wet flies, and worms.

Directions: The lake is located on the west side of the village of Cazenovia. US 20 skirts its south shore.

Additional information: The affluent residents of Cazenovia are a protective lot and would like to keep the lake to themselves, sometimes even posting FOR CAZENOVIA RESIDENTS ONLY signs at the entrances to the lake's three public access sites. However, the NYS Department of Transportation owns a tiny parking area at the intersection of US 20 and NY 92 that offers parking for about twenty cars, a beach launch, shore-fishing access, and picnic tables. Nearby Chittenango Falls State Park (see 150D), a fee area, offers camping.

Contact: New York State Department of Environmental Conservation Region 7 and Madison County Tourism.

149. Tuscarora Lake (Erieville Reservoir) *(see map on page 251)*

Key species: Largemouth bass, walleye, and yellow perch.

Description: Built in 1850 to provide water for the Erie Canal, this lake covers 340 acres, averages 21 feet deep, and has a maximum depth of 43 feet. Its shore is almost completely developed with private residences.

Tips: Ice fish for large walleyes by jigging minnows.

The fishing: Boasting a great deal of shallow-water habitat, this place is loaded with largemouth bass ranging from 14 to 18 inches long. Work spinnerbaits and Texas-rigged worms around shallow structure like docks and ancient tree stumps. Walleyes are stocked by a local club and reach trophy size—fish up to 14 pounds have been reported. Most are taken through the ice on big minnows; however, in spring and fall they hit Rat-L-Traps and Bomber Long "A"s at night. In summer some are taken by drifting leeches and worms. Yellow perch running from 8 to 12 inches are targeted with worms and 2-inch scented curly-tailed grubs spring through fall and through the ice with small minnows and grubs.

Directions: Head east out of Cazenovia on US 20 for about 3 miles to Nelson, then turn south on Erieville Road and travel for about 4 miles.

Additional information: An ice-fishing derby is held each year, with proceeds going to the stocking of the lake. There is no official public access, but many people fish off the long earthen dam on the north end and off the shoulder of Tuscarora Road on the south end.

Contact: New York State Department of Environmental Conservation Region 7 and Madison County Tourism.

150. Chittenango Creek *(see map on page 251)*

Key species: Brown trout, brook trout, and walleye.

Description: Spawned by Tuscarora Lake and doubled in size by tributaries that flow into it in Nelson Swamp, this creek meanders north for about 30 miles. On the way it tumbles over Chittenango Falls and picks up Limestone and Butternut Creeks, then pours into Oneida Lake at Bridgeport.

Tips: Dead-drift Wooly Worms in late summer.

The fishing: One of Central New York's finest trout streams, Chittenango Creek gets stocked annually with about 14,000 browns. The vast majority averages 8 inches, but more than 2,000 are two-year-olds averaging 14 inches. Worms and salted minnows are the local baits of choice. Worms are especially effective in pocket water after a rain. Though few in number, wild brook trout range from 6 to 12 inches and hit the same baits as the browns. Walleyes spawn in the creek and hang around in the pools near Bridgeport until June.

Trout season is year-round in the stretch from US 20 in Cazenovia to the Conrail railroad line a couple miles downstream of Chittenango. Fishing is prohibited from the Conrail line to the mouth from March 16 until the first Saturday in May.

Directions: NY 13 parallels the creek from a couple miles south of Cazenovia to Chittenango.

Additional information: Much of the stream is open to public fishing. There are numerous informal shoulder pull-offs on NY 13 between Cazenovia and Chittenango.

Contact: New York State Department of Environmental Conservation Region 7 and Madison County Tourism.

150A. Nelson Swamp Unique Area Public Access *(see map on page 251)*

Description: This site is on an abandoned railroad grade, which crosses the creek and parallels it for a couple hundred yards.

The fishing: This part of the stream runs through a huge swamp. Slow moving, spotted with deep holes, lined with undercut banks crowned in heavy brush and thick woods, and littered with windfalls, the area is remote, offering solitude and a good chance at catching savvy 20-plus-inch trout.

Directions: Take US 20 east out of Cazenovia for about 1 mile and turn right on Stone Quarry Road. At the stop sign about 1 mile later, head straight on Nine Road for about 0.5 mile; the parking area will be on the left, before the bridge.

Additional information: This area is considered unique because of its unusual vegetation, including patches of old-growth forest—one contains the world's oldest eastern white pine.

150B. Gorge Trail Public Access *(see map on page 251)*

Description: This abandoned railroad grade parallels the creek for about 2 miles. A popular hiking path, the trailhead has parking for about five cars.

Directions: In the heart of Cazenovia, take NY 13 to Clark Street, cross the bridge, and park on its northeast corner.

150C. Public Access *(see map on page 251)*

Description: This site has parking for about ten cars.

Directions: On NY 13, about 3 miles north of Cazenovia.

150D. Chittenango Falls State Park *(see map on page 251)*

Description: This 192-acre park has twenty-two no-frills campsites, hot showers, playgrounds, hiking trails, and fishing access to the pocket water and deep pools above the falls and the spectacular gorge below it. The campground is open from mid-May through mid-October; a day-use fee is charged noncampers.

Directions: Head north out of Cazenovia on NY 13 for about 4 miles.

151. Old Erie Canal State Park *(see map on page 258)*

Key species: Black bass, chain pickerel, northern pike, bullhead, sunfish, and carp.

Description: Originally opened in 1825 and expanded several years later, this marvel of nineteenth-century engineering sliced through the state, connecting Lake Erie at Buffalo with the Hudson River at Albany, a distance of 363 miles. Today most of the canal is filled in, and small sections have been turned into parks. Old Erie Canal State Park is the longest, running 35 miles from Syracuse to Rome.

Tips: Chum a spot with canned corn, then come back in an hour and fish for carp.

The fishing: Smallmouth bass averaging 12 inches and largemouth bass running from 12 to 14 inches hit spinnerbaits and twitch baits. Northern pike up to 24 inches seem to gravitate to the wide waters where they take Johnson silver spoons worked along cattail mats and through weed beds. Chain pickerel average 16 inches and like worms on spinner rigs cranked over weed openings and around windfalls. Sunfish up to 8 inches and bullheads averaging 10 inches can be caught just about anywhere on worms. Carp range from 12 to 20 inches and hit worms, bread balls, and baked potato.

Directions: NY 5 parallels the waterway from DeWitt to Canastota; numerous public access sites, with parking for a couple cars each, are available at the bridges of most roads striking north from the highway. CR 76 runs along the canal's dike from Canastota to Durhamville, where NY 46 picks it up and hugs it into the outskirts of Rome.

Additional information: Green Lakes State Park (see site 144) on NY 290, offers a campground and cabins. The old canal drains into the New Erie Canal in New London, leaving the park's last 5 miles a patchwork of swamps and marsh. In remote areas the old towpath, or heelpath (an emergency route that paralleled the south bank), serves as recreational trails. Several wide waters swell Clinton's Ditch between DeWitt and Pools Brook, a couple miles east of Kirkville. Fabulous aqueducts built of cut limestone carry the canal over Butternut, Limestone, Chittenango, and Oneida Creeks, and countless smaller but equally impressive culverts carry it over brooks and springs. A free descriptive brochure containing a map showing all access sites is available at the park office.

Contact: New York State Department of Environmental Conservation Region 7 and Old Erie Canal State Park.

Old Erie Canal State Park

152. East Branch Fish Creek *(see map on page 261)*

Key species: Brown trout, rainbow trout, and brook trout.

Description: Pouring out of the high reaches of Tug Hill Plateau, the East Branch of Fish Creek drops about 1,600 feet on its circuitous 30-mile trip to its juncture with the West Branch, a mile south of the village of Blossvale. Fast, wide, relatively shallow, and punctuated by countless pools and channels, this freestone stream resembles a western river more than an eastern creek. Tirelessly running through the "Hill," it cuts Central New York's most spellbinding gulf, a druidic setting where sheer cliffs tower anywhere from 20 to 50 feet above the water, offering a truly wild fishing experience.

Tips: Nymphs and streamers help prevent the heartbreak of rough fish.

The fishing: The upper section above East Branch (Rome) Reservoir (site 153) is stocked yearly with about 3,300 browns and 1,000 rainbows averaging 8 inches and 1,180 9.5-inch brookies. Most are caught the first few weeks of the season. The greatest survival rates are found among the browns, followed by the rainbows, primarily because they find their way into the relatively safe reservoir. They return to the creek to spawn—browns in the fall, rainbows in the spring. The fishing is better below the impoundment. A little more accessible, the state stocks this stretch each year with about 8,900 8-inch browns. They hit worms, tiny spinners, and spoons. Although stockies are a lot like anglers, sticking close to the road, the farther you go into the backcountry, the better your chances of getting a large fish.

Directions: The creek is paralleled (north to south) by Creek Road, Coal Hill Road, and Blossvale Road.

Additional information: Downstream of East Branch Reservoir trout season is open from April 1 through November 30. Fishing is prohibited from the mouth to the NY 69 bridge in Taberg from March 16 to the first Saturday in May to protect spawning walleyes. Since the late 1990s a private group, the Fish Creek Atlantic Salmon Club, has been annually stocking about 25,000 Atlantic salmon fry into some of the creek's tributaries. Although it's too early to tell if their restoration attempt is successful, anglers regularly report catching landlocked salmon.

Contact: New York State Department of Environmental Conservation Region 6, Oneida County Convention and Visitors Bureau, and Tug Hill Commission.

152A. Osceola Road (CR 46) Bridge Public Access

Description: This bridge crosses the creek a few hundred feet upstream of its mouth on East Branch Reservoir. Shoulder parking for about ten cars.

The fishing: Above the bridge the water goes through a system of deep pools, fast chutes, and shallow ripples. Most of the trout are browns and rainbows ranging from 8 to 10 inches, but some wild brook trout running from 6 to 12 inches are also present. They hit worms, nymphs, and spinners.

Directions: Head north out of Taberg on Coal Hill Road for about 7.5 miles. A few hundred feet after going through the sharp curve, turn left on Creek Road. Travel for about 5 miles to the stop sign on CR 46, turn right, and continue for a couple hundred yards.

152B. Public Access

Description: A single-lane blacktop road leads to a small parking area at the foot of the ruins of an ancient bridge. Parking for about five cars.

The fishing: Upstream of this site the creek flows through the heart of the Tug Hill Plateau wilderness, picking up numerous tributaries. Brook trout become more common the deeper in you go.

Directions: The 0.5 mile-long access road is off CR 46, 0.2 mile east of site 152A.

152C. East Osceola State Forest

Description: Primitive camping is allowed in this 1,974-acre state forest.

Directions: Head west on CR 46 (Osceola Road) for about 8 miles from site 152A.

152D. E. Frederick W. Parker Jr. (CR 67A) Bridge Public Access

Description: This site has shoulder parking and stone steps leading down to the creek.

The fishing: Deep within the canyon, this site's rapids and deep pools hold good numbers of browns in the 10- to 14-inch range. They take emergers and terrestrials in the quiet water and nymphs and streamers in the pocket water.

Directions: Head north out of Taberg on Coal Hill Road (which turns into CR 67A) for about 7.5 miles.

152E. Point Rock Creek Public Access

Description: Access and shoulder parking at the bridge. Wilderness anglers reach a remote section of the East Branch gorge by wading—and fishing—Point Rock Creek for 0.5 mile to its mouth.

The fishing: The state annually stocks about 1,200 8-inch brown trout into this tiny freestone stream. They respond to nymphs and worms.

Directions: Continue east on CR 67A from site 152D for about 0.25 mile, turn south on Point Rock Road, and travel about 0.5 mile to the bridge.

Additional information: This is one of the tributaries the Fish Creek Atlantic Salmon Club stocks with landlocked salmon.

East Branch, West Branch, and Main Stem Fish Creek · East Branch Reservoir · Mad River (Oneida County)

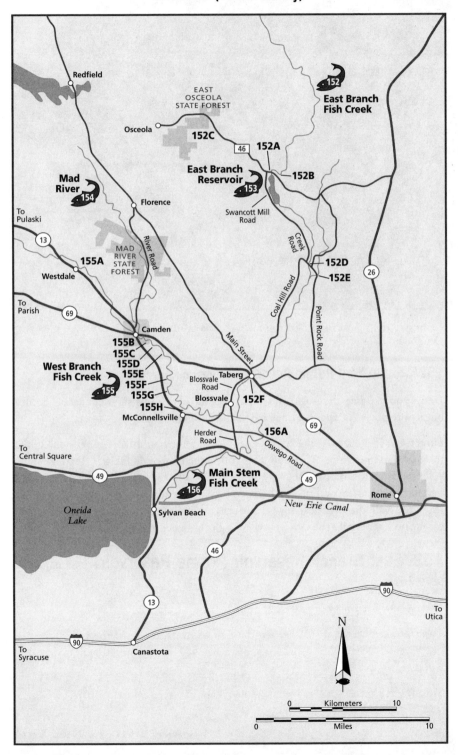

Casting to rising browns at East Branch Fish Creek (site 152).

152F. Stone Wall Public Access *(see map on page 261)*

Description: A popular put-in site for spring kayakers, this shoulder access point is on private property and can be posted at any time.

Directions: From I–90 exit 34 in Canastota, head north on NY 13 for about 12 miles to NY 49 and turn east. After about 5.5 miles, turn north on Herder Road. Roughly 4.3 miles later, just before Taberg, you'll come to a farmer's field on the right. About a hundred yards beyond its north end, you'll find a slot in the woods. Park on the shoulder, walk down the dip into the forest, and follow the creek downstream to an old stone wall, where the cliff is low enough to descend to the water.

153. East Branch Reservoir (Rome Reservoir) *(see map on page 261)*

Key species: Brown trout and bullhead.

Description: Formed in 1960 when the city of Rome dammed the East Branch of Fish Creek for an additional water supply, this 400-acre impoundment is ringed by woods.

Tips: Right after ice-out, suspend minnows about 3 feet below bobbers.

The fishing: The state annually stocks 4,000 6.5-inch browns. They end up ranging from 8 to 12 inches, but 4-pounders are caught regularly. They are mostly targeted with worms, minnows, and Rooster Tail spinners. Some rainbows are also available and reach the same size as the browns. The bullheads average 6 inches and respond to worms fished on bottom, especially in the spring.

Directions: From I–90 exit 34 in Canastota, head north on NY 13 for about 12 miles to NY 49 and turn east. About 5.5 miles later, turn north on Herder Road (which turns into Blossvale Road) and follow it for about 5 miles to Taberg. Turn left at the stop sign, then right onto Coal Hill Road several hundred yards later. After about 7.5 miles, the road banks a sharp right (it's CR 67A at this point). Continue for a few hundred feet, turn north on Creek Road, and continue for a couple miles.

Additional information: A fishing access site on Swancott Mill Road (Creek Road in Lewis County) has parking for about twenty cars. Gas-powered motors aren't permitted on the reservoir. Camping isn't allowed in Swancott Mill State Forest to protect Rome's water supply. However, primitive camping is allowed in nearby East Osceola State Forest (site 152C), a 1,974-acre area accessible off Osceola Road (CR 46), 8 miles west of the Osceola Road/Swancott Mill Road intersection.

Contact: New York State Department of Environmental Conservation Region 6 and Tug Hill Commission.

154. Mad River (Oneida County) *(see map on page 261)*

Key species: Brown trout and brook trout.

Description: This fast-flowing stream is West Branch Fish Creek's largest tributary, feeding it on the southern outskirts of Camden.

Tips: Wear a Bug-Out head net from mid-May through mid-June.

The fishing: This river gets stocked with roughly 3,300 8-inch browns annually. They end up ranging from 8 to 14 inches and take worms and spinners. Wild brook trout up to 12 inches are available in the upper reaches and take the same baits as browns.

Directions: River Road crosses the stream a couple of times and parallels it in several spots between Camden and Florence.

Additional information: Access and parking for ten cars is at the NY 69 bridge in Camden. Primitive camping is allowed in Mad River State Forest, about 5 miles north of Camden on River Road.

Contact: New York State Department of Environmental Conservation Region 6 and Oneida County Convention and Visitors Bureau.

155. West Branch Fish Creek (see map on page 261)

Key species: Brown trout and walleye.

Description: Pouring out of Kasoag Lake, this stream runs over the southern edge of Tug Hill Plateau. Flowing south for 25 miles on a relatively gentle path of mild rapids and long, deep pools, it joins the East Branch in Blossvale, forming the Main Stem. Mostly wide, flat, and deep, this creek is ideal for fly fishing from a canoe.

Tips: Most any white fly catches trout all summer long.

The fishing: About 5 miles shorter than the East Branch, but far more accessible, this stream gets stocked annually with about 13,950 brown trout averaging 8 inches. Life is decent, and quite a few reach the 12- to 16-inch range—and even larger. Post-spawn walleyes ranging from 18 to 21 inches can be caught below the dam in McConnellsville for most of May on jigs and worms.

This creek's trout season extends to November 30. From the mouth upstream to the McConnellsville dam, fishing is prohibited from March 16 through the first Saturday in May to protect spawning walleyes. The minimum length for walleyes is 18 inches, until October 1, 2004, when it becomes 15 inches. The daily limit is three.

Directions: NY 13 parallels much of the stream.

Contact: New York State Department of Environmental Conservation Region 6 and Oneida County Convention and Visitors Bureau.

155A. Public Access

Description: This site is located at a dam. There is a canoe launch, manicured lawns suitable for the physically disabled, and parking for about thirty cars.

Directions: Take NY 13 north out of Camden for 3.5 miles to Westdale, then turn right (east) on Cemetery Road (at the 20-ton bridge sign).

155B. Public Fishing Platform

Description: Situated at a bridge just upstream of the dam in the village of Camden, this site has a large wheelchair-accessible fishing platform and is popular with family groups. Parking for about fifty cars is across the street.

Directions: On NY 69 west, less than a block past the intersection with NY 13.

155C. Forest Park

Description: This sprawling facility has a long, winding road leading to several spots from which the West Branch is accessible. A narrow one-way road runs through the park.

Directions: Located on Ripley Road on the southern edge of the village of Camden.

Fly fishing at the Westdale Dam on West Branch Fish Creek (site 155A).

Additional information: This village park is dedicated to local folks. It has numerous shelters, each with its own picnic tables and grills and many with swing sets.

155D. Brewer Road Public Access

Description: Informal access at the bridge and shoulder parking for about ten cars.

Directions: Brewer Road is off NY 13, 0.5 mile south of Camden. The bridge is 0.8 mile down the road.

155E. Blakesly Road Public Access

Description: Informal access at the bridge and shoulder parking for about ten cars.

Directions: Blakesly Road is off NY 13, 1.1 miles south of Camden. The bridge is 0.7 mile down the road.

155F. Buell Road Public Access

Description: A bridge used to cross the creek here. Shoulder parking for about six cars.

Directions: Buell Road is off NY 13, 1.2 miles south of Camden. The creek is 0.8 mile down the road.

155G. Trestle Road Public Access *(see map on page 261)*

Description: Formal state access site on the east side of the bridge with parking for ten cars.

Directions: Trestle Road is off NY 13, 2.4 miles south of Camden.

155H. McConnellsville Public Access *(see map on page 261)*

Description: A dam at the Harden Furniture Factory forms a long, quiet pool upstream; a staircase of rapids and pools is down below. Informal shoulder parking.

Directions: Head south out of Camden on NY 13 for 4.4 miles. Turn east on McConnellsville Road, then immediately left at the post office.

Additional information: No trespassing on the dam. This is a good site to launch canoes.

156. Main Stem Fish Creek *(see map on page 261)*

Key species: Brown trout, walleye, northern pike, largemouth bass, smallmouth bass, channel catfish, yellow perch, black crappie, sunfish, and brown bullhead.

Description: Formed by the East and West Branches converging just downstream of Blossvale, this is Oneida Lake's largest tributary, contributing nearly half the lake's water. Wide and deep, it lazily snakes toward the lake on the most circuitous route imaginable.

Tips: Cast YUM tubes into windfalls and brush.

The fishing: The Main Stem holds some huge brown trout over 20 inches. Savvy beasts, they're tough to catch, and those that don't die of old age end up being pleasant surprises for folks targeting walleyes with worms and hard minnowbaits. Although walleyes are in the stream year-round, the best numbers are here in May and June and again in the fall. Ranging from undersize to 22 inches, they are taken by drifting worms and minnows or by throwing Rebels, Rat-L-Traps, and jigs. Northern pike up to 36 inches and largemouth bass ranging from 2 to 5 pounds share weed edges, submerged timber, and undercut banks. Both respond to minnows and spinnerbaits. Smallmouth bass hang out along drop-offs and in deep pools, where they take crayfish and wide-bodied crankbaits like Excalibur Fat Free Fingerlings and Fat Free Shallows. Channel catfish up to 20 pounds are available and take large minnows, cut bait, and gobs of worms. Perch up to 12 inches, crappies ranging from 9 to 14 inches, bullheads running 8 to 14 inches, and sunfish averaging 8 inches are plentiful. Small minnows and 2-inch scented curly-tailed grubs work great for perch and crappies. Worms are best for sunfish and bullheads.

All fishing is prohibited from March 16 until the first Saturday in May to protect spawning walleyes. The minimum length for walleyes is 18 inches, until October 1, 2004, when it becomes 15 inches. The daily limit is three.

Directions: The stream is paralleled (north to south) by Herder Road, NY 49, Haskins Road, and Vienna Road. Toward the end, it runs along the eastern boundary of Sylvan Beach and feeds the New Erie Canal about 1 mile east of Oneida Lake.

Additional information: The creek flows into the Erie Canal on the outskirts of Sylvan Beach, one of the most popular summer resorts in Central New York. There are several private campgrounds and marinas with ramps.

Contacts: New York State Department of Environmental Conservation Region 6 and Oneida County Convention and Visitors Bureau.

156A. Meadows Road Public Access

Description: By this point the creek is slowing down—one local calls it "the last landing." There are still some fast-flowing areas, but they get shorter and the pools in between are deeper and longer.

Directions: Take NY 13 north out of Sylvan Beach for about 2 miles to its confluence with NY 49 and turn right. After 6 miles, turn left on Herder Road, then east on Oswego Road about 1 mile later. Continue for 1 mile, turn right immediately after crossing Fish Creek, park at the end of the cul-de-sac, and take the footpath down to the river.

157. Oneida Lake *(see map on page 268)*

Key species: Walleye, northern pike, black bass, tiger muskie, channel catfish, white bass, sheepshead, yellow perch, sunfish, and bullhead.

Description: Spilling into four counties, this 51,091-acre lake is the largest body of water totally contained within the state's borders. It averages 22 feet deep and has a maximum depth of 55 feet.

Tips: In autumn cast ThunderSticks or Bomber Long "A"s from the surf at dusk.

The fishing: New York's most famous walleye fishery, this place has fallen onto hard times lately. Exotic organisms like zebra mussels and water chestnuts (there's a new one every year) are driving the walleyes to constantly shift their behavior patterns. One year they're deep to escape the intense sunlight brought into the depths by zebra mussels filtering algae out of the water. The next season they're taking cover under water chestnuts. The only constant is the state-of-the-art walleye hatchery on the north shore, which annually stocks more than 161,000,000 walleye fry and 103,000 5-inchers into the lake. At the turn of this century, authorities estimated the keeper (18 inches) walleye population at about 250,000, down 50 percent from thirty years ago. Still, tradition dies hard, and the lake has a dedicated following of walleye anglers who take them with every popular technique, from drifting and trolling worms to tossing bucktail jigs and bladebaits, casting crankbaits, and trolling plugs ranging from Hot 'N Tots to Red Fins. The minimum length for walleyes is 18 inches, until October 1, 2004, when it becomes 15 inches. The daily limit is three.

Oneida Lake · Panther Lake

Smallmouth bass in the 1.5- to 4-pound range share the deep water with "eyes" in summer, moving up onto shoals at night. They can't seem to pass up spinnerbaits, jigs, minnows, and crayfish. Historically this shallow lake was a northern pike and largemouth bass hot spot, but construction of the Barge Canal drained much of the surrounding wetlands, greatly diminishing the shallow habitats both these species occupy and spawn in. Lately their numbers seem to be rebounding. Bucketmouths reaching up to 6 pounds and northerns between 22 and 36 inches rule the weedy bays and tributary mouths. They like minnows, YUM tubes, spinnerbaits, and buzzbaits. Tiger muskies aren't common, but when you get one chances are it'll be 15 pounds or better. Target them with large in-line bucktail spinners and minnow-imitating crankbaits like Mann's S-t-r-e-t-c-h series and strange acting ones like Lazy Ikes.

Channel cats up to 20 pounds prowl the deep water and take cut bait and large minnows. Sheepshead ranging from 14 to 24 inches are popularly targeted with crayfish around the entrances to the Erie Canal on both ends of the lake. In addition, many are taken incidentally by anglers tossing jigs for bronzebacks and walleyes along drop-offs and in the shipping channel. Bullheads up to 14 inches swarm into tributary mouths in early spring. They are targeted at night in early spring by bank anglers still-fishing with worms on bottom, under what can be described as a carnival-like atmosphere illuminated by Coleman lanterns. There isn't a winter that goes by that doesn't form safe ice on the lake, and folks love walking on it and fishing for yellow perch averaging 9 inches. Locally called jacks, they take minnows and grubs. Lately, monster white bass have made a noticeable appearance. Ranging from 0.75 to 2 pounds, they run in schools and are often mistaken for suspended walleyes. They take just about any minnow-imitating lure. They also take worms baited on jigheads and retrieved steadily at a moderate clip.

A word about burbot: This lake has a good population ranging from 12 to 18 inches. Seldom targeted, they are often taken by icers going for perch and walleyes with minnows. Unfortunately most anglers don't know what they are—indeed, how delicious they are—and simply leave them on the ice to die. This is a terrible waste of a tasty native fish.

Directions: Take I–81 north from Syracuse for 11 miles to exit 31 in Brewerton. NY 49 parallels the north shore and NY 31 runs the length of the south shore.

Additional information: Fed and drained by the New Erie Canal, close proximity to Syracuse and the resort village/theme park of Sylvan Beach on the east shore makes Oneida Lake one of Central New York's most popular summer destinations.

Contact: New York State Department of Environmental Conservation Region 7, Oneida County Convention and Visitors Bureau, Madison County Tourism, Syracuse Convention and Visitors Bureau, and Oswego County Promotion & Tourism.

Angler holding a typical Oneida Lake white bass.

157A. Brewerton Public Access *(see map on page 268)*

Description: Brewerton offers two wheelchair-accessible sites, one on each side of the I–81 bridge. Parking for fifty cars at the south site and twenty-five cars at the north site.

Directions: For the south site, take I–81 exit 31 (Brewerton), bear west on Bartell Road, and take the first right onto Kathan Road. For the north site, stay on Bartell Road for about 1 mile, turn right on US 11, cross the bridge over the Oneida River about 1 mile later, hook a right at the traffic light onto CR 37, and travel about 500 yards to the foot of the I–81 bridge.

157B. Oneida Shores County Park *(see map on page 268)*

Description: Covering 340 acres, this fee area offers sixty-five campsites (twenty-five with electricity and water), a swimming beach, a bathhouse, showers, and a paved boat launch with parking for about fifteen rigs. The campground is open from the first weekend of May through mid-October. Free day use is allowed off-season.

Directions: From I–81 exit 31 (Brewerton), head east on Bartell Road for about 1 mile to the park.

Contact: Onondaga County Parks.

157C. South Shore Boat Launch *(see map on page 268)*

Description: This site offers two paved ramps and parking for thirty-five rigs.

Directions: Take I–81 north from Syracuse for about 8 miles to exit 30 (Cicero). Turn east on NY 31 and travel for about 10 miles (1 mile east of Bridgeport).

157D. Verona Beach State Park *(see map on page 268)*

Description: This 1,735-acre fee area offers thirty-five campsites, hot showers, flush toilets, 3,300 feet of sandy beach, surf fishing, and hiking trails.

Directions: Head north out of Canastota (I–90 exit 34) on NY 13 for 8 miles.

157E. Sylvan Beach Public Access *(see map on page 268)*

Description: This resort village offers surf-fishing access, several hundred yards of access on the walls of the New Erie Canal, a huge municipal parking lot, and shoulder parking on the pier.

The fishing: The beach is a popular surf-fishing site for autumn walleyes.

Directions: Sylvan Beach is about 1 mile north of site 157D.

157F. Godfrey Point Public Access *(see map on page 268)*

Description: This site has two paved ramps and parking for thirty rigs.

Directions: Head north out of Brewerton on I–81 for 4 miles to exit 32 (Central Square), and take NY 49 east for about 11 miles (1 mile east of the hamlet of Cleveland).

157G. Phillips Point Public Access *(see map on page 268)*

Description: This site offers a beach launch suitable for small trailered craft, parking for twenty rigs, and surf fishing.

The fishing: This is a local hot spot for bullheads in spring. In addition, it is a productive surf-fishing spot for post-spawn and autumn walleyes.

Directions: From Central Square (I–81 exit 32), take NY 49 east for 3 miles, turn right onto Toad Harbor Road, then turn left about 3 miles later on McCloud Drive and travel 1 mile to its end.

Additional information: This site is part of the Three Mile Bay Wildlife Management Area, and no camping or off-road driving is allowed.

158. Panther Lake *(see map on page 268)*

Key species: Largemouth bass, smallmouth bass, walleye, black crappie, tiger muskie, and chain pickerel.

Description: This 119-acre lake averages 12 feet deep and drops to a maximum depth of 21 feet. Its shore is heavily developed with cottages and homes.

Tips: In summer it's best to fish this lake during the week.

The fishing: Largemouth bass ranging from 2 to 4 pounds respond to soft-bodied jerkbaits and Texas-rigged worms worked in the vegetation on the north and west sides. Smallmouths go from 1 to 3 pounds and like Rat-L-Traps and scented soft baits on drop-shot rigs worked along breaks. Walleyes aren't plentiful, but they average 5 pounds and are primarily taken through the ice on Swedish Pimples and minnows. Black crappies are the lake's most popular panfish, with a lot of 10-inchers available. They respond to minnows and Marabou Tail Stump Jumpers. The state stocks several hundred 9-inch tiger muskies yearly. Survival isn't the greatest, but keepers range from 30 to 36 inches. They take large minnows and Mepps bucktail spinners. The lake's nastiest natural predator is the chain pickerel. These feisty battlers reach 25 inches and can be taken on crankbaits and spinnerbaits and by ripping worms through the shallows on spinner harnesses.

Directions: Head west out of Camden on NY 69 for about 7 miles, turn south on CR 17, and continue for about 3 miles.

Additional information: A paved single-lane boat ramp is on CR 17. Privately owned by the Pine Grove Inn across the street, it has been free for years, and as of press time the proprietor intended to keep it that way. Parking for twenty cars is available.

Contact: New York State Department of Environmental Conservation Region 7 and Oswego County Promotion & Tourism.

159. New Erie Canal: Rome to Tonawanda *(see maps on pages 274, 276, 278, 281, and 283)*

Key species: Black bass, northern pike, walleye, tiger muskie, channel catfish, black crappie, sunfish, yellow perch, white perch, white bass, rock bass, brown bullhead, and American eel.

Description: Originally named the Barge Canal, this waterway replaced the Old Erie Canal in 1918. Stretching for roughly 210 miles, from Lock 21 west of Rome to Tonawanda on the Niagara River, the western half of the waterway averages 12 feet deep and is at least 200 feet wide in canalized creeks (Tonawanda) and rivers (Oneida, Seneca, and Clyde) and 75 feet wide in earth cuts. It starts out atop the divide separating the Mohawk and Oneida River drainages, descends 50 feet on two locks to reach Oneida Lake's level, then goes through another lock to step down 7 feet to the level of the Seneca and Oswego Rivers. In Baldwinsville it starts an ascent that will elevate it 187 feet, via 12 locks, to the Niagara River. Along the way it bypasses natural oxbows with cuts. The longest, flattest stretch, known as the Long Level, runs from Lock 34 in Lockport to Lock 33 in Henrietta, a distance of about 60 miles.

Tips: Use a Lindy No-Snag Slip Sinker to drag night crawlers or YUM Shakin' Worms on bottom in the holes in the rapids next to locks for walleyes and bronze-backs.

The fishing: Bucketmouths up to 6 pounds and bronzebacks up to 4 pounds are the most plentiful game fish. The largemouths tend to hang out along riprap and in swampy and marshy areas lining the canal, while the smallmouths like rapids, breaks, and the channel floor. Both can be caught in these habitats on minnows, crayfish, spinnerbaits, Slug-Gos, Mann's Goblins and Ghosts, and Texas- and Carolina-rigged worms. Northern pike typically range from 20 to 28 inches, but 40-inchers are possible. The largest pikesauruses are caught in the section running from Onondaga Lake's outlet west to Macedon, an area rich in backwaters and tributaries. They respond to large minnows, buzzbaits, spinnerbaits, and crankbaits like Rebel Minnows. Walleyes ranging from 15 to 28 inches are present throughout the canal. However, the greatest populations are found in three areas: between Lock 21 (the second lock east of Oneida Lake) and Palmyra, the Rochester area, and from Lockport to the Niagara River. They hang out on drop-offs and the channel floor by day and suspend or move up onto shelves and shoals and into rapids in the evening. They hit bucktail jigs, scented curly-tailed grubs and 4-inch worms, crankbaits like Wally Divers and Mann's Accu-Tracs, and night crawlers bounced on bottom with Mepps SpinFlexes and drifted or trolled on spinner harnesses. Tiger muskies have recently been stocked heavily, especially in the Oneida and Cross Lakes sections. Fish for them with large minnows and their imitations and with Mepps bucktail spinners.

New Erie Canal: Rome to Brewerton

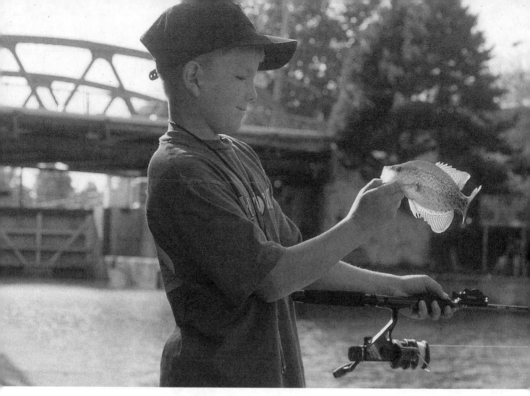

Summer lunch caught fresh from the New Erie Canal (site 159).

Catfish in the 15- to 20-inch range are most common, but monsters the size of miniature Minotaurs are caught regularly. They like meat—worms, minnows, cut bait, and shrimp—fished on bottom. The canal is loaded with crappies exceeding 9 inches, yellow perch ranging from 6 to 10 inches, rock bass up to 10 inches, and white perch and white bass running anywhere from 4 to 14 inches. Schools of white bass and white perch hang out everywhere, still water and fast. Crappies suspend around docks, swimming platforms, and timber and below locks. Yellow perch like drop-offs and deep water, and rock bass prefer riprap and rocky rapids. They all take minnows, small lures, streamers, and poppers. Bluegills and pumpkinseeds averaging 6 inches are plentiful. They like shallow habitats and will even create their own by suspending near the surface in the deep water below canal walls. These sunfish are partial to worms and wet flies. Brown bullheads between 6 and 12 inches are common. They like worms still-fished on bottom, especially around marshes in spring, and in rapids below dams in early summer. American eels averaging 30 inches are commonly caught on minnows and worms fished on bottom at night for catfish and bullheads. They are especially plentiful in the Seneca and Oneida Rivers. Bonus brown and rainbow trout, many over 20 inches, can be found around tributary mouths in the spring.

In the Seneca River the minimum length for northern pike is 22 inches. In addition, the state is trying to restore Cross Lake's walleye fishery and has imposed a special 18-inch minimum length and daily limit of three in the section of the Seneca

New Erie Canal: Brewerton to Lyons

River running from Jordan Road (the first bridge over the canal west of the lake) to Plainville Road (the first bridge over the canal east of the lake).

Directions: I–90 and NY 31 parallel the waterway.

Additional information: A two-day or season pass is required to go through locks. The Erie Canal Heritage Trail, a recreation path, opens much of the waterway to shore fishing. There are no public campgrounds on the canal, but numerous private campgrounds are nearby.

Contact: New York State Department of Environmental Conservation Regions 7, 8, and 9 and New York State Canal Corporation.

159A. Brewerton Public Access *(see map on page 274)*

Description: Parking for about forty cars and access, including a handicapped ramp, to approximately 200 yards of canal wall.

Directions: From I–81 exit 31 (Brewerton), head west on Bartel Road for about 0.5 mile and turn right on US 11. Continue for about 0.3 mile, turn left just before the bridge onto Benett Street, and take the first right.

159B. Caughdenoy Public Access

Description: Located on the tip of the Oneida River's largest oxbow, this site offers parking for twenty cars and shore-fishing access above and below flood gates.

The fishing: Walleyes spawn in the rapids, making this a Central New York hot spot for the first month of the season. Ruins of an Old Erie Canal–era lock are at the foot of the bridge on the south side of the river, and the hole at the end of the lock wall holds northern pike in May and post-spawn black bass. The pool below the floodgates is notorious for holding huge channel catfish.

Directions: Head west on CR 37 out of Brewerton for about 3 miles to its end, turn left on CR 12, and travel about 0.25 mile.

159C. Oneida River State Fishing Access

Description: This site has a double-wide paved ramp, parking for ten rigs and fifteen cars, and 200 feet of shore-fishing access.

Directions: Head south out of Phoenix on CR 57 for about 2 miles to Three Rivers. Cross the bridge over the Oneida River, make an immediate left onto Maider Road and travel 0.4 mile, then turn left on Bonstead Road. The launch is a mile away, under the double bridges.

159D. Baldwinsville Lions Park

Description: This site has a paved ramp, parking for about ten rigs, additional space for about twenty cars, and a couple hundred yards of shore-fishing access, including the mouth of Crooked Brook and several hundred yards upstream.

New Erie Canal: Lyons to Rochester

Directions: Take Syracuse Street (NY 48) south out of Baldwinsville. Go through the VanBuren Road traffic light at the edge of town and turn left onto Lion's Parkway a few hundred feet later.

159E. Port Byron State Fishing Access *(see map on page 276)*

Description: This site offers a gravel single-lane launch ramp suitable for small motorized craft, parking for about thirty rigs, and shore access.

Directions: On NY 38, about 3 miles north of Port Byron.

159F. Clyde Boat Launch *(see map on page 276)*

Description: This site has a paved launch, parking for thirty rigs, and shore-fishing access.

Directions: On Water Street in Clyde.

Additional information: This launch is about 1 mile downstream from the mouth of the longest stretch of the Clyde River (site 109), a stream whose sources were diverted to feed the canal. As a result, what's left of the original Clyde is a snaking, stagnant, shallow backwater loaded with fallen timber and vegetation—the ideal haunt of largemouth bass, northern pike, and panfish.

159G. Abby Park

Description: This site offers a paved ramp, parking for about ten rigs, picnic areas, a playground, and toilets.

Directions: On Water Street (off NY 14 on the north side of the canal) in Lyons.

159H. Arcadia Widewaters Canal Park

Description: This site has a paved double-lane launch ramp, parking for about ten rigs, shore fishing, picnic facilities, a playground, and toilets.

The fishing: More than twice as wide as most of the western half of the canal, this spot gets a lot of fishing pressure. Nonetheless, it still manages to maintain good populations of largemouths in the 2- to 4-pound range, northerns averaging 4 pounds, and lots of sunfish, perch, and keeper crappies.

Directions: About 1 mile west of Newark on NY 31.

159I. Palmyra Aqueduct Park

Description: This community park offers a paved ramp, parking for ten rigs, several hundred yards of shore-fishing access, rest rooms, playgrounds, and picnic facilities.

The fishing: Situated on the site of a lock spillway and the mouth of a creek, this park's fast water loads up with panfish in early spring and is the local hot spot for post-spawn walleyes and black bass.

Directions: On NY 31 on the western edge of Palmyra.

Additional information: The old Erie Canal ran through here, and the scenic ruins of the aqueduct over Ganargua (Indian for "muddy waters") Creek punctuate the western end of the park.

159J. Lock 30 Canal Park (see map on page 278)

Description: This park offers a paved ramp, parking for fifty rigs, shore-fishing access, grills, picnic tables, and rest rooms.

The fishing: The steady current in the side channel carrying excess water around the lock always has smallmouth bass and channel cats.

Directions: Located on NY 31F in Macedon.

159K. Town of Perinton Boat Launch (see map on page 278)

Description: This site has a hard-surface ramp, loading docks, parking for fifteen rigs, and shore-fishing access.

Directions: At the Ayrault Road bridge in Fairport (within the town of Perinton).

159L. Lock 32 Public Access (see map on page 278)

Description: This site offers a paved ramp, parking for about thirty rigs, and shore-fishing access.

The fishing: Located at the foot of the lock, this site contains a culvert and discharge pipes that generate a continuous current, making the spot attractive to smallmouth bass ranging from too small to 16 inches and channel catfish up to 20 inches.

Directions: Take the access road on the southeast corner of the NY 65 bridge in Pittsford.

159M. San Souci Canal Park

Description: This site features a double-lane paved launch, parking for about thirty rigs, a handicapped fishing ramp, a shelter, picnic tables, and a toilet.

Directions: Take NY 31 west out of Brockport for about 2 miles and turn right on County Line Road.

159N. Bates Road Launch

Description: This site has a paved double-lane ramp and parking for thirty rigs.

Directions: At the Bates Road bridge in the hamlet of Medina.

159O. NY 31 Public Access

Description: This site offers a paved ramp and parking for fifteen rigs.

New Erie Canal: Brockport to Lockport

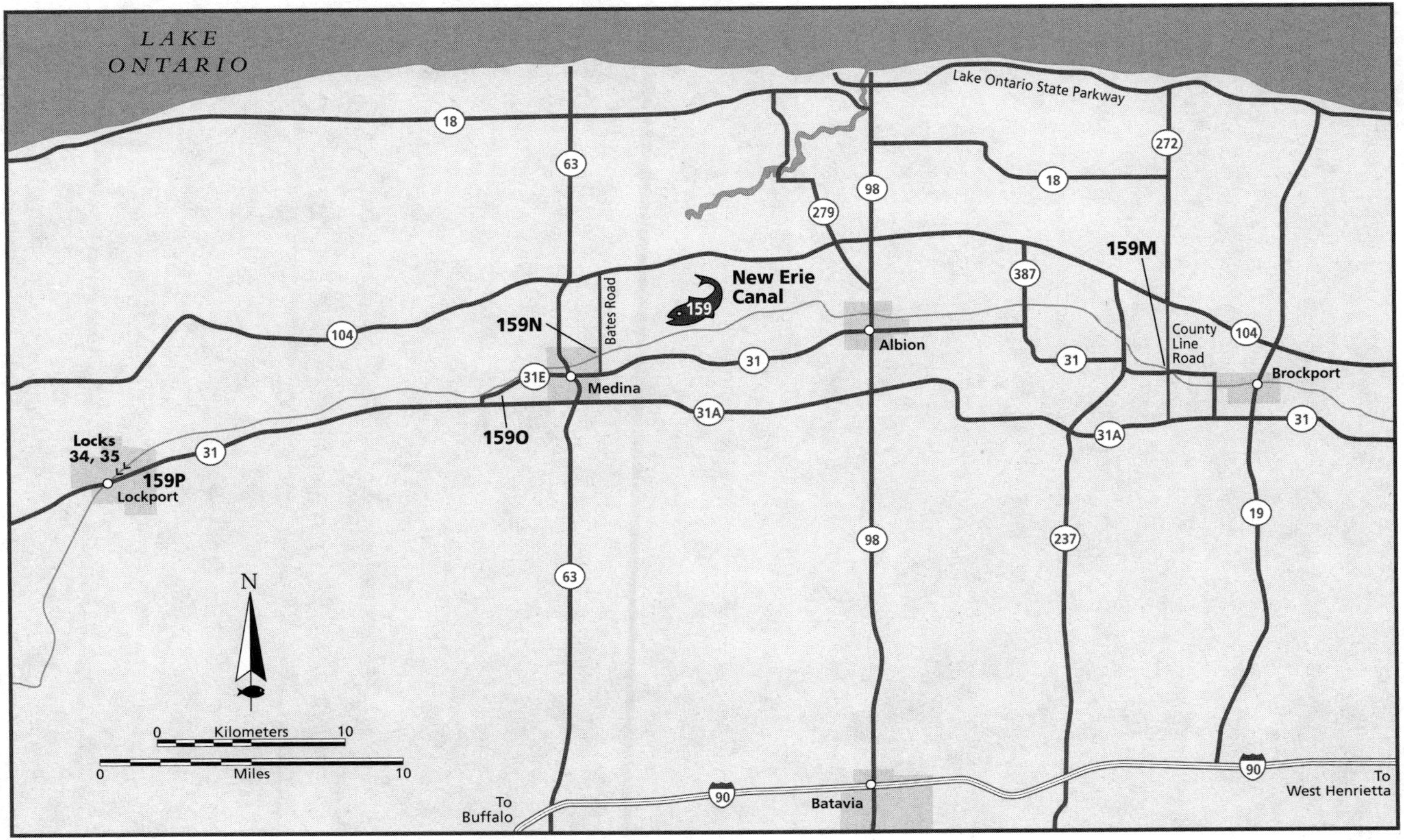

LAKE ONTARIO

Lake Ontario State Parkway

Brockport

County Line Road

159M

New Erie Canal

159

Bates Road

159N

Medina

159O

Albion

Lockport

Locks 34, 35

159P

To West Henrietta

Batavia

To Buffalo

N

Kilometers 10

Miles 10

Old Erie Canal locks next to the New Erie Canal in Lockport (site 159P).

New Erie Canal: Lockport to North Tonawanda

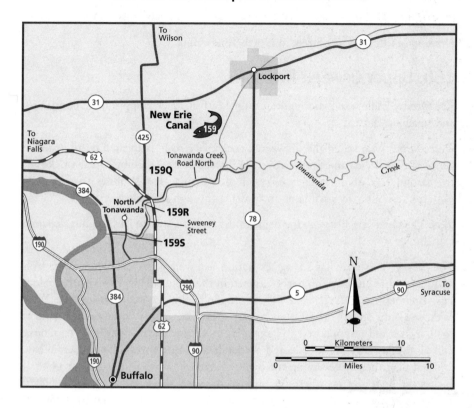

Directions: About 3 miles west of Medina on NY 31E.

159P. Nelson C. Goehle Park (Widewaters Marina) *(see map on page 281)*

Description: This site offers a paved double-lane ramp, parking for about twenty-five rigs, shore fishing, rest rooms, and a picnic area.

Directions: Located on Market Street in Lockport.

159Q. West Canal Park & Marina

Description: This site offers a paved ramp, parking for thirty rigs, shore fishing, and picnic tables.

Directions: On Tonawanda Creek Road North in North Tonawanda.

159R. North Tonawanda Botanical Gardens Boat Launch

Description: This site offers a paved ramp, parking for thirty rigs, picnic tables, and toilets.

Directions: Off Sweeney Street in North Tonawanda.

159S. City of North Tonawanda Boat Launch *(see map on page 283)*

Description: This site offers a paved ramp, parking for twelve rigs, and shore fishing.

Directions: Off Sweeney Street in North Tonawanda.

160. Upper Oswego River

Key species: Walleye, northern pike, channel catfish, black crappie, largemouth bass, and smallmouth bass.

Description: Also called the Oswego Canal, this stream is formed by the convergence of the Oneida and Seneca Rivers at Three Rivers. Draining Oneida Lake and the eastern half of the Finger Lakes, it flows north for 22 miles to feed Lake Ontario, tumbling over six dams and passing through six locks.

Tips: The fast water between the dams in the city of Oswego harbors huge channel catfish.

The fishing: This river has a long reputation as a walleye fishery. They range from 15 to 27 inches and are popularly targeted in the rapids below dams with bucktail jigs, Bomber Long "A"s, and jigheads tipped with scented plastics like YUM Walleye Grubs and YUM Wooly Curltails. Northern pike typically range from 18 to 36 inches and respond best to large minnows fished at the mouths of tributaries and along the edges of weeds and wetlands and to spinnerbaits and crankbaits worked over the shelves lining the banks. Channel catfish running from 14 to 18 inches can be found anywhere for most of the year; however, they enter rapids in full force to spawn in late May and stay through mid-July. Locals target them with night crawlers cast across the current and allowed to sweep down to the edge. Smallmouth bass in the 12- to 15-inch range share the rapids with walleyes early and late in the season. In summer they join the river's larger bronzebacks (up to 20 inches) on drop-offs, where they hit minnows, crayfish, and jigs. Largemouths up to 22 inches occupy the edges of swamps, tributary mouths, the inside channels of islands, windfalls, and the edges of water chestnuts. They hit surface lures, jig-'n'-pigs, spinnerbaits, and Texas-rigged worms. Black crappies up to 14 inches hang out around brush, timber, and docks; at tributary mouths; and below locks. They hit small minnows, 2-inch YUM Wooly Beavertails, and Beetle Spins.

Directions: CR 57, NY 48, and NY 481 parallel the river.

Additional information: The Lower Oswego River, from its mouth to the first dam, is covered in site 35 in the Great Lakes Region section.

Contact: New York State Department of Environmental Conservation Region 7 and Oswego County Promotion & Tourism.

Upper Oswego River · Lake Neatahwanta

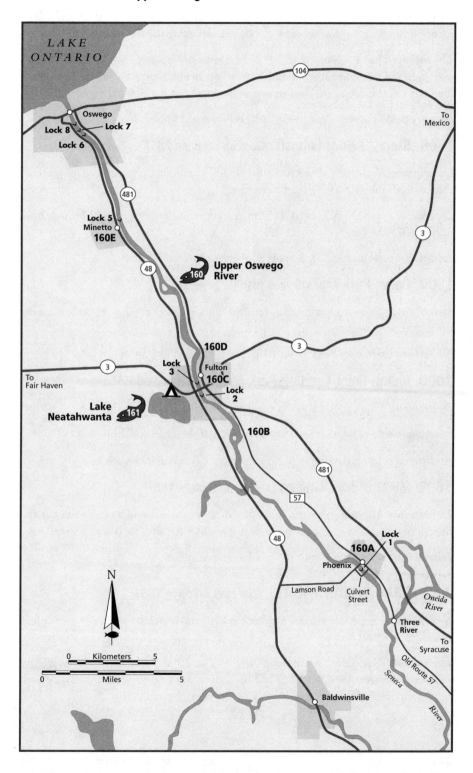

LAKE ONTARIO

Oswego

Lock 8
Lock 7
Lock 6

481

Lock 5
Minetto
160E

48

160

Upper Oswego River

160D

To Mexico

104

3

3

3

Lock 3
Fulton
160C

Lock 2

To Fair Haven

Lake Neatahwanta

161

160B

481

57

48

Lock 1

160A

Phoenix

Lamson Road

Culvert Street

Oneida River

Three River

To Syracuse

Old Route 57

Seneca River

Baldwinsville

N

0   Kilometers   5

0   Miles   5

160A. Public Access *(see map on page 285)*

Description: This site has a paved ramp, parking for twenty-five rigs, and hundreds of yards of shore-fishing access below floodgates and along the old riverbed and canal.

The fishing: The rapids in the village of Phoenix hold post-spawn walleyes through mid-June and again in October and November. In summer walleyes spend most of their days in the deep canal but return to the rapids in the evening.

Directions: At the drawbridge on Culvert Street in Phoenix.

160B. Stop 28 Boat Launch *(see map on page 285)*

Description: A no-frills shore site, suitable for launching cartop and small trailered craft with shoulder parking for fifteen rigs.

Directions: From the NY 481/CR 57 intersection on the south side of Fulton, head south on CR 57 for just under 1 mile.

Additional information: This site is above the city's two locks.

160C. Canal Park Marina *(see map on page 285)*

Description: This site has fifteen transient slips and sits on a river walk running through downtown.

Directions: On South First Street (between the locks) in Fulton.

160D. Indian Point Landing Park *(see map on page 285)*

Description: This site has a paved ramp and parking for fifteen rigs.

Directions: Off NY 481 on the northern edge of the city of Fulton.

Additional information: This site is below the city's two locks.

160E. Minetto Boat Launch *(see map on page 285)*

Description: Although this site has a paved ramp, turnaround space is limited and the county classifies it as a cartop launch. Shoulder parking for about six rigs.

Directions: On the west bank in the village of Minetto.

161. Lake Neatahwanta *(see map on page 285)*

Key species: Largemouth bass, northern pike, yellow perch, white perch, sunfish, black crappie, and bowfin.

Description: Neahtahwanta means "little lake near the big lake" in Iroquois. This 750-acre lake averages 6 feet deep and has a maximum depth of 12 feet. Two-thirds of its shoreline is forested, and the remainder is manicured parks.

Tips: Ice fishing for panfish is hottest one hour before and after sunset.

The fishing: This productive warm-water fishery's largemouth bass average 4 pounds, and its northerns run from 4 to 8 pounds. Locals target them with minnows, spinnerbaits, and stickbaits. Bluegills and pumpkinseeds typically go 4 to 7 inches and respond to worms and 1-inch scented curly-tailed grubs. Yellow perch and white perch averaging 7 inches and black crappies running up to 11 inches are plentiful and are mostly taken with emerald shiners (locally called buckeyes), flathead minnows, 2-inch Rebel Minnows, and Crappie Thunders. Each of these panfish takes spikes, mousies, and other grubs through the ice. Neahtahwanta has a larger than average population of bowfin, a toothy, hard-fighting critter that locals call dogfish. An ancient species that scientists call a living fossil, bowfins aren't particularly handsome or good tasting so they're seldom targeted, but many up to 2 feet long are caught incidentally on minnows.

Directions: The lake is bordered by NY 3, on the west side of Fulton.

Additional information: Public access with shoulder parking is plentiful on the north and east banks. North Bay Campground, a fee area, offers thirty-five no-frills sites, thirty-five sites with water and electricity, a paved ramp, parking for ten rigs, a swimming beach, and playgrounds. The campground is open from mid-May through mid-September, and a day-use fee is charged noncampers in-season.

Contact: New York State Department of Environmental Conservation Region 7 and Oswego County Promotion & Tourism.

162. East Branch Salmon River *(see map on page 288)*

Key species: Brook trout and rainbow trout.

Description: This branch flows off Tug Hill Plateau and drains into the Salmon River Reservoir.

Tips: The best fishing is in May.

The fishing: The state annually stocks about 900 brookies averaging 9 inches and 1,800 rainbows averaging 8 inches. Most are caught by local meat anglers early in the season. Still, some survive and 12-inchers—some even bigger—are available by late summer. Both species hit worms and salted minnows in spring, nymphs in summer, and Wooly Worms in autumn.

Directions: Head south out of Redfield on CR 17 for about 0.5 mile. Turn east on Waterbury Road and travel 3 miles, then turn south on Ryan Road. Continue a little over 1 mile, turn east on CR 44 and travel 2 miles, then turn north on CR 46 and go to the bridge in Osceola.

Additional information: Camping is permitted on the state land a few hundred yards upstream of the bridge. Black flies often get so thick from May through mid-June, they can run unprotected anglers off the stream.

Upper Salmon River, Branches, and Reservoirs - Mad River (Oswego County)

163. Mad River (Oswego County)

Key species: Brook trout.

Description: This stream springs out of the Tug Hill Wildlife Management Area and quickly picks up numerous feeders, becoming a small river by the time it feeds the North Branch of the Salmon River in Battle Hill State Forest, north of Redfield.

Tips: After a rain drift a worm on bottom, tight to submerged logs and boulders.

The fishing: This river used to get stocked with brookies, but much of it flows through private property, and recent access problems have caused the state to discontinue stocking it. Still, most of the brooks streaming through Tug Hill Plateau contain brook trout. When they outgrow their home range, they scatter in search of larger haunts, and many end up in the Mad River. Ranging from 4 to 12 inches, they are partial to worms, salted minnows, and Mepps Spin Flies.

Directions: CR 17 parallels the river's west bank.

Additional information: Primitive camping is permitted in Battle Hill State Forest.

Contact: New York State Department of Environmental Conservation Region 7.

163A. Otto Mills State Fishing Access

Description: This site is on the edge of state land and has parking for about four cars. You have to walk the old Otto Mills Drive about 1,000 yards to its end at the river.

Directions: Head north out Redfield on CR 17 for about 3 miles. Turn east onto Otto Mills Drive and travel for about 0.5 mile.

164. North Branch Salmon River

Key species: Brook trout.

Description: This stream springs from Tug Hill Plateau and pours into the north end of the Salmon River Reservoir in Redfield.

Tips: Cast black all-purpose nymphs into the heads and tails of pools.

The fishing: Each year the state releases in excess of 3,000 brook trout averaging 9 inches. Combined with the river's natives, they make this one of Oswego County's most productive streams. The fishing is best from late April through May, when the trout hit worms and salted minnows. Come summer, terrestrials, nymphs, caddis, emergers, and moth patterns work well.

Directions: Harvester Mill Road and CR 17 parallel the stream.

Additional information: From May through mid-June the black flies are often thick enough to drive you off the stream. The easiest way to deal with them is to douse yourself with insect repellent. However, health-conscious anglers find mesh garments like Bug-Out Outdoorwear only slightly less convenient and a lot healthier.

Contact: New York State Department of Environmental Conservation Region 7.

164A. Public Access *(see map on page 288)*

Description: This undeveloped site has parking for about four cars.

Directions: Head north out of Redfield on Harvester Mill Road for about 1 mile to the first bridge.

164B. Public Access *(see map on page 288)*

Description: This site has parking for about eight cars.

Directions: Head north out of Redfield on Harvester Mill Road for about 2 miles to the second bridge.

164C. Public Access *(see map on page 288)*

Description: This site has parking for five cars.

Directions: At the CR 17 bridge, about 3.5 miles north of Redfield.

164D. Public Access *(see map on page 288)*

Description: This site has parking for five cars.

Directions: Head north out of Redfield on CR 17 for about 5 miles and turn west on Caster Drive.

165. Salmon River Reservoir (Redfield Reservoir) *(see map on page 288)*

Key species: Black bass, black crappie, sunfish, rock bass, brown bullhead, brown trout, brook trout, and rainbow trout.

Description: Created in 1914 when a power dam was built on the Salmon River, this reservoir covers 3,379 acres, averages 20 feet deep, and has a maximum depth of 57 feet.

Tips: Work Texas-rigged scented worms like Mister Twister Exudes in the reservoir's stump fields.

The fishing: Primarily a warm-water fishery, largemouth bass ranging from 1 to 5 pounds are plentiful and strike crayfish, minnows, and soft jerkbaits like Slug-Gos and Fin-S fish. Smallmouths have recently been illegally introduced and are gaining a foothold. Averaging about 1.5 pounds, they are primarily targeted by drifting minnows and crayfish. Crappies are abundant, and locals know how to keep it secret. Averaging a whopping 10 inches, many over 14 inches are taken each year, primarily on buckeye and flathead minnows. Bluegills and pumpkinseeds averaging 7 inches are common and take poppers, flies, worms, and tiny grubs like spikes. Rock bass averaging a solid 7 inches are abundant over the numerous rock fields and hit worms and minnows. Bullheads range from 8 to 14 inches and are a popular rite of spring for locals fishing with worms on the bottom at night.

A few large trout (brown, rainbow, and brook), migrants from tributaries like the Salmon River, are available. Indeed, there are enough 20-inchers of each species to attract locals who still-fish for them with worms in the early spring off points. In addition, a dedicated following targets these trout in warm weather by trolling small spoons in open water by day or casting crankbaits along the shoreline around dawn and dusk. Trout season is year-round.

Directions: Head east out of Pulaski on CR 2 for about 10 miles.

Additional information: Primitive camping is permitted on the state land off CR 2.

Contact: New York State Department of Environmental Conservation Region 7.

165A. Falls Road Day Use Project

Description: This site has a beach launch, picnic facilities, parking for about twenty-five cars, and shore-fishing access.

Directions: Head east out of Pulaski on CR 2 for about 9 miles and turn right on Dam Road. Travel for 1.2 miles and turn left at the four corners.

Additional information: Dam Road isn't plowed in winter.

165B. Jackson Road Public Access

Description: This site has a double-wide concrete launch, parking for about forty rigs, and shore-fishing access.

Directions: Jackson Road is about 9.5 miles east of Pulaski, off CR 2.

Additional information: The lower half of Jackson Road isn't plowed in winter.

165C. Little America Public Access

Description: This site has parking for about thirty cars and shore-fishing access.

Directions: Take CR 2 east out of Pulaski for just under 11 miles, turn right on C.C.C. Drive, and travel for about 0.5 mile.

Additional information: The lower portion of C.C.C. Drive isn't plowed in winter. This site's steep banks make launching even small canoes difficult. There are several hardened, no-frills campsites above the east side of the parking lot and one on the road leading to the access site.

165D. Hall Island State Forest Public Access *(see map on page 288)*

Description: This site has upper and lower parking lots that accommodate a total of forty cars. If the upper barrier is closed, you have to park and walk 0.8 mile to the reservoir.

Directions: Head south on NY 13 from Pulaski for about 6.5 miles to Altmar. Turn left on Cemetery Road (at the SALMON RIVER FISH HATCHERY sign) and continue straight (the road turns into CR 22 north) for 3.2 miles to CR 30. Turn south and travel for 0.3 mile, bear left on Pipe Line Road, and travel 2.2 miles to the parking area and access road on the left.

Additional information: This is a popular night-fishing spot for early-season bullheads. Primitive camping is allowed in the surrounding state forest.

166. Upper Salmon River *(see map on page 288)*

Key species: Rainbow trout and brown trout.

Description: This portion of the river spills out of Salmon River Reservoir and runs through a 2-mile gorge, tumbles over the spectacular Salmon River Falls about halfway, and feeds Lighthouse Hill Reservoir.

Tips: The best trout fishing is early in the season, downstream of the Salmon River Falls.

The fishing: The section above Salmon River Falls has poor habitat and is best suited for anglers more concerned with pristine scenery and solitude than trout. Below the cataract, however, the stream gets spawning runs of browns and rainbows, some of which stay afterwards. Here the river flows over the ancient riverbed and is wide and shallow, nothing more than mere ripples over broken sheets of rock for most of its length. However, there are some fishy pools, runs, and rifts if you don't mind taking a long walk up the spectacular gorge. Fish here can range anywhere from 8 to 20 inches. None are stocked but migrate up from Lighthouse Hill Reservoir. They respond well in the spring to worms.

Directions: Head east out of Altmar on CR 22 for 3.4 miles to Bennett Bridges (the double white bridges); the natural river flows under the second bridge.

Additional information: The Lower Salmon River is site 37, in the Great Lakes Region section.

Contact: New York State Department of Environmental Conservation Region 7 and Oswego County Promotion & Tourism.

166A. Salmon River Falls Unique Area

Description: This 112-acre preserve has parking for thirty cars. The 150-foot descent to the river below the falls is steep, rugged, and extremely difficult.

Directions: Continue north on CR 22 from Bennett Bridges (see site 166) for about 1 mile to Falls Road. Turn right and travel for 1.5 miles.

167. Lighthouse Hill Reservoir *(see map on page 288)*

Key species: Rainbow trout, brown trout, largemouth bass, bluegill, yellow perch, and brown bullhead.

Description: This 164-acre impoundment averages 25 feet deep and has a maximum depth of 50 feet. Its shoreline is forested, except for powerhouses on the east and west ends.

Tips: From May through mid-July work nymphs through the rapids at the mouth of the power company's tailrace.

The fishing: The state stocks about 5,000 rainbow trout averaging 9 inches annually. They grow to range from 10 to 16 inches and respond to worms, Berkley Trout Bait, and spinners in the spring and to dry flies fished at dusk and dawn in summer. Brown trout, descendants of former stocking programs, are also available. These truly wild fish range from 6 to 20 inches and are usually caught incidentally by folks targeting rainbows at Bennett Bridges or drifting minnows and casting minnow-imitating crankbaits for largemouth bass. Bucketmouths range from 1 to 4 pounds and take spinnerbaits and Carolina-rigged worms fished in 5 to 20 feet of water. Yellow perch up to 10 inches, bluegills between 4 and 7 inches, and brown bullheads averaging 10 inches hit worms.

Directions: Head south out of Pulaski on NY 13 for 6.8 miles to Altmar. Turn left on Cemetery Road (at the SALMON RIVER FISH HATCHERY sign) and continue straight (it turns into CR 22) for 3.4 miles to the double bridges.

Additional information: The Salmon River Project Bennett Bridges Day Use Site has parking for about thirty cars, a beach launch, and several hundred yards of shore-fishing access on the reservoir and at the mouths of the old Salmon River and the power company canal.

Contact: New York State Department of Environmental Conservation Region 7 and Oswego County Promotion & Tourism.

THOUSAND ISLANDS REGION

W hile the Thousand Islands are generally considered a feature of the St. Lawrence River, the outcrops responsible for this geological wonderland stretch south to a point midway between the river and Tug Hill Plateau. This rugged area is pocked with lakes. All but four of those listed here (Perch Lake, Sixtown Pond, Lake Bonaparte, and Sylvia Lake) belong to the Indian River Lakes group, eighteen glacial gems set dead center on the southern edge of the St. Lawrence lowlands. Their close proximity to one another, coupled with their diverse physical characteristics, offer time-strapped anglers a wide variety of habitats containing every species indigenous to the state. The local New York State Department of Environmental Conservation office publishes a free brochure, *Fishing the Indian River Lakes: Official Maps and Guide.*

Set in an economically depressed area, many Indian River Lakes are subject to commercial ice fishing. Locals single out certain lakes in a given year, depleting the number of adult yellow perch and sunfish. As a rule, game fish numbers aren't fazed.

168. Perch Lake

Key species: Northern pike, yellow perch, black crappie, and sunfish.

Description: Fed by Gillette Creek and a smaller brook on the north end, this 540-acre lake's average depth is 4 feet, and its maximum depth, a small hole out in the middle, drops to 10 feet. Totally surrounded by the Perch River Wildlife Management Area, its shoreline is undeveloped.

Tips: Use an ice shanty or nylon shelter to protect yourself from the wind.

The fishing: After being a private commercial fishery for most of the last century, this lake was opened to the public in 1994. But there's a catch: It's only open to ice fishing. The average yellow perch is 8 inches long, pumpkinseeds and bluegills range between 5 and 10 inches, and black crappies run between 9 and 11 inches. They all take tiny ice jigs tipped with grubs. While northern pike up to 40 inches have been caught in research nets, most range between 3 and 8 pounds. They are normally taken with large minnows fished below tip-ups.

Directions: From Watertown, take NY 12 north for about 3 miles and turn right onto Mustard Road. At its end, about 1 mile later, bear left onto Perch Lake Road and follow it for about 5 miles to the access road on the left.

Additional information: The lake is open to ice fishing only from December 1 to March 1. The Perch River Wildlife Management Area is a nesting site for bald

Perch Lake

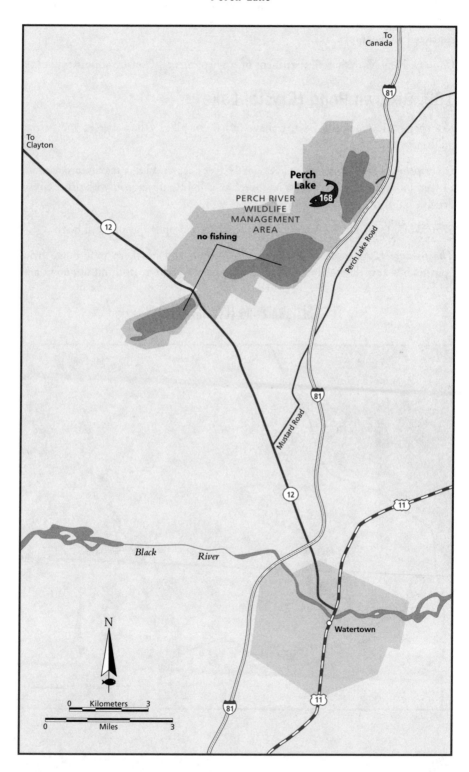

eagles, and the lake is closed during warm weather to protect them. The access road is plowed, and at its end is a parking lot for about fifty cars. You must sign in at the parking lot's unmanned station because this is a special-regulation area. Access is restricted to the upper lake.

Contact: New York State Department of Environmental Conservation Region 6.

169. Sixtown Pond (Crystal Lake)

Key species: Largemouth bass, walleye, northern pike, yellow perch, and brown bullhead.

Description: This 172-acre lake averages 14 feet deep and has a maximum depth of 24 feet. Largely ringed by reeds, its shoreline is lightly developed with private residences.

Tips: Work Texas-rigged worms along the edges and openings of weed beds.

The fishing: Largemouth bass average 14 inches, and northern pike range from "pin-pike"—less than 18 inches—to respectable 26-inchers. Both hit minnows and

Sixtown Pond (Crystal Lake)

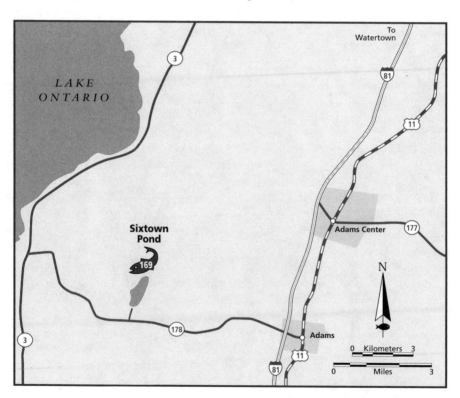

minnow-imitating crankbaits such as Rebel Minnows and Excalibur Fat Frees. The state has recently stocked walleyes, and anglers regularly report catching fish ranging from 18 to 20 inches by drifting and trolling worms on harnesses and by jigging scented curly-tailed grubs on bottom. Bullheads ranging from 8 to 12 inches and yellow perch averaging 7 inches are plentiful and respond to worms still-fished on bottom. The minimum length for walleyes is 18 inches, and the daily limit is three.

Directions: Head west out of Adams on NY 178 for 5.4 miles and turn right on the gravel road.

Additional information: The state access site offers shore fishing, a beach launch suitable for cartop craft, and parking for twenty cars.

Contact: New York State Department of Environmental Conservation Region 6.

170. Indian River *(see map on page 298)*

Key species: Brook trout, brown trout, walleye, northern pike, black bass, channel catfish, and black crappie.

Description: Stretching for over 100 miles, this stream grows quickly, from creek-size in the village of Indian River to a respectable river by the time it feeds the Oswegatchie River, 2 miles downstream of Black Lake. Although it has some killer drops, like the ones in the villages of Theresa and Rossie, Indian River is generally a mild-mannered stream.

Tips: Drift live bait.

The fishing: The state annually stocks roughly 300 brook trout averaging 9.5 inches and 1,000 brown trout averaging 8 inches into the upper reaches, around the villages of Indian River and Natural Bridge. The water is creek-size here, and wading anglers tossing worms, salted minnows, or nymphs are treated to brookies ranging from 10 to 13 inches and browns up to 18 inches long.

Below Natural Bridge the river becomes a warm-water fishery. Walleyes generally run less than 22 inches. Most locals catch them by drifting worms (plain and harnessed) or casting bucktail jigs and crankbaits. Both species of black bass are well represented. Smallmouths range from 12 to 15 inches, and largemouths can go as large as 6 pounds, particularly downstream of Rossie. Drifting with minnows and crayfish and working Carolina- or Texas-rigged worms around structure are the most productive methods for taking both species. Northern pike range from 18 to 30 inches, but beasts up to 40 inches are caught each year. Most are taken on large shiners and suckers or by casting spinnerbaits. The pool below the falls in Rossie is famous for black crappie in the 9- to 12-inch range, especially in the spring. Fish buckeye or flathead minnows below bobbers or jig 2-inch scented tubes and grubs. There are enough monster channel catfish up to 20 pounds in the river below Rossie Falls to attract a dedicated following who still-fish on bottom in deep holes and channels with clumps of worms, minnows, shrimp, cut bait, and even chicken parts.

Indian River

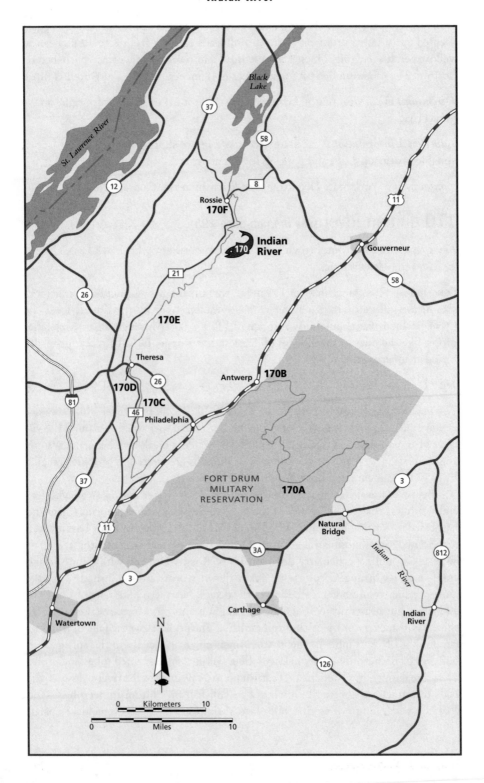

The minimum length for black bass is 10 inches from the source to Rossie Falls. Downstream of this cataract to the Oswegatchie River, the minimum size for black bass is 15 inches. Also, downstream of Rossie Falls the minimum length for walleyes is 18 inches, and the daily limit is three.

Directions: The river runs alongside US 11, NY 37, CR 21, CR 3, CR 6, and CR 4 at various points. NY 3 crosses the river in Natural Bridge.

Additional information: The trout section runs mostly through private property, and the only access is at bridges and the shoulder of the road. The regional Department of Environmental Conservation office publishes a free sixteen-page pamphlet, *Fishing and Canoeing the Indian River,* containing maps, locations of rapids, and public access sites.

Contact: New York State Department of Environmental Conservation Region 6, Fort Drum, Indian River Lakes Chamber of Commerce, and St. Lawrence County Chamber of Commerce.

170A. Fort Drum Public Access

Description: Home of the army's 10th Mountain Division, this 107,265-acre military base has 25 miles of the Indian River running through it. Most of it is in the "high impact area" and off limits to civilians. But a couple of highly productive stretches containing walleyes, northern pike, and smallmouth and largemouth bass are open to the public.

Additional information: Along with all of the state regulations, you'll be expected to abide by Fort Drum Regulation 420-3 (stuff like no fishing downrange of the infantry during target practice). Fort Drum's publication *Angling Opportunities on Fort Drum* contains a map and descriptions of twenty-eight sites open to the public. You must possess the pass you are issued, for a fee, at all times. One day, three-day, and season passes are available. Primitive camping is allowed at some sites.

Contact: Fort Drum.

170B. Antwerp Public Access

Description: This small, grassy landing on the southeast corner of Antwerp's Main Street bridge is suitable for bank fishing and launching cartop craft onto the long, narrow impoundment between two dams. Parking for about three cars is available.

Directions: From Watertown, take US 11 north for about 20 miles to Antwerp, then turn right (east) onto CR 194 and follow it for about 0.25 mile.

170C. Public Access

Description: This site has parking for ten cars and shore-fishing access and is suitable for launching cartop craft.

The fishing: On a slowly moving portion of the river, this site is popular with canoe

Fishing at the old mill on the Indian River in Rossie (site 170F).

anglers targeting walleyes, smallmouth bass, northern pike, and panfish.

Directions: Two miles south of Theresa on CR 46.

170D. Public Access (see map on page 298)

Description: This town-owned site has a paved ramp, parking for three cars, and a picnic table.

The fishing: The site is on an especially scenic flat stretch known for bass, walleyes, and northerns.

Directions: At the NY 26 bridge in Theresa.

Additional information: In late summer the water at this ramp often drops to about a foot below the ramp. This leaves a foot or so drop at the end of the asphalt, making it unsuitable for launching large, trailered craft—unless, of course, you have a monster truck with really high clearance.

170E. Indian River Wildlife Management Area Public Access (see map on page 298)

Description: This site has a beach launch for small trailered craft and parking for five cars.

The fishing: A mild-mannered, fairly straight stretch of river runs through the wildlife management area. Marsh borders much of this section, making it a productive northern pike, largemouth bass, and panfish spot.

Directions: From Bridge Street in the heart of Theresa, get on Red Lake Road. Follow it for 3.7 miles and turn left on Nelson Road. The launch is 0.2 mile down the gravel road.

170F. Public Access *(see map on page 298)*

Description: A manicured lawn gently slopes down to the river, providing easy launching of cartop craft and about 500 feet of open bank-fishing access suitable for safe family outings.

The fishing: This site's still water surrenders walleyes, northerns, and bass to folks casting crankbaits and spinnerbaits.

Directions: Located on CR 3, about 1 mile south of the hamlet of Rossie.

171. Red Lake *(see map on page 302)*

Key species: Walleye, northern pike, black bass, black crappie, yellow perch, bluegill, and brown bullhead.

Description: At 396 acres, this lake is one of the larger ones in the Indian River chain. It's also one of the deepest, averaging 27 feet and dropping to 45 feet in the middle. Its habitats range from undercut marsh mats to steep drop-offs at the bases of scenic cliffs.

Tips: Cast curly-tailed grubs and soft plastic minnows rigged on spinner forms.

The fishing: The state maintains a walleye presence by stocking hundreds of thousands of fry annually. They end up growing to range from 15 to 25 inches and respond to ThunderSticks, Cotton Cordell's Spot Minnows, and worms trolled or drifted on spinner harnesses. This lake is loaded with northern pike; unfortunately, most are "ax handles," just over the minimum size. They take Rat-L-Traps and Bomber Long "A"s. Pike up to 20 pounds exist and are invariably taken through the ice on large minnows. Smallmouths range from 1.5 to 4 pounds, and largemouths can run a pound or two larger. Work rattling crankbaits along drop-offs for bronzebacks, and rip soft plastic worms and slugs through the surface film near vegetation and timber for bucketmouths. Black crappies range from 9 to 12 inches, and yellow perch go 7 to 12 inches. Both take small minnows and Beetle Spins. Bluegills running 5 to 10 inches and brown bullheads up to a staggering 16 inches are plentiful. Both take worms, and the sunnies have a taste for poppers and wet flies, too.

Directions: From Watertown, take I–81 north for about 15 miles to exit 49 (La Fargeville), then take NY 411 east for about 4 miles (it turns into NY 26). In the heart of Theresa, take a left onto Bridge Street, then a quick left onto Red Lake Road and continue for about 4 miles.

Indian River Lakes

Angler holding a Red Lake walleye (site 171).

Additional information: The state fishing access site at the end of Red Lake Road has a beach launch and parking for about ten rigs.

A significant minority of the lake's yellow perch is infested with grubs, resulting, some say, from the lake's abundant waterfowl. While the larvae don't seem to affect the fish's flavor—indeed, one old-timer claims "they give the perch fillets the same insect protein you get from trout"—they're unsightly.

Contact: New York State Department of Environment Conservation Region 6 and Indian River Lakes Chamber of Commerce.

172. Moon Lake

Key species: Tiger muskie, northern pike, walleye, largemouth bass, and black crappie.

Description: This 200-acre lake averages 12 feet deep and has a maximum depth of 20 feet. Half the shoreline is developed with summer cottages; the other half is a scenic mixture of marsh, forest, and outcrops.

Tips: Work tiny jigs and tubes around brush and sunken timber for crappies.

The fishing: Best known as a crappie hot spot, Moon Lake gets heavy ice-fishing pressure. Still, every winter sees enough 9-inchers taken on minnows and grubs to draw anglers back year after year. The state annually stocks several hundred 9-inch tiger muskies. Though few make it past their first year, the survivors end up running from 30 to 40 inches. They are mostly taken incidentally by anglers casting crankbaits for northerns and bass. Northerns up to 25 inches are fairly common and respond to spinnerbaits and large minnows. Largemouth bass typically range from 1.5 to 4 pounds and hit buzzbaits and jerkbaits. Locals complain the walleyes are becoming increasingly rare, but when you get one it's usually over 22 inches. They take worms and crankbaits. The minimum length for walleyes is 18 inches, and the daily limit is three. Motors over ten horsepower are prohibited.

Directions: From Theresa, take Red Lake Road for about 3 miles, hook a right onto Moon Lake Road, and travel for 1.4 miles.

Additional information: A fishing access site on Moon Lake Road offers a beach launch and parking for ten cars.

Contact: New York State Department of Environmental Conservation Region 6 and Indian River Lakes Chamber of Commerce.

173. Muskellunge Lake *(see map on page 302)*

Key species: Largemouth bass, northern pike, black crappie, bluegill, and brown bullhead.

Description: Blanketing 275 acres, this lake averages 11.5 feet deep, and its maximum depth is 25 feet. Shaped like a medieval battle ax, it is set deep in spectacularly rugged country, whose cliffs ring much of the lake's mostly undeveloped shoreline. Two scenic islands rise out in the middle.

Tips: Cast spinnerbaits and buzzbaits for largemouths and northerns.

The fishing: Bucketmouths in the 15- to 20-inch class are common. Jerkbaits such as Mann's Loudmouths and MirrOlure Minnows are productive. Northern pike typically range 18 to 22 inches, but 3-footers are available. Most are taken on large shiners, either drifted, free-lined, or fished below bobbers. Devoid of free public access, this lake doesn't get the heavy ice-fishing pressure its sister lakes do. Crappies ranging from 9 to 12 inches and bluegills up to 10 inches are plentiful. The crappies take small minnows suspended below pencil floats and marabou jigs fished plain or tipped with soft plastic grubs or tubes. The sunnies like worms, flies, poppers, Berkley Power Wigglers, and 1-inch Power Grubs. Brown bullheads range from 10 to 14 inches and, incredibly, are popularly taken in broad daylight with worms still-fished on bottom. A few walleyes are also available. They are normally taken on minnows and crankbaits targeting other species. The minimum length for walleyes is 18 inches, and the daily limit is three.

*The Indian River lakes
are loaded with large
northern pike.*

Directions: From Theresa, take CR 22 east for about 5 miles. Turn left on New Connecticut Road and travel 2.4 miles, then turn left at the sign bearing GENE'S FISHING CAMP, MUSKELLUNGE LAKE, NATURE'S FISH BOWL. Continue on this gravel pot-holed road for just under 1 mile to the boat launch at Gene's Fishing Camp.

Additional information: Gene's Fishing Camp, a privately owned fee area offering the only public access to the lake, is open from May 1 to October 24. The owner allows ice-fishing access to anglers who make arrangements with him during his regular season.

Contact: New York State Department of Environmental Conservation Region 6 and Indian River Lakes Chamber of Commerce.

174. Payne Lake *(see map on page 302)*

Key species: Northern pike, walleye, largemouth bass, yellow perch, black crappie, bluegill, and brown bullhead.

Description: This 160-acre lake averages 6.5 feet deep and has a maximum depth of 15 feet. A spectacular cliff runs along most of its west bank.

Tips: Use jigs tipped with grubs or perch eyes immediately after first ice.

The fishing: The shallow lake's greatest draw is its populations of panfish: yellow perch averaging 10 inches, black crappies up to 12 inches, bluegills ranging from 7 to 10 inches, and brown bullheads up to 14 inches. Ice fishing with live grubs is the most popular method of taking the perch, sunfish, and crappies. Bullheads are primarily targeted with worms in spring. Good populations of northern pike ranging from 18 to 25 inches and largemouth bass running from 12 to 15 inches are also present. Both of them respond to spinnerbaits, Rat-L-Traps, and minnow-imitating crankbaits. In addition, the bass like crayfish and jig-'n'-pigs. The state maintains a walleye presence by stocking hundreds of thousands of fry annually. "This is the second best walleye lake in the Indian River chain," says state fisheries biologist Frank Flack. They range from 15 to 23 inches and like worms trolled on spinner harnesses, bucktail jigs, and crankbaits. Recently the state has been stocking about 300 9-inch tiger muskies annually, but it's too early to tell how they are doing.

Motors over ten horsepower are prohibited.

Directions: Head north out of Theresa on CR 22 for about 8 miles.

Additional information: The state access site on CR 22 offers a concrete ramp, parking for thirty rigs, and bank fishing. Primitive camping is permitted in the 1,600-acre Pulpit Rock State Forest, on the west shore opposite the launch.

Contact: New York State Department of Environmental Conservation Region 6 and Indian River Lakes Chamber of Commerce.

175. Sixberry Lake *(see map on page 302)*

Key species: Lake trout, walleye, smallmouth bass, bluegill, yellow perch, and land-locked Atlantic salmon.

Description: Largely undeveloped, this 115-acre lake is ringed by a forest of ever-greens and white birch clinging to steep, rugged banks sporting striking granite out-crops. Triangular in shape, the lake averages 45 feet deep, and its maximum depth is 90 feet.

Tips: Drift over deep water and vertically jig spoons for lakers.

The fishing: This two-story fishery offers some awfully big cold-water and warm-water species for a lake its size. Each year the state stocks about 2,500 6.5-inch lake trout. They typically reach between 4 and 8 pounds and are targeted by locals with spoons and minnows fished deep behind Christmas tree and Seth Green rigs. Walleyes generally run between 2 and 5 pounds, but trophies up to 11 pounds are caught regularly. They'll take jigs tipped with worms and floating/diving crankbaits like ThunderSticks and Mann's Loudmouth Jerkbaits. Smallmouth bass average 2.5 pounds and take minnows and crayfish drifted on bottom along breaks. Toward the end of the last century, the state annually stocked 500 6-inch land-locked Atlantic salmon for a while to study the feasibility of more intensive stock-ing. The program ended in 2000, says state fisheries biologist Frank Flack. Still, some 15- to 20-inch salmon should be around until 2006 or so. They are known to take streamers, small spoons, and crankbaits like Rebel Holographic Minnows and Excalibur Ghost Minnows. Bluegills ranging from 5 to 8 inches and yellow perch averaging 9 inches are commonly taken by still-fishing with worms or fly fishing with wet flies and poppers.

Motors exceeding ten horsepower are prohibited.

Directions: Head north out of Theresa on Alex Bay Road, turn right 100 yards later onto CR 21 (English Settlement Road), travel for about 4 miles, then turn west on Sears Road and continue for about 0.25 mile.

Additional information: The state access site on Sears Road has a single-lane paved ramp, parking for about ten cars, and shore-fishing access. A private campground is next to the boat launch.

Contact: New York State Department of Environmental Conservation Region 6, 1000 Islands International Tourism Council, and Indian River Lakes Chamber of Commerce.

176. Lake of the Woods *(see map on page 302)*

Key species: Lake trout, lake whitefish, northern pike, smallmouth bass, bluegill, rock bass, landlocked Atlantic salmon, and rainbow trout.

Description: Remote and lightly developed, this 166-acre lake is more than it seems. Indeed, it's only about 1,500 feet wide, but it averages 43 feet deep and drops to a maximum depth of 80 feet in the middle. Its wooded shoreline is steep. Up and down the beach, branches of submerged timber reach out of the waves like phantom limbs.

Tips: Ice fish with minnows suspended below tip-ups for lake trout.

The fishing: The state stocks about 2,900 6.5-inch lakers annually. They pig out on the lake's freshwater shrimp and end up averaging a very respectable 5 pounds. Locals go after them by deep-trolling minnowbaits like Red Fins and Junior ThunderSticks and small spoons behind wobblers. About 250 6.5-inch Atlantic salmon were stocked yearly as the twentieth century waned. Although they were replaced in 2001 with a rainbow trout stocking program, salmon in the 15- to 20-inch range should be around until at least 2005. They hit flatlined streamers and free-lined garden worms drifted over deep water. Just recently the state has been annually releasing 500 rainbows averaging 9 inches. Survival is decent, and "bows" up to 15 inches are available now, but they should get bigger. They take dry flies cast along the shoreline at dusk and dawn, Berkley Trout Bait suspended about 18 inches off the floor, worms, and streamers. This is one of the few lakes around that still have whitefish. They range from 16 to 22 inches and are targeted, mostly in winter, with ice-fishing flies tipped with a kernel of corn. Northern pike range from 18 to 25 inches and take minnows, jerkbaits, and Rat-L-Traps. Smallmouth bass in the 12- to 16-inch range are common and respond to spinnerbaits retrieved slow and deep or yo-yoed and allowed to occasionally bounce bottom. Sunfish and rock bass up to 0.75 pound can be counted on to hit worms and surface poppers anytime.

Lake trout can be taken year-round. Motors over ten horsepower are prohibited.

Directions: Take CR 21 (English Settlement Road) north out of Theresa. About 7.5 miles later, at the stop sign in Chapel Corners, turn left on Cottage Hill Road. Take the next right, 0.4 mile later, onto Burns Road and follow it for 0.8 mile, then turn right on the dirt road at the FISHING ACCESS SITE sign.

Additional information: The fishing access site has a beach launch and parking for about twenty rigs.

Contact: New York State Department of Environmental Conservation Region 6, Indian River Lakes Chamber of Commerce, and 1000 Islands International Tourism Council.

177. Grass Lake (see map on page 302)

Key species: Black bass, northern pike, walleye, bluegill, black crappie, brown bullhead, and tiger muskie.

Description: This 320-acre lake averages 15 feet deep and drops to a maximum depth of 55 feet. Paradoxically its western arm only averages 3 feet deep. Its splendid environs range from pristine marsh to steep, forested hills lightly developed with environmentally sensitive seasonal residences.

Tips: Work weedless floating lures like Mann's Ghosts and Goblins in and around vegetation.

The fishing: State fisheries biologist Frank Flack considers this the best Indian River lake for autumn bass "mainly because it's the least fished." Bronzebacks typically range from 12 to 20 inches, and bucketmouths can reach 6 pounds. Both wantonly strike spinnerbaits and buzzbaits early in the season but wise-up quickly, and come fall, they are best approached with finesse with baits such as 2-inch YUM Wooly Curltails, Shakin' Worms, and Wooly Beavertails. Northern pike do well in this food-rich habitat, averaging a cool 24 inches. Twenty-eight-inchers are common, and pikeasauruses stretching over 36 inches are available. They like minnows, rattling crankbaits, and spinnerbaits. The walleyes are typical for the chain, ranging anywhere from too small to 24 inches. They take minnow-imitating crankbaits like Bass Pro Shop's XPS Extreme Minnows worked along the shore early in the season and at dusk, and vertically jigged bladebaits and YUM Walleye Grubs bounced on bottom in deep water during the heat of the day. Bluegills running up to 10 inches and crappies averaging 11 inches are abundant. Crappies hit streamers, and the bluegills are partial to tiny poppers. Both take marabou jigs and wet flies. Bullheads ranging from 8 to a whooping 16 inches respond enthusiastically to worms. Over the past couple years, the state has been stocking 400-plus 9-inch tigers. The results aren't in yet, but with all the food around, they should do very well. Go for them with bucktail in-line spinners and shallow running crankbaits such as 4.5-inch Rebel Holographic Minnows.

The minimum length for walleyes is 18 inches, and the daily limit is three. Motors over ten horsepower are prohibited.

Directions: From site 176, continue north on Burns Road for about 2 miles to the county line. Turn right on the single-lane dirt road and travel for 0.4 mile, bear left and drive for 0.2 mile, then bear right and travel for 0.1 mile.

Additional information: The state fishing site offers a beach launch and parking for three rigs.

Contact: New York State Department of Environmental Conservation Region 6 and 1000 Islands International Tourism Council.

178. Crystal Lake *(see map on page 302)*

Key species: Northern pike, black bass, black crappie, bluegill, yellow perch, brown bullhead, and maybe walleye.

Description: Spilling over 122 acres, this lake offers a lot for its small size. Averaging 21 feet deep and dropping to a maximum depth of 40 feet, only about 30 percent of its scenic shoreline is developed. The remainder is either striking cliffs crowned in forest or bottomland woods.

Tips: Work fast-diving lures like Mann's Little Georges and Mini Fins along drop-offs.

The fishing: Northern pike ranging from 18 to 22 inches are plentiful and respond to minnows and soft jerkbaits. Smallmouth bass commonly go between 12 and 15 inches. They like ribbed soft plastics like YUM Wooly Curltails and Finesse Tubes and live crayfish dragged slowly on bottom. Largemouth bass running from 1.5 to 3 pounds hang out wherever they can find shallow structure and respond to Texas-rigged worms and scented tubes like YUM Vibra Kings. Black crappies only average 8 inches, but enough keepers are available to make crappie dinners for two realistic goals. Most anglers target them with minnows and grubs, primarily in the spring and through the ice. Yellow perch up to 9 inches, sunnies from 5 to 8 inches, and bullheads up to 12 inches are abundant and respond to worms. The state recently started stocking walleyes to the tune of 4,000 fingerlings annually. At press time it was too early to determine the program's success.

Directions: Head south out of Redwood on NY 37 for 0.7 mile, turn left on the unmarked road at the CRYSTAL LAKE CAMPGROUND sign, and travel for 0.4 mile.

Additional information: There is no free public access on the lake; however, Crystal Lake Campground offers a beach launch for a fee. The launch is open from May 15 through October 15.

Contact: New York State Department of Environmental Conservation Region 6 and Indian River Lakes Chamber of Commerce.

179. Millsite Lake *(see map on page 302)*

Key species: Lake trout, northern pike, largemouth bass, smallmouth bass, yellow perch, landlocked Atlantic salmon, brown trout, and rainbow trout.

Description: This 500-acre lake is the third largest in the Indian River chain. Averaging 42 feet deep and dropping to a maximum depth of over 70 feet, its clear, cold water is splattered with islands and skirted by a wooded shoreline embellished with splendid outcrops.

Tips: Cast crankbaits parallel to shore in the spring.

The fishing: The state manages this lake as a two-story (warm- and cold-water) fishery. Millsite is notorious for northern pike in the 30- to 40-inch range. Even more remarkable is its lake trout, which typically reach 10 to 13 pounds. Both species reach Herculean proportions by feeding on the lake's ciscos. Locals target them with live minnows fished deep for the lake trout and 3 to 5 feet beneath floats for northerns. Smallmouth bass run from 1 to 2.5 pounds and hit salted tubes and curly-tailed grubs. Largemouths up to 5 pounds lurk around shallow structure and respond to Zara Spooks and jig-'n'-pigs. Yellow perch reach up to 14 inches in the lake's shoreline habitats and take worms, small minnows, and 2-inch curly-tail grubs.

The state stocked hundreds of 6.5-inch landlocked Atlantic salmon annually at the end of the last century to study their movements through the Indian River lakes chain and to determine if large-scale introduction was feasible. Frank Flack, senior fisheries biologist for the state, reports that they were last stocked in 2000. In 2001 a rainbow trout stocking program was initiated, and several hundred 8-inchers were released. In 2002 the rainbows were replaced with 450 9-inch browns. At press time 2003's stocking report wasn't available. Some rainbows, browns, and salmon ranging from 15 to 20 inches will probably be around through 2005 and should respond to flatlined Junior ThunderSticks and streamers and free-floating worms and minnows.

Motors exceeding ten horsepower are prohibited.

Directions: From the south side of Redwood, head east on Cottage Hill Road for about 1 mile.

Additional information: The state beach launch off Cottage Hill Road has a hard-surface ramp and parking for ten cars.

Contact: New York State Department of Environmental Conservation Region 6 and Indian River Lakes Chamber of Commerce.

180. Butterfield Lake (see map on page 302)

Key species: Walleye, northern pike, largemouth bass, smallmouth bass, yellow perch, black crappie, bluegill, and bullhead.

Description: This 1,005-acre body of water is the second largest Indian River lake. It averages 15 feet deep, has a maximum depth of 50 feet, boasts numerous islands, and has a steep, mostly forested shoreline accented in outcrops.

Tips: In spring work bucktail jigs, plain or tipped with 3-inch Power Grubs or minnows, along weed edges and drop-offs for northerns and walleyes.

The fishing: A winding coastline and numerous islands stretch this 2-plus-mile-long lake's shoreline to over 10 miles. Combined with its shallow water, all this edge habitat makes for a highly productive warm-water fishery. Over the past few years, the state has been heavily stocking the place with walleyes. The figures for 2002 were 4,600,000 fry, 5,510 2-inchers, and 14,500 4-inchers. Many survive to range between 15 and 23 inches. They'll strike C.C. Shads, ThunderSticks, worms trolled on spinner harnesses, and bucktail jigs. Northern pike grow from 18 to 30 inches and are mostly targeted with spinnerbaits and large minnows. Largemouths up to 5 pounds like Texas-rigged worms pitched into weed openings. Bronzebacks up to 4 pounds prowl the drop-offs on the south end and respond to jigs and Carolina-rigged 4-inch worms. Black crappies in the 9- to 14-inch range and yellow perch up to 12 inches take small minnows or curly-tailed grubs jigged or worked on spinner forms. Bluegills the size of cup saucers hit garden worms in early spring, wet flies and poppers in summer, night crawlers in autumn, and mousies and spikes through the ice. Bullheads up to 16 inches swarm into the shallows in spring and can't resist a juicy worm squirming in the mud.

Angler showing off a pair of typical crappies that the Indian River lakes are famous for.

Directions: The lake is on the eastern border of the hamlet of Redwood. Stine Road follows the lake.

Additional information: The state launch in Redwood has a concrete ramp, parking for fifty rigs, and toilets.

Contact: New York State Department of Environmental Conservation Region 6 and Indian River Lakes Chamber of Commerce.

181. Hyde Lake *(see map on page 302)*

Key species: Tiger muskie, walleye, northern pike, and largemouth bass.

Description: This 198-acre lake averages 11.5 feet deep and has a maximum depth of 18 feet. A spectacular cliff towers over most of the east shore. The north and south basins are shallow, with the south basin averaging 3 feet deep for about 100 feet out. The east and west sides, however, drop quickly to 15 feet deep.

Tips: Work large bucktail spinners over the gentle drops on the north and south ends for norlunge.

The fishing: This is the best bet in the Indian River lakes for catching a keeper tiger muskie. Trophies over 40 inches are reported periodically. Northern pike in the 18- to 25-inch range are common. Both of these members of the pike family are caught on large minnows, Rat-L-Traps, and minnowbaits like MirrOlures and Mann's Loudmouth Jerkbaits. The state had stocked thousands of walleye fingerlings in the recent past, but results weren't encouraging, and none were released in 2002. Still, a few "eyes" up to 22 inches long are present and are often caught on jigs and finesse worms dragged on bottom for bass. The lake has good populations of largemouth bass in the 12- to 18-inch range, with many growing larger. They're partial to shallow water, where they hit buzzbaits and surface walkers.

The minimum length for walleyes is 18 inches, and the daily limit is three. Motors over ten horsepower are prohibited.

Directions: From the village of Theresa, take NY 26 north for about 4 miles to Funda Road and turn left.

Additional information: The state fishing access site on Funda Road has a beach launch and parking for about fifteen rigs.

Contact: New York State Department of Environmental Conservation Region 6 and Indian River Lakes Chamber of Commerce.

182. Clear Lake *(see map on page 302)*

Key species: Northern pike, black bass, walleye, black crappie, yellow perch, sunfish, and bullhead.

Description: This 180-acre lake averages 20 feet deep and has a maximum depth of 44 feet. Its shoreline is largely developed with private residences.

Tips: Work soft jerkbaits like YUM Houdini Shads through the northern shallows for post-spawn pike and black bass.

The fishing: This popular warm-water fishery boasts good numbers of northern pike. Most go around 2.5 pounds, but 10-pounders—and even better—are available. They hit live minnows and minnow-imitating crankbaits such as Bomber Long "A"s. Largemouth bass ranging between 1.5 and 3 pounds and smallmouths in the 1- to 2-pound class are well represented. While the bucketmouths tend to gravitate toward the shallows and the bronzebacks prefer drop-offs, either one can be caught in both places. They share a common taste for crayfish, spinnerbaits, 3-inch YUM Wooly Beavertails, and Berkley Power Grubs. Though not overly abundant, walleyes running from 18 to 22 inches are present and like Rat-L-Traps and Cicadas retrieved steadily or yo-yoed in deep water. Black crappies averaging 9 inches and yellow perch ranging between 7 and 10 inches are partial to minnows and curly-tailed grubs. Bluegills between 5 and 10 inches and bullheads reaching up to 14 inches thrive in this habitat and respond to worms.

The minimum length for walleyes is 18 inches, and the daily limit is three.

Directions: Head south out of Alexandria Bay on NY 26 for 6.6 miles, turn left on Clear Lake Road, and continue for 0.8 mile.

Additional information: A hard-surface public launch is at the end of Clear Lake Road. There is no formal parking lot, but shoulder parking is permitted a couple hundred yards up the road.

Contact: New York State Department of Environmental Conservation Region 6 and Indian River Lakes Chamber of Commerce.

183. Black Lake

Key species: Black bass, walleye, northern pike, muskellunge, black crappie, yellow perch, rock bass, bluegill, bullhead, and channel catfish.

Description: Covering over 10,980 acres, Black Lake is the largest in this highly productive group. Roughly 20 miles long, averaging 8 feet deep, dropping to a maximum depth of 29 feet, and punctuated with scenic islands, its warm, clean, weedy water makes it the most fruitful largemouth bass and crappie fishery in the state.

Tips: In spring and autumn drift worms around the causeway for walleyes.

The fishing: The largemouth bass fishing is legendary—5-pounders are common. They respond to everything from Texas-rigged worms pitched into windfalls and weed openings, to crankbaits and spinnerbaits worked around docks, bass bugs and Mann's Goblins bounced off lily pads, and jig-'n'-pigs worked in slop. Smallmouths

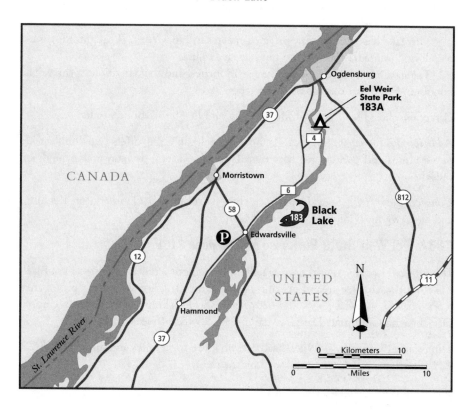

aren't as plentiful, but there's still a lot of them. They like minnows, crayfish, and scented curly-tailed grubs and finesse worms and tubes dragged on bottom, especially in channels and around island drop-offs. After being all but wiped out in the last century, allegedly by crappies feeding on their fry, walleyes are staging a comeback—with human intervention. Over the past several years, the state has stocked a total of a couple hundred thousand fry and tens of thousands of fingerlings—30,000 and 22,400 respectively in 2002. While there's no proof it's "payback time," crappie numbers are down slightly, and the "eyes" seem to be thriving. Indeed, 2- to 3-pounders are becoming so plentiful, word is getting out and anglers are increasingly targeting them, with good results, on crankbaits, jigs, and worms.

Northern pike easily reach 10 pounds and are mostly caught with large minnows. Muskies, though few, average about 30 pounds. Troll for them with large crankbaits. This lake is considered one of the best crappie waters in the Northeast. Slabs typically range from too short to 11 inches, with some 15-inchers available. They like minnows, 2-inch Berkley Power Grubs, YUM Wooly Beavertails, and small hard lures like Cotton Cordell's Spot Minnows and ¼-ounce Silver Buddies. Perch ranging from 6 to 12 inches are common and hit the same baits the crappies like. Bluegills reaching 10 inches and bullheads up to 16 inches like worms. Catfish up to 20 pounds hug the lake's channels and deep holes and hit large minnows, clumps of worms, cut bait, and shrimp.

This lake has sturgeon, a protected species in New York. If caught, they must be released immediately, with no unnecessary injury.

The minimum length for walleyes is 18 inches, and the daily limit is three. The minimum length for black bass is 15 inches.

Directions: Head south out of Morristown on NY 58 for about 6 miles.

Additional information: Black Lake Boat Launch, on CR 6, offers two double-wide paved ramps and parking for fifty rigs. There are several private campgrounds on the lake.

Contact: New York State Department of Environmental Conservation Region 6 and St. Lawrence County Chamber of Commerce.

183A. Eel Weir State Park *(see map on page 315)*

Description: Located on the Oswegatchie River, about 2 miles downstream of Black Lake's outlet, this fee area offers thirty-eight campsites, hot showers, a picnic area, a playground, a paved ramp, and 600 feet of shore-fishing access. Open Memorial Day through Columbus Day; free day use is allowed off-season.

Directions: From Edwardsville, head east on CR 6 for 8 miles and turn right on CR 4. The park is 2 miles down the road on the right.

184. Pleasant Lake

Key species: Walleye, northern pike, black bass, yellow perch, bluegill, and brown bullhead.

Description: This 204-acre lake averages 22 feet deep and has a maximum depth of 32 feet.

Tips: Drag YUM Shakin' Worms on bottom along gently sloping drop-offs.

The fishing: Pleasant Lake offers an above average warm-water habitat. The state maintains a walleye presence by stocking several thousand fingerlings each year. Survival in this predator-rich environment is so-so, but enough live to the minimum 18 inches to make pursuing them worthwhile. Walleyes typically run from 18 to 22 inches and are mostly targeted with bucktail jigs, fished plain or tipped with a worm or scented grub, and crankbaits such as Rat-L-Traps and Bomber Long "A"s. Northern pike averaging 22 inches are common and respond to minnows and Slug-Gos. Populations of smallmouth and largemouth bass are pretty equal. Bronzebacks generally run between 12 and 15 inches and prefer soft plastics like curly-tailed grubs and finesse worms and hard crankbaits worked in deep water. The bucket-mouths like soft plastic jerkbaits, 10-inch worms, and snakes worked through and

Pleasant Lake · Yellow Lake · Sylvia Lake · Lake Bonaparte

around cover and structure in shallow water. The lake's yellow perch easily reach 10 inches, its bluegills average 7 inches, and its bullheads go anywhere from 8 to 14 inches. The perch hit small jigs, in-spinners, and minnows; the sunnies like worms, wet flies, and 1-inch curly-tailed grubs; and the bullheads respond to worms.

Directions: Head east out of Rossie on CR 8 for 3.2 miles. Turn right on Pleasant Lake Road and travel 0.2 mile, then turn right on Pleasant Lake Road Number 2 and travel 0.2 mile to the launch at the bend in the road.

Additional information: The town launch isn't marked and only has room for launching, not bank fishing. Parking for three rigs is at the shoulder along the guardrail.

Contact: New York State Department of Environmental Conservation Region 6 and St. Lawrence County Chamber of Commerce.

185. Yellow Lake (see map on page 317)

Key species: Northern pike, largemouth bass, black crappie, sunfish, yellow perch, and bullhead.

Description: Averaging only 4 feet deep and boasting a couple of spots in the middle that drop to a maximum depth of 13 feet, this 480-acre lake is prime warm-water habitat. With less than 10 percent of its shoreline developed, this is one of the best spots in the state for solitary fishing experiences framed in scenic granite outcrops crowned with precariously perched timber.

Tips: Cast large plugs in the deep center on the northern half of the lake for huge pike.

The fishing: Relatively isolated, hard to get to, and rich in marsh and shallow water that minnows love, this place boasts great populations of large northern pike and largemouth bass. Pike range from 18 to 40 inches, with an unusually large number stretching the tape to over 36 inches. Bucketmouths typically range from 3 to 6 pounds, but quite a few go a couple pounds heavier. Both take large minnows, soft plastic slugs, buzzbaits, ThunderSticks, and Rat-L-Traps. Black crappies, bluegills, and pumpkinseeds normally run from 0.5 to 0.75 pound, and yellow perch and bullheads go 8 to 14 inches. Fly fish for the sunfish, crappies, and perch with wet flies, tiny streamers, and poppers. Bullheads hang out in the shallows and take worms still-fished on bottom, especially in the spring and on hot summer nights. (If you're going to night fish, wear insect-proof clothing like Bug-Out Outdoorwear over your regular clothes.)

Motors over ten horsepower are prohibited.

Directions: From the NY 26/CR 22 intersection in Theresa, take CR 22 east for 9.5 miles to CR 25 and turn left (north). At the Y in the road 1 mile later, continue straight onto CR 10 and travel for 4 miles, then bear right onto Liscum Road, which

The Indian River lakes are notorious for their huge panfish.

turns into Hall Road. The state's fishing access site is on the right, several hundred yards later.

Additional information: The fishing access site is separated from the parking area by about 0.25 mile of pasture on which the state owns easement rights. You'll have to walk, going through two S-shaped fences designed to block cattle, so make sure the craft you bring can be lifted about 5 feet. The access site itself is just a narrow channel through marsh, unsuitable for bank fishing in the spring. Primitive camping is allowed in the Yellow Lake State Multiple Use Area hugging the southeastern half of the lake. Completely surrounded by private land, the only way to reach the area is by boat.

Contact: New York State Department of Environmental Conservation Region 6 and Indian River Lakes Chamber of Commerce.

186. Sylvia Lake *(see map on page 317)*

Key species: Rainbow trout, lake trout, smallmouth bass, yellow perch, and sunfish.

Description: Its shoreline half developed with residences, this 313-acre lake averages 70 feet deep and has a maximum depth of 142 feet.

Tips: Troll spoons through the deep areas on Seth Green rigs.

The fishing: Managed as a cold-water fishery, this place has resident populations of lake trout ranging from 2 to 5 pounds. In addition, each year the state stocks anywhere from 3,000 to 5,000 rainbows averaging 9.5 inches. Both species are taken by trolling spoons. Smallmouth bass range from 0.5 to 3 pounds. Fish for them along drop-offs in 10 to 25 feet of water by dragging jig worms and Carolina-rigged 4-inch worms. Yellow perch range from 6 to 12 inches, and bluegills and pumpkinseeds average 7 inches. Both take worms, and the perch like small lures and minnows, too.

Directions: Head south out of Gouverneur on NY 812 for about 7 miles, then turn west on Pumphouse Road. Enter the talcum mine's grounds and make an S-turn. At the end of the company's property, the paved road turns to gravel for the remaining 0.7 mile to a state fishing access site.

Additional information: The fishing access site has a few hundred feet of shore access and parking for about ten rigs. There is no formal launch, but the beach drops quickly and locals launch trailered craft here.

Contact: New York State Department of Environmental Conservation Region 6.

187. Lake Bonaparte (see map on page 317)

Key species: Lake trout, brown trout, walleye, smallmouth bass, largemouth bass, northern pike, yellow perch, and burbot.

Description: This lake's shoreline is heavily developed with private residences. Covering 1,286 acres, it averages 30 feet deep and has a maximum depth of 75 feet.

Tips: In the spring run spoons parallel to shore for trout and northern pike.

The fishing: Managed as a two-story fishery, the state annually stocks about 1,800 lake trout averaging 6.5 inches and 3,000 brown trout averaging 9 inches. Survival isn't great, but some reach between 1 and 4 pounds. Lakers are targeted with silver spoons trolled deep. Browns respond best, especially in the spring, to silver and perch-colored crankbaits like Rapala Minnows and ThunderSticks trolled close to shore. In 1997 the state started a five-year walleye stocking program in which 25,000 fingerlings would be stocked annually. In 1999 the number was doubled because the fish hatchery at Oneida Lake had a banner year, producing three times its average. By 2001 creel surveys showed keeper walleyes were available, suggesting the species was taking. Even if they do start reproducing naturally, the lake's crappies and bass will probably keep their population low—maybe even wipe them out again. Still, 4- to 7-pound survivors of the stocking program should be available until 2010 or so. They hit worms drifted on harnesses, curly-tailed grubs, and crankbaits.

Largemouth bass range from 1.5 to 5 pounds and are normally taken in the bays with Texas-rigged worms and soft jerkbaits. The best bucketmouth habitat is Fort Drum's Mud Lake and around the channel connecting it to the west side of Lake

Bonaparte. Back in the main lake, smallmouths range between 1 and 2.5 pounds and can be taken on drop-offs with crayfish, minnows, and jigs. Northern pike run from 18 to 36 inches and are targeted with large minnows. Perch range from 6 to 12 inches and take worms, minnows, and 2-inch Mister Twister Exude grubs during warm weather and minnows and live grubs jigged through the ice. Burbot averaging 2 pounds respond to minnows fished on bottom.

The minimum length for brown trout is 9 inches. Trout can be taken year-round. The minimum length for walleyes is 18 inches, and the daily limit is three. A pass is needed to fish on Fort Drum property.

Directions: Head east out of Watertown on NY 3 for about 11 miles, then bear east on NY 3A. About 5 miles later, get back on NY 3 east and travel for 15.4 miles, then turn left onto North Shore Road. At the T in the road 0.2 mile later, turn left and continue for 3.5 miles.

Additional information: The day-use area off North Shore Road has a concrete launch, parking for fifteen rigs, several hundred feet of shore-fishing access, and a toilet. There are three no-frills campsites across the street; a permit, available from the local forest ranger, is needed to use them.

Contact: New York State Department of Environmental Conservation Region 6, Fort Drum, and Lewis County Chamber of Commerce.

Appendix

I n most cases, fishing information can be obtained toll-free by contacting county tourism offices or regional councils such as the 1000 Islands International Tourism Council. If that doesn't work or if you require detailed, site-specific information like stocking reports and future management plans, contact the fisheries office in the regional Department of Environmental Conservation office.

Visitor Bureaus, Visitor Associations, and County Tourism Offices

Allegany County Tourism
County Office Building, Room 208
7 Court Street
Belmont, NY 14813
(800) 836–1869
tourism@alleganyco.com
www.alleganyco.com

Buffalo Niagara Convention & Visitors Bureau
617 Main Street, Suite 400
Buffalo, NY 14203-1496
(888) 228–3369
www.visitbuffaloniagara.com
For the *Greater Niagara Hot Spot Fishing Map: Erie and Niagara County Fishing Guide,* call (866) 345–FISH or visit www.northeastoutdoors.com.

Cattaraugus County Department of Economic Development, Planning, and Tourism
303 Court Street
Little Valley, NY 14755
(800) 331–0543
www.co.cattaraugus.ny.us

Cayuga County Tourism
131 Genesee Street
Auburn, NY 13021
(800) 499–9615
(315) 947–6348 (fishing hotline)
www.cayuganet.org/tourism

Chautauqua County Visitors Bureau
P.O. Box 1441
Chautauqua, NY 14722
(800) 242–4569
ccvb@cecomet.net
www.tourchautauqua.com

Cortland County Visitors Bureau
34 Tompkins Street
Cortland, NY 13045
(800) 859–2227
www.cortlandtourism.com

Finger Lakes Visitors Connection
25 Gorham Street
Canandaigua, NY 14424
(877) 386–4669
www.visitfingerlakes.com

Greater Rochester Visitors Association
45 East Avenue
Rochester, NY 14604
(800) 677–7282
www.visitrochester.com

Ithaca/Tompkins County Convention & Visitors Bureau

904 East Shore Drive
Ithaca, NY 14850
(800) 284–8422
www.ithaca.ny.us/commerce

Madison County Tourism, Inc.

P.O. Box 1029
Morrisville, NY 13408
(800) 684–7320
www.madisontourism.com

Niagara County Tourism and Convention Corporation

139 Niagara Street
Lockport, NY 14094
(800) 338–7890
www.niagara-usa.com

Oneida County Convention and Visitors Bureau

P.O. Box 551
Utica, NY 13503-0551
(800) 426–3132
www.oneidacountycvb.com

Orleans County Tourism

14016 Route 31
Albion, NY 14411
(800) 724–0314
(716) 589–3220 (fishing hotline)
www.orleansny.com/tourism

Oswego County Promotion & Tourism

County Office Building
46 East Bridge Street
Oswego, NY 13126
(315) 349–8322
(800) 248–4386 (Fish-n-Fun line)
www.co.oswego.ny.us

Seneca County Tourism

One Di Pronio Drive
Waterloo, NY 13165
(800) 732–1848
www.co.seneca.ny.us/tourism

Steuben County Conference and Visitors Bureau

5 West Market Street
Corning, NY 14830
(866) 946–3386
www.corningfingerlakes.com

Syracuse Convention and Visitors Bureau

572 South Salina Street
Syracuse, NY 13202-3320
(800) 234–4797
www.syracusecvb.org

Tioga County Tourism

188 Front Street
Owego, NY 13827
(800) 671–7772
www.seetioga.com

Wayne County Office of Tourism/History

P.O. Box 131
Lyons, NY 14489
(800) 527–6510
(315) 946–5466 (fishing hotline)
www.tourism.co.wayne.ny.us

Wyoming County Tourism Promotion Agency

P.O. Box 502
Castile, NY 14427
(800) 839–3919
www.wyomingcountyny.com

Chambers of Commerce

Broome County Chamber of Commerce Convention & Visitors Bureau
P.O. Box 995
Binghamton, NY 13902-0995
(800) 836–6740
www.binghamtoncvb.com

Chemung County Chamber of Commerce
400 East Church Street
Elmira, NY 14901
(800) 627–5892
www.chemungchamber.org

Genesee County Chamber of Commerce
210 East Main Street
Batavia, NY 14020
(800) 622–2686
www.geneseeny.com

Henderson Harbor Chamber of Commerce
P.O. Box 468
Henderson Harbor, NY 13651
(888) 938–5568

Indian River Lakes Chamber of Commerce
Town Clerk's Office
Commercial and Main Streets
Theresa, NY 13691
(315) 628–5046

Lewis County Chamber of Commerce
7383-C Utica Boulevard
Lowville, NY 13367
(800) 724–0242
www.lewiscountychamber.org

Livingston County Chamber of Commerce
4235 Lakeville Road
Building 2, Suite A
Geneseo, NY 14454
(800) 538–7365
www.livchamber.com

St. Lawrence County Chamber of Commerce
Drawer A
Canton, NY 13617
(315) 386–4000
slccoc@northnet.org
www.stlawrencechamber.org

Schuyler County Chamber of Commerce
100 North Franklin Street
Watkins Glen, NY 14891
(800) 607–4552
www.schuylerny.com

Yates County Chamber of Commerce
2375 Route 14A
Penn Yan, NY 14527
(800) 868–9283
www.yatesny.com

Regional Councils, Associations, and Commissions

Finger Lakes Association
309 Lake Street
Penn Yan, NY 14527
(800) 548–4386
www.fingerlakes.org
www.madeinthefingerlakes.com

Seaway Trail, Inc.
109 Barracks Drive
Sackets Harbor, NY 13685
(800) 732–9298
www.seawaytrail.com

1000 Islands International Tourism Council
Box 400
Alexandria Bay, NY 13607
(800) 847–5263
www.visit1000islands.com

Tug Hill Commission
Dulles State Office Building
317 West Washington Street
Watertown, NY 13601-3782
(888) 785–2380
www.tughill.org

New York State Department of Environmental Conservation

Fisheries Office
NYSDEC Region 6
State Office Building
317 Washington Street
Watertown, NY 13601-3787
(315) 785–2261

Fisheries Office
NYSDEC Region 7
1285 Fisher Avenue
Cortland, NY 13045-1090
(607) 753–3095

Fisheries Office
NYSDEC Region 8
6274E Avon-Lima Road
Avon, NY 14414-9519
(585) 226–5334

Fisheries Office
NYSDEC Region 9
182 East Union, Suite 3
Allegany, NY 14706-1328
(716) 372–0645

State Parks

State parks generally charge a day-use fee from Memorial Day through Labor Day. Reservations for camping can be made by calling the New York State Camping Reservation System at (800) 456–2267 or on-line at www.reserveamerica.com.

Allan H. Treman State Marine Park
Taughannock Boulevard
Ithaca, NY 14850
(607) 272–1460

Allegany State Park
2373 ASP Route 1, Suite 3
Salamanca, NY 14779
(716) 354–9121

Burnham Point State Park
34075 Route 12E
Clayton, NY 13624
(315) 654–2324

Buttermilk Falls State Park
R.D. 10
Ithaca, NY 14850
(607) 273–5761

Canandaigua Lake State Marine Park
Lakeshore Drive
Canandaigua, NY 14424
(716) 394–9420 (in-season)
(315) 536–3666 (off-season)

Cayuga Lake State Park
2678 Lower Lake Road
Seneca Falls, NY 13148
(315) 568–5163

Cedar Point State Park
36661 Cedar Point State Park Drive
Clayton, NY 13624
(315) 654–2522

Chittenango Falls State Park
2300 Rathbun Road
Cazenovia, NY 13035
(315) 655–9620

Clark Reservation State Park
Jamesville, NY 13078
(315) 492–1590

Eel Weir State Park
R.D. 1
Ogdensburg, NY 13669
(315) 393–1138

Evangola State Park
Route 5
Irving, NY 14081
(716) 549–1802

Fair Haven Beach State Park
Route 104A
Fair Haven, NY 13604
(315) 947–5205

Fillmore Glen State Park
Route 38
Moravia, NY 13118
(315) 497–0130

Four Mile Creek State Park
Youngstown, NY 14174
(716) 745–7273

Golden Hill State Park
Barker, NY 14012
(716) 795–3117

Grass Point State Park
c/o Cedar Point State Park
36661 Cedar Point State Park Drive
Clayton, NY 13624
(315) 654–2522

Green Lakes State Park
7900 Green Lakes Road
Fayetteville, NY 13066-9658
(315) 637–6111

Hamlin Beach State Park
Hamlin, NY 14464
(716) 964–2462

Jacques Cartier State Park
P.O. Box 380
Morristown, NY 13664
(315) 375–6317

Keewaydin State Park
43165 Route 12
Alexandria Bay, NY 13607
(315) 482–3331

Keuka Lake State Park
3370 Pepper Road
Bluff Point, NY 14478
(315) 536–3666

Kring Point State Park
25950 Kring Point Road
Redwood, NY 13679
(315) 482–2444

Lakeside Beach State Park
Waterport, NY 14571
(716) 682–4888

Letchworth State Park
1 Letchworth State Park
Castile, NY 14427
(716) 493–3600

Long Point State Park (Cayuga Lake)
Finger Lakes Region Office of Parks,
Recreation and Historic Preservation
2221 Taughannock Park Road
Trumansburg, NY 14886

Long Point State Park (Lake Ontario)
7495 State Park Road
Three Mile Bay, NY 13693
(315) 649–5258

Mary Island State Park
c/o Cedar Point State Park
36661 Cedar Point State Park Drive
Clayton, NY 13624
(315) 654–2522

Old Erie Canal State Park
R.D. 2, Andrus Road
Kirkville, NY 13082
(315) 687–7821

Robert H. Treman State Park
R.D. 10
Ithaca, NY 14850
(607) 273–3440

Robert Moses State Park
P.O. Box 548
Massena, NY 13662
(315) 769–8663

Sampson State Park
6096 Route 96A
Romulus, NY 14541
(315) 585–6392

Selkirk Shores State Park
Route 3
Pulaski, NY 13142
(315) 298–5737

Seneca Lake State Park
P.O. Box 665
Geneva, NY 14456
(315) 789–2331

Southwick Beach State Park
8119 Southwicks Place
Henderson, NY 13650
(315) 846–5338

Taughannock Falls State Park
2221 Taughannock Park Road
Trumansburg, NY 14886
(607) 387–6739

Watkins Glen State Park
P.O. Box 304
Watkins Glen, NY 14891
(607) 535–4511

Wellesley Island State Park
44927 Cross Island Road
Fineview, NY 13640
(315) 482–2722

Westcott Beach State Park
P.O. Box 339
12224 Route 3
Sackets Harbor, NY 13685
(315) 938–5083

Wilson-Tuscarora State Park
Wilson, NY 14172
(716) 751–6361

County and Town Parks

Monroe County Parks Department
171 Reservoir Avenue
Rochester, NY 14620
(716) 256–4956
(716) 872–5326 (camping reservations)
www.co.monroe.ny.us

Onondaga County Parks
P.O. Box 146
Liverpool, NY 13088
(315) 451–7275

Park Station Recreation Center
2 West Beaver Pond Road
Erin, NY 14838
(607) 739–9164

Town of Camillus Parks and Recreation
4600 West Genesee Street
Syracuse, NY 13219
(315) 487–3600
www.townofcamillus.com

Indian Territories

Cattaraugus Indian Reservation
Seneca Nation of Indians
Route 438
Irving, NY 14081
(716) 532–4900
sni@localnt.com

Onondaga Nation of Indians
Route 11A
Nedrow, NY 13120
(315) 492–1922

Seneca Nation of Indians
Clerk's Office
P.O. Box 231
3582 Center Road
Salamanca, NY 14779
(716) 945–1790

More Contacts

Fort Drum
Outdoor Recreation
Building P-11115
North Memorial Drive
Fort Drum, NY 13602
(315) 772–6106 or (315) 772–5169

New York State Canal Corporation
P.O. Box 189
Albany, NY 12201-0189
(800) 422–6254

Reliant Energy
225 Greenfield Parkway, Suite 201
Liverpool, NY 13088
(315) 413–2800
www.reliantenergy.com
For information on water releases at power plants on the Salmon and Black Rivers, call the Waterline at (800) 452–1742.

U.S. Coast Guard
Marine Safety Office
1 Fuhrmann Boulevard
Buffalo, NY 14203
(716) 843–9570

About the Author

Spider Rybaak is the son of Ukrainians who were deported by the Nazis to work as slave laborers. In 1949, with three children in tow, they legally immigrated to America. Spider learned early in life the spiritual, emotional, and practical benefits of fishing. A freelance outdoor writer and photographer, Spider's work has been published in *In-Fisherman, Outdoor Life, Great Lakes Angler, Fishing and Hunting News, American Legion,* and *Boating Life.* He is also the author of *Fishing Eastern New York* (Globe Pequot, 2003). Spider resides in Central New York with his best friend, Susan, and their ten cats.

ESSENTIAL GUIDES FOR EVERY ANGLER

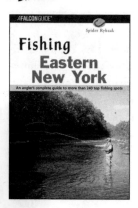

FISHING EASTERN NEW YORK
Spider Rybaak
This book guides readers to over 370 fishing locales in New York State.
$16.95
0-7627-1100-0

FISHING MAINE
Tom Seymour
Eighty-one of the best places to fish, both fresh- and saltwater.
$12.95
1-56044-514-9

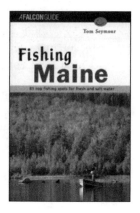

ALL ABOUT FLIES
Chuck and Sharon Tryon
A terrific revision to the classic *Figuring Out Flies.*
$14.95
1-59228-030-7

THE BEAVERKILL
The History of a River and its People
Ed Van Put; Introduction by John Merwin
An in-depth history of America's most famous trout stream.
$26.95
70 historic photos
1-58574-691-6

101 FLY-FISHING TIPS
Practical Advice from a Master Angler
Lefty Kreh
"One of the most talented and knowledgeable fly fishers of this century." —John Goddard
$14.95
1-58574-035-7

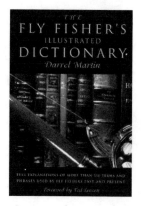

ESSENTIAL GUIDES FOR EVERY ANGLER

FLY FISHING MADE EASY, 3RD
A Manual for Beginners with Tips for the Experienced
Michael Rutter and Dave Card

For beginners eager to land their first fly-caught fish and for more experienced anglers looking to advance their skills.
$17.95
0-7627-0750-X

GOOD FLIES
Favorite Trout Patterns and How They Got That Way
John Gierach

A great writer, some great flies—and more practical and amusing observations on flies and fly tying.
$14.95
1-58574-611-8

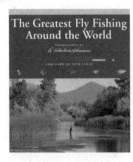

THE GREATEST FLY FISHING AROUND THE WORLD
R. Valentine Atkinson

$40.00 Hardcover
full color throughout
1-59228-086-2

IN THE RING OF THE RISE
A Startling Look at Trout Behavior and Riseforms
Vincent C. Marinaro

"An angling classic."
—Fly Fisherman
$19.95
1-58574-377-1

INSTINCTIVE FLY FISHING
A Guide's Guide to Better Fishing
Taylor Streit

$24.95 Hardcover
1-59228-190-7

ESSENTIAL GUIDES FOR EVERY ANGLER

THE L.L. BEAN ULTIMATE BOOK OF FLY FISHING
M. Lord, D. Talleur, and D. Whitlock

A spectacular, full-color guide, brought to you by one of the most trusted names in the outdoors.

$40.00 Hardcover
full color
1-58574-632-0

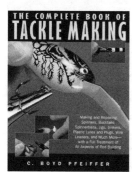

THE COMPLETE BOOK OF TACKLE MAKING
C. Boyd Pfeiffer

The most thorough work ever published on making and caring for fishing tackle. 800 illustrations.

$19.95
1-55821-721-5

A. K.'S FLY BOX
A. K. Best; Introduction by John Gierach

"I learned most of what I know now and use about fly tying from my old friend A. K. Best." —John Gierach

$40.00 Hardcover
1-55821-362-7

CATHY BECK'S FLY-FISHING HANDBOOK
REVISED AND UPDATED
Cathy Beck; Foreword by Lefty Kreh

"Cathy Beck is such an accomplished fly fisher that both women and men can learn much from the pages of this book." —Lefty Kreh

$18.95
1-58574-484-0

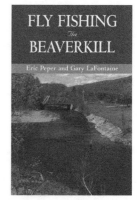

FLY FISHING THE BEAVERKILL
Eric Peper and Gary LaFontaine

This is a must for fly fishers going to the Beaverkill River.

$12.95
1-58574-773-4

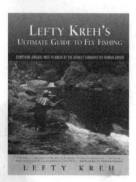

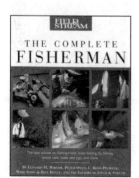

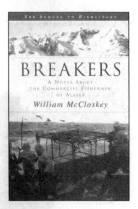

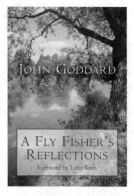

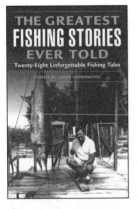